LANGUAGE CULTURE TYPE

Language Culture Type

INTERNATIONAL TYPE DESIGN

IN THE AGE OF UNICODE

Edited by John D. Berry

WITH A SPECIAL SECTION

SHOWING THE WINNERS IN BUKVA:RAZ!,

THE TYPE DESIGN COMPETITION

OF THE ASSOCIATION TYPOGRAPHIQUE

INTERNATIONALE

ATypI • Graphis

First published in New York, 2002, by the Association Typo-
graphique Internationale (ATypI), 10 Ridgeway Road, Redhill,
Surrey, RH1 6PH, United Kingdom; and Graphis, Inc., 307
Fifth Avenue, 10th Floor, New York, New York 10016, USA.

Design by Maxim Zhukov. Page make-up by John Hudson.
Distributed by Publishers Group West. Printed in the UK.

ISBN 1-932026-01-0

Contents

[v]

Acknowledgements
Thanks to the following for their help in making this project possible: Adobe Systems for providing an early copy of InDesign 2.0 to facilitate the typsetting; Matthew Carter for donating his typefaces Fenway and Vincent; ParaType for donating New Letter Gothic, and the ITC Cyrillic fonts; Masterfont for donating Hebrew fonts; DecoType and Linotype Library for donating Arabic fonts; Andrey Andreyev, Mark Batty, Lev Mazin, Nikita Ordynskiy and Vladimir Yefimov for permitting us to use their photographs from the bukva:raz! competition judging and the Judges' Soirée in Moscow.

Foreword

THIS BOOK is a major project of the Association Typographique Internationale and is part of ATypI's continuing outreach program. It is a monument to contemporary typographic creativity throughout the world. In these pages you will find examples of the best work that has taken place in typeface design over the five-year period 1996–2001. More than one hundred examples of typefaces, featuring fourteen different alphabets and writing systems, are displayed.

Since 1957, ATypI has been a forum and a catalyst to promote excellence in typography, type design, type technology, and education. More recently the work of ATypI has focused on its international conferences. These take place annually, each in a different city, thus far either in Europe or in the Americas. Each conference has been an evolving combination of discussion groups, forums, lectures, and exhibitions.

The main purpose of ATypI conferences has been to provide an environment where practitioners of the lettering arts can come together to share views and concerns and to find ways of promoting excellence in typographic communications. This has been accomplished effectively, but over time there has been considerable technological and market change, which has modified the demand for typefaces, the nature of typefaces that will be commercially successful, and the role of the people who design them and sell them.

ATypI members have become increasingly aware that the value of ATypI's contribution and effectiveness can and must be enhanced by projecting its activities beyond the comparatively ephemeral nature of the conference environment. Other initiatives have been developed that have the quality of building blocks, thereby providing a more permanent structure to encourage growth and innovation within the Association. Among these building blocks has been ATypI's publications program. There have been newsletters, journals, and books, but none on the scale of this project.

The idea for *Language Culture Type* started to develop in 1999. There were several strands that led us to our conclusion.

We wanted to find a way to promote cultural pluralism, encourage diversity, and provide a co-operative environment for the development of truly international typographic communications.

We were aware that the United Nations was planning 2001 as the Year of Dialogue among Civilizations, an important initiative that fit well with our own aspirations.

The idea of a well planned and internationally organized open competition, with enough winners to provide an onlooker with a good sense of the trends in international typeface design, started to take shape.

It seemed an obvious choice to reach out beyond the conference, to make the competition happen, and to publish a book that would act as a comprehensive vehicle to show what we had found, and to explain its importance to a wider audience.

The result is this publication – but as with all the best projects, the story does not end here. This book represents not so much an end as a new beginning. Our survey of international type design over the last five years is reported in this book in such a way that we hope that it will have lasting relevance and continue to be a useful reference tool for many years to come. As a first attempt this is something of an experiment, but it is our intention to repeat this initiative in another five years. It will be interesting to compare developments over that time; not just in design trends, but also exploring the effect of cultural and political shifts.

Mark Batty
President, ATypI

Preface

WRITTEN COMMUNICATION around the world is accomplished almost entirely with type – not just in the traditional form of typography in books, magazines, and printed ephemera (advertisements, flyers, posters, tickets, labels, and so on) but on television and movie screens, in many kinds of public signage and wayfinding, and in all the myriad ways in which we now use digital fonts. The number of people who design type is small – a few hundred, perhaps – but the number who use it has become vast. Type matters.

Despite the dominance of English in the world today, and especially its preponderance on the Internet, only a portion of that global communication is done in English, or even in the Latin alphabet. The distribution of languages around the world is uneven, and any attempt to map them must of necessity lie, through oversimplification. People speak more than one language, whether well or badly; people move around, and learn or forget; people play with their language, making jargon and inventing new terms; people hear new words on television or radio, or in the local marketplace, and adapt them to their own use. Almost all the languages in the world today can be written, even those that were once purely oral; and once a language is written, there develops a constant back and forth between its written forms and its spoken forms, each influencing the other. In order to communicate in our many tongues, we need type.

The number of writing systems in the world is large, although a few have become especially widespread: the Latin alphabet, the Cyrillic, the Arabic; the Chinese ideographic system; Japanese syllabic writing; Devanagari and its relatives in India. Some scripts, such as the Hebrew and Greek alphabets, have a high profile even though the number of people speaking their languages is relatively small. Other writing systems are used by multitudes, but are not widely known outside their native areas.

All of these writing systems started out as handwriting, but today they are all reproduced – and widely read – as type. Now that we can send digital text to each other, we find ourselves up against a technological problem: how to make sure that the text we send can be read correctly when it is printed on paper, or when it appears on someone else's computer screen. Anyone who has tried to use accented characters in an e-mail message knows how uncertain this can be.

The year 2001 was declared, by the United Nations, the 'Year of Dialogue among Civilizations.' The events of 2001 made it clear just how important that dialogue can be, and how much we suffer if it's neglected or misunderstood. As part of this Year of Dialogue, the Association Typographique Internationale (ATypI) sponsored an international competition for the best type designs of the previous five years — in all alphabets and writing systems, used in any language, from anywhere in the world. The competition was organized in New York and Moscow, an office was set up in Moscow, and the whole project was given the somewhat playful name bukva:raz! ('letter:one!' in Russian). The judging was done in December 2001 by an international jury of distinguished typographers and type designers, who chose the 100 best type designs out of those submitted. The winning designs are shown in this book, along with information on the typefaces and their designers. To put them in context and provide some depth of information about a few of the different scripts shown here, we asked type experts from around the world to write essays on several different writing systems and the problems of designing type for them.

The voices heard in these essays are diverse and individual. This is not a definitive 'official' overview. In the spirit of the book's ecumenical nature, we have made no attempt to homogenize them into a single style, and we have followed the authors' preferences in using either American or British spelling conventions. (For clarity, though, we have adopted a consistent style of punctuation.) Although considerable thought has been given over the years to coming up with agreed-upon definitions for typographic terms like 'character', 'glyph', 'letter', and so on, we have left it up to each writer to decide how to use them. The purpose of this looseness is not to create cacophony, but to allow each voice to be heard in its own cadences and accents.

The proportion of Latin and non-Latin typefaces among the bukva: raz! winners is not a reflection of the distribution of scripts or typefaces in the world. It is simply a reflection of the typefaces that were entered — and, among those, of which ones the jury chose. Not surprisingly, in an information world currently dominated by Western European languages, there were more Latin typefaces than any other kind. But such things are fluid; in another year, the mix might change. *Language Culture Type* is a benchmark of where we stand today in both the craft and the technology of making typefaces for use in global communication.

John D. Berry

Language Culture Type

ROBERT BRINGHURST

Voices, languages and scripts
around the world

I

DROP A WORD in the ocean of meaning and concentric ripples
form. To define a single word means to try to catch those ripples.
No one's hands are fast enough. Now drop two or three words in
at once. Interference patterns form, reinforcing one another here and can-
celing each other there. To catch the meaning of the words is not to catch
the ripples that they cause; it is to catch their interaction. This is what it
means to listen; this is what it means to read. It is incredibly complex, yet
humans do it every day, and very often laugh and weep at the same time.
Writing, by comparison, seems altogether simple, at least until you try.

Writing is the solid form of language, the precipitate. Speech comes
out of our mouths, our hands, our eyes in something like a liquid form
and then evaporates at once. It appears to me that this is part of a natural
cycle: one of the ways the weather forms on the ocean of meaning. What
else are the words we drop like pebbles in that ocean if not condensing
droplets of evaporated speech, recycled bits of the ocean of meaning itself? Yet language can also solidify – into iridescent, sharp, symmetrical
crystals, or into structures more like hailstones or shale beds or mud. In
solid as in liquid form, the intersecting meanings may reinforce each
other or rub each other out.

To bring the metaphor ashore, writing is language *displaced* from
the mode of immediate gesture or speech to the mode of the memento –
something like the seashells and the driftwood and the footprints on the
beach. Writing is leftovers – but of a kind some people prize as highly as
they do the original meal or parent organism itself.

And what is language? Language is what speaks us as well as what
we speak. Through our neurons, genes and gestures, shared assump-
tions and personal quirks, we are spoken by and speak many languages
each day, interacting with ourselves, with one another, other species,
and the objects – both natural and man-made – that populate our world.
Even in silence, there is no complete escape from the world of symbols,
grammars and signs.

[3]

Like other creatures, humans are heavily self-absorbed. We frequently pretend (or self-righteously insist) that language belongs to humans alone. And many of us claim that the only kind of human language, or the only kind that matters, is the kind that is born in the mouth. The languages of music and mathematics, the gestural languages of the deaf, the calls of leopard frogs and whales, the rituals of mating sandhill cranes, and the chemical messages coming and going day and night within the brain itself are a few of the many reminders that language is actually part of the fibre of which life itself is spun. We are able to think about language at all only because a license to do so is chemically written into our genes.

In the next few pages, nevertheless, I will use the words *language* and *writing* most of the time in rather selfishly human terms.

II

Linguists distinguish with some care (though never with perfect consistency or success) between *languages* and *dialects*. Languages are analogous to species. They may have borrowed much from one another or have sprung from the same root, but time has redesigned them. Speakers of one must temporarily regress and learn a whole new set of skills before they understand the speakers of another. Mentally and socially, to learn another language, you must *pass again through childhood*. Dialects, however, are the subspecies of language. A fluent speaker of a language can move to another dialect without much loss of cultural seniority.

Dialects almost always have regional roots, but dialects, like languages, can cut their local ties and become the mobile hallmark of certain ethnic groups or social classes. If they retain some isolation, they are likely, over time, to grow into different languages. If not, educational campaigns or population shifts may flatten them instead.

A script in itself is not a language; it is a system of representation, sufficient to catch some (but never all) of a language in its net. Human language, for its own sake, has no need of being written so long as it is spoken. Languages can and do attain at least as much sophistication, and as great a pitch of eloquence, in oral cultures as in cultures rich in printed books. And for 95% of their time on earth, members of the species *Homo sapiens* evidently felt no need for the managerial control over language that a writing system permits. Still, language can and does adapt to writing, just as plants and animals adapt to farming and ranching. Standing row on row, like corn and squash or squawking chickens, in memos, periodicals and books, there are varieties of language that would never exist or survive without the protection afforded by writing.

Languages divide and subdivide, forming families and branches, like the phylogenetic trees of animals and plants. Scripts do the same – but scripts are quintessentially *invented*, and languages are quintessentially not. The world of manuscript and print requires artificial sustenance – organized training of the young: in other words, a school – while spoken languages sustain themselves and flourish wherever humans live. These are some of the reasons why the phylogenetic trees of the world's scripts and the world's languages don't match.

Languages and scripts, like plant and animal species, are also subject to change. Their territories grow and shrink and subdivide and fuse, but there are none that are not mortal, none that will not someday be extinct.

Reading comes first. The reading of tracks and weather signs is a fundamental mammalian occupation, practised before primates started walking on their hind legs, much less writing. And writing, in a sense, is always on the verge of being born. All of us who speak by means of gesture, or who gesture as we talk, are gesturing toward writing. But it is a rare event for instincts such as these to crystallize into a system that can capture and preserve the subtleties of speech in graphic form. Such a system can only mature within a culture prepared to sustain it. Starting from scratch, with no imported models, people have made the shift from oral to literate culture at least three times but perhaps not many more than that. In Mesopotamia about 5,000 years ago, in northern China about 4,500 years ago, and in Guatemala and southern Mexico about 2,000 years ago, humans created a script and a scribal culture, apparently without imported models of any kind.

In each case, the writing began with pictures – which as they came to stand for words and then for syllables, grew increasingly abstract. In each case, the originating society was already highly organized, with a heavy investment in agriculture, architecture, social institutions and political centralization. And in each case, so far as we can tell, writing was first used in the work of political, economic or religious administration. Its use for literary purposes came later.

Writing *in the literary sense* is one of the world's most solitary crafts, but it is only pursued on the margins of highly organized and centralized societies.

Literature – meaning storytelling and poetry – involves the use of language more for purposes of discovery than for purposes of control. It is a part of language itself: present, like language, in every human community. There are no natural languages without stories, just as there are none without sentences. Yet literature is not the cause of writing. Literature *in the written sense* represents the triumph of language over writing: the subversion of writing for purposes that have little or nothing to do with social and economic control.

[5]

Writing, as Leonard Bloomfield wisely observed, is 'an outgrowth of drawing.' But in growing out of drawing it turns into something else. There are intermediary stages between the two, but when writing has fully distinguished itself from drawing, it has the following characteristics:

1. *Writing is abstract.* Pictures can be made by playing games with writing, but in writing itself no significant pictorial content remains. In Eric Gill's famous phrase, 'letters are things, not pictures of things'. Some very eminent non-readers of Chinese have wanted to think otherwise, but this is true for Chinese characters as well as Latin script. Non-readers seek out every wisp of pictorial residue in the characters because looking at the pictures is much easier than learning to read in Chinese. For those who read and write with ease, these associations vanish. Fluent readers of Chinese do not in fact see pictures of horses and mountains in their texts any more than fluent readers of English see pictures of I-beams, D-rings, T-squares, vees of geese or S-shaped links of chain. Such child's play intrudes upon the reverie of reading.

2. *A writing system is codified.* It consists of a repeating set of symbols sufficient to the language that it serves. Twelve Latin letters are enough to write Hawaiian. To write a lengthy Chinese text, thousands of glyphs may be required. But whatever system is used, writers can write what has never been written before without inventing further symbols. New symbols can of course be borrowed or created but very rarely have to be.

3. *These symbols are defined in terms of something else.* The something else is usually speech but needn't be speech. What it has to be is language.

4. *The system is stylistically as well as symbolically self-contained.* As a calligraphic tradition develops, the symbols start to talk to one another, nourished by the dialogues of writers with their tools. The line of the scribe, like the stroke of the painter, the gesture of the dancer or the touch of the musician, then becomes in itself another means of speaking. Latin script did not begin with the system of stems and branches, ascenders and descenders, bowls and counters now familiar to lettering artists and typographers; Arabic script did not begin with its now canonical initial, medial, terminal and independent forms; and Chinese script did not begin with the seven basic strokes now taught to apprentice calligraphers nor the set of basic glyphs (the 214 radicals) which has, since the Míng Dynasty, formed the cornerstone of Chinese lexicography. Scripts acquire internal grammars of this kind as they mature, by being written.

Sūn Qiánlǐ, a Táng Dynasty calligrapher, put it this way: *dǎo zhī zé chuán zhù, dùn zhī zé shān tuǒ:* 'Where the brush leads, springs flow; where it halts, the mountains stand'.

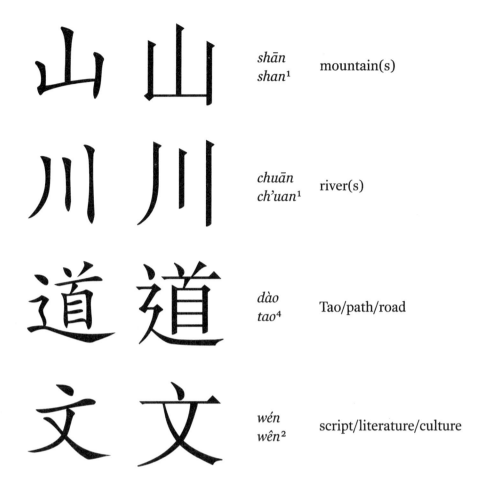

山	山	*shān* shan¹	mountain(s)
川	川	*chuān* ch'uan¹	river(s)
道	道	*dào* tao⁴	Tao/path/road
文	文	*wén* wên²	script/literature/culture

Figure 1. 'Mountains and rivers are the script [*or* pattern *or* literature *or* culture] of the Tao': an abbreviated quotation from the opening chapter of *Wén xīn diāo lóng* [*The Literary Mind and the Carving of Dragons*] by Liú Xié (c. 465–522). The Chinese characters in column 1 are *kăitĭ* ('model glyphs', based on Hàn Dynasty brushwork). Those in column 2 are *sòngtĭ* ('Sòng glyphs', based on woodblock printing of the Sòng and Míng Dynasties). In column 3, the pinyin romanization is given first, Wade-Giles romanization below. The tones of Mandarin Chinese (level, falling, dipping or rising) are marked by diacritics in pinyin, by superscript numerals in Wade-Giles. *Tao,* though usually spelled with a *t* in English, is always pronounced with a *d* by Mandarin speakers (just as *tofu* is pronounced with a *d* by all speakers of Japanese).

III

If writing is only rarely invented from scratch, it is often reinvented by example, and often vigorously spread. Politics, religion and commerce are crucial factors here again. Linguists, artists, visionaries, kings, even novelists and poets, have *designed* many scripts, but it is missionaries, teachers, traders, administrators and immigrants – both conquerors and refugees – who actually spread them around. By these means, Latin, Arabic, Chinese, Cyrillic, Greek and Hebrew scripts have circumnavigated the world, and specimens of Egyptian and Mayan hieroglyphs and of Mesopotamian cuneiform have found their way to libraries, schoolrooms, museums and souvenir shops thousands of kilometers from home.

The Latin, Greek, and Cyrillic alphabets are the three most prominent members of what we might call the Eurasian family of scripts. Like the Latin, Greek and Russian languages, they spring from a common root. But one of these alphabets has been tied for 3,000 years to a single language. The other two have been systematically spread, both voluntarily and by force. The Spanish, Portuguese, Dutch and British empires, and of course the Christian church, have left hundreds of Latin-based scripts in their wake. The Soviet Union left behind it dozens of scripts based on Cyrillic. In the same way, the spread of Islam has provoked dozens of scripts that are based on Arabic.

Cyrillic is in consequence now used for six of the surviving Slavic languages and for many Central Asian and Siberian tongues whose palette of sounds is fundamentally different. Arabic script, though Semitic in origin, is widely used for non-Semitic languages, including Persian, Urdu, Kashmiri, Kurdish, Malay, and African languages such as Tamazight. Latin script is used not only for Romance languages such as Portuguese and French but for all the Germanic and Scandinavian languages, for all the Slavic languages not written in Cyrillic, and for many more outside the Indo-European family: Finnish, Estonian, Turkish, Hungarian, Basque, Vietnamese, and more than a thousand African, Polynesian and Native American languages. Meticulous systems have also been devised for the romanization and cyrillization (transposition into Latin and Cyrillic) of Chinese, Hebrew, Greek, Korean, Sanskrit, and many other languages equipped with scripts of their own.

Where scripts are perceived not as tools for the free use of individuals but as vectors of religious or political authority, shifts in power are sometimes quickly mirrored by shifts in script. Turkish was written in Arabic script from the 12th or 13th century until 1928, when a government decree forced a shift to the Latin alphabet. Tajik was first written in Arabic, then for a time in Latin letters, but in the Soviet era, these scripts were replaced by Cyrillic. In 1991, when Tajikistan declared its independence, efforts were underway to return to Arabic script. Continuing shifts in the balance of power are still having an effect on how (and where and whether) Tajik children learn to write.

Even systems of romanization are sometimes perceived as politically charged. Despite its many practical advantages and nearly worldwide acceptance, there are governments, institutions and individuals who will not use the pinyin system for romanizing Mandarin Chinese, on the grounds that the system's initial sponsors were Marxist.

A writing system consists of a set of symbols, a set of definitions for the symbols (that is, a graphic lexicon), and rules for their use (a graphic syntax). The symbols, most of the time, are realized as glyphs, which are visible, repeatable marks and shapes, constrained by the propensities and limits of the human hand and eye. Except by association, there are no Marxist (or Christian or Muslim or Jewish) scripts, any more than there is a Marxist or Christian arithmetic, or in music, a communist C-sharp.

Cultural factors, including religion and politics, do indeed affect how writing looks, but their effects are often remarkably independent of the script that is in use. Industrial civilization, for example, during the early and mid 20th century, gave us typefaces such as Helvetica and Akzidenz Grotesk, with their tiny aperture, absence of serifs, blunt terminals, bold and invariant stroke, short extenders, large x-height, and slightly squashed counters set on a rigidly vertical axis. The same industrial civilization gave us Greek, Cyrillic, Hebrew, Devanagari, Japanese and Chinese types with similar characteristics: a global epidemic of Helveticas. No one can determine, by examining these fonts, the religious or political opinions of their designers or manufacturers. What one can determine is that all of them embody an aesthetic reminiscent of the forklift and the freight car: heavy industry and centralized production. All are aesthetically linked, in other words, to a world in which Marxist thought could flourish.

An equally global post-industrial aesthetic, later in that century, gave us, for each of these scripts, types that are lighter in weight though very similar in form. (Latin versions can be found in the font catalog under several names, including Helvetica Light.) Here again, it is impossible to tell, by looking at the type, the religious or political ideas of its designers, but all these fonts are aesthetically linked to a world of greater automation and lighter, faster transport: one where factories are airier, work more often sedentary, shift times often shorter, and where references to Marx, whether in or out of fashion, rarely inspire inquisitorial zeal.

Stylistic changes of that kind – dark to light or squarish to roundish, short-limbed to long-limbed, serif to sans, and so on – are part of the life history of almost every script, and over time the changes can be numerous and great. Chinese, Indic, Arabic, Hebrew, Greek, Cyrillic and Egyptian scripts have histories as intricate and various as Latin script – enough to guarantee no end of pleasant tasks for the art historian of letters.

The subtler changes often look to me more interesting and meaningful than catastrophic shifts. People very rarely choose what species of script they are going to write. A system of writing is thrust upon most by local tradition, and on some by a dictator's whim, a colonial invasion, or a missionary's passion. How individuals and their societies use the system they are given is what tells us who they are. Out of the endless search for perfect form have come the inscriptional caps of Trajan's column, humanist romans and italics; the *naskhi, thuluth* and *ruq'a* forms of Arabic; the script of Qumran and the Tuscan rabbinical hand; the *kǎishū* or 'model script' of Wèi and Jìn Dynasty China, the Wild Grass or Crazy Grass tradition known as *kuángcǎo* in China and as *kyōsō* in Japan; the Ume and Uchen scripts of Tibet, and many more.

Scripts consisting of spare, unserifed Euclidean figures – lines, angles, dots, circles, arcs, squares, and so on – have sprung up many times. The early scripts of Italy, Spain and Greece are examples. So are the Massilian (Berber) scripts of North Africa, dating back perhaps to the 5th century BCE, and so are the Brahmi script, created in northern India, perhaps at the behest of the Buddhist emperor Aśoka in the 3rd century BCE, the Scandinavian futhark (runic script), which probably dates from the first century CE, the original Hangul script introduced in Korea in 1446, the Algonquian syllabic script created in central Canada around 1840 by James Evans, and Brahmi's modern descendant, the Miao script created in Indochina in the early 1900s by James Pollard. Their early forms have much in common, but each has its own history.

The early European scripts grew by slow degrees into all the different forms of Greek and Latin script: rustics, uncials, square capitals, the Carolingian minuscule, the humanist hands of 15th-century Italy, and the enormous take-out menu of low-priced digital type that now resides on most computers. Brahmi developed into Devanagari, Bengali, Malayalam, Telugu, Thai, Tibetan, and all the other forms of Indic writing. The Massilian scripts have never had much use apart from brief inscriptions, letters, labels and ornamentation, yet the system has survived, almost unchanged, in the Tifinagh script, still used for the same purposes, chiefly by the Tuareg. The futhark was widely used in northern Europe without much formal change – but like Massilian, it was evidently never used for texts of any length. It survives, like Tifinagh, not as a medium of literature nor even administration, but as a plaything and a form of symbolic ornament. Those who might have written in runes now write in Latin script instead, and those who might have written in Massilian now either dwell in one of the world's few surviving oral cultures or do their more serious writing in Arabic script. In short, runic and Massilian scripts have remained in the realm of handicraft or folk art, while the scripts of southern Europe (like those of China, Japan and the Muslim world) have been for many centuries the object of professional attention.

The most striking contrast, however, is between the fate of Hangul and Algonquian syllabics. When Hangul was introduced, Koreans had no writing system of their own. Those who were literate had learned to read and write Chinese instead – and then adapted Chinese glyphs in some degree to write Korean. The Hangul script was designed and tested in private, then presented fully formed, backed by the authority of the king. Four centuries later, another such system was presented, fully formed, to the Cree and Ojibwa of Ontario and Manitoba, backed by the authority of the resident Methodist missionary. Phonologically, Hangul is more sophisticated by far than Algonquian syllabics, but both systems were tailored to the languages involved and easy for native speakers to learn. What both these systems lacked was a scriptorial tradition and a sense of graphic poise. Both were introduced in a form resembling first-graders' sticks-and-balls.

Within a single generation, Hangul was transformed by its own users. The script's essential geometric plan and rational basis were maintained, but it was written with a Chinese brush. Principles of movement and fluidity, balance and asymmetry were borrowed from Chinese calligraphic tradition, which many Koreans already understood.

In the Algonquian world, however, no other form of writing was in use when Evans introduced his system. Cree hunters familiar with any form of calligraphy were few and far between. As an agent of social change, the Algonquian script has been a success. It is still preferred by many Cree and Ojibwa despite the inroads later made by Latin script, and in the 1850s, Evans's missionary colleagues adapted it to Inuktitut (the language of the Inuit or Eskimo). In the Eastern Canadian Arctic, it is now the major script for much administrative work and is used for literature as well. Yet Algonquian and Inuktitut syllabics still have not developed a fluent cursive form nor a calligraphic tradition. As missionary scripts, they were initially intended more for reading hymns and gospels than for writing indigenous texts, and they were cut and cast in type with missionary zeal before their users could impart a human touch. Most people writing Inuktitut now use a keyboard and computer in preference to a pencil or pen, further insulating the script from the humanizing force of writing patiently and lovingly by hand. It remains to be seen how the script may now develop through the medium of digital design.

IV

When exported from one language to another, a writing system almost always undergoes some change. The basic Latin alphabet, for instance, is only 20 letters: ABCDEFGHILMNOPQRSTUX. (Latin scholars often count three more: Etruscan K, which was used at first and then rejected, and Greek Y and Z, which were borrowed by bilingual Roman writers when required.) On its way to modern English, this efficient, simple system acquired a lower case, a set of Arabic (in reality, Indian) numerals, and a dozen or so marks of punctuation. It also added several letters: *j k v w y z.* To accommodate French, it has added *à â ç é è ê ë î ï j ô œ ù û ü v y z.* In adapting to Norwegian, it has dropped *c q x* and added *å œ ø v y z.* For Tahitian, it has dropped *b c d g l q s x* and added only *v.* It is the mark of a modern and cosmopolitan language to make some room for foreign words, and the mark of a modern and cosmopolitan script to make some room for foreign letters. The fact remains that *b c d l* and *s* are foreign letters in Tahitian, and *k* and *w* foreign letters in French, just as *ç ł* and *ø* are foreign letters in English.

In adapting to modern Russian, the old Cyrillic alphabet has dropped more than a dozen older letters and added й э я [*short i, e, ya*]. For Macedonian, it has added ѓ ј љ њ ќ џ è ѝ [*gje, je, lje, nje, kje, dzhe, grave e, grave i*] and retained the old Cyrillic ѕ [*dze*], which is no longer used in Russian. To suit the needs of Persian, the Arabic script adds پ چ ژ گ [*peh, cheh, zheh, gaf*]. It adds the same letters for Kurdish (though the preferred Kurdish form of *cheh* is چ) and another four as well: ر ڤ ڵ ۆ [*retroflex r, veh, velar l, o*]. In Kurdish, however, the script is differently used. All vowels, both long and short, are written in Kurdish – not as diacritics but as full-size, baseline characters. Only long vowels are written on the baseline in Arabic and Persian. What this means is that Arabic script has *become alphabetic in Kurdish* though it is *not* alphabetic in Arabic, Urdu or Persian.

Arabic script, unlike Latin and Cyrillic, very rarely loses any letters in adapting to new languages. The reason is that it arrives as the script of the Koran, which faithful Muslims are expected to read or recite in the original, not in translation. Any language that accepts Arabic script is likely to be spoken in a culture that accepts Islam. Any culture that accepts Islam inherits a sacred text written in Arabic and therefore needs all the Arabic letters, including ض [*ḍâd*], which represents a voiced, pharyngealized dental stop (emphatic *d*). Arabic is the only language in the world in which this phoneme plays a role, but its symbol now appears in the standard character sets of several dozen languages.

The scripts of English, French, Macedonian, Persian and Kurdish are, in essence, 'graphic dialects' of Latin or some other parent script. Most scripts are of this kind – mere variants of other scripts – and are none the worse for that. Writing systems are rarely created from scratch where an existing script can comfortably be borrowed or adapted. In order to be written, every language needs a set of characters sufficient to bridge the gap between one speaker and another, but there is no linguistic reason why it needs a script exclusively its own.

To millions of people nevertheless, script is a badge. Hebrew script, to many, is a badge of Jewishness, Arabic script a badge of the Islamic faith, Devanagari script a badge of Hindu pride, Cyrillic script a badge of Slavic solidarity or Soviet nostalgia, and Sinhalese and Tamil scripts the sym-

ا	alif	ا	â
ب	bâ'	ب	
		پ	peh
ت	tâ'	ت	
ث	thâ'	ث	
ج	jîm	ج	
		چ	cheh
ح	ḥâ'	ح	
خ	xâ' / khâ'	خ	
د	dal	د	
ذ	dhal	ذ	
ر	râ'	ر	
		ڕ	ṛeh
ز	zây / zayn	ز	
		ژ	zheh
س	sîn	س	
ش	shîn	ش	
ص	ṣâd	ص	
ض	ḍâd	ض	
ط	ṭâ'	ط	
ظ	ẓâ'	ظ	
ع	'ayn	ع	
غ	ghayn	غ	
ف	fâ'	ف	
		ڤ	veh
ق	qâf	ق	
ك	kâf	ك	
		گ	qâf
ل	lâm	ل	
		ڵ	ḷâ'
م	mîm	م	
ن	nûn	ن	
ه	hâ'	ه	a/e
و	wâw	و	u
		ۆ	o
ى	yâ'	ى	ê

Figure 2. The basic Arabic character set (far left) is a syllabary now consisting of 28 consonants and eleven (largely optional) diacritics, three of which are the basic signs for vowels.

The derivative of this script used for Kurdish (near left) is an alphabet. In Kurdish script, there are six additional consonants, and four of the borrowed Arabic signs are redefined as vowels. Two additional Kurdish vowels are written as digraphs: long *u* as double *wâw*, long *i* as double *yâ*. The five greyed letters in the Kurdish list are used only for writing Arabic words.

Velar l (here transcribed as *ḷ*) occurs in both Arabic and Kurdish, but only in Kurdish does it have a graphic symbol of its own (*ḷâ'*). In Arabic, this phoneme occurs in only one word, *Allah*. In Kurdish it is more extensively used.

[13]

bols of two Sri Lankan factions now bitterly opposed. But badges are re-movable. Where associations such as these are fervently pursued, a script occasionally proves to be more like a brand, or indeed like a prison tattoo, re-engraved on the brain with every letter written and every letter read.

The number of languages actively written in two scripts is not, at present, very large, but the tension that exists where several of these languages are spoken is enough to give one pause. Serbo-Croatian, for example, is commonly written in Latin script by Croats, in Cyrillic script by Serbs. Tajik is now written in both Arabic and Cyrillic, Malay in both Arabic and Latin – the choice again depending mostly on political or religious affiliation. Kashmiri and Sindhi are generally written by Hindus in Devanagari and by Muslims in Arabic script. Hindi and Urdu – the one a major language of India, written in Devanagari, the other a major language of Pakistan, normally written in Arabic script – might more accurately be described as one language or as three. Literary Urdu and literary Hindi are specialized forms, largely distinct from one another and from Hindi/Urdu in its normal spoken form. Before the partition of Pakistan and India, this colloquial language – which is spoken by 300 million people or more – was known as Hindustani. Religious and political division have left it no accepted name of its own. It is referred to in Pakistan as Urdu and in India as Hindi, and is written in two scripts, yet underneath these names and scripts, no language barrier really exists. It is often said that the purpose of script is to extend and enhance communication, but scripts are sometimes used instead to establish or enforce a demarcation.

Phonetic scripts such as the IPA (International Phonetic Alphabet) are not tied to any particular language – and unlike any 'natural' script, they are really designed for use by linguistic outsiders. Native speakers do not need the finicky instructions about tongue position and voicing that phonetic scripts provide. The IPA, one might suppose, is a perfectly neutral and objective way of writing. Yet even this script, designed to scientifically record what strangers say, is sometimes used as a tribal badge, to segregate the academic linguist from the rest of humankind.

Humanist traditions around the world tend to rely on a different assumption: not that all members of a group should speak or write with a single voice, but that a single individual can speak and write with many different voices. Different ways of writing serve then as the emblems of different ways of speaking, and different ways of speaking help to classify and order information, not to classify or stereotype the speaker.

One of the great books of the Renaissance is Leonhard Fuchs's botanical work *De Historia stirpium*, published by the Basle printer Michael Isengrin in 1542. Four scripts are used throughout the text. Two of the four are bicameral (that is, they include an upper and lower case); the other two are tricameral (upper case, lower case and small caps). So there are ten sets of characters in constant use. The main text is in Latin, set in a serifed roman, upper & lower case. Some information, especially plant names, is also given in German and Greek, with the German words in u&lc fraktur, the Greek in u&lc cursive Greek. The sidenotes – in Latin again – are u&lc italic. Main heads are set in roman capitals (from the same font as the text). Run-in heads and running heads are set in spaced small caps, Latin or Greek, as the language demands. Four other fonts appear on a regular basis. Subheads are in small caps larger than those in the running heads. Another fraktur, also larger and of more elaborate cut, is used for German captions to the illustrations, side by side with Latin captions in text-size roman caps. A four-line ornamented initial marks the start of every chapter – and this again is sometimes Latin, sometimes Greek.

Polyphonic music was in vogue all over Europe in Fuchs's time, and there is something polyphonic in the typography of his book. Many voices speak from the page at once. Each speaks a separate part, but they are graphically in tune. The effect is vigorous and harmonious, not chaotic.

Even in Germany, the mixing of roman and blackletter types is now rarer than it was. But in most of the places where Latin script is used, it is standard practice to mix roman with italic and small caps (and/or bold and bold italic). Each is given a separate job to do. This is a legacy from printers such as Isengrin, who pioneered the route. Great resources and intense work are required to do all this with handcut metal type. Mixing scripts and sizes in the digital world is easy – but doing it as well as a 16th-century master printer is something else again.

In Chinese, Arabic, Hebrew, Armenian and Devanagari, true italic type does not exist, and different calligraphic styles are rarely mixed as closely as roman and italic are in Latin script. Bold type is sometimes used for emphasis, however, and good Chinese and Japanese typographers will sometimes build a very subtle pattern of mixed sizes on one page.

Only a few writing systems – Latin, Greek, Cyrillic, Armenian – have developed bicameral form, but every script that is heavily used develops multiple styles, including some that are more formal, interrupted and precise, and some that are more cursive. Using one script for heads, another for text is common enough. But mixing two such scripts *like this,* in the midst of a single-language sentence, was a late development even in Latin script. It began in 16th-century mathematical texts, to mark symbolic letters (as in: draw a line from *a* to *b*). The use of italic to isolate phrases, such as the titles of books, began with the practice of changing type to mark a change in language. A Latin title cited in French text or vice versa was cause for a shift between roman and italic. In time, the change of font was taken to mark a logical shift instead of a linguistic one. In 1559, at Lyon, Jean de Tournes printed a revered French text (Jean Froissart's *Chroniques*), annotated as though it were a Greek or Latin classic. Like the text, the scholarly sidenotes are in French, but they switch back and forth between roman and italic to distinguish editorial *emendations* from editorial *remarks*. In 1559, this was a revolutionary step. Mixing roman and italic on one line in one language did not become a widespread practice for another hundred years. (Most German printers avoided it long after that.)

Greek type has existed in both cursive and upright forms since roughly 1475, but using these together *in a single line of type* was rare indeed until the late 20th century. The typographic habits of Greek, Cyrillic and Latin script have been converging slowly for two centuries, and are now converging rapidly, under the spell of English, French and German models. Similar experiments are occurring in other scripts as well. In Korean, for instance, oblique Hangul type is occasionally used in imitation of Latin italic.

Japanese, however, has a tradition of mixing scripts and types that is at least as highly developed as the Latin system and fundamentally different. Japanese has been written in Chinese characters since the third or fourth century CE. Around the tenth century, Japanese syllabic script came into use, and this now has two forms. Chinese characters (called in Chinese *hànzì*, in Japanese, *kanji*) remain the foundation of Japanese writing. Cursive syllabic script, called *hiragana,* is used for writing syntactical particles and all the grammatical inflections that Chinese does not have but Japanese can't do without. More angular syllabics, *katakana,* are used for words and names borrowed from other languages, for irony and emphasis (much like italics) and for any Japanese word the writer does not wish to (or know how to) write in *kanji.* In addition, modern Japanese makes frequent use of roman characters, *romaji.* These are employed for European names, citations and addresses, for many abbreviations, and increasingly for slogans and quotations. To this set of four basic scripts, others may be added. Greek and Cyrillic scripts, for instance, are found in scientific work. Devanagari and Tibetan are much used in Buddhist studies.

v

No one appears to have made a careful count of writing systems known throughout the world. Ignoring for the moment all the systems invented for private use by individuals (of which there may be thousands), the tactile scripts for the blind, and all the cryptographic and stenographic systems (a thousand at least), there appear to be only about a hundred species-level systems (such as Chinese, Latin, Cyrillic, Bengali and Arabic) that are now in current public use. At least a hundred more – maybe closer to a thousand more – are dormant, undeciphered or lost and forgotten. But the number of distinct subsystems (on the level of Spanish and French, Ukrainian and Russian, Persian and Kurdish, Cree and Inuktitut) is growing year by year and is potentially much larger than the number of human languages to be written. Humans speak about 6,000 languages at present. A century ago, most of these had never been written. Now, nearly all of them have – though only a few hundred possess a self-sustaining scriptorial tradition.

The number of languages spoken by humans is, however, dropping at a very rapid rate, and the number of people devoted to reading the languages of the past is not apparently increasing. Uses could be found for 10,000 scripts. But if, in the near future, humans will speak only a few hundred or few dozen privileged languages – and if only a few scholars, who cannot really speak them, will read what is written in all the rest – then a few scripts are all we need. Languages that have no native speakers, and no more than a few eccentric readers, might just as well, alas, be written in phonetics.

In 1996, two linguists, Peter Daniels and William Bright, published an analytical catalog of *The World's Writing Systems,* claimed by its publisher to cover 'all scripts officially used throughout the world – as well as their historical antecedents'. *Officially,* here, is a wistful but meaningless word. In truth, though it exceeds 900 pages, the catalog omits thousands of writing systems, including some (Zuni and Navajo, for instance) that are the vehicles of 'unofficial' major world literatures. The best that can be said is that Daniels & Bright is much the most impressive effort yet toward a monumental, uncompleted task.

A number of scholars (including Daniels and his teacher I.J. Gelb) have been concerned with the systematic classification of writing systems. The taxonomy I will outline here draws heavily on the work of Gelb and Daniels but is in some respects at variance with both. I have found it workable and useful, but there is no guarantee that this or any other taxonomy is effectively complete – for new scripts can always be created, and a number of undeciphered (hence unclassified) scripts survive from the distant past.

Writing systems can be characterized as *semographic, syllabic, alphabetic* or *prosodic.* These four terms or *hues of meaning* form a simple taxonomic wheel. Finer distinctions are certainly possible, and in some instances useful. *Syllabic* can be subdivided, for instance, into *logosyllabic* and *alphasyllabic.* Prosodic can be divided into *semoprosodic* and *alphaprosodic.* But no such term, no matter how ponderous, is in itself a satisfactory classification. The reason is that writing systems are like lichens: they are compound entities. Every developed system belongs to *more than one* of the four primary categories.

Coarser distinctions are possible too. Beneath this four-part taxonomy, a two-part taxonomy is lurking. In essence, when writing a spoken language, one can focus on *meanings* or on *sounds*. Sounds can be written as clumps (the sonorous units called syllables) or parsed, at least roughly, into phonemes and written as consonants and vowels. If the writing of meanings ran on a parallel track, then meanings could also be written as clumps (the conceptual units called words) or parsed into morphemes and written as lexical roots, affixes and inflections. The morphemes of 'meaning', for instance, are *mean + -ing,* and the morphemes of 'meanings' are *mean + -ing + -s.* Each of these could have its symbol. But no known writing system works in quite that way.

When people approach the task of writing by trying to represent what they *mean*, not what they *say*, they produce an alternative to speech and not a record of it. Very often, they start with pictures – conceptual triggers that point or allude to things or ideas. Later on, as the need to write sounds becomes more pressing, these images may be used to represent the sound of the word that names the meaning – but then they are no longer symbols of meaning but symbols of sound. After writing with sounds is established, people sometimes look for ways to make the meaning clearer. Often they do so by giving the writing a pattern or shape – not pictorial shape, but a pattern or shape found in the act of thinking itself, or in the sounds by which that thinking is expressed. These shapes and patterns are prosodic. They are written not with pictures but, as a rule, with punctuation. This may be a little clearer if we go around the taxonomic wheel spoke by spoke.

In *semographic* systems, separate symbols represent units of meaning, which sometimes include entire phrases or polysyllabic words. Mathematical writing systems are routinely semographic. The systems now in common use for arithmetic, algebra and the calculus are almost purely so. No *literary* script is entirely semographic, but Egyptian, Mayan and Chinese writing is semographic in part. Numerals, currency signs, and the per cent sign are semographic glyphs routinely used in many scripts that are otherwise syllabic or alphabetic.

In a sense, of course, a semographic script is supralinguistic. It makes no difference (for some purposes) whether the symbol *2* is pronounced as *two, dos, deux, zwei, ni,* δύο or שנים. Yet many kinds of statements can be written in semographic scripts with great precision, and all such statements can have equally precise realizations in spoken language. (The statement *1 + 1 = 2,* for example, will be differently pronounced in

English, Greek and Hebrew, but it possesses in each case a quite specific and precise linguistic formulation.)

In *syllabic* systems, each sign represents a syllable, which is usually treated as an unanalyzable whole. In logosyllabic scripts, there may be many signs for a given syllable, each with a different meaning. Egyptian and Mayan hieroglyphs are logosyllabic in part. Chinese script is primarily logosyllabic for Mandarin Chinese, but *the same script* is largely semographic when used for Japanese. (The reason is that, when reading Japanese, the phonetic components of the Chinese glyphs, the *kanji*, are frequently ignored, and the monosyllabic Chinese glyphs often read as Japanese polysyllables.)

In other syllabic scripts there is one symbol per syllable, but the symbols are not based on any system that acknowledges the underlying presence of consonants and vowels. Katakana, hiragana and Cherokee are scripts that are syllabic in this rather purist sense.

In alphasyllabic systems, syllables are recognized as units but are represented by symbols that acknowledge an awareness of underlying consonants and vowels. This can be done in a number of ways. In Devanagari, Tibetan, Malayalam, Burmese and other Indic scripts, the basic symbol represents a consonant and implies by default a simple vowel. Diacritics are added to represent a change in that associated vowel. In Ethiopic, the basic symbol represents a consonant, and the associated vowel is shown by systematic *distortion* (e.g., by shortening the left or right side of the base character). In Canadian syllabics (Cree, Chipewyan, Dakelhne and Inuktitut writing), the basic symbol represents a consonant, and its *orientation* (facing up, down, left or right) reveals the vowel. In Korean Hangul script, consonants and vowels are fully analyzed and each has its own grapheme, but these component symbols are recombined in compound glyphs or clusters that each portray a syllable.

Consonantal scripts such as Arabic and Hebrew are often assigned to a separate category. I believe that it makes better sense to regard them as a special case of alphasyllabic writing. In these scripts, just as in Devanagari, the basic symbol represents a consonant. The companion vowel (or its absence) *can* be represented by a diacritic, just as in Devanagari, though in practice, with consonantal scripts, these diacritics are usually left off. Some such systems – the Massilian scripts of North Africa, for instance – have no vowel signs at all. Others (e.g., liturgical Hebrew and modern Aramaic) have been effectively transformed, through consistent use of vowel signs, into full-fledged alphasyllabaries.

In *alphabetic* systems, the syllable is invisible; nothing is represented except the separate consonants and vowels. Latin, Greek and Cyrillic are alphabetic systems – but in their normal working form, with numerals,

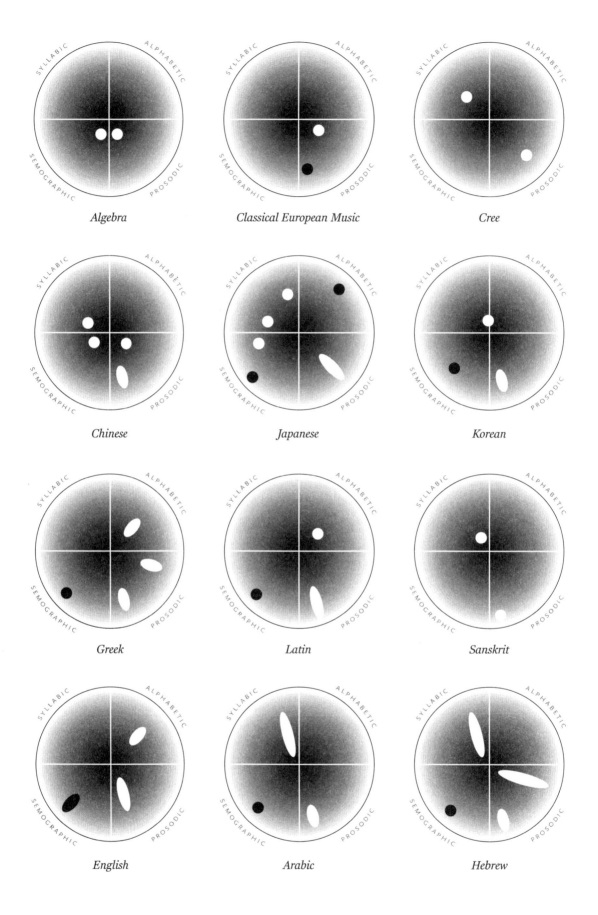

Algebra

Classical European Music

Cree

Chinese

Japanese

Korean

Greek

Latin

Sanskrit

English

Arabic

Hebrew

punctuation and other analphabetic symbols, they are far from being purely alphabetic. (Both Korean Hangul and liturgical Hebrew have been called alphabetic, because they do, each in their own way, systematically indicate both consonants and vowels. I call them alphasyllabic instead, because, like Devanagari, they are essentially syllabic in organization.)

The Latin, Greek and Cyrillic scripts are almost universally called alphabets. It is useful, though, to remember that what makes any set of glyphs an alphabet is not the glyphs themselves but *how they're used*. Latin script is used syllabically, not alphabetically, in acronyms such as RCAF and FBI. It is used semographically, not alphabetically, in numerals such as XIV and MMIII. On the other hand, in some early Egyptian inscriptions there are instances of genuinely alphabetic writing using hieroglyphs. (Most hieroglyphic texts are partly semographic, partly syllabic.) Arabic script is used alphabetically for Kurdish and Kashmiri, and some writers use it alphabetically for Pashto. Hebrew script has been used alphabetically, especially for writing Yiddish and Spanish. If the syllable clusters of Korean Hangul are dismantled and the components arranged in a line (as has sometimes been proposed), the result is alphabetic Korean. Yet all these scripts – Arabic, Hebrew, Korean – are normally syllabic.

Prosodic writing systems focus not on words, syllables or phonemes but on what linguists like to call 'suprasegmentals'. These are intonational features such as pitch, duration, emphasis and pause. Musical notation is fundamentally prosodic, though not always purely so. Literary writing systems are never purely prosodic, just as they are never purely

Figure 3 (opposite). Taxonomic wheels for the writing systems used in twelve of the world's languages. In this chart, the language designations are specific and the scripts implied are those in modern use, in typographic form. (Latin means Latin language in modern Latin script; Arabic means Arabic language in modern Arabic script, and so on.)

Every script has several components. The more accurately any component registers what happens in the language, the closer it approaches to the centre of the wheel. White dots represent essential features of the script, black dots its optional components. The components that are classified as optional in these charts are (1) beams and bar lines in musical notation; (2) romaji in Japanese; (3) numerals and symbols such as dollar signs and yen signs in Japanese, Korean, Greek, Latin, English, Arabic and Hebrew.

Stretched dots are a way of acknowledging, albeit imprecisely, that usage often varies among different kinds of texts. Numerals play a greater or lesser role in different genres of English writing. Written Arabic and Hebrew can be more or less thoroughly syllabic, depending on how fully vowels are marked. Hebrew can be more or less thoroughly prosodic, depending on the use of cantillation marks and Masoretic accents. More prosodic information is written into verse texts, as a rule, than into prose. Greek spelling is phonemically more accurate for classical Greek than for modern Greek, and English spelling phonemically more accurate for early texts than for later ones. The polytonic Greek script used for classical texts gives more alphaprosodic information than the modern monotonic script.

semographic, but a strong prosodic component has developed in many writing systems which began with no prosodic symbols at all. The lineation of Greek and Latin verse, the single and double bars of Sanskrit verse, the tonic accents added to Greek texts by Alexandrian scribes, the Masoretic accents and Tiberian cantillation marks applied to the Hebrew of the Torah during medieval times, and the tonemarks created in 13th-century Indochina for Sukothai (the parent script of Thai and Lao) are all prosodic symbols of importance to the history of script. Comma, colon, semicolon, long dash, full stop, parentheses, square brackets, question, exclamation and quotation marks are the survivors from a larger flock of symbols used as prosodic markers by many generations of European scribes. They are now routine components of every European script and of many Native American, Asian and African writing systems too. In bicameral scripts, the systematic use of capitals is yet another established form of prosodic marking – and so is italicization.

Semographic and *prosodic* are not so much opposite ends of a spectrum as adjacent points on a circle – but between these two adjacent points, the circle may be either broken or whole. How a statement is inflected can contrast or coincide with what it otherwise might mean. Besides that, meaning has its prosody – conceptual, not audible – which the prosody of speech appears at times to know but little of. If we look more closely at prosodic scripts (or the prosodic components of scripts), a division appears. There are signs that represent the prosody of speech, and signs that represent the prosody of meaning. We can call them *alphaprosodic* and *semoprosodic* signs. The distinction exists in the writing of music and mathematics just as it does in the writing of speech – but in mathematical notation, semoprosodic comes first; the reverse is the case in musical notation. In early manuscripts of European music, all signs are alphaprosodic. In a modern European musical score, the notes and rests and ties portray the prosody of sound, but the bar lines and beams (e.g., the heavy horizontals connecting groups of eight notes) are semoprosodic signs. They tell us how the music is *thought*, not how it sounds.

As usual in the world of writing systems, the difference is not in the signs themselves; it is in how the signs are used. That ubiquitous yet invisible symbol known nowadays as the *hard return* is often an alphaprosodic symbol in verse but semoprosodic in grocery lists, computer scripts and literary prose. Square brackets and parentheses are usually semoprosodic in literary texts, just as in mathematical notation. But the most important semoprosodic symbol in general use is the wordspace. It is needless in Chinese, where nearly every syllable – and therefore every symbol – is a word, but essential in mathematics. Many scripts have done without it, but those that have absorbed it have all kept it. It is crucial to silent reading (which is, in essence, semoprosodic reading). For that reason, it is crucial to reading *speed*.

In a normal string of English text, alphabetic symbols will outnumber semographic and prosodic symbols roughly five to one (and 75% or 80% of the non-alphabetic signs will be the spaces between words). Yet on a normal QWERTY keyboard, there more semographic and prosodic signs than alphabetic letters.

Writing, in short, is many things, used in many different ways by different people. In itself, it is both less and more than language. More because it can develop into rich and varied forms of graphic art. Less because, much as we love it, it is not an inescapable part of the human experience or the perennial human condition. If language is lost, humanity is lost. If writing is lost, certain kinds of civilization and society are lost, but many other kinds remain. Humans lived on the earth successfully – and so far as we know, quite happily – for a hundred thousand years without the benefit of writing. They have never lived, nor ever yet been happy, so far as we know, in the absence of language.

Recommendations for further reading

Bloomfield, Leonard. 1933. *Language*. New York: Holt.

Bringhurst, Robert. 1994. 'On the Classification of Letterforms.' Claremont, Calif.: *Serif* 1: pp. 30–39.

Chang Ch'ung-ho & Hans H. Fraenkel, ed. 1995. *Two Chinese Treatises on Calligraphy*. New Haven: Yale University Press.

Coulmas, Florian. 1989. *The Writing Systems of the World*. Oxford: Blackwell.

Daniels, Peter T., & William Bright, ed. 1996. *The World's Writing Systems*. New York: Oxford University Press.

DeFrancis, John. 1989. *Visible Speech: The Diverse Oneness of Writing Systems*. Honolulu: University of Hawaii Press.

Diringer, David. 1962. *Writing*. London: Thames & Hudson.

Gaur, Albertine. 1984. *A History of Writing*. London: British Library.

Gelb, I.J. 1963. *A Study of Writing*. 2nd ed. Chicago: University of Chicago Press.

Herrick, Earl M. 1974. 'A Taxonomy of Scripts.' Cleveland: *Visible Language* 8.1: pp. 5–32.

Jensen, Hans. 1970. *Sign, Symbol, Script*, translated by George Unwin. London: George Allen & Unwin.

Katzner, Kenneth. 1975. *The Languages of the World*. New York: Funk & Wagnalls.

Sapir, Edward. 1921. *Language: An Introduction to the Study of Speech*. New York: Harcourt, Brace & World.

Senner, Wayne M., ed. 1989. *The Origins of Writing*. Lincoln: University of Nebraska Press.

JOHN HUDSON

Unicode, from text to type

I. TYPE IN THE WORLD

INTERNATIONAL TYPE DESIGN typically implies one of two things: the design of type by people in many nations for their own scripts and languages, or the design of type by people in one nation for the scripts and languages of another. It may also refer to the work of type designers working internationally, calling to mind the itinerant punchcutters who followed the spread of printing and publishing across Europe, or the apprentices who gravitated to the geographical centres of the trade: a typographical migration that resulted in the first Roman types, made by two Germans, and the most esteemed Dutch oldstyle type, designed by a Hungarian. All three senses of the term are represented in the contemporary work celebrated in this book. In none of these senses is international type design a new thing.

The type specimens of the major European foundries of the 18th century display an abundance of 'exotic' types, mostly produced for academic publishers, and their number increases in the 19th century with the proliferation of missionary societies and presses printing religious texts in many hundreds of languages. Religious missions then, as before and since, provided both a demand for new types for indigenous writing systems and invented new writing systems where none existed. 19th century missionaries to North American aboriginal peoples were particularly inventive in the latter regard, but this too was nothing new. The most successful of the missionary writing systems must surely be the much older Cyrillic script, devised by missionaries to the Slavs in the 9th century: the modern Cyrillic script is used to write more than sixty languages across Eastern Europe and Eurasia. Similarly, the Armenian script was invented by the cleric Mesrop Maštoc, around 400 AD, for the translation of Greek and Syriac scriptures into his native tongue. The writing and printing of the Arabic script, variants of which are used to write dozens of languages from West Africa to South East Asia, spread with the progress of Islam.

[24]

It is in the nature of type design to follow in the baggage train. It is a secondary industry, and over 550 years it has played its rôle in the logistics of publishing, religion, advertising, politics, and business and, lately, 'information technology'. If, as I believe, type design is going through a truly international renaissance at the beginning of the 21st century, it is in large part enabled by the desire of the computer industry to sell hardware and software to people who speak languages other than English. The computer industry has not replaced older markets for type design (although it has revolutionised them, along with most other things), but by making every computer user in the world a customer for new typefaces – however indirectly, through the licensing of fonts to hardware and software companies for 'bundling' with their products – software developers have enormously expanded the demand for new and better digital fonts internationally. Type and typography are now intimately involved – they are implicated – in the internationalisation of computing and so in the cultural and economic developments that this process supports. As Robin Kinross, author of *Modern Typography*, observes:

> the era of DTP [desktop publishing] ushers into typography the phenomenon that we now call globalization. Perhaps it is one of the rather early instances of this, just as printing itself was a forerunner of the processes of mass-production and industrialization. There are elements in DTP itself that allowed and encouraged this. I mean: its essentially electronic nature, enabling the sharing of data across devices, and thus across countries and continents. And the development of DTP must have been partly driven by processes that were beginning to happen anyway – the rise of transnational corporations.[1]

This essay explores the relationship of text and type in the context of international software development and, in particular, in the context of the Unicode character encoding standard. It is, necessarily, a technical essay, and might at first seem out of place in a volume celebrating the artistic achievement of typeface designers. It certainly isn't necessary to understand anything about fixed-width encoding or bidirectional algorithms in order to appreciate the beauty of a typeface: much of what this book has to say can be reckoned by looking at the pictures. In a recent article for the Microsoft Typography website,[2] I defined typography as the functional application of beauty to the articulation of text. In the same way that I think a misapprehension is involved in trying to separate beauty from functionality in typography, so it is a mistake to consider the art of type design separate from the technology of type manufacture and use. Gutenberg's types finely emulated the *textura* manuscript book hand fashionable in mid-15th century Germany, but they are part of the history of typography, not of calligraphy, because of the technology that produced them. Digital technology has revolutionised the way in which type is designed, manufactured and used, and by understanding that technology – and the direction in which that technology is moving – we can understand what is possible today in type design and typography. This understanding can inform and enhance our appreciation of the type designer's art.

II. 0074006500780074

A computer is a machine that stores and manipulates numbers, which means that text, in order to be entered, stored, edited and typeset on a computer, must be expressed as a sequence of numbers. These numbers must, in turn, be mapped to character input methods, e.g. to keyboard keys, and to the visual representation of the characters in a font. A character encoding standard, such as Unicode, defines the relationship between the smallest units of written language necessary for entering and storing text – i.e. characters – and the numbers that represent them in computer encoded text. There are many standard – and some not so standard – character encodings available for computers and fonts to employ. Most encodings are specific to certain scripts and languages and to specific computer operating systems or applications. The basic nature of a character encoding is determined by its size, and this is determined by the number of bytes that the encoding assigns to each character. A byte is a unit of memory or data, usually reckoned as equal to eight bits,[3] and as such individual bytes were at a premium in early, slow computers with very limited memory and storage capacities. Bytes are not something that software engineers are keen to waste, even on today's very fast personal computers, so many character encodings employ a single byte to represent each character. Such encodings are typically referred to as 8-bit encodings, and sometimes as single-byte encodings. Good examples of common 8-bit encodings are ISO 8859-1, Windows CP 1252 and the Apple Mac Roman character set, all of which are designed to support the same set of Western European languages but which, frustratingly, differ in their actual assignment of numbers to characters. The number of bytes assigned to each character limits the overall size of the character encoding to the number of unique numbers than can be expressed in that quantity of bytes. This means that 8-bit encodings are limited to 256 characters: the total number of unique character identifiers that can be expressed as single bytes. This number is calculated by counting in base 16 (hexadecimal), starting at zero: 0 1 2 3 4 5 6 7 8 9 A B C D E F. In an 8-bit encoding, each byte is represented by two hexadecimal digits, which produces a grid of 256 character positions, or codepoints.

One of the many problems of 8-bit encodings is the unavoidable ambiguity of different encodings using the same numbers to represent

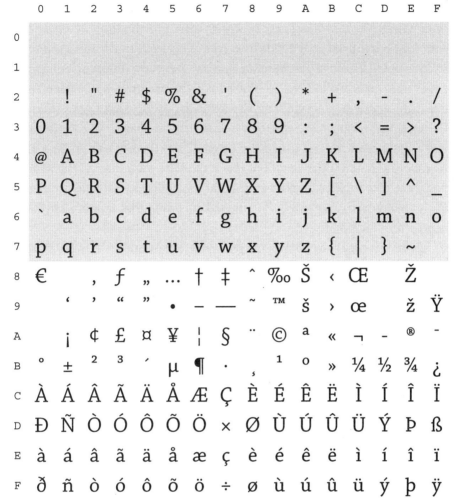

Figure 1. Example of an 8-bit character encoding: Windows Codepage 1252. Note that not all 256 codepoints are occupied by a visible character; some codepoints are reserved as control characters, a few are empty, and two codepoints, 20 and A0, are occupied by the *space* and *non-breaking space* characters respectively. The grey area represents the ASCII 7-bit encoding, which is a subset of most 8-bit encodings.

different characters. For example, comparing only Microsoft's Windows codepages, we can see that the same codepoint, F0, represents a different character in almost every 8-bit encoding:

đ   CP 1250 (Central European)

p   CP 1251 (Cyrillic)

ð   CP 1252 (Western European)

π   CP 1253 (Greek)

ð   CP 1254 (Turkish)

ך   CP 1255 (Hebrew)

́   CP 1256 (Arabic)

š   CP 1257 (Baltic)

đ   CP 1258 (Vietnamese)

This means that, in order to be able to correctly display a document on a computer, it is necessary to know which of these many character sets has been used to encode the text. The problem is compounded by the need to move documents around between different computer platforms – from Windows to Macintosh, for example – on which even the 8-bit encodings supporting the same group of languages differ. As Robin Kinross observes, electronic data can be shared 'across devices, and thus across countries and continents', but there needs to be a way to ensure that what the recipient receives is the same text as the sender has sent. This implies one of two things: the ability to translate from one 8-bit encoding to another, or a standard encoding that is shared by both sender and recipient.

There are other problems inherent in the limitations of 8-bit character sets, especially when we look beyond the relatively simple requirements of most European languages. Many of the world's writing systems require more than 256 characters. The Ethiopic syllabary, for example, consists of some 345 characters. The catalogue of modern and historic Han characters – the Chinese writing system variously employed as Chinese *hanza*, Japanese *kanji*, and Korean *hanja* – now numbers more than 80,000 characters (not all of these Han characters have been included in character encoding standards, but all are candidates for encoding). Obviously, for such scripts, single 8-bit encodings are insufficient.

There are two ways to increase the number of characters that can be represented in a given encoding. The first is to build collections of 8-bit encodings, in which a character is identified by both its position in an 8-bit character set and by the identity of that particular character set. The second method – easier to manage and to implement but generally requiring a greater number of overall bytes to encode any given piece of text – is to increase the number of bytes that are used to represent each character. This means moving, as a first step, from 8-bit, single-byte encoding to a 16-bit, double-byte encoding. This increases the number of available unique codepoints from 256 (16×16) to 65,536 (256×256).

In 1986, engineers from Xerox and Apple began discussing a common solution to the challenges of encoding Chinese and, in particular, to ways in which existing double-byte Japanese encodings could be leveraged to provide an easy migration path to extended Chinese. This notion, expressed as Han unification – treating Chinese and Japanese writing systems not as separate scripts but as different expressions of the same script – became one of the key principles in proposals that would result in the Unicode Standard. Over the following year, these discussions expanded to consider the idea of a universal, fixed-width[4] character encoding standard for all of the world's scripts and languages.

Toward the end of 1987, Joe Becker at Xerox coined the term Unicode, from 'unique, universal, and uniform character encoding'. The first version of the Unicode Standard was published in 1990, by which time the original ad hoc committees had evolved into the Unicode Consortium, with representation from many of the world's largest software companies with a stake in internationalisation.

Earlier, in 1984, the International Organization for Standardization (ISO) had formed a working group to develop a similar universal character encoding standard: ISO/IEC 10646. The main difference between the Unicode and ISO standards is that the Unicode Consortium is an industry organisation, with direct representation from member companies, while WG2, the working group responsible for ISO/IEC 10646, is made up of representatives from national standardisation bodies. In 1991, sensibly realising the futility of maintaining two universal yet incompatible character encodings, WG2 and the Unicode editorial body – the Unicode Technical Committee, or UTC – agreed to merge the two standards, reconciling their differences. There are still two standards, but their character repertoires are maintained and extended cooperatively, and Unicode is recognised by ISO as the official way to implement ISO/IEC 10646.

This very potted history leaves out many details, and fails to acknowledge the many men and women who have made the Unicode standard their work for more than fifteen years.[5] What even the most condensed history of Unicode and ISO/IEC 10646 makes clear is the common realisation, in the mid-1980s, that software internationalisation would require a universal character encoding to provide a unique indentifier for each character in the world's many writing systems. Today, the Unicode Standard is fast becoming the most widely used character encoding standard worldwide. It is the native character set for Microsoft's NT-based operating systems, Windows 2000 and XP, and for Apple's OS X. It is the default character set for the World Wide Web Consortium's XML standard. Adobe's powerful and well-respected suite of design applications is gradually being converted to handle Unicode text, and new Unicode-based text processing software seems to be released almost monthly. The Unicode conferences, which once happened annually, now take place twice each year, in different locations around the globe, to meet the demand for information about the standard.

Observant readers may have noticed that the estimated number of Han characters that are candidates for encoding – more than 80,000 – exceeds the number of single codepoints available in a 16-bit encoding. It became apparent, as the standard developed, that 65,536 codepoints were not going to be sufficient to encode all of the world's writing systems. In version 2.0 of the standard, 1996, the Unicode Consortium published an extension mechanism using pairs of double-byte codepoints to identify triple-byte characters. Effectively, this mechanism transforms Unicode into a 32-bit encoding, capable of providing unique identifiers for 1,114,111 characters. It is thought that this will be enough. Most of the characters currently encoded in Unicode are in the first 16-bit area, called the Basic Multilingual Plane or BMP. The Supplementary Planes have begun to be populated with additional mathematical characters, musical symbols, historical and artificial scripts, and with Han characters that are not in extensive modern use.

III. TEXT AND TYPE

Problems of cross-platform incompatibility, textual ambiguity and inadequate support for many writing systems – problems inherent in the limitations of single-byte text processing – are exacerbated when the intent is not simply to enter, store and display text but to articulate it using a sophisticated typographic system. Font developers and vendors in the early days of desktop publishing recognised the need to support traditional elements of typographic design such as ligatures, smallcaps and superior letters, but were forced to do so within a character encoding and text processing model that relied on 8-bit character sets. Large software companies like Adobe defined private standards for supplementary fonts – 'expert sets' –, while others took a more cavalier approach and hijacked codepoints within standard character sets to encode ligatures and other typeforms essential to good typography. Employing an Adobe expert set font to typeset, for example, the word *office* with an appropriate *ffi* ligature requires the user to switch fonts and to change the text of the word so that the letter sequence *ffi* is replaced by the character codepoint in the expert set that corresponds to the desired ligature. In this instance, using the Adobe expert set mapping, the text string is changed from *office* to *oYce;* the result looks fine when printed, but in the memory of the computer the text had ceased to be meaningful. Effectively, there is little to differentiate this approach to digital typography from earlier, mechanical typesetting; indeed, it can be seen as the application of a mechanical paradigm to a digital technology. Typeforms are selected by their appearance from a font of semantically empty characters. All the advantages of the merging of typesetting with text processing that should characterise digital typography – the ability to search, sort, spellcheck or re-use the text – are abandoned in order to make the document look the way it should on the page. When this kind of typographically driven textual dismemberment meets the multilingual demands of internationalisation and the exchange of documents between different computer operating systems and applications, the impact of 8-bit character encoding on text can be impressively destructive.

Impressions of the whole journey are described in *Podróż do Ziemi Świętej z Neapolu* (1836-39), of which *Grób Agamemnona* is a part. After coming back from the East, Słowacki stayed in Florence for two years before going to Paris, which was the center of Polish culture at that time. However, the poet did not find approval. His poetry, differing from the accepted model of Mickiewicz's poetry, instead of optimism brought negative and ironic opinions about the Polish exiles and their chances to win independence.

```
Impressions of the whole journey are described in
Podróż do Ziemi Œwiêtej z Neapolu (1836-39), of which
Grób Agamemnona is a part. After coming back from
the East, S³owacki stayed in Florence for two years
before going to Paris, which was the center of Polish
culture at that time. However, the poet did not Wnd
approval. His poetry, diVering from the accepted model
of Mickiewicz's poetry, instead of optimism brought
negative and ironic opinions about the Polish exiles
and their chances to win independence.
```

Figure 2. A short extract from a biography of the Polish romantic poet Juliusz Słowacki, written by Michał Kosmulski. Four different 8-bit fonts are required to typeset the few lines of text, including both Western and Central European fonts and an Adobe 'expert set' font. Below this is the typeset text as it appears when copied and pasted into a single-byte text editor, showing the damage to the text wrought by the limitations of single-byte language support and by use of expert set elements such as ligatures.

The Unicode Standard does not directly address the challenges of typographic sophistication, but by providing robust and unambiguous plain text encoding it provides a firm foundation for even the most complex typography. It does so by making a division between the encoding of text and the display of text. Rather than attempting to encode all the typographic variants of characters — ligatures, smallcaps, swash letters, contextual positioning forms, etc. — that might be required to typeset any document in a given script and language, Unicode encodes only those characters that are necessary to input and store plain text that may subsequently be displayed using as much or as little typographic sophistication as required. For some writing systems, such as the use of the Latin script for the English language, this plain text encoding is typified by a one-to-one relationship between the stored characters and the minimum standard of human readability.[6] English text does not require ligatures or smallcaps to be readable: it needs them to look good and to articulate its meaning more fully. Other writing systems, such as Arabic and the many South Asian scripts classified as Indic, require higher level processing to render the stored text with appropriate typeforms in order to be readable. Such writing systems are commonly referred to among text processing and internationalisation experts as complex scripts. Some examples of complex script processing are provided later in this essay.

The division between the encoding and display of text is expressed in Unicode by distinguishing characters from glyphs. In manual and mechanical typesetting practice, it was typical to use the term character to refer to any individual typographic element; for instance, an *ffi* ligature would be referred to as a character, even though it represented three letters that would themselves be called characters. This simple terminology reflects the nature of typeforms in these typesetting processes: the semantic relationship of the *ffi* ligature to the letters *f* and *i* exists only in the mind of the person setting the type, so there is no need to distinguish it as a different kind of element. When typesetting is married to computer text processing, however, the term character acquires a more precise meaning and refers only to an encoded element of text, not to the typeform or forms that are used to display that element. The latter are referred to as glyphs, and the relationship of glyphs to characters is varied. A character might be displayed by a single glyph or by more than one glyph, or a single glyph might represent more than one character. Because it seeks to only encode characters necessary for plain text, the Unicode standard does not need to provide codepoints for all the possible glyphs that might be used to display that text. So, for example, the *ffi* ligature does not need to be encoded, because the individual letters *f* and *i* are encoded, and this is sufficient for plain text.[7]

The text processing distinction between simple and complex scripts can be generalised in terms of the relationship of glyphs to characters in normal readable text. In simple scripts, there is a one-to-one relationship between the stored character codes of plain text and the glyphs needed to represent that text in a minimally readable form. Effectively, plain text and readable text are the same thing for simple scripts. Complex scripts, such as Arabic, are typified by complex relationships of characters to glyphs, and plain text in these languages is sub-readable: a reader might be able to decipher plain text, but it is not the normal standard of readability expected of the script. The relationship of characters to glyphs in complex scripts might involve obligatory ligatures, contextual forms, or the adjustment of the position of glyphs relative to each other. In addition, as we shall see in the Devanagari script example later in this essay, complex script text processing can involve manipulation of the order of characters prior to glyph processing.

In figure 3 the character sequences on the left are displayed in 'logical order', from left to right, the order in which the character codes are stored

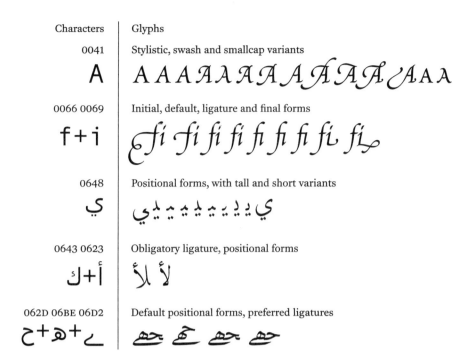

Figure 3. Divers relationships of characters to glyphs. Top, typographic and ornamental variants for Latin letters; below, orthographic and typographic variants for Arabic letters.

in the computer. However, the Arabic glyphs are rendered from right to left. In addition to assigning codepoints to characters, the Unicode Standard also provides rules and guidelines for implementing character-level layout of text, including control of display order for bidirectional text. In addition to a unique identifier, each character in Unicode is assigned a variety of character properties. These include a bidirectionality property that determines the display order of the character relative to other characters in the same text. There are nineteen different bidirectional categories in the standard, determining how characters are displayed in accordance with the Unicode bidirectional algorithm. These categories can be generalised in terms of strong, weak and neutral directionality. An Arabic letter, for example, will have a strong right-to-left direction property, while a Latin letter will have a strong left-to-right. This means that sequences of Arabic letters will always be displayed from right to left, and Latin letters from left to right. Other characters, however, are assigned weak directionality, meaning that their display order might change relative to adjacent characters with strong directionality. Some characters have neutral directionality, and inherit directly from preceding characters without affecting subsequent characters. Obviously, this kind of text layout information is required for multilingual texts in which words in languages such as Arabic, written from right to left, are مندمج in the midst of left-to-right text. Less obviously to non-native readers, the scripts that most people think of as right-to-left writing systems – Arabic, Hebrew, Syriac, Thaana – involve bidirectional layout internally. While words in these scripts are written from right to left, numbers, including dates, are written from left to right.

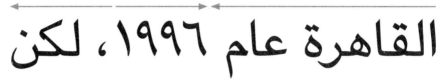

القاهرة عام ١٩٩٦، لكن

Figure 4. Bidirectional Arabic text. The words read from right to left, the numbers from left to right.[8]

Complex script processing generally requires manipulation of both characters and glyphs. While specifying some aspects of this processing, the Unicode Standard does not force software developers to cut the cake in only one way. Deciding which aspects of complex script shaping to handle at the character level and which at the glyph level determines how responsibility is shared among operating system, application and font developers. For example, the bidirectional algorithm is applied in recent versions of the Mac operating system by Apple Text Services for Unicode Imaging (ATSUI), but most other aspects of complex script processing – e.g. reordering of text elements for Indic script – are handled at the glyph level using Apple Advanced Typography (AAT), an extension of the TrueType font format. This approach puts the greater burden of responsibility on font developers. OpenType technology, jointly developed by Microsoft and Adobe, is also based on an extension of the TrueType format, but more evenly distributes the responsibility for script and language support. All character processing requirements and recommendations in the Unicode Standard are the responsibility of the operating system or individual application, which reduces the amount and complexity of glyph processing that needs to be provided by font developers.

There are, of course, pros and cons and trade-offs in both approaches. The AAT font intelligence model is internally more powerful and flexible than OpenType, and the general purpose engine that processes AAT font features does not require independent knowledge about particular writing systems. This means that fonts can be developed for any Unicode encoded script without worrying about whether the system or application has knowledge of the shaping requirements for that script. However, some key aspects of AAT font intelligence, e.g. contextual glyph substitution, are considerably more difficult to develop than the OpenType equivalent, and AAT is poorly supported by font development tools. The very small number of applications that made use of ATSUI/AAT prior to Mac OS X, and the continued lack of support in major application suites from other vendors, has not encouraged much AAT development out-side Apple and a small number of niche localisation developers. Apple's overall market share may be insufficient to promote the technology in a world in which cross-platform compatibility is increasingly important. Unicode enables the seamless exchange of text between different oper-ating systems, and the existence of two different font technologies to display that text seems increasingly anachronistic.

The OpenType model obliges font developers to work within a sys-tem of character level support that preconfigures text ready for glyph processing. For internationalisation, this means that font support for individual scripts and languages is dependent on character processing support at the system or application level. In Microsoft Windows 2000 and XP, complex script processing is generally handled via the Unicode Script Processor (Uniscribe).[9] Uniscribe contains a number of individual script shaping engines that apply character level pre-processing to text and then apply specific OpenType Layout glyph substitution and posi-tioning features. The principle function of Uniscribe is to provide basic correct text shaping, i.e. to raise complex script text from the plain text level stored in the computer to a human-readable level. Most subsequent typographic refinement – e.g. the use of discretionary, non-obligatory ligatures or swash forms – needs to be user-controllable within applica-tions, either through direct interaction with glyph processing features in the font, or by calling additional Uniscribe processing. This architecture greatly simplifies the task of font development for complex scripts, but it also means that fonts cannot be developed for a script until an appropri-ate shaping engine is available in Uniscribe.[10] Although it is a younger technology than AAT, OpenType Layout for complex scripts is already supported in a greater number of major applications. Due to the rela-tive ease of development and superior tool support, a large amount of OpenType font design and production is now taking place, particularly among Indic and Arabic developers.

The original TrueType font format and rendering software was developed by Apple in the late 1980s, was released in the early 1990s, and was soon after licensed by Microsoft. Although Adobe's Type 1 PostScript font format had been, and remained, the favourite of digital typesetters, graphic designers and other design and publishing profes-sionals, TrueType became the system font format for both the Mac and Windows operating systems. Although for a long time PostScript fonts were better supported in pre-press output devices, and so gained a repu-tation for greater reliability, TrueType had a number of advantages over the Type 1 format. Two of these advantages relate directly to our topic, and have influenced the subsequent development of font technology at

Apple, Microsoft and Adobe. In April 1988, when Unicode was still in its infancy, Apple decided to incorporate the new encoding standard into the TrueType specification by making support for multi-byte character mapping central to the new format. The Type 1 font format is limited to a single-byte, 8-bit character set, and so suffers from the limitations and attendant text processing problems discussed earlier. By building multi-byte encoding support into the TrueType specification, Apple provided a solid foundation for future development of the format. The second advantage of TrueType is the tabular structure of an 'sfnt' font, the file format defined by Apple.[11] A TrueType or other 'sfnt' font is made up of a collection of individual tables, each containing specific font data. For example, the 'glyf' table contains TrueType outline information for each glyph in the font, the 'kern' table contains horizontal metric adjustment values for pairs of glyphs, and the 'cmap' table maps glyphs in the font to character codes. Type rendering and layout software accesses information from different tables as needed. By accessing the 'cmap' table, for instance, software knows which glyph to display when you type a character; by accessing a glyph substitution table, such as the OpenType 'GSUB' table described below, software knows what to do with that glyph when you apply a layout feature to it such as smallcaps or swash. The tabular structure of the 'sfnt' file means that it is relatively easy to extend the capabilities of the format by adding new tables. This is what Apple did with AAT (then called GX Typography) in the early 1990s, and what Microsoft and Adobe have done with OpenType.

The OpenType specification describes a variety of new required and optional tables, but only two concern us in this discussion: the OpenType Layout tables 'GSUB' and 'GPOS'. These tables contain information, respectively, for glyph substitution and glyph positioning. This information is processed by OpenType-savvy applications by examining runs of glyphs in text and matching lookups in the tables to features applied, for instance, by a shaping engine such as Uniscribe or directly by the user. For example, the GSUB table might include a set of lookups mapping uppercase Latin glyphs to corresponding smallcap forms, associated with the *Small Capitals from Capitals* <c2sc> OpenType Layout feature. When this feature is applied to text by the user, in Adobe InDesign for example, the software examines the text and matches uppercase glyphs to the <c2sc> lookup input in the GSUB table and substitutes the appropriate smallcap output glyphs. By carefully organising the order in which different lookups are applied, font developers can enable layout features to interact in powerful ways. For example, having applied a feature that substitutes smallcaps, the user might then apply another feature to substitute swash forms or other variants of those smallcaps. The GSUB table

GSUB lookup type 1, simple

GSUB lookup type 2, multiple

GSUB lookup type 3, alternate

GSUB lookup type 4, ligature

Figure 5. Basic, non-contextual, glyph substitution lookup types.

Segunda 2ª Octavo 8º

Figure 6. Example of contextual glyph substitution using the *Ordinals* <ordn> layout feature. The feature is applied to the entire run of text, but the *a* and *o* are only replaced by ordinal forms when they follow a numeral.

supports different lookup types that provide one-to-one, one-to-many, one-to-one-of-many, many-to-one, and contextual substitutions.

Lookups in the GPOS table operate in a similar fashion. Software examines the text for glyphs included in GPOS lookups, and adjusts the positioning of these glyphs. Glyph positioning can be used to handle a variety of functions: positioning accents above letters, or stacking accents one above another; adjusting the vertical position of glyphs, e.g. shifting punctuation, to align better with uppercase or smallcap settings; changing the default sidebearings of glyphs or adjusting pairs of glyphs to increase or decrease the space between them; or aligning attachment points between different glyphs, which is very useful for cursive scripts such as Arabic and for handwriting fonts.

To understand better how Unicode text is processed and displayed by script shaping engines and font layout information, let's look at a single word in the ancient Sanskrit language of India, as typeset in the Devanagari script using R.K. Joshi's Raghu OpenType font.[12] This word, प्रज्ञेनात्मनास्माल्लोकादुत्क्रम्यामुष्मिन्स्वर्गे, transliterated *prajñenātma-nāsmāllokādutkramyāmusminsvarge,* is taken from the final sentence of the *Aitreyopanishad,* one of the classical Hindu spiritual texts collectively known as the Upanishads.[13]

The text is entered in a common Windows application like MS Word, using a phonetic Sanskrit keyboard layout, and as each character is entered it is stored and the run of text is passed to the Unicode Script

Processor (Uniscribe). Uniscribe determines, by looking at the character codes, that the text is in the Devanagari script, so knows to process the text using its Indic shaping engine. Devanagari, like the many other scripts generally classified as Indic, is an alphasyllabic writing system. Each consonant carries an inherent vowel – the short *a* – and in order for that vowel to be suppressed or another vowel to be used, the consonant is modified by the presence of a vowel killer (*halant* or *virama*) or a dependant vowel sign (*matra*). Additionally, consonants may join with each other to form conjunct clusters, in the same way that the letter sequence *tch* represents a distinct consonant sound in the English word *fetch*. Consonant clusters might be represented by using modified forms of the initial consonants (half forms) or by a ligature form, depending on the font and the style of representation desired by the user. The Unicode Devanagari block encodes only full forms of consonants, and vowels as both independent forms (seldom used, except at the beginning of words) and as *matras*. Because half forms and ligatures are not encoded, they need to be shaped during glyph processing, using OpenType GSUB lookups. Some *matras* and the consonant *ra* require additional handling to position them relative to consonants or conjuncts. Because the text is entered using a phonetic keyboard, spelling out the consonants and vowels as they are spoken, this is the order in which the characters are stored in the computer. However, one of the Devanagari *matras,* the short *i,* is properly displayed to the left of the consonant or conjunct that it follows phonetically; this means that the order of text involving this character has to be changed. Similarly, the consonant *ra* which takes a special form relative to other consonants or conjuncts, often needs to be reordered. Because these actions are part of the basic shaping of text, following rules laid out in the Unicode standard, this reordering is done by Uniscribe at the character level, rather than at the glyph level in font lookups.

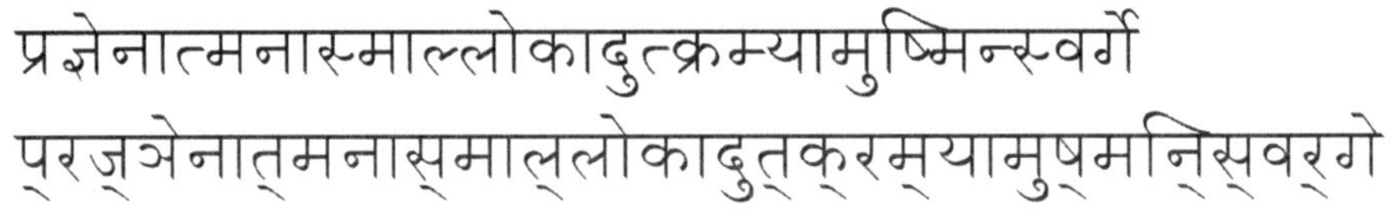

प्रज्ञेनात्मनास्मल्लोकादुत्क्रम्यामुष्मिन्स्वर्गे

पुरज्ञेनातुमनासुमाल्लोकादुतकुरमयामुषमनिसुवरगे

Figure 7. Our Sanskrit sample word correctly displayed, top, and as plain text without any shaping, below. Without shaping, the word is represented by the default glyph forms of the Unicode text; this is barely decipherable, and certainly not readable.

As should be apparent even from this brief and incomplete summary of the features of the Devanagari alphasyllabary, the basic unit of writing is the syllable, so Uniscribe's Indic shaping engine begins by analysing the text and splitting the character string into syllables. These character clusters are then analysed in turn, and characters such as the *ra* consonant short *i matra* that need to be reordered prior to glyph processing shifted. Note that this reordering takes place in a buffered storage layer, as part of the display of the text: the original text string is never altered, which means that it can continue to be searched, spellchecked etc.

Here is the stored sequence of Unicode codepoints encoding our sample word, divided into syllable clusters by Uniscribe as indicated by the grey vertical bars. The codepoints to pay attention to for are U+0930, the *ra* consonant, and U+093F, the *i matra*. The frequently occurring code point U+094D is the vowel killer (*virama* or *halant*); when this appears between two consonants, it indicates that they form a conjunct.

```
092A 094D 0930 | 091C 094D 091E 0947 | 0928 093E | 0924
094D 092E | 0928 093E | 0938 094D 092E 093E | 0932 094D
0932 094B | 0915 093E | 0926 0941 | 0924 094D 0915 094D
0930 | 092E 094D 092F 093E | 092E 0941 | 0937 094D 092E
093F | 0928 094D 0938 094D 0935 | 0930 094D 0917 0947
```

Here is the buffered sequence of Unicode codepoints, after Uniscribe has reordered the *ra* and *i matra*. The affected characters are highlighted in bold, their original positions in the syllable indicated by a bullet

```
092A 0930 094D • | 091C 094D 091E 0947 | 0928 093E | 0924
094D 092E | 0928 093E | 0938 094D 092E 093E | 0932 094D
0932 094B | 0915 093E | 0926 0941 | 0924 094D 0915 0930
094D • | 092E 094D 092F 093E | 092E 0941 | 093F 0937 094D
092E • | 0928 094D 0938 094D 0935 | • 0917 0947 0930
094D
```

प्र ज्ञे ना त्म ना स्मा ल्लो का दु त्क्र म्या मु ष्मि न्स्व र्गे

Figure 8. The individual syllables of our Sanskrit sample word.

At this stage, character processing is complete, and Uniscribe begins glyph shaping for each syllable cluster by applying GSUB and GPOS lookups associated with a number of Indic script layout features. The features and lookups applied are to a degree font-dependent. Here are the layout features applied to each syllable using Professor Joshi's Raghu font; a different font might apply slightly different features, e.g. more or fewer ligature forms for conjuncts.

092A 0930 094D : *pra* : The 'Below-Base Forms' feature is applied to replace the 0930 (*ra*) and 094D (*halant*, vowel killer) with a default below-base form of 0930 (*vattu*). The 'Below-Base Substitutions' feature is then applied to 092A (*pa*) and the default below-base form (*vattu*) to render the required ligature.

091C 094D 091E 0947 : *jñe* : The 'Akhand' feature is applied to replace 091C (*ja*) 094D (*halant*) 091E (*nya*) with the necessary ligature. The 'Above- Base Mark Positioning' feature is applied to position 0947 (*e matra*, vowel sign) above the ligature.

0928 093E : *na* : No OpenType Layout features applied.

0924 094D 092E : *tma* : The 'Half Forms' feature is applied to the combination 0924 (*ta*) 094D (*halant*) to substitute the half form of 0924 (*t*).

0928 093E : *na* : No OpenType Layout features applied.

0938 094D 092E 093E : *sma* : The 'Half Forms' feature is applied to the combination 0938 (*sa*) 094D (*halant*) to substitute the half form of 0938 (*s*).

0932 094D 0932 094B : *llo* : The 'Half Forms' feature is applied to the combination 0932 (*la*) 094D (*halant*) to substitute the half form of 0932 (*l*).

0915 093E : *ka* : No OpenType Layout features applied.

0926 0941 : *du* : The 'Below-Base Mark Positioning' feature is applied to position 0941 (*u matra*) below 0926 (*da*).

0924 094D 0915 0930 094D : *tkra* : The 'Half Forms' feature is applied to the combination 0924 (*ta*) 094D (*halant*) get the half form of 0924 (*t*). The 'Below-Base Form' feature is applied to 0930 (*ra*) and 094D (*halant*) to replace it with a default below base form of 0930 (*vattu*). The 'Below-base Substitutions' feature is then applied to 0915 (*ka*) and the default below base form (*vattu*) to render the required ligature.

092E 094D 092F 093E : *mya* : The 'Half Forms' feature is applied to the combination 092E (*ma*) 094D (*halant*) to substitute the half form of 092E (*m*).

092E 0941 : *mu* : No OpenType Layout features applied.

093F 0937 094D 092E : *smi* : The 'Pre-Base Substitutions' feature is applied to get the desired glyph variant of 093F (*i matra*); this feature substitutes one of five different *i matras* in the Raghu font that are designed to fit over different widths of consonants and conjuncts.

0928 094D 0938 094D 0935 : *nsva* : The 'Half Forms' feature is applied to the combinations 0928 (*na*) 094D (*halant*) and 0938 (*sa*) 094D (*halant*) to substitute the respective half forms of 0928 (*n*) and 0938 (*s*).

0917 0947 0930 094D : *rge* : The 'Reph' feature is applied to replace 0930 (*ra*) and 094D (*halant*) with a default glyph for the *reph* (the above-base form of *ra*). The 'Above-Base Substitutions' feature is then applied to 0947 (*e matra*) and the *reph* to substitute them with a composite. The 'Above-Base Mark Positioning' feature is applied to position the composite above 0917 (*ga*).

Of course, all this is invisible to the user and happens very fast. The user is aware only of typing his or her language as it is spoken, and seeing the text displayed and printed as expected, according to the orthographic and typographic traditions embodied in the typeface design. The relationship of text to type made possible by Unicode – and by the new font formats, shaping engines and applications that implement Unicode – is rich and complex. It is a the result of a massive cooperative effort of linguists, text encoding experts, software engineers, font developers and, at the centre of it all, the talented type designers of many countries who preserve in their work the heritage of the world's many and varied writing systems.

IV. A VOICE IN THE WORLD

For we speak as others have spoken before us. And a sense of language is also a feeling for ways of living that have meant something.[14]

At the beginning of this essay, I suggested that the involvement of type and typography in the internationalisation of computing implicates type designers in the cultural and economic developments of globalisation. This is inevitable. Type design is an art and a craft, but it is also a business. The internationalisation of software made possible by the Unicode standard is an opportunity for many type designers and font developers. There is money to be made. But around the world, people both rich and poor are beginning to understand that globalisation must be about more than trade deals, international finance and the quest for profits: that globalisation of business must be informed and tempered by the meeting of cultures, dialogue among civilisations, and increased respect for the heritage, rights and aspirations of a global citizenship. Throughout its history, type design has been an activity taking place at the intersection of ideas. It exists to serve the written word, the record of ways of living that have meant something. If type design is implicated in globalisation, we can hope that it will be a humanising influence and a witness to older and enduring values.

Acknowledgements

I would like to thank John Jenkins and Ken Whistler, members of Unicode Technical Committee, for reviewing some sections of this essay and providing helpful advice, and Peter Lofting for his balanced discussion of the technical strengths and developmental weaknesses of AAT fonts.

[41]

The views finally expressed are, of course, those of the author, and any errors or omissions are his own. I would also like to thank Apurva Joshi for assisting me in preparing the Devanagari example of complex script rendering, and Dr Anthony Stone for providing the Latin transliteration.

Notes

1. Kinross, Robin. *The reinvention of printing: the coming of desktop publishing in the 1980s.* A talk given at the 'Re-Marking the text' conference, St Andrews, Scotland, July 20, 2001. www.typotheque.com/stuff/articles/DTP.html

2. Hudson, John. *OpenType Typography for European Scripts.* Microsoft Typography. www.microsoft.com/typography/otfntdev/standot/euroscripts.htm

3. The term byte was coined by Werner Buchholz in 1956, during the development of the IBM Stretch computer. A byte was originally defined as 1 to 6 bits, but IBM settled on an 8-bit byte later that year, and this was adopted as a standard for later computers.

4. A fixed-width encoding uses byte sequences of the same length to represent all characters, regardless of how few bytes are actually required. In a variable-width encoding, the number of bytes used to represent each character varies and generally utilises the smallest number of bytes necessary. For example, in a double-byte encoding, the first 256 characters could be expressed as single bytes, since the first byte of a double-byte representation would equal zero. In a variable-width encoding, the first 256 characters would be represented by one byte each, while the next 65,280 characters would be represented by two bytes each. In a fixed-width encoding, every character would be represented by two bytes. The advantage of a variable-width encoding is that languages that can be encoded using characters in the first 256 codepoints take up only half the storage and memory space of other languages. However, this requires a mechanism to distinguish between single-byte text strings and double-byte text strings. Does the hexadecimal string 74657874 represent a sequence of four single-byte characters or two double-byte characters: the English word text or the Chinese characters 琠硴? In a fixed-width encoding, this ambiguity is removed.

5. A more detailed history of the Unicode Standard and its relationship to ISO/IEC 10646 can be found at the Unicode Consortium's website: http://www.unicode.org/unicode/consortium/consort.html

6. Not all languages that employ the Latin script share this simple characteristic. Many African languages employ tonal diacritics that are encoded in Unicode only as combining marks, not as precomposed combinations of letters and diacritics. In order to achieve a minimal acceptable level of human readability, such languages require glyph substitution or positioning similar to that employed for complex scripts such as Arabic.

7. Although it is not necessary for Unicode to provide a codepoint for a ligature such as *ffi*, this glyph and a small number of other 'presentation forms' are encoded in the standard. Although it is a principle of Unicode to encode only plain text characters, it is also a principle to provide one-to-one codepoint mappings for older character sets, to enable easy roundtrip conversions of text between Unicode and pre-existing standards. Since some of these older character sets were not limited to plain text characters, some ligatures are encoded for the

Latin, Armenian, Hebrew and Arabic scripts. The use of these presentation form codepoints is not encouraged, and some software may choose to apply canonical decomposition rules to reduce a character such as *ffi* to the plain text codepoints for the sequence *f f i*.

8. The numbers in this illustration are displayed using the traditional Arabic forms, which Arabs have traditionally called Indic numbers in recognition of their origin. Europeans, meanwhile, have traditionally referred to the numbers in common use since the 15th century as Arabic numbers, again in recognition of their origin. So European numbers are Arabic numbers and Arabic numbers are Indic numbers. To add to the confusion, the forms of numbers have evolved since their adoption by Europeans, so the date in this illustration that looks as if it might be 1997 in European numbers is actually 1996 in Arabic numbers. All this and much more is explained in Georges Ifrah's fascinating book *The Universal History of Numbers: From Prehistory to the Invention of the Computer* (New York, 1999).

9. Uniscribe is a dynamic link library (DLL) that ships with the Windows operating system and with Internet Explorer. A DLL is a collection of small programs that can be called by a larger program to perform a specific task or series of tasks. The principal advantage of DLLs is that they are only loaded into random access memory when called, otherwise keeping memory free for other processes. Uniscribe contains a collection of text layout APIs that control how text is displayed. API is an abbreviation for application programming interface, a function, or set of functions, that applications use to take advantage of system components. For example, almost all Windows applications that process plain use the common TextOut or ExtTextOut system APIs to draw text.

10. Three other developments deserve at least brief mention in this context. The Summer Institute of Linguistics, which supports linguists and translators dealing with minority languages around the world, has developed its own Unicode-based font technology, Graphite, and a small number of applications to provide basic word processing capabilities. Graphite provides the flexibility of Apple's AAT technology on the Windows platform, and allows SIL to bypass the Uniscribe shaping engine requirement; SIL make use of both OpenType and Graphite, as support permits or demands. Meanwhile, contributors to the FreeType project, an open-source font rendering system increasingly used in Linux and other flavours of UNIX, have been developing script shaping engines to implement Unicode complex script character processing; the intention of such engines is to mirror the system/font relationship of Uniscribe, which will make OpenType Layout more widely useable. Finally, Adobe, Microsoft's partner in the development of the OpenType specification, have chosen to build their own core text processing engines, in order to end their reliance on operating system components. Adobe's OpenType focus to date has been on European and East Asian scripts, with no systematic support for Indic or Arabic OpenType Layout.

11. With the inclusion of PostScript outlines in OpenType fonts, the 'sfnt' file structure has become a *de facto* industry standard. The merging of TrueType and PostScript font technology in this way results in some awkward terminology. Although an OpenType font shares the same file structure as a traditional TrueType font, it may be 'TrueType flavour' or 'PostScript flavour' (the latter is often referred to as CFF flavour, in reference to Adobe's Compact Font Format, the particular PS outline expression used in OpenType fonts). While the term 'sfnt

font' is too probably technical to gain broad popularity, it remains the most accurate name to apply to the class of fonts that use the TrueType table structure but that can contain different kinds of glyph outlines.

12. Professor Joshi's Raghu typeface was selected as a winner in the *bukva:raz!* competition. See specimen on pages 312–313.

13. The *Aitreyopanishad* is a meditation on the singular spirit that created the universe out of His own being, and was written around 550 BC. The sample word comes from the conclusion of the third and final section of this Upanishad, translated by F. Max Müller, the eminent 19th century German Sanskritist: 'He [Vamadeva], having by this conscious self stepped forth from this world, and having obtained all desires in that heavenly world, became immortal, yea, he became immortal'.

14. Rhees, Rush. *Without Answers.* Routledge & Kegan Paul. London, 1969. p.150

MAXIM ZHUKOV

ITC Cyrillics: 1992-

A CASE STUDY

T HERE SEEMS TO BE a steadily growing demand for non-Latin typefaces these days. Cyrillic typography is now experiencing a revival – both in post-Soviet Russia and worldwide. The number of people involved in Cyrillic type design is increasing. The reasons are many: political changes in countries where Cyrillic is used, and the liberation of the press; democratisation of type design tools; and the globalisation of written communications, to name a few. This last phenomenon has been further enhanced by the adoption of Unicode, a new character encoding standard that includes Cyrillic, an 'umbrella' covering a great number of character sets which belong to various scripts of the world.

Type designers and font manufacturers are increasingly expected to produce fonts that include character sets reaching far beyond the boundaries of the usual 256-character Windows ANSI, or Macintosh, complement. With this background in mind, the pioneering experience of the International Typeface Corporation and ParaType in planning and building a comprehensive library of digital Cyrillics may prove interesting to those involved in, or concerned with, multilingual typography.

ITC: LES LIAISONS DANGEREUSES

ITC's 'Russian connection' dates back more than twenty years. Over this time the company has been interested in Russian design heritage as part of world typographic culture, and ITC provided continuous support to Soviet designers through sponsorship of individuals, activities, and events. These activities proved vital in the development of the typographic design profession in the Soviet Union. The many exhibitions, competitions, publications, and conferences that ITC has sponsored or been involved in have included the exhibition *Typographica USSR*, *Calligraphia USA/USSR*, the Herb Lubalin Student Design Competitions, and a survey of Soviet typography in the book *Typographic Communications Today*, put together by Ed Gottschall and published by ITC and MIT in 1987. In addition, the visits to the Soviet Union of ITC's top people (Ed

[45]

Gottschall in 1984, Aaron Burns in 1985, Mark Batty and Laurie Burns in 1990) contributed significantly to the process of Russian typographic revival, which started gaining momentum even before the advent of perestroika and glasnost and the end of the USSR.

And so it was that ITC became the first type foundry in the USA to start an ambitious new venture with ParaType (then ParaGraph), a newborn Russian company that quickly emerged as an industry leader in developing Cyrillic digital fonts.

IN THE BEGINNING...

The history of the ITC Cyrillic library goes back to the late 1980s. At that time ITC had a consultative body, the Type Review Board (TRB). It convened several times a year to discuss possible additions to the ITC type library, and to exchange views on directions and trends in typeface development. The Board was made up of senior company managers (Aaron Burns, Mark Batty, Allan Haley) and such eminent type gurus as Colin Brignall, Cynthia Hollandsworth, Mike Parker, Erik Spiekermann, and Sumner Stone, among others.

In May 1988, I made a presentation to the ITC Type Review Board on the possible extension of the ITC type library to a number of non-Latin scripts: Arabic, Cyrillic, Devanagari, Greek, and Hebrew; the visuals for my proposal were prepared by my old friend Vladimir Yefimov. After a lively discussion at the TRB meeting, a decision was made to have the Cyrillic versions of the most popular ITC typefaces devised by a contractor in Moscow, namely ParaType.

Following several meetings and other communication between the managers of ParaType and ITC, the project finally took off the ground. It was overseen by Allan Haley and Ilene Strizver at ITC, and by Andrei Skaldin, Alexei Dobrokhotov, and Emil Yakupov at ParaType. ITC asked me to act as an advisor and co-ordinator, and to assume responsibility for the quality of the ITC Cyrillics – to test, review, and evaluate the betas, and to provide directions for improving and fine-tuning the designs.

AVANT GARDE HEADS THE PACK

The mainstream development work on the ITC Cyrillics project started in earnest in 1992, with, quite aptly, the flagship ITC typeface, Avant Garde Gothic. The companion Cyrillic version was designed by Vladimir Yefimov, the principal designer at ParaType. The choice of Avant Garde was both symbolic and practical.

This neo-constructivist design originated with the New York magazine *Avant Garde*, the title of which echoed the name given to the Russian revolutionary art movement. The typeface was designed by Herb Lubalin, whose father Joseph came to America from Russia in 1903. So the creation of ITC Avant Garde Gothic Cyrillic completed a small historical circle.

The development of ITC Avant Garde Gothic Cyrillic was intended as a cornerstone in building a Cyrillic 'core set' of the thirty-five fonts included in PostScript-driven laser printers and image-setters: the first four of the thirty-five were the type styles of ITC Avant Garde Gothic.

For the same reason, the initial set of Cyrillics also included the extensions of two other ITC typefaces that were part of the 'PostScript 35': ITC Bookman and ITC Zapf Chancery Medium.

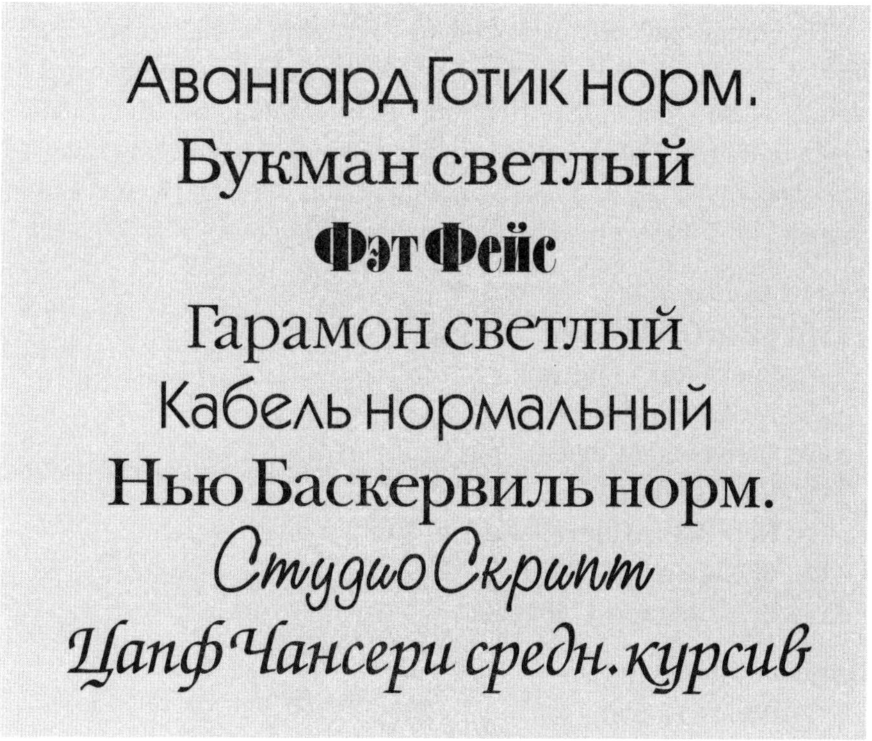

Авангард Готик норм.
Букман светлый
Фэт Фейс
Гарамон светлый
Кабель нормальный
Нью Баскервиль норм.
Студио Скрипт
Цапф Чансери средн. курсив

Figure 1. First set of ITC Cyrillics, spring 1994 (top to bottom).
ITC Avant Garde Gothic Cyrillic, by Vladimir Yefimov; original by Herb Lubalin and Tom Carnase, 1970; André Gürtler, Christian Mengelt and Erich Gschwind, 1977. ITC Bookman Cyrillic, by Lyubov' Kuznetsova and Tagir Safayev; original by Edward Benguiat, 1975. ITC Fat Face Cyrillic, by Vladimir Yefimov and Gennady Baryshnikov, original by Herb Lubalin and Tom Carnase, 1970.
ITC Garamond Cyrillic, by Alexander Tarbeev; original by Claude Garamond, 1532; Jean Jannon, 1621; Morris Fuller Benton, 1919; Tony Stan, 1975, 1977. ITC Kabel Cyrillic, by Tagir Safayev; original by Rudolf Koch, 1927; Victor Caruso, 1976. ITC New Baskerville Cyrillic, by Tagir Safayev; original by John Baskerville, 1757; John Quaranta, Matthew Carter et al., 1978. ITC Studio Script Cyrillic, by Elvira Slysh; original by Pat Hickson, 1990. ITC Zapf Chancery Cyrillic, by Vladimir Yefimov and Gennady Baryshnikov; original by Hermann Zapf, 1979.

PACKAGING THE ITC CYRILLICS

Many ITC typefaces developed in the 1970s and 1980s are, in fact, extended families, comprising many weights (up to five in ITC Avant Garde Gothic, ITC Kabel, and ITC Bauhaus), with matching italics, small caps, alternate glyph sets, and so on. In order to meet the immediate needs of a market hungry for digital fonts, issuing complete families did not seem the right thing to do in the first years of the ITC/ParaType venture. With limited resources and under heavy time pressure, we felt that releasing more typefaces in abridged versions, rather than fewer typefaces in the full range of styles, was more appropriate.

The design and production of the ITC Cyrillics had to be divided into stages, in which packages of assorted typefaces, often batched as standard 'four-packs' of related fonts ('normal/italic/bold/bold italic'), would be issued. The packages had to be composed as carefully balanced combinations of text and display, serif and sans-serif, and formal and informal. This thinking resulted in the composition of the first four sets:

First set (Spring 1994):
    ITC Avant Garde Gothic (4 fonts);
    ITC Bookman (4 fonts);
    ITC Fat Face (1 font);
    ITC Garamond (4 fonts);
    ITC Kabel (5 fonts);
    ITC New Baskerville (4 fonts);
    ITC Studio Script (1 font);
    ITC Zapf Chancery (1 font).

Second set (Spring 1995):
    ITC Anna (3 fonts);
    ITC Bauhaus (5 fonts);
    ITC Beesknees (1 font);
    ITC Benguiat Gothic (4 fonts);
    ITC Garamond Narrow (4 fonts);
    ITC Machine (2 fonts);
    ITC Officina Sans (4 fonts);
    ITC Officina Serif (4 fonts).

Third set (Winter 1995):
    ITC Franklin Gothic (8 fonts);
    ITC Korinna (4 fonts);
    ITC Flora (2 fonts);
    ITC Garamond (4 additional fonts);
    ITC Garamond Narrow (2 additional fonts).

Fourth set (Summer 1997):
ITC Benguiat Gothic (4 additional fonts);
ITC Korinna (4 additional fonts);
ITC Friz Quadrata (4 fonts);
ITC True Grit (1 font).

ITC Stenberg, ITC Banco, ITC Charter, ITC Bodoni 72, and ITC Franklin Gothic (Condensed, Compressed and X-Compressed) were added to the Cyrillic collection later: in 1997, 2000, 2001, and 2002, respectively.

STYLE-SELECTION ROULETTE

Naturally, the ParaType designers had to be quite particular in making their choices, selecting those designs which in their view had indisputable priority, and seemed to address the most urgent needs of the Russian (as well as non-Russian) typographic community. It was inevitable that many of these choices centred on classical styles of proven worth, such as ITC New Baskerville, ITC Garamond, and ITC Franklin Gothic – whose use, it was hoped, would transcend fleeting fashion.

Choosing display designs presented a special challenge, due both to the volatile nature of demand and, again, to the limited resources of ParaType. It was very important to be selective, to be sure of the market potential before investing time, labour, and money in the development of certain typefaces. This was particularly difficult in view of font-software and copyright piracy: display fonts are the favourite prey of bootleggers.

THE CONCOMITANTS

Gradually, the ITC Cyrillic product line grew into a substantial typeface collection. Its development, having been a formidable feat from the production standpoint, had brought up a number of important issues of both a practical and theoretical nature.

1. *Russian typographic terminology* proved inadequate. Major changes in the course of history always affect language: perestroika, glasnost, and subsequent post-Soviet developments created many new words, expressions, and terms. Some of them were short-lived, transient: they either had little, if any, relevance to the new realities, or just offered new names for old things. Other words were here to stay, because they stood for phenomena, entities, and values which had not existed before. The glossary of Russian typography expanded: *кернинг* ('kerning'), *трекинг* ('tracking'), *фонт* ('font'), among others. Many new terms found their way into the type lingo some terms out of necessity, and others because they were fashionable.

A whole new set of type terms had to be compiled and agreed upon, in order to simplify communication at various stages in the project. For example, straightforward and unambiguous definitions of various font 'weights' were needed. The lack of consistency in modern Western typographic classification created difficulties. The list of possibilities is long: Ultra Light, Extra Light, Thin, Light, Roman, Normal, Regular, Book, Medium, Semibold, Demi, Bold, Heavy, Extra Bold, Black, Extra Black, Ultra.... In the case of the Cyrillics, when the weight range went beyond the standard Soviet combination of *светлый* and *полужирный* ('regular' and 'bold'), the lack of suitable existing terminology created a difficult practical problem.

2. *The naming of the typefaces* presented challenges. Translated into Russian, or transliterated in Cyrillic, some typeface names either did not make sense or proved confusing, such as ITC Avant Garde Gothic, ITC Beesknees, or ITC True Grit. Very specific rules of transliteration had to be adopted in order to derive credible Russian versions of the original ITC typeface names. For example, we had to render 'Benguiat' as *Бенгет* ('Benghet', not 'Benghiyat'), 'Officina' as *Официна* ('Ofitsina', not 'Offisina'), and 'Friz' as *Фриц* ('Frits', not 'Freez').

3. *The main challenge*, however, was neither terminological, nor phonetic. Designing Cyrillic extensions proved difficult and demanding. On the one hand, in extending the character set beyond the original font complement, it is imperative to preserve the design concept and the visual identity of the typeface. On the other hand, one must observe the established conventions of glyph construction with regard to the style category, and/or to the aesthetics of the historical period of the design in the Russian typographic tradition.

ADAPTATION VS. CREATION?

Adaptation of a type design to a different script, as laborious and arduous a job as it is, is sometimes underestimated and undervalued – as if it were an inferior job, not worthy of the attention of a creative designer. Why this underestimation?

A translation
How do you measure the quality of an 'adaptation' of a typeface to a foreign script (a writing system different from the one it was originally designed for)? Consider the translation of verse as an analogy. A translator strives to retain as much as possible of the spirit, the style, and the flavour of the original piece. Keeping the author's metre, the cadence, the rhyme scheme, the division into stanzas, etc., is certainly imperative; re-

АННА НОРМАЛЬНЫЙ

Баухауз средний

БИЗНИЗ

Бенгет Готик нормальный

Гарамон узкий светлый

МАШИН ПОЛУЖИРНЫЙ

Официна Санс нормальный

Официна Сериф нормальный

Figure 2. Second set of ITC Cyrillics, spring 1995 (top to bottom).
ITC Anna Cyrillic, by Vladimir Yefimov and Svetlana Yermolaeva; original by Daniel
Pelavin, 1990. ITC Bauhaus Cyrillic, by Elvira Slysh and Tatiana Lyskova; original
by Herbert Bayer, 1925; Edward Benguiat and Victor Caruso, 1975. ITC Beesknees
Cyrillic, by Elvira Slysh and Tatiana Lyskova; original by David Farey, 1990.
ITC Benguiat Gothic Cyrillic, by Alexander Tarbeev; original by Edward Benguiat, 1979.
ITC Garamond Narrow Cyrillic, by Alexander Tarbeev; original by Claude Garamond,
1532; Jean Jannon, 1621; Morris Fuller Benton, 1919; Tony Stan, 1975, 1977; Bitstream
Inc., 1988-91. ITC Machine Cyrillic, by Vladimir Yefimov and Gennady Baryshnikov;
original by Tom Carnase and Ronne Bonder, 1970. ITC Officina Sans Cyrillic,
by Tagir Safayev; original by Erik Spiekermann, 1990. ITC Officina Serif Cyrillic,
by Tagir Safayev; original by Erik Spiekermann and Just van Rossum, 1990.

creating at least some of the original acoustic and graphic effects, such
as alliterations, assonances, anaphorae, is desirable.

At the same time, the piece should sound natural in the language of
translation – as if it were originally written in that language. Therefore,
all language rules, as different as they may be from the original, must be
followed and observed.

Of course, any comparison can only go so far, and beyond a certain
point it inevitably fails. A poet only infrequently thinks of the translation
of his verse into other languages. A literary work is normally created as
a self-contained, closed structure, not really meant for further reprocess-
ing, recycling, or repurposing. The same is also true for a typeface design,
whose visual features are firmly rooted in a specific script, and often a
specific language. It is a fact, however, that additional characters or alternate glyphs can be added to the original character set as necessary. Thus,

[51]

as opposed to a literary piece, and most works of art not based on the serial principle, a typeface is normally an open, expandable structure.

An elaboration

Local language extensions of the character set of a font are often considered an unimportant production routine: adding accents for Swedish or Lettish, or extra characters for Polish or Turkish. Creating ligatures or alternates is more challenging. Still more challenging is developing character glyphs for related scripts: Greek and Cyrillic. The three alphabets – Latin, Greek, and Cyrillic – share many letter forms, e.g., A B E H I K M O P T X, though the same shapes often represent different sounds. The construction of glyphs in Latin, Cyrillic, and [uppercase] Greek follows the same pattern, and the glyphs share many visual features (e.g., the height, the weight, the contrast, the stress), and even design elements (the serifs, the stems, the bars, the bowls, the terminals, etc.). Therefore, creating non-Latin extensions, or expanding the original font complement, is very often a sophisticated exercise in glyph combinatorics.

Figure 3. Greek, Latin, Cyrillic (Russian). Identical glyph shapes. Typeface: PT Pragmatica.

Figure 4. Latin, Cyrillic. Identical glyph shapes (Macintosh, codepages 201 and 251). Typeface: PT Pragmatica.

Obviously, no impenetrable wall exists between the expansion of the Latin-based character set and the creation of additional glyphs for Cyrillic. And still, there is a certain point at which quantity turns into quality: the D F G L N Q R U V W Y Z get replaced by the Б Г Д Ж З И Й К Л П У Ф Ц Ч Ш Щ Ъ Ы Ь Э Ю Я, and voilà – a new entity emerges: a Cyrillic.

A re-creation

However, Cyrillic characters, of which so many have the same shape as Latin, have relationships all of their own. They invariably produce visual results that look very different from the texture of the copy typeset in the related Latin fonts; and the presence of the peculiar non-Latin letters, like the Ж or the Я, is not the only explanation for that: even in the Latin script, the texture, the colour, and the rhythm of the type pages dramatically vary with different languages.

The development of non-Latin 'extensions' calls into being autonomous, mostly self-sufficient, character sets. They may be used in combination with the Latin characters, if the copy calls for it; however, most of the time it does not, and the Cyrillic letters are used alone. The user of the Cyrillic 'typeface adaptation' – a typographer or reader – does not think of it as an 'extension' to something else: he judges it by its own merits, no matter how perfect the [Latin] original design might be. Thus, in designing the Cyrillic extension, every effort has to be made to provide not only for its visual compatibility with its Latin master version, but also for the maximum harmony and integrity within the Cyrillic complement.

This is why in many cases the development of non-Latin extensions can be seen as an activity no less challenging than the creation of new, 'original' designs: it is just that the 'rules of the game' have already been set by the author of the source version, and the designer working on the extension must play by those rules, having no control over the 'given' visual features of the typeface. Here is where the comparison with literary translation comes into play again: most readers have no way of comparing the translation with the original; its accuracy largely remains on the translator's conscience.

'IT TAKES A RUSSIAN...'

There is a wide-spread belief that a good Cyrillic typeface can only be designed by a person fluent in a language using Cyrillic: for example by a Russian, a Bulgarian, a Kazakh. Of course, knowledge of languages helps. And yes, there are special cases. One of them is designing an informal script typeface, based on everyday handwriting. In such instances, in order to achieve a free, natural, and spontaneous flow of letters in a type line, it takes a good deal of daily writing practice in the given script, combined with language proficiency. However, in most cases language proficiency is not critical: what is indispensable is an understanding of Cyrillic letterform construction, and of the variations and correlations that exist in the design of its glyphs.

What makes designing Cyrillic type different is the fact that Cyrillic more often than Latin allows for alternate glyph versions within the same typeface. However, the use of certain letter forms requires the use of other glyphs, related to them in shape. This interdependence of glyph shapes is not peculiar to Cyrillic: it is just as applicable to any script, including Latin. And yet the shapes of Cyrillic glyphs vary much more than in Latin-based typefaces. Consequently, the wider choice of alternates makes consistency and co-ordination crucial in styling a Cyrillic type.

Knowledge of typical Cyrillic character combinations, their frequency, the average word length – peculiar to certain languages, and common to them all – is also most helpful.

THE CANONS OF STYLE

As with Latin-based types, there are details in the treatment of the Cyrillic letter forms peculiar to the specific categories of style classification. For example, the isosceles *delta*-like Λ and *lambda*-like Λ appear to be more appropriate in the context of an 'old-style' than of a 'modern' serif typeface (compare it to the straight-legged R and the caudate Q in an old-style roman vs. their bow-legged and the bob-tailed counterparts in a modern Latin typeface).

It is a fact that most type designs, no matter how original, can be traced to a certain stylistic type, if only for the sake of classification; this is useful in analysing their visual features, both when studying the existing designs, and when planning new ones.

THE TAXONOMY OF TYPE

The 20th century's typographic history was marked by a revival and/or a reinterpretation of many designs going back to various periods of Western typographic and calligraphic history – from the Middle Ages to Art Déco. That recycling of historical designs, and the development of new ones – either based upon tradition or breaking away from it – contributed to the development and fine-tuning of various systems of typeface classification.

In turn, this has led to the intellectualisation of type design, which has become a much more rationalist activity. The shapes of glyphs – down to their smallest details – have ended up being rather firmly associated with certain typeface categories and subcategories.

Франклин Готик нормальный
Коринна нормальный
Флора средний
Гарамон нормальный
Гарамон нормальный узкий

Figure 5. Third set of ITC Cyrillics, winter 1995 (top to bottom).
ITC Franklin Gothic Cyrillic, by Isay Slutsker and Tatiana Lyskova; original by
Morris Fuller Benton, 1903; Victor Caruso, 1980. ITC Korinna Cyrillic, by Lyubov'
Kuznetsova; original by H. Berthold, 1904; Edward Benguiat and Victor Caruso,
1974. ITC Flora Cyrillic, by Emma Zakharova and Vladimir Yefimov; original by
Gerard Unger, 1985. ITC Garamond Cyrillic (4 additional fonts), by Alexander
Tarbeev; original by Claude Garamond, 1532; Jean Jannon, 1621; Morris Fuller
Benton, 1919; Tony Stan, 1975, 1977. ITC Garamond Narrow (2 additional fonts),
by Alexander Tarbeev; original by Claude Garamond, 1532; Jean Jannon, 1621;
Morris Fuller Benton, 1919; Tony Stan, 1975, 1977; Bitstream Inc., 1988-91.

Many systems of typeface classification are based upon the 'period'
principle: such as Renaissance, Baroque, Neoclassical. Soviet typography has largely been unaffected by that revivalist approach. Very few
typefaces have been created based on historical styles, and even fewer
good typefaces.

GARALDES? RÉALES? CONNAIS PAS...

Soviet typography was hardly rich in choices. For seven decades,
only a dozen typefaces were available to most printers and publishers.
The design of those types being a non-issue, even the system of typeface
classification remained basic – unlike the elaborate, mostly period-style-
based systems in the West. Soviet typographers never had their Vene-
tians or Transitionals, their *Garaldes* or *Réales*.

In Soviet times very few new typefaces were introduced into typographic usage. (Many more had been trashed, done away with, for their
alleged 'bourgeois decadent aesthetics'.) Today, with the ongoing large-
scale development of Cyrillic versions of typefaces originally created for
Latin script, the Russian typographic palette is quickly growing richer
in variety and sophistication. In the last five years more faces have been
added to the Russian typographic repertory than in the seventy-four
years of Soviet rule.

As we observed earlier, there are specific rules governing the design of typefaces that belong to different categories – very subtle at times, yet quite distinctive. Soviet designers' experience of period revivals was limited to a handful of typefaces; no wonder their stylistic palette remained underdeveloped, imprecise and unsophisticated. Historical references were vague and muddled; designers took great liberties in interpreting the prototypical shapes of the letter forms. Various and numerous ways of drawing the same letter were often considered interchangeable: they were loosely, if at all, assigned to certain historical and formal categories. The only way to secure the integrity of the design was the consistency of using the same features throughout the entire font complement: many of them are indeed interrelated. To repeat the earlier example, you would not normally have a trapezoid Д and a triangular Λ in the same typeface: they should be both trapezoid (ДЛ), or both triangular (ΔΛ).

A REVIVAL? A REDESIGN? A RE-CREATION?

In developing a Cyrillic 'revival' typeface based on an historical model, editing is indispensable, and of a greater importance than in designing a Latin face. Because of its much shorter history, modern Cyrillic type had considerably less time to reach design maturation than Latin. The romanised ('Civil') style was started in 1708 by Peter the Great, and its letter forms came to [relative] fruition only by the end of the 18th century, at which point they were much closer to the present-day convention.

Direct replicas of early Russian types, with little or no editing — similar to Latin replicas such as ATF Caslon ['Old Face'], Monotype Fournier, or Linotype Janson – are impractical. There were no attempts at creating them. But if there had been, the results would certainly look as quaint as the types of Schweynheim and Pannartz, or of Erhard Ratdolt, or as any other such 'under construction' styles. The need for very tactful and delicate editing gives special importance to the designer's knowledge of, and sensitivity to, the historical details and the subtleties of style. However, for want of significant practice, those needful qualities had no real chance to develop. That is why so many Soviet 'revival' designs look either amateurish or arbitrary.

CYRILLIC, A TYPOGRAPHIC LATECOMER

Modern Cyrillic typography caught up with its Western sister part-way: Civil Type was styled after the post-Baroque/pre-Transitional Dutch fonts of the late 17th century, a kind of *morte-saison* in Western typographic history. From then on, the design of Cyrillic typefaces followed the pattern of the aesthetic evolution in European typography: Empire –

Бенгет Готик средний
Коринна сверхжирный
Фриц Квадрата норм.
Тру Грит

Figure 6. Fourth set of ITC Cyrillics, summer 1997 (top to bottom).
ITC Benguiat Gothic Cyrillic (4 additional fonts), by Alexander Tarbeev; original
by Edward Benguiat, 1979. ITC Korinna Cyrillic (4 additional fonts), by Lyubov'
Kuznetsova; original by H. Berthold, 1904; Edward Benguiat and Victor Caruso,
1974. ITC Friz Quadrata Cyrillic, by Alexander Tarbeev; original by Ernst Friz,
1965; Victor Caruso, 1974; Thierry Puyfoulhoux, 1994. ITC True Grit Cyrillic,
by Vladimir Yefimov; original by Michael Stacey, 1995.

Romantic – Victorian – Art Nouveau, etc. But the earlier style periods
(prior to the Petrine reform) left no trace on the forms of Cyrillic type.

Nevertheless, there is certainly a way to make up for this historical
deficiency. Through extrapolation of modern Cyrillic design conventions
to pre-Petrine times, and their judicious application to the shaping of
glyphs that are complementary to those that have the same forms in
Latin and Cyrillic (e.g., the capitals A B C E H M O P T X), credible results
can be achieved in creating Cyrillic typefaces styled like, say, early Humanist faces, or French Old Styles, or Dutch Old Styles. Another major
reference is the design of early Greek types: there are many identical, or
similar, [capital] letters in the Cyrillic and Greek typographic alphabets
(А Г Е М Н О Р Т Ф Х). With the many alternatives that exist in the construction of certain Cyrillic letter forms, there is enough room for choosing the shapes that blend best into the context of the chosen period style.

THE АБВ OF CYRILLIC TYPE DESIGN:
A REASSESSMENT

Typography and type design in post-Soviet Russia are now experiencing
a rebirth. However, current practice highlights either a vagueness or
a want of common conventions with regard to the particulars of glyph
construction.

The need for a reliable and generally acceptable code of design rules
is made more urgent by the growing demand for non-Latin typefaces.
More and more people are designing Cyrillic types: the reason is not only
the democratisation of design tools, but also the globalisation of written

Language Culture Type

communications. The continuing process of typeface development on a massive scale provides ample opportunity for redefining the style conventions of Cyrillic type design. Its visual vocabulary is being constantly revised, updated, and fine-tuned as more typefaces belonging to various design categories are worked on.

In many cases the rules, standards, and correlations are being either rediscovered, or deduced and newly established as such. Very often past experience, if available at all, is of little help in addressing specific real-life situations. Decisions are made in the heat of the production process, and later, if proven sound, are considered as models in similar cases. Successful precedents are being generalized into rules, or rather guidelines, thus facilitating the development of new designs. Having the visual conventions in place is actually liberating: it helps the designer set aside the common, generic features of the design (which are, in a sense, taken for granted) and concentrate on what constitutes its true identity.

RUSSIAN TYPOGRAPHIC RENAISSANCE

The building of the ITC Cyrillic library, with the thoroughly planned diversity of its components, has a secondary agenda of finding solutions to the many problems posed by their belonging to various design categories, including those which are new to Cyrillic typography. The scope of the design problems to be addressed in contemporary typeface development are wide, wider than at any other point in Russian typographic history. Solutions have to be found in the simultaneous development of typefaces as different as Humanist script and Geometric sans, or Transitional roman and Art Nouveau titling.

The large-scale production of new typefaces, including the Cyrillic versions of those originally created for Latin script, has brought about a new interest in the theory of typeface design, and in the Russian typographic and calligraphic legacy. One significant aspect of the post-Soviet typographic renaissance is a surge in theoretical and historical studies.

'CYRILLIC? NO PROBLEM.'

There are a number of foundries in present-day Russia and its former sister republics, and ParaType is not alone in exploring Cyrillic type design. It is just that the ParaType design team appears to be the strongest in the nation, with more professional experience than its competitors. The core team that was involved in the development of the ITC Cyrillic typefaces included Lyubov' Kuznetsova, Isay Slutsker, Tagir Safayev, Alexander Tarbeev, and Vladimir Yefimov.

Professionalism calls for, among other things, responsibility and attention to detail. Many newcomers to the business of type design are ei-

[58]

СТЕНБЕРГ ЖИРНЫЙ

Банко светлый

Чартер нормальный

Бодони 72 нормальный

Figure 7. Latest additions to ITC Cyrillic library, as of 15 April 2002 (top to bottom). ITC Stenberg, original by Tagir Safayev, 1996; ITC Banco Cyrillic, by Tagir Safayev, 2000; original by Roger Excoffon, 1952; Phill Grimshaw, 1997. ITC Charter Cyrillic, by Vladimir Yefimov, 1999; original by Matthew Carter, 1987, 1993. ITC Bodoni 72 Cyrillic, by Dmitry Kirsanov, 2000; original by Janice Fishman, Holly Goldsmith, Jim Parkinson, Sumner Stone, 1994.

ther unable to see, or reluctant to admit, that the problems the ParaType designers are struggling to solve are real. They happily churn out digital fonts by the dozen, slapping together Cyrillic glyphs from bits and pieces of the Latin letterforms. And of course, the unlicensed Cyrillic versions of the ITC typefaces were all 'done' by them and offered to the ever-hungry Russian software market a while ago. Not one of them seems to care about, and to spend so much time on, fine-tuning the design, the way ParaType does. But here we are dealing with a clear case of unfair competition, when one party tries to play by the rules, and the other one does not even care if rules exist.

HISTORY, FAST FORWARD?

There is a widespread delusion among some design professionals that the basic Cyrillic alphabetic character shapes (as opposed to glyphs) are manageable and malleable and that they can, and should, be 'improved'. Modern Cyrillic was styled after the Western model, or at least such was the intention of its august reformer, Peter the Great. For some people it therefore follows that if Cyrillic is lacking in certain design features standard in Western roman typefaces, then this can logically be seen as a shortcoming of the script.

Yes, in Cyrillic type the difference in glyph construction between the upper and the lower case is small; yes, there are not many extenders in its lower case; yes, there are many more verticals in Cyrillic than in Latin. Whether this is truly a deficiency is debatable especially in light of the continuous experiments in the West with so-called unicase type designs, as demonstrated by the work of many renowned masters: Herbert Bayer,

Jan Tschichold, A.M. Cassandre, Bradbury Thompson, W.A. Dwiggins, and most recently Zuzana Licko.

What is not debatable, however (at least, to the ParaType designers), is that Cyrillic typography must not be forced into a 'new, improved' look. In contrast to the energetic approach of Peter the Great and all his zealous followers, ParaType designers preach sensitivity, tactfulness, and patience in the face of history. They see their mission as collecting, studying, and organizing the tools and devices of Cyrillic typography, not as their hasty replacement. They believe in evolution, not revolution: they saw too many of the latter in their lifetime. 'Let's give history a chance' – isn't that a truly revolutionary approach under these circumstances?

AFTERWORD

ITC as we knew it ceased to exist on 31 December 1999. Since then its Cyrillic programme has been indefinitely suspended, due to the continuing change of ownership, and restructuring of production activities. A great number of typeface projects were put on hold – some of them at very advanced stages of development. At the time of writing it is still not clear whether this survey is a progress report or a post-mortem. Whichever it turns out to be, one thing is clear: the development of ITC Cyrillics can already be considered a notable venture that marked the beginning of a new and exciting chapter in the historical development of Russian typography and type design.

Acknowledgements

I would like to thank my friends Mark Batty and Vladimir Yefimov for their generous help and guidance in my putting together this essay.

Further reading

Gherchuk, Yuri. *The art of lettering in the Soviet Union*. Moscow: Sovietsky Khudozhnik, 1983. [Published in conjunction with the exhibition 'Typographica USSR: The art of lettering, calligraphy and type design in the Soviet Union'. The exhibition was co-sponsored by the Artists Union of the USSR, the International Typeface Corporation, and the Herb Lubalin Study Center for Design and Typography of the Cooper Union for the Advancement of science and Art; it was held at the Arthur A. Houghton, Jr. Gallery, at the Cooper Union in New York City, in early 1985.]

Burns, Laurie. 'Typographica USSR'. *Print* XXXIX:III (May/June 1985), pp. 86–95.

Gottschall, Edward, ed. *Typographic communications today*. Cambridge: MIT Press, 1989.

Calligraphia USA/USSR. Exhibition catalogue. New York: International Typeface Corporation, 1991. [The exhibition was co-sponsored by the Artists Union of the

USSR, the International Typeface Corporation, and the United Nations Educational, Scientific and Cultural Organization (UNESCO); it opened at the Central Artist's House in Moscow in November 1990; it was exhibited throughout the United States from 1992 to 1994; it was held at the United Nations headquarters in January 1994, and at Somar Gallery in San Francisco in September 1994.]

Batty, Mark. 'Calligraphia'. *U&lc*, Vol. 18, No. 3 (Fall 1991), pp. 20–23.

[Haley, Allan.] 'ITC Cyrillic series'. *U&lc*, Vol. 20, No. 4 (Spring 1994), pp. 23–29.

Brenner, Jane. 'Jottings'. *Alphabet: the Journal of the Friends of Calligraphy*, Vol. 20, No. 2 (Winter 1995), p. 32.

[Zhukov, Maxim.] 'ITC Cyrillics: The sequel'. *U&lc*, Vol. 21, No. 4 (Spring 1995), pp. 36–37.

Zhukov, Maxim. 'Type design in Russia'. *Reports of the Country Delegates. 1995–1996*. The Hague: Association Typographique Internationale, 1996.

Zhukov, Maxim. 'Towards an open layout: A letter to Volodya Yefimov'. *Type*, Vol. 1, No. 1 (Spring 1997), pp. 23-45.

Zhukov, Maxim. 'Typographic design in Russia: 1997'. *Reports of the Country Delegates. 1996-1997*. Reading: Association Typographique Internationale, 1997.

Zhukov, Maxim. 'Typographic design in Russia: 1998'. *Reports of the Country Delegates. 1997–1998*. Lyons: Association Typographique Internationale, 1998.

Berry, John D. 'Russian eclectic'. *Print* LIII:III (March/April 1999), pp. 176–182.

Zhukov, Maxim. 'Kyrillitsa lives!'. *U&lc*, Vol. 25, No. 4 (Spring 1999), pp. 32–35.

Zhukov, Maxim. 'Russia'. *Reports of the Country Delegates. 1999–2000*. Leipzig: Association Typographique Internationale, 2000.

AKIRA KOBAYASHI

How do the Japanese read?

D O THE JAPANESE read from left to right, or from right to left? This is the most frequently asked question about Japanese script. The answer is that we read both ways. To be more precise, we have two directions of writing: horizontal and vertical. Most of our glyphs are designed in a square, and can be set either horizontally or vertically. For more than a thousand years, all text was set vertically. Horizontal setting is a fairly recent innovation. When the text is set horizontally, we read from left to right, as Western people do. When the text is vertically set, we read from top to bottom, beginning from the line that is at the right side of the column. Thus I can say that we read from right to left.

Japanese is a complicated system of writing. We have basically three scripts: Chinese ideographic symbols called kanji (that means Chinese letter) and two phonetic alphabets called hiragana and katakana. In daily use, we use only about two thousand kanji symbols and about eighty each hiragana and katakana glyphs. I'm not even sure how many kanji I can read and write. Certainly there will be hundreds that I can read but cannot spell correctly. Still, the Japanese language is expanding – we have already included the Latin alphabet and Arabic numerals among our characters, and these have now been standard for decades. I assume that an average 7-year-old in Japan can at least read both hiragana and Katakana, Arabic numerals from 0 to 9, a handful of kanji and a few words of English splashed across his or her T-shirts.

The second question is often, 'How big is the Japanese personal computer keyboard?' The answer is: we have the same size keyboard with the same number of keys as a Westerner has in his or her office. Then how do we manage typing so many characters? It is not too difficult: imagine that you need to type a % symbol but there is no key for % available, but you know how to spell it. What you need to do is, type *p-e-r-c-e-n-t* and then hit the enter, or return, key. The computer converts the word written in phonetic signs into another symbol in a fraction of second, and then the % symbol appears. Sometimes it is as easy as that, but sometimes you have to find the correct symbol among more than ten possible candi-

て、もちろんすべてがいい
が、MoMA、グッゲンハ
役割というのはかなり重要

イギリスの Reading で
行なわれた ATypl 総会
では、多数の参加者が

イギリスのReadingで行なわれたATypl総会では、多数の参加者が

イギリスのレディングで行なわれたATypI総会では、多数の参加者が

イギリスのReadingで行なわれたATypI総会では、多数の参加者が

Figure 1. Japanese text in kanji and hiragana phonetic symbols, a Western name, Guggenheim, transcribed into katakana phonetic symbols.

Figure 2. Examples of mixed setting. Top: Horizontal setting with a Western place name and a contraction in the Latin alphabet. In this example I show Japanese and Latin scripts together, but usually Western place names would be transcribed into katakana. Middle: Vertical setting using the same text. It looks rather strange because it is not common to set names (especially not contractions) in the Latin alphabet sideways. Bottom: Typical vertical setting. Here the Western place name is rendered in katakana and a contraction in a special set of 'vertical' Latin alphabet. Now the Western names are little bit more friendly to a Japanese eye, even if most of you do not agree. (The three examples are set in TypeBank Gothic, for which the horizontal Latin typeface was designed by the author.)

dates that have the same pronunciation but separate meanings. Usually word-processing software automatically chooses the right candidate by the context, or selects and shows characters by order of frequency of appearance in typical text.

Like the kanji characters, which we borrowed from China a couple of thousand years ago, Latin letters are now a crucial part of our writing system. We use them in our text in Japanese, often to describe a name of an organisation such as IOC and OPEC. Replacing such acronyms with kanji, to say the name in full, is possible but rather inefficient. A news presenter says 'sekiyuyushutsukokukikou' for OPEC and nearly bites his tongue. Japanese are very fond of contractions. Generally kanji is very efficient. In newspapers, 'Japanese-American relationships' requires only four kanji, but for OPEC the Latin alphabet is preferred because the result is shorter, and probably easier to pronounce.

So, here we have two directions of writing, four and half different scripts (three Japanese systems and a Western one that includes Arabic numerals) and all can happen at once on the same page. Vertical setting, preferred by novels and newspapers, can also include some Western words or names. Such words are usually transcribed into our katakana phonetic symbols, but acronyms or other organisational names will be set vertically in Latin letters if they are shorter that way.

In figure 1, we see Japanese text in kanji and hiragana phonetic symbols, a Western name, Guggenheim, transcribed into katakana phonetic symbols, and 'MoMA' (a contraction of 'Museum of Modern Art') set vertically. Obviously the space after the first M appears too wide, but that is not a serious problem for Japanese readers. We are used to overlooking these gaps, because it is almost inconspicuous among Japanese letters that are usually monospaced and allow gaps between them. Latin ascenders and descenders can also cause awkward letter combinations. In order to avoid collision, we have a special set of Latin alphabets. I must emphasize that they are not designed for setting words, but rather for the contractions that require letter-by-letter recognition. Unfortunately, one of the most disasterous letter combinations in vertical setting I can think of would be 'ATypI'.

FIONA ROSS

An approach to non-Latin type design

IN THE CLOSING quarter of the twentieth century, the requirement of producing a Bengali digital typeface unwittingly prompted a radical shift in approach to non-Latin type design by one of the major font manufacturers. The influence of this approach is still evident in the non-Latin fonts in widespread use today. It was the request, in 1978, by the Indian newspaper group Ananda Bazar Patrika Limited, for Linotype-Paul Ltd to produce a Bengali font for the Linotron 202 digital typesetter that precipitated the adoption of a new method of developing type for Indian and other complex scripts.

The preliminary work on the Linotype project[1] revealed firstly the unsatisfactory state of current Bengali typography and type-design; and secondly, the paucity of research into Bengali typeforms – aside from several histories of printing presses in Bengal and early Indian imprints. It was also clear that it was necessary to make good the deficiency in historical research in order to understand, arrest, and reverse the trend of gradual deterioration of the elegant Bengali script into awkward typeforms (compare figures 1, 2, overleaf). In other words, to appreciate how the printed forms had arrived at their current shapes, it was essential to view them from an historical perspective and to assess whether factors influencing their design were still pertinent in the digital era.

Research showed that in the context of Indian typefounding history, European political and religious interests were the motivating forces behind the establishment of the first vernacular presses and typefoundries in the Indian subcontinent. Foreign hegemony and the activities of missionary bodies in India since the sixteenth century encouraged not only the development of type designs betraying foreign, i.e. European, traits but also the practice of mixed-language setting, one language usually being set in Latin types.

In the late eighteenth century, apart from the printing of regulations, the Governor General of Bengal, Warren Hastings (1732–1818), advocated the publication of grammars, dictionaries, and exam papers in order to promote 'the cultivation of a right understanding and a medium

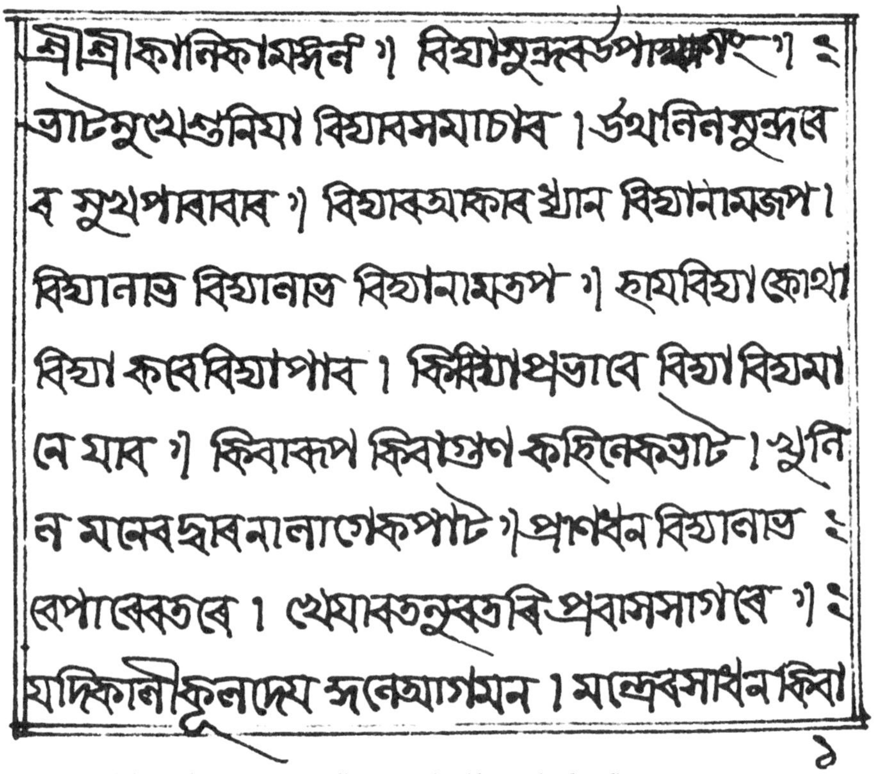

Figure 1. Eighteenth century Bengali manuscript (decorative hand). From BL MS Add 5593 – *Vidyāsundara*, British Library (enlarged).

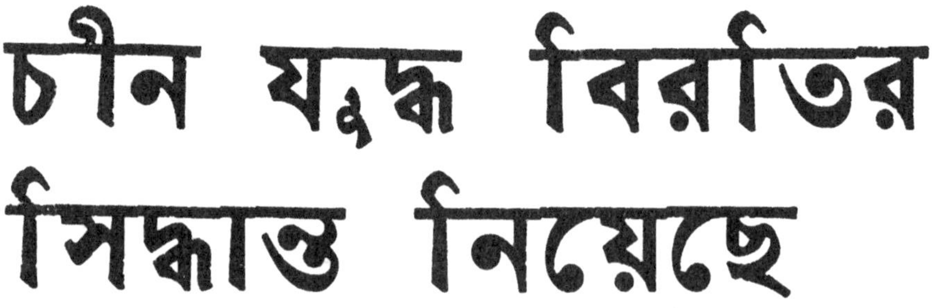

Figure 2. Headline from *Ananda Bazar Patrika* newspaper composed with hot-metal Linotype font (reduced).

of intercourse ... between the Natives of Europe who are to rule, and the Inhabitants of India who are to obey'.[2] Such publications, in which Bengali types first appeared, were directed chiefly at East India Company servants. Thus the types, which often represented the Indian script in a simple style of letter-formation, were not designed with the native reader in mind.[3] Furthermore, the typography of the imprints was styled on Western models, and in the case of Bengali, the lettershapes of the first fonts contravened the customary stroke sequence of the penned hand. The notion of a baseline was conceived for ease of mixing with Latin types; Latin punctuation made its appearance in non-Latin texts; and interword spacing was introduced.

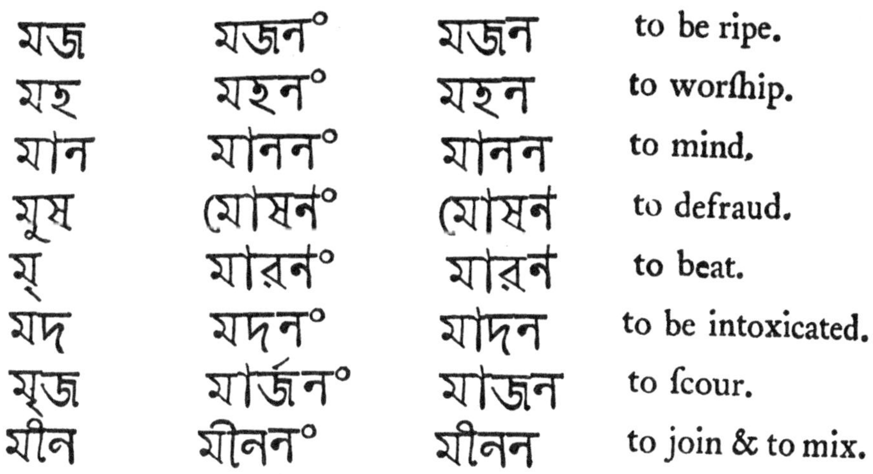

যজ্ঞ	যজন°	যজন	to be ripe.
যহ	যহন°	যহন	to worſhip.
যান	যানন°	যানন	to mind.
মুষ	মোষন°	মোষন	to defraud.
য্	যারন°	যারন	to beat.
যদ	যদন°	যাদন	to be intoxicated.
মৃজ	মার্জন°	মাজন	to ſcour.
মীন	মীনন°	মীনন	to join & to mix.

Figure 3. N.B. Halhed, *A Grammar of the Bengal Language* (Hoogly, 1778).

The mission presses, while also producing dictionaries, grammars, and text books to instruct the foreigner in the vernacular languages, were principally occupied with the printing of (often inaccurate) translations of Christian texts. Since the prime objective of the missionaries was the promulgation of their faith as widely as possible, they had little interest in the art of typography. Between 1801 and 1832 the Serampore Mission Press published 'over two hundred and twelve thousand volumes in forty languages'.[4] But the Serampore Missionaries, who dominated Bengali printing in the nineteenth century, seemed unaware of the poor quality of their fonts. Their first fonts, for the most part, appeared to comprise inferior copies of those produced for East India Company imprints. Innovation in type design was chiefly restricted to reducing the character height in order to economize on paper whilst printing more matter. *A Memoir of the Translations for 1813* (p. 20) stated: 'It seems an important question, how the greatest number of clear and legible copies can be furnished at the least expense.'

The fonts and imprints produced by foreigners in India were augmented by type and publications produced in Europe. But European imprints showing Indian fonts were not intended for Indian nationals, and polyglot editions of the Lord's Prayer were rarely intended to support the proselytizing activities of missionaries abroad. Rather they served as type specimens and seemed designed to boast the richness of the printing establishment to its local public, having a markedly European appearance, and therefore appealing more to Western perceptions of letter design and typography. One Bengali font of 370 characters cut in England, but first employed in 1826 by the Baptist Mission Press, saw over a century of use. Its longevity can be attributed to the professionalism of its typefounder, Vincent Figgins (1766–1844), who saw the necessity

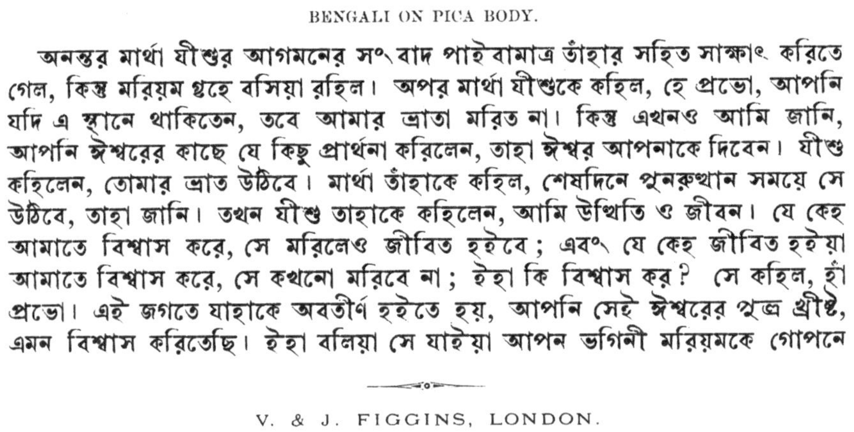

BENGALI ON PICA BODY.

অনন্তর মার্থা যীশুর আগমনের সংবাদ পাইবামাত্র তাঁহার সহিত সাক্ষাৎ করিতে গেল, কিন্তু মরিয়ম গৃহে বসিয়া রহিল। অপর মার্থা যীশুকে কহিল, হে প্রভো, আপনি যদি এ স্থানে থাকিতেন, তবে আমার ভ্রাতা মরিত না। কিন্তু এখনও আমি জানি, আপনি ঈশ্বরের কাছে যে কিছু প্রার্থনা করিলেন, তাহা ঈশ্বর আপনাকে দিবেন। যীশু কহিলেন, তোমার ভ্রাত উঠিবে। মার্থা তাঁহাকে কহিল, শেষদিনে পুনরুত্থান সময়ে সে উঠিবে, তাহা জানি। তখন যীশু তাঁহাকে কহিলেন, আমি উত্থিত ও জীবন। যে কেহ আমাতে বিশ্বাস করে, সে মরিলেও জীবিত হইবে ; এবং যে কেহ জীবিত হইয়া আমাতে বিশ্বাস করে, সে কখনো মরিবে না ; ইহা কি বিশ্বাস কর ? সে কহিল, হাঁ প্রভো। এই জগতে যাহাকে অবতীর্ণ হইতে হয়, আপনি সেই ঈশ্বরের পুত্র খ্রীষ্ট, এমন বিশ্বাস করিতেছি। ইহা বলিয়া সে যাইয়া আপন ভগিনী মরিয়মকে গোপনে

V. & J. FIGGINS, LONDON.

Figure 4. V. & J. Figgins, 'Bengali on Pica Body'; New Specimens; Oriental Types (London, 1884).

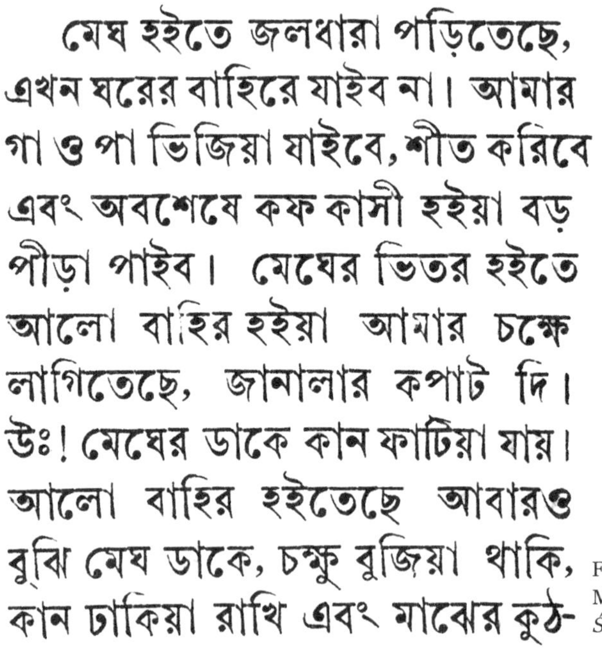

মেঘ হইতে জলধারা পড়িতেছে, এখন ঘরের বাহিরে যাইব না। আমার গা ও পা ভিজিয়া যাইবে, শীত করিবে এবং অবশেষে কফ কাসী হইয়া বড় পীড়া পাইব। মেঘের ভিতর হইতে আলো বাহির হইয়া আমার চক্ষে লাগিতেছে, জানালার কপাট দি। উঃ! মেঘের ডাকে কান ফাটিয়া যায়। আলো বাহির হইতেছে আবারও বুঝি মেঘ ডাকে, চক্ষু বুজিয়া থাকি, কান ঢাকিয়া রাখি এবং মাঝের কুঠ-

Figure 5. Bengali text; Madanamohana Tarkālaṅkāra, *Śiśuśikṣā* (Calcutta, 1864).

of cutting extra kerning sorts. It is a neat and readable typeface, but its rather uninspiring design owes little to Bengali calligraphy (figure 4).

From the second half of the nineteenth century, the standard of type design and typography for Indian scripts was raised by the products of indigenous presses and foundries (only one such foundry is known to have existed in Bengal in 1856[5]). Differences in letter formation are visible between fonts cut by indigenous artisans and those of European origin. Two works published in Calcutta during this time assisted in establishing a standard Bengali character set for printed works, viz. *Śiśuśikṣā* (1849) and *Varṇaparicaya* (1855) by Īśvaracandra Vidyāsāgara and Madanamohana Tarkālaṅkāra (the founders of the Sanskrit Press). These works enjoyed immense popularity, running to well over a hundred editions before the turn of the century (figure 5). The *Varṇaparicaya*

provi... explains the necessity... ng obsolete forms.
Vidy... composing school-
book... or quality work. But
the... their mark: known
vari... tin punctuation was
com... just a headline for
Nor... ority of imprints follow... Sanskrit pundit and
resp... unctuation and the
hyp... nfluence did not di-
I min... increasing demand
for... scripts, hence the
forr... ns. The restrictions
of h... a profound impact
(sor... because, *inter alia,*
the... accurate placement
of d... achieve readability.
New... y the limited range
of characters and character elements available on hot-metal machines
to generate all the required Bengali letterforms. The new convention of
setting vowel signs separately from their host characters was introduced,
and this became the standard typographic practice for more than half a
century, appearing even in magazine and book publications (figure 6).

A new approach to type design was needed, to counter the steady
degradation of Bengali typography – which appeared set to continue,

12 point (12△472)　　　　　　　　১২ পয়েন্ট

লাইনোটাইপের মুদ্রণ-সম্ভাবনা বিশ্বপ্রসারী। সাড়ে আটশতেরও অধিক সংখ্যক ভাষা এবং উপভাষায় ইহার 'কী-বোর্ড' দ্বারা অক্ষরবিন্যাস সম্ভব। ব্রিটিশ এবং মার্কিন লাইনোটাইপ সংস্থাগুলির দ্বারা প্রবর্তিত অন্যান্য অক্ষর-বিন্যাস পদ্ধতির মধ্যে শ্রেয় এই 'স্লাগ' পদ্ধতির অক্ষরবিন্যাস পৃথিবীর বহু জাতি এবং ভাষার যে উপকার সাধন করিয়াছে, তাহাই ইহার সাফল্যের প্রকৃষ্ট প্রমাণ। তাঁহাদের অক্লান্ত প্রচেষ্টা এবং তাহার সহিত প্রত্যেক দেশের অভিজ্ঞ ব্যাক্তিদের অমূল্য উপদেশের ফলেই লাইনোটাইপ আজ সারা পৃথিবীতে সংবাদ-পত্র, পুস্তক এবং অন্যান্য যাবতীয় মুদ্রণের কাজে ব্যবহৃত হইতেছে। প্রথমে 'রোমান' হরফে মুদ্রণের উদ্দেশ্যেই লাইনোটাইপ আবিষ্কৃত হইয়াছিল, কিন্তু আজ ইহা বাংলার মত নানা ছাঁদের অক্ষরবিন্যাসে সক্ষম। শুধু সক্ষমই নহে, এ-যন্ত্র অতি সহজে এবং অপূর্ব দ্রুতগতিতে কাজ সম্পাদন করিতে সক্ষম। দক্ষিণ হইতে বামে পাঠ্য অক্ষরবিন্যাসও ইহার দ্বারা অত্যন্ত সহজসাধ্য। প্রমাণ 'গ্যালী'র স্থলে একটি সামান্য বিপরীতমুখী কৌশলের দ্বারা ইহা সম্ভব করা

Figure 6. Hot-metal type specimen: Linotype Bengali No. 2.

ইলেকট্রনিক শিল্প স্থাপনের কাজ জুনেই শুরু হচ্ছে

Figure 7. Headline from *Ananda Bazar Patrika* newspaper composed with Linotron 202 Linotype Bengali font (enlarged).

due to the customary convention of adapting existing typefaces to new technologies rather than creating original designs. When Linotype-Paul was commissioned to assist Ananda Bazar Patrika Limited in its conversion from hot-metal composition to digital typesetting, it became evident to the Department of Typographic Development that the easy option of converting the Linotype hot-metal Bengali fonts directly to digital format should be avoided. Thanks to this change in attitude, when Linotype-Paul began its first digital font of Bengali types in 1978, the pattern of imitation that had permeated the development of the printed Bengali character was arrested.

The company realized that the huge investment in the technical development of digital photocomposition warranted new investment in the area of type design and non-Latin typography. The designers therefore studied the Bengali typographic tradition, to appreciate the origins of contemporary typeforms and to assess their relevance in current typographic practice. This would be particularly valuable in determining the criteria that promoted readable Bengali typeface designs on poor-quality newsprint in areas of relatively low literacy.

The study of the evolution of the printed Bengali character led to the preferment of the decorative manuscript hand over the then-current typeforms for the styling of the digital lettershapes.[6] The approval by Ananda Bazar Patrika Limited to re-shape three elemental character shapes in the hot-metal font provided licence to re-design the entire font according to the brief given, viz., that of producing a newspaper text typeface and accompanying bold font, which would eventually be used for book production (figure 7). Crucially, Linotype-Paul determined that it was important to strive for quality comparable to that of Latin fonts rather than to maintain compatibility with earlier systems of non-Latin composition. This could only be achieved by exploiting the advantages of the new technology by means of a typesetting scheme capable of implementing the design desiderata for the new Bengali fonts.[7]

*

The advent of photocomposition had provided the opportunity to reverse the decline in typographic quality incurred by mechanization, but
it had no perceptible influence on Bengali composition until the 1970s.
The first film fonts for the Northern Indian scripts were produced outside India and were copies of foundry or hot-metal types. Perhaps the
lack of linguistic knowledge on the part of Western font manufacturers
made them reluctant to tamper with non-Latin designs whose metal
forms had been found to be 'acceptable'.

Nevertheless, early experiences in filmsetting were informative regarding the possibilities and implications of photocomposition for vernacular setting. One feature of great significance was the development
of software to achieve typographic enhancements that could emulate,
where appropriate, the calligraphic hand. Software facilitated improvements in kerning, diacritical positioning, and justification – all vital to
non-Latin typesetting. Furthermore, the V-I-P Arabic typesetting system[8]
demonstrated the feasibility of selecting contextual forms[9] by means of
specific software.

Software was to play an even more vital role in digital typesetting: it
emancipated the font repertoire from the rigid confines of specific input
systems with limited output codes. The development of software logic at
Linotype-Paul that could select contextual forms in any script heralded
the demise of the large non-Latin keyboards of the photocomposition
era. Linotype's invention of the *Phonetic Keyboard* for Indian scripts in
1978 not only enabled complex scripts to be set from standard equipment, but provided unprecedented flexibility in designing new typefaces
for digital composition (figure 8).

4. Conjuncts are keyed phonetically via the *Conjunct Key;* the sequence is as follows:

a) Conjunct formed of two consonants:
   Conjunct Key ক + ক = ক্ক
b) Conjunct formed of three consonants:
   Shift *Conjunct Key* ন + দ + র = ন্দ্র

Figure 8. Phonetic keying sequence – from Fiona Ross 'Indian Scripts for
Photocomposition' (July, 1979), unpublished Linotype in-house document.

Among other advantages, a designer could question the limitations
of the character set, since now the font repertoire (by means of software) could contain up to 500 sorts. These would be accessed by specific
phonetic keying sequences, from a keyboard comprising only the basic
characters of the syllabary, punctuation, numerals and typographic symbols.[10] A type designer could also question the appropriateness of inhar-

monious proportions, since character widths were no longer restricted. And a designer could question the peculiar positioning of subscripts and superscripts that had became fixed in metal, since software could now place these according to calligraphic practice. In short, long-standing errors no longer needed to be perpetuated, and inherited outmoded technical limitations could be jettisoned.

Clearly, such an approach was not solely applicable to Bengali typography but to that of all vernacular scripts. Ananda Bazar Patrika converted to digital typesetting in 1981 using the Bengali digital fonts and typesetting program produced by Linotype-Paul. It also commissioned Linotype to adopt the same approach for a Devanagari digital typeface and to produce a phonetic keyboard combining three languages, viz. Bengali, Devanagari, and English – a hitherto impossible feat. Thus the methodology developed for the design of the Bengali typeface and composing scheme became the blueprint for the development of other fonts by the company.

The application of this methodology was significant in many ways. It led to the extension by 300 characters of the Linotype Devanagari fonts designed by Matthew Carter. The use of half forms (common components) to create Devanagari characters was abandoned, except in cases of the additional consonantal combinations required for loan words. It led to the revision of the Gujarati hot-metal typeface licensed from the Monotype Corporation; and to the new designs for Malayalam, Telugu, Kannada, and Sinhala scripts (figure 9). The typesetting scheme for Bengali was extended to produce a single typesetting program for composing all South Asian scripts. Thai type design and composition came under similar scrutiny, particularly with regard to justification routines.

This approach to type design, whereby issues concerning the cultural heritage, linguistic fidelity, and technical composition were addressed by a team usually comprising native speakers, typographers, designers,

నోరు పెట్టుకొని గెలవవే ఊరగంగాన మ్మా అని చివరకు హడావుడి చేసీచేసీచార్లెస్ స్కిల్లియేకేసుగ ల్చాడు. బెడ్ఫో ర్డ్మైర్ లోచార్లెన్స్కిల్లీ అనే 40

నోరు పెట్టుకొని గెలవవే ఊరగంగాన మ్మా అని చివరకు హడావుడి చేసీచేసీచార్లెస్ స్కిల్లియేకేసుగెల్చాడు. బెడ్ఫో ర్డ్మైర్ లోచార్లెన్స్కిల్లీ అనే 40 సంవత్సరాలఆసామి

Figure 9. Telugu type specimen: Linotype Tamara light and bold.

خط نستعلیق کے بانی اور موجد فارسی زبان کے ایک عالم تھے سلطان محمود

بھمانی نے انھیں قطب الملک کا خطاب عطا کیا تھا چنانچہ اسی مناسبت

سے انھوں نے اس خط کو قطب شاہی کالقب دیا اس کے بعد سے

خطاطوں اور علماء کی مختلف نسلوں کے درمیان ترقی کی منازل طے کر

Figure 10. *Nasta'liq* type specimen: Linotype Qalmi.

and programmers, also paved the way for the development of Linotype's *nasta'liq* composing system.[11] Digital typesetting not only offered the possibility of multilingual composition with different reading directions, but it could also handle multiple-level scripts and multiple base-jumps. It was, therefore, possible to devise a scheme whereby the Arabic *nasta'liq* style could be composed from a standard keyboard to an Urdu layout. Utilizing approximately 400 glyphs (sorts), the font would generate the numerous forms necessary for typesetting *nasta'liq*. The result was Qalmi, a modern, compact style of *nasta'liq* designed for newspaper text typography (figure 10). It was necessarily table-driven: i.e. it was heavily reliant on software that selected the appropriate sorts, dots, etc., to generate thousands of character combinations. The composition program was sensitive to the diagonal progression of joined sequences, automatically selecting diminished lettershapes at higher levels, thereby allowing more economical letterspacing.

The techniques advocated by the Typographic R&D Department at Linotype-Paul for developing non-Latin typestyles were confined neither to a specific script nor to a particular technology. When Arabic fonts were being converted to PostScript format, the typefaces were reassessed, and appropriate revisions undertaken, such as the re-fitting of medial forms, the application of improved kerning logic, and the addition of extra ligatures. In the case of Amharic, new keyboarding practices were implemented to complement a new typeface.

Evidence of the influence of the first digital Indian font and composing system is not simply in the numerous pirated copies or derivatives. Non-Latin fonts have been viewed from a new perspective during the last two decades: the adoption of a phonetic-style keyboard has become standard for most non-Latin scripts; and significant improvements to the positioning of vowel signs and kerning has been visible in the majority of vernacular publications.

However, technical advances – even those of twenty years ago – have not been fully embraced by all type designers and font developers. Many current digital fonts are simply conversions of less-than-satisfactory non-Latin metal or film fonts. Instead of allowing software to select well-designed contextual forms, the unhappy conjunction of common components appears frequently in contemporary Devanagari texts. Accents on 'stalks', as in the Malayalam script, which had been introduced for linecasting, are still in use. Oversized subscripts in the Telugu script – designed to avoid metal-type breakage – and other such peculiarities are ever visible. Perhaps this is due to the convenience of requiring no extra research or time to develop new font synopses. Perhaps some font developers are catering to user or reader conservatism. Perhaps in a few cases it results from limited linguistic knowledge or imagination. Fear of piracy also renders relatively large investments in non-Latin projects unappealing. Maybe a combination of some, or all, of these factors has hindered the growth of high-quality non-Latin font libraries.

Although printing by means of prefabricated letterforms in non-Latin scripts dates back to the 11th century AD,[12] it is not until the digital era that some non-Latin scripts, in particular Indic, have been rendered correctly in print. There is still much more that can be achieved typographically for complex scripts by implementing numerous features that could produce, say, digital calligraphy to a desirable quality, or that could render sacred writings accurately in print and in multimedia endeavours.[13]

The development of OpenType fonts and Unicode text processing is facilitating computer-mediated information interchange between an increasing number of writing systems, encouraging font designers and developers to redefine character sets and to reconsider issues of readability for many languages. The potential for non-Latin typography to gain comparable quality and status to that of Latin is achievable in the 21st century – as long as type designers are predisposed to the view that, irrespective of the writing system, innovations in design can parallel developments in typesetting technology.

Acknowledgements

Figures 1 and 5 are reproduced courtesy of the British Library Board. Figure 3 is reproduced courtesy of the School of Oriental and African Studies, London University. Figures 6, 8–10 are reproduced courtesy of Linotype Library GmbH. Figure 4 is reproduced by kind permission of the St Bride Printing Library. Much of the information for this essay has been drawn from the author's book, as cited in footnote 10.

Notes

1. Undertaken by the author.
2. Nathanial B. Halhed, *A Grammar of the Bengal Language* (Hoogly, 1778), p. ii.
3. The first successful font of Bengali types was produced by Charles Wilkins, in India, for Halhed's *Grammar*. Wilkins used approximately 170 sorts to represent the Bengali script; see figure 3.
4. G.A. Grierson, 'The Early Publications of the Serampore Missionaries: A Contribution to Bibliography', *Indian Antiquary* XXXII (June 1903), p. 241.
5. At the Girīśa Vidyāratna Press.
6. This study was undertaken in consultation with Dr Tarapada Mukherjee, Lecturer in Bengali at the School of Oriental and African Studies (London University), who acted as consultant on Bengali orthography.
7. The author was to design the typesetting scheme and provide the artwork brief; Tim Holloway was commissioned to design the artwork.
8. Produced by Linotype-Paul Ltd; the software was devised and written by Dr Mike Fellows, who also created and wrote the software for the Linotron 202 non-Latin fonts.
9. Initial, medial, final, and isolated forms as well as ligatures.
10. See F. G. Ross, *The Printed Bengali Character and its Evolution* (Richmond, 1999) pp. 216-220.
11. Patent no: GB2208556B; inventors Mike Fellows, Tim Holloway and Fiona Ross; property of Linotype Library GmbH.
12. See Albertine Gaur, *A History of Writing* (London, 1984), p. 198.
13. It is not within the scope of this essay to discuss potential typographic features, such as variable length curved kashidas in Arabic. Each feature merits detailed discussion.

GERRY LEONIDAS

A primer on Greek type design

A T THE 1997 ATYPI CONFERENCE at Reading I gave a talk with the
title 'Typography & the Greek language: designing typefaces in a
cultural context'. The inspiration for that talk was a discussion
with Christopher Burke on designing typefaces for a script one is not
linguistically familiar with. My position was that knowledge and use of a
language is not a prerequisite for understanding the script to a very high,
though not conclusive, degree. In other words, although a 'typographically attuned' native user should test a design in real circumstances, any
designer could, with the right preparation and monitoring, produce com-
petent typefaces. This position was based on my understanding of the
decisions a designer must make in designing a Greek typeface. I should
add that this argument had two weak points: one, it was based on a small
amount of personal experience in type design and a lot of intuition, rather than research; and, two, it was quite possible that, as a Greek, I was
making the 'right' choices by default. Since 1997, my own work and that
of other designers – both Greeks and non-Greeks – proved me right.

The last few years saw multilingual typography explode. An obvious arena was the broader European region: the Amsterdam Treaty of
1997 which, at the same time as bringing the European Union closer to
integration on a number of fields, marked a heightening of awareness
in cultural characteristics, down to an explicit statement of support for
dialects and local script variations. Furthermore, the assignment of can-
didate-for-entry status to several countries in central and eastern Europe,
and the tightening of relationships with other countries in the region,
foregrounded not only the requirements of the extended Latin script,
but the different flavours of the Cyrillic script in use within the broader
European area. In this context, the Greek script is a relatively minor, if
indispensable, player. However, in a reflection of its history in the last
five centuries, there is a huge interest for Greek typography from outside
the boundaries of the Greek state. There are considerable Hellenic communities in Europe, North America, and Australia; a significant number
of academics working on ancient, Byzantine, and modern Greek; and an
important worldwide market for bilingual ecclesiastical texts.

[76]

Despite sizable gaps in published research, the development of the Greek typographic script up to the twentieth century is well established, at least for the non-historian. The twentieth century, on the other hand, is not as well documented, and even less well researched – a regrettable fact, since it is a far more volatile and interesting period for Greek typography. Here, I will very briefly go over a few key contributions to Greek type design up to the end of the nineteenth century, before expanding on more recent developments.

GREEK LETTERFORMS UP TO THE FIFTEENTH CENTURY

Varied, but clearly related, inscriptional and scribal strands of development were established, spanning all the way from pre-classical times through the Hellenistic years and the ascendancy of Orthodox Byzantium. Inscriptional letters were not cut at the larger sizes common in Imperial Rome; the development of Byzantine hagiographical and secular lettering did not follow the logic of the brush-stroke construction as outlined by Catich in his *Origin of the Serif*.

An uncial hand developed for writing on softer materials, which branched into official and vernacular varieties, the latter with a strong cursive character. Such hands were increasingly adopted by the mercantile classes, secular writers, and non-patristic ecclesiastical writers. Letters from older hands were used for versals and titles.

After the sack of Constantinople in 1204 by the fourth Crusade, the western, largely Venetian, occupation of many lands, particularly Crete and Cyprus, facilitated the migration of Greek scribes to the Italian peninsula. This movement turned into a flood after the fall of Constantinople in 1453 to the Ottoman Turks. It was the cursive hand that these scribes brought to the West, and put to use as tutors, editors, and printers.

THE FIRST GREEK TYPEFACES

The first printers to cast Greek type used the hands of Italian humanists as models. Typefaces of this group tend to have upright letterforms, with nearly circular counters, and monoline strokes with occasionally bulging or tapering terminals. There are few ligatures, and letterforms are positioned within a clearly defined vertical band – in other words, there is minimal kerning. Although some letterforms were consistently troublesome for western punch-cutters, texts are easily readable and the texture of the page is generally even. This style reached its zenith in the typeface by the Spaniard Arnaldo Guillen de Brocar (figure 1, overleaf), famously used in the Complutensian Polyglot Bible.

Scribal models for Greek typefaces were not as established as for Latin ones, where the varieties of blackletter were dominant in patristic and

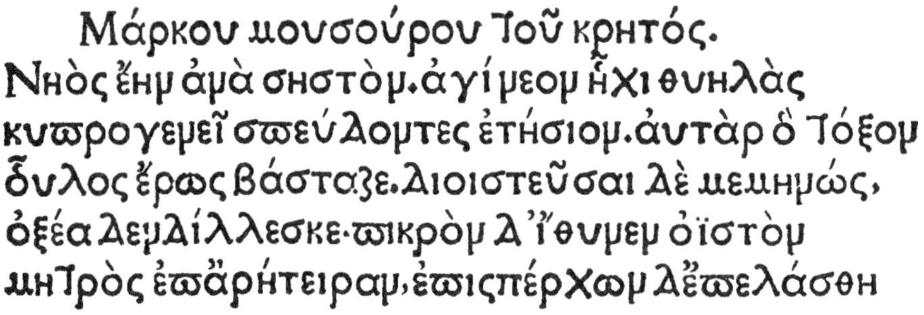

Μάρκου μουσούρου Ίοῦ κρнτός.
Νнὸς ἔнμ ἁμὰ σнστὸμ.ἀγί μεομ ἤχι θυнλὰς
κυϖρο γεμεῖ σϖεύ Λομτες ἐτήσιομ.ἀυτὰρ ὀ Ίόξομ
ὄυλος ἔρως Βάστα3ε.Διοιστεῦσαι Δὲ μεμнμώς,
ὀξέα Δεμ Δί λλεσκε·ϖικρὸμ Δ ἲθυμεμ ὀϊστὸμ
μнΊρὸς ἐϖάρήτειραμ,ἐϖιςπέρχωμ Δἔϖελάσθн

Figure 1. Typeface by the Spaniard Arnaldo Guillen de Brocar. This is one of the
three main strands of early Greek type styles. Despite its simplicity and clarity, it
fell victim to the commercial success of the Aldine model.

ecclesiastical texts, and the early humanists' version of littera antiqua
were standard in classical texts and treatises. Despite the considerable
involvement of non-Greek scholars in – mostly Venetian and Florentine –
publishing enterprises, the refugee scribes and scholars had significant
authorial and editorial presence, even when they did not assume the role
of publisher or printer. It is not difficult to imagine that their manuscripts
would be seen as fitting models for the cutting of new typefaces.

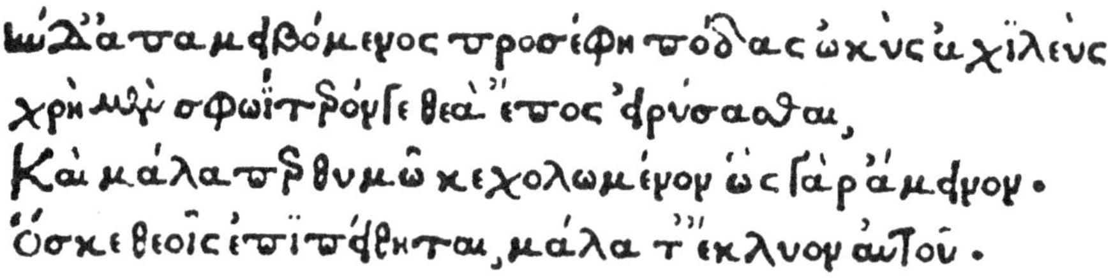

Figure 2. Typeface by Demetrios Damilas. This strand of early Greek type
styles, in some ways a stylistic precursor to de Brocar's, combined regularity
with fluidity without indulging in over-complexity.

This first style of types modelled on the hands of the Greek refugees
is exemplified by the type of Demetrios Damilas, which appeared in 1476
(figure 2). Each letterform is clearly differentiated, although there are
more ligatures and abbreviations. Some regularity and circularity has
been traded for a closer correspondence to the variety and vigour of energetic handwriting. One could say that these types mirror the scribe's
familiarity with the letterforms. The strong distinction between minuscules for text and capitals for versals or titles must have made it easier for
printers to use capitals from different typefaces, not to mention borrow-
ing what could be used from a Latin fount.[1]

The turning point for Greek types is 1495, the year Aldus Manutius
published his first Greek text. Technical considerations aside,[2] Aldus's
importance lies in his choice to follow the hand of the Greek scribe Immanuel Rhusotas (figure 3) in all its complexity. This necessitated a huge
number of contractions, ligatures, and alternate sorts (figure 4). Aldus's

three subsequent typefaces were essentially attempts to simplify the design and eliminate ligatures and contractions. Unfortunately, and to the regret of generations of compositors, it would take a couple of centuries for punchcutters of Greek to take serious steps in turning a scribal script into a typographical one suitable for typesetting by hand.[3]

The typefaces that mirrored the handwriting style of contemporary scholars must have contributed to the commercial success of the Aldine editions as much as their novel format and Aldus's drive to publish Aristotle's works. The result was that the style became the accepted face of printed Greek erudition, and was imitated widely, in complexity comparable to the originals.

We should note that the prominence of the Aldine style eclipsed other alternatives, most notably the practically contemporary design of Zacharias Kalliergis (figure 5, overleaf). This typeface has wider spacing, more open counters, and curved strokes that develop without crowding or closing in on themselves. Altogether more space is allowed for the elaboration of strokes – and, despite being based on a scribal hand, there are concessions to typographical necessity. Kalliergis' typeface influenced some later designs, but its legacy was not lasting; a regrettable development by any measure.

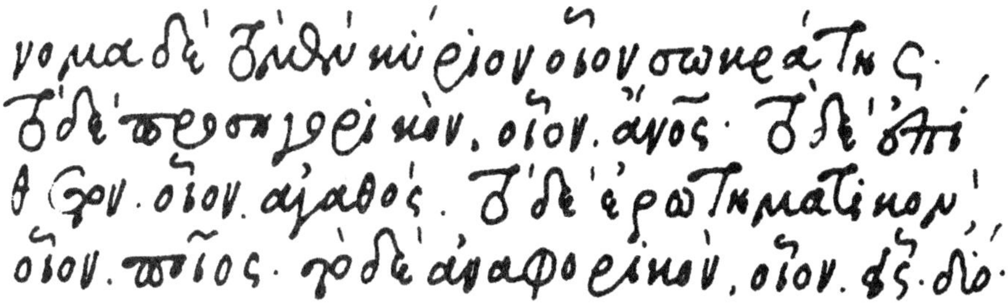

Figure 3. The hand of the Greek scribe Immanuel Rhusotas, which Aldus used as a model for Griffo to cut his Greek types. The fluidity is characteristic of a proficient scribe's hand.

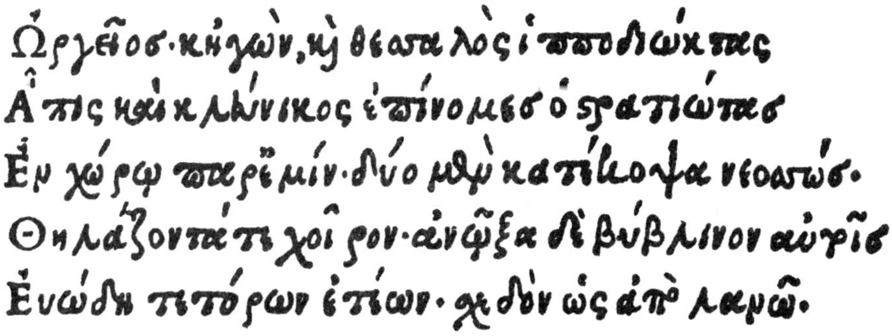

Figure 4. First Greek typeface by Aldus Manutius. The decision to provide a sufficient number of ligatures, contractions, and abbreviations to replicate the texture of the handwritten text would burden the Greek typographic script with undesirable complexity for centuries.

In the 1540s Claude Garamond cut a Greek typeface (figures 6a, 6b) in three sizes drawing on the Aldine spirit, but this time based on the hand of another Greek scribe, Angelos Vergikios. The types are more open and upright, and strokes flow easily into one another. One could say that the smoothness of the curves and the transitions from one letter to the next bring to mind the shift in the French interpretations of Griffo's italics. To the compositors' continuing despair, the founts were equipped with hundreds of ligatures and contractions. Garamond's type-

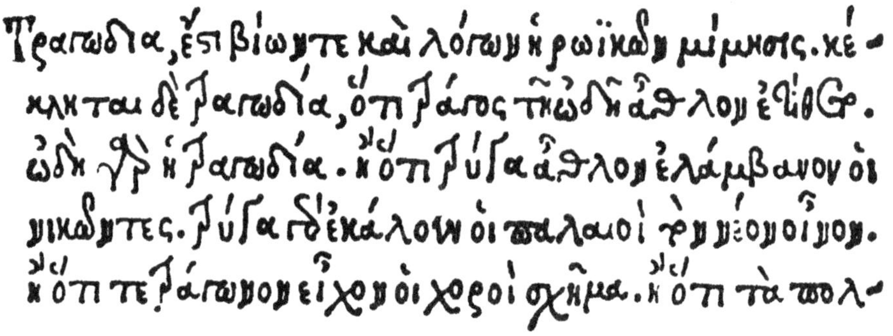

Figure 5. Typeface of Zacharias Kalliergis. Another victim of Aldus's business acumen, this was probably the most promising of all the strands of early Greek type: it is fluid but uncomplicated, elegant yet susceptible to regularisation.

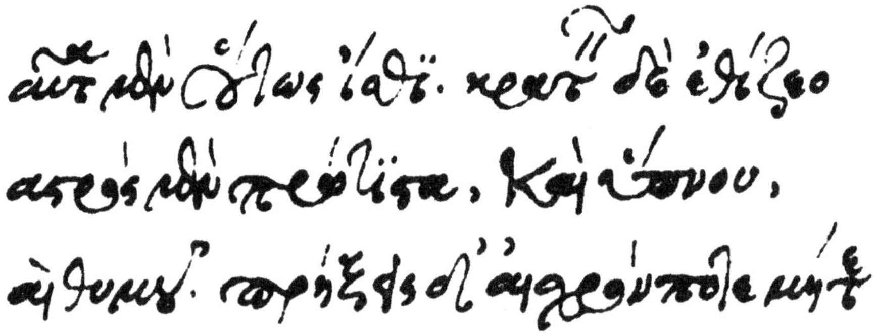

Figure 6a. The writing of the scribe Angelos Vergikios. Despite its elegance, this hand has all the marks of a script that is unsuitable for conversion to a typographic alphabet. That it was the model for the widely copied *grecs-du-roi* was, with hindsight, unfortunate.

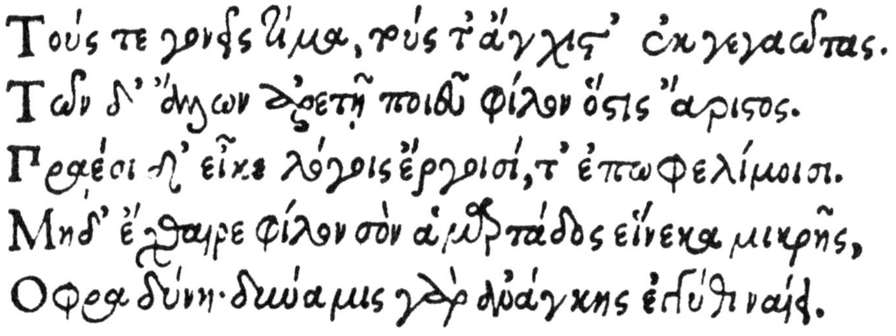

Figure 6b. Claude Garamond's *grecs-du-roi*.

faces were an immediate and long-lasting success: printers hastened to secure copies or close approximations, and the style dominated Greek typefaces well into the 18th century.

For the two centuries after Garamond, the main development was the inevitable abolishment of most of the ligatures and contractions. The issue was not simply one of just not using the extra sorts; if a punchcutter had intended a typeface with, for example, a double *gamma* ligature, the possibility of two single *gamma* sorts side-by-side would not have been anticipated. If we take into account the extent to which typefaces relied on ligatures and alternate sorts, simply omitting these features would truncate the design. It was not until 1756 that Alexander Wilson cut a successful typeface that followed the established models while doing away with all but the most basic ligatures and contractions (figures 7a, 7b) The new trend did not catch on as easily as compositors might have hoped, but eventually Greek typefaces were liberated from the more complex scribal remnants.

The eighteenth century saw printers like Baskerville and Bodoni transplant elements from the writing masters' style and the Modern types to their Greeks, with, on the whole, unfortunate results.[4] An inclined variety

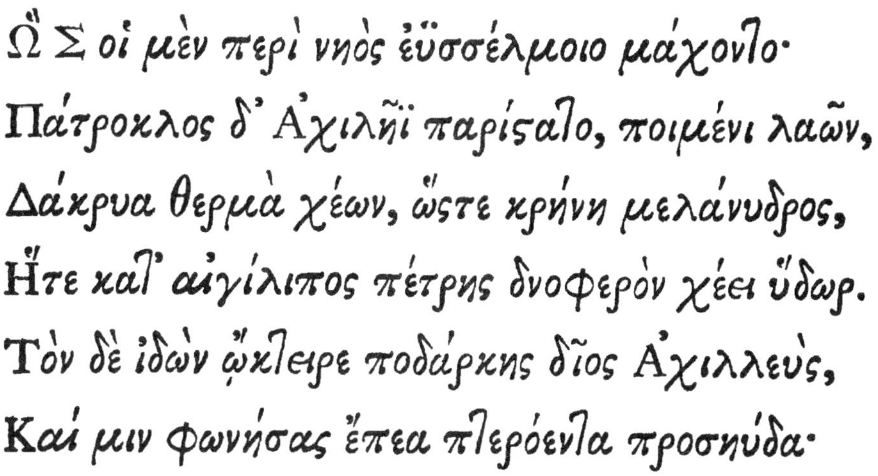

Ὣ Σ οἱ μὲν περὶ νηὸς ἐϋσσέλμοιο μάχονΊο·
Πάτροκλος δ᾽ Ἀχιλῆϊ παρίσαΊο, ποιμένι λαῶν,
Δάκρυα θερμὰ χέων, ὥστε κρήνη μελάνυδρος,
Ἥτε καΊ᾽ αἰγίλιπος πέτρης δνοφερὸν χέει ὕδωρ.
Τὸν δὲ ἰδὼν ᾤκΊειρε ποδάρκης δῖος Ἀχιλλεὺς,
Καί μιν φωνήσας ἔπεα πΊερόενΊα προσηύδα·

Figure 7a. Alexander Wilson's Greek typeface for the Foulis Press.

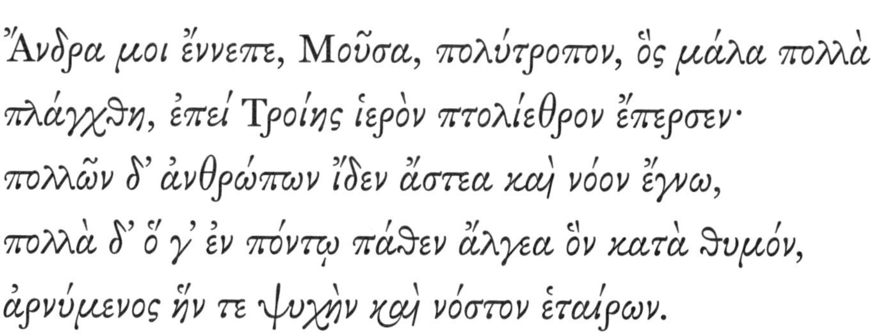

Ἄνδρα μοι ἔννεπε, Μοῦσα, πολύτροπον, ὃς μάλα πολλὰ
πλάγχθη, ἐπεὶ Τροίης ἱερὸν πτολίεθρον ἔπερσεν·
πολλῶν δ᾽ ἀνθρώπων ἴδεν ἄστεα καὶ νόον ἔγνω,
πολλὰ δ᾽ ὅ γ᾽ ἐν πόντῳ πάθεν ἄλγεα ὃν κατὰ θυμόν,
ἀρνύμενος ἥν τε ψυχὴν καὶ νόστον ἑταίρων.

Figure 7b. A digital version of Wilson's typeface designed by Matthew Carter.

with some distinct traces of Bodoni's style was developed by German printers for textbooks of Greek authors; the style survives to this day.

However, one of the most important figures from the early 19th century was the Frenchman Ambroise Firmin Didot, a fervent philhellene and supporter of the early attempts to establish printing in Greece (Didot trained a Greek printer and donated one of the first presses to operate on liberated Greek soil). His types, which dominated Italy as well as, eventually, the lands of the emerging Greek state, are distant descendants of the *grecs du roi*, but have evolved a consistent style of their own (figure 8). The upright stance and relative thickness of the strokes impart solidity, while the ductal character conveys liveliness and speed. Eventually, the Didot style would prove more resilient than the Bodoni-clones, providing the basis for what became the most widely used typeface in the twentieth century within Greece.

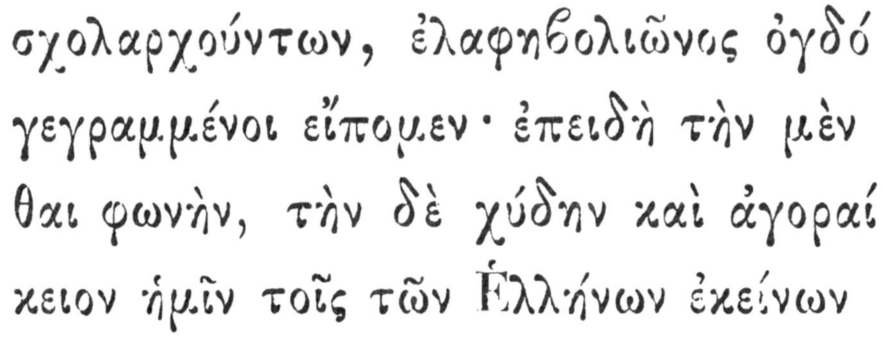

σχολαρχούντων, ἐλαφηβολιῶνος ὀγδό γεγραμμένοι εἴπομεν· ἐπειδὴ τὴν μὲν θαι φωνὴν, τὴν δὲ χύδην καὶ ἀγοραί κειον ἡμῖν τοῖς τῶν Ἑλλήνων ἐκείνων

Figure 8. A Greek by Ambroise-Firmin Didot, from an 1875 edition. Note that the breathings and accents are, unusually, over the capital vowels. This example is a good compromise between strongly scribal characteristics (the pointed *theta*, the long-terminal *delta*, the imposing *gamma* and *lambda*, and the variable ascender heights) and the cleaned-up, more homogenized look of the later Monotype Series 90.

A completely different strand was initiated by the Cambridge Hellenist Richard Porson, who designed a typeface based on his own handwriting, cut by Richard Austin in 1806 (figure 9). The design was a radical departure from contemporary styles: the curves are simplified and the structure and alignment of characters more regularised. The modulation of the strokes is more consistent, and there are some new interpretations, like the lunate *epsilon* (present in several manuscripts, most commonly as part of ligatures), the *kappa*, and the simpler *perispomeni*. The terminals are varied: some taper, some end in drop-like bulbs, and some are sheared. The design is somewhat inconsistent in the balancing of white regions, both in closed counters and around open characters like the lambda. Appropriately for this style, there were no ligatures or contractions. Porson's design showed the way forward for the next generation of Greek typefaces, re-stating the case for abandoning the *grecs*

τ᾽ ἐπιτύχοιεν ξυνελάμβανον τοῦ μὴ ἐξάγγελτοι γενέ-
σθαι, καὶ προσβαλόντες πρῶτον Κωρύκῳ τῆς ἠπείρου
καὶ ἀφέντες ἐνταῦθα αὐτούς, αὐτοὶ μὲν προξυγγενό-
μενοι τῶν ξυμπρασσόντων Χίων τισί, καὶ κελευόντων
καταπλεῖν μὴ προειπόντας ἐς τὴν πόλιν, ἀφικνοῦνται

Figure 9. Richard Austin's typeface, based on the hand of the Hellenist Richard
Porson. Note the tear-drop terminals of vertical strokes, the lunate *epsilon,* the
'headless' *lambda,* and the concave *perispomeni.*

du roi influence and regularising the strokes of letterforms. It was widely
copied (and modified) and still enjoys considerable success, albeit within
Greece only for shorter runs of text.

THE TWENTIETH CENTURY

Although typefoundries existed from the very first years of the modern
Greek state, the turn of the twentieth century saw Greece importing most
of its printing equipment, as well as essentially all the models for text
typefaces, from Europe. We can identify two main strands: an upright
style drawing on Didot's Greeks, and an inclined style with direct references to German typefounders. Notwithstanding the vicissitudes of typographic fashion, upright and inclined typefaces were considered equal
for text material.

From around 1910 onwards, Lanston Monotype and Mergenthaler
Linotype began to make Greek typefaces available for machine composition. The involvement of these companies was instrumental in clarifying
character sets, especially in relation to alternate forms (primarily the
alpha, beta, epsilon, theta, kappa, pi, rho, and *phi*). Another, more elementary, influence of Monotype and Linotype was the complete redefinition
of the relationship between primary and secondary typefaces: until that
point, Greek typesetters used spacing between letters to signify emphasis
in a text. Less frequently, an alternate typeface might be used. Monotype
and Linotype shifted inclined Greeks towards a role equivalent to italics
in Latin typography, a decision that must have been driven by marketing as much as technical reasons. Both adopted the Didot style for their
uprights; and Monotype's Series 90 became the definitive text typeface
of the twentieth century. Numerous – and hugely varied in quality – digital versions are still very popular for literature, while some lower-run or
luxurious editions are typeset with the hot-metal versions. An inclined
typeface with clear German roots and few exact design correlations with
the Didot style, which until that time was a text typeface in its own right,
became the Series 91, the designated secondary italic (figure 10).

αβϐγδεζηθϑικλμνξοπρστυφφχψως

αβϐγδεζηθϑικλμνξοπϱστυφφχψως

Figure 10. Monotype's Series 90 and 91 Greeks. The surviving names for the
two styles are indicative: the Didot style is still called *aplá*, which means 'simple'
(but also, in Greek vernacular, 'default') and the cursive variation of the inclined
types was until the early 1990s called *Lipsías*, which means 'from Leipzig'.

Although types were cut in Greece throughout the period of mechanical typesetting, any original designs were limited to display typefaces;
very few typefaces used for text failed to conform to either the Didot or
to the (German) inclined paradigm. One characteristic common to both
hand-set type specimens from the early part of the century and the surviving specimens from pre-digital phototypesetters is the very narrow
selection of text typefaces, and the relative profusion of display designs.
Perhaps not surprisingly, few of the latter have survived the test of time.

In 1927, Victor Scholderer designed the New Hellenic for Monotype
(figure 11). With some modifications, this has enjoyed moderate success
outside Greece, and rather more within, where it has also had the hon-
ourable role of a variation having been used in primary school first readers for nearly three decades.

αβγδεζηθικλμνξοπρστυφχψως

ΑΒΓΔΕΖΗΘΙΚΛΜΝΞΟΠΡΣΤΥΦΧΨΩ

αβγδεζηθικλμνξοπρστυφχψως

ΑΒΓΔΕΖΗΘΙΚΛΜΝΞΟΠΡΣΤΥΦΧΨΩ

Figure 11. Victor Scholderer's New Hellenic in Monotype's digital version,
with the scribal form of *Omega*. Below it, a local version of questionable
pedigree. Note the *xi*, final *sigma*, *Theta*, and *Psi*.

In the years up to the Second World War, most attempts at new Greek
typefaces designed by non-Greeks – admittedly not numerous, but some
by highly credited designers like Eric Gill and Jan van Krimpen – were
misconceived, and failed to dent the hegemony of the Didot style. However, this did not open up the road to Greek designers: although Greek
printers relied heavily on foundry type that was generally produced lo-
cally, any originality in domestic production continued to be limited to
display types.

The fifties changed all that. Greece was becoming an industrialized
country with a rapidly expanding urban population, so it's no surprise

to see new designs for the emerging middle-class markets. The Gill Sans family (figure 12) designed by the Monotype drawing office was widely imitated, and, together with a small number of other sans serifs, provided the workhorses of the periodical press and advertising of the time.

αβγδεζηθικλμνξοπρστυφχψως

ΑΒΓΔΕΖΗΘΙΚΛΜΝΞΟΠΡΣΤΥΦΧΨΩ

αβγδεζηθικλμνξοπρστυφχψως

ΑΒΓΔΕΖΗΘΙΚΛΜΝΞΟΠΡΣΤΥΦΧΨΩ

αβγδεζηθικλμνξοπρστυφχψως

ΑΒΓΔΕΖΗΘΙΚΛΜΝΞΟΠΡΣΤΥΦΧΨΩ

αβγδεζηθικλμνξοπρστυφχψως

ΑΒΓΔΕΖΗΘΙΚΛΜΝΞΟΠΡΣΤΥΦΧΨΩ

Figure 12. Monotype's digital Gill Sans (upper pair) is seriously compromised by the *alpha, gamma, zeta, lambda, mu, tau, chi, psi,* and both *sigmas.* The pirated version (one of many) improves somewhat on the *alpha, zeta,* and final *sigma,* but is wide of the mark in its *beta, gamma, theta, lambda, tau, phi,* and *chi,* most of which are plainly wrong. Note also the *Xi,* with the vertical joining stroke.

The other major family of the fifties was Times Greek (figures 13a, 13b, overleaf). Capitals excepted, the Greek versions share little with the Latin ones. Regardless, the ubiquity of Times Greek (in all its guises) in the last thirty-odd years, both within and outside Greece, is undeniable, if far from deserved. We must keep in mind that Latin typefaces of the time were very much influenced by the regularising approach then in favour; this approach, however, was primarily implemented in new designs or interpretations of fin-de-siècle sans serifs. It is questionable whether the Times family was a good choice for such treatment. Applying a 1950s approach to the style of a 1930s typeface (with sixteenth-century roots) was inauspicious for Times Greek. The homogenised counters and normalised typeform widths with add-on scribal flourishes and terminals leave a lot to be desired, and the unresolved stress angles and compressed or extended counters testify to a program that failed to adapt conclusively the Latin original's characteristics to the Greek.

The early seventies saw the arrival of the Greek Optima, which was to carve its own niche in Greek magazine publishing, and, more importantly, one of the most influential designs of the post-junta period: the Greek Helvetica (figure 14, p. 87). This was one of the first new Greek

αβγδεζηθικλμνξοπρστυφχψως

αβγδεζηθικλμνξοπρστυφχψως

αβγδεζηθικλμνξοπρστυφχψως

αβγδεζηθικλμνξοπρστυφχψως

αβγδεζηθικλμνξοπρστυφχψως

αβγδεζηθικλμνξοπρστυφχψως

Figure 13a. Different versions of Times Greek with associated italics. Some italic fonts are little more than slanted, compressed versions of the uprights. The alternate forms of letters (e.g. the *alpha, gamma, kappa, upsilon, phi, psi*) suggest one possible route for differentiating effectively between the primary and secondary fonts.

Figure 13b. Lowercase *alphas* from alternate digital versions of Times Greek typefaces (the grey is Monotype Times New Roman, the outline is Linotype Times Ten. The *alpha* is the most common letter in Greek texts, and the size and shape of its counter have a profound effect on the appearance text. Ironing out the corner in the counter of the *alpha* precipitated a straightening of the right half of the typeform into a single vertical stroke; together these constitute one of the most unfortunate developments in Greek type design.

typeface designed directly for phototypesetting; on the whole, the few available phototypes had been re-issues of hot-metal designs. Helvetica went hand-in-hand with the new style in magazine and advertising, if with a few years' delay from the rest of Europe. Through mainly the periodical press, Helvetica became part and parcel of the new, 'cleaner', European aesthetic promoted to urban readers from that time onwards well into the next decade. It is clear that Matthew Carter, who designed these fonts, was asked to produce typefaces that 'looked like the Latin [western] ones', an understandable request in the political and cultural context of Greece in the early 1970s. However, the serifed typefaces of the group developed at the time (Baskerville, Century Schoolbook, and Souvenir) revealed the problems with this approach that trouble Greek typefaces to this day.

All in all, however, the seventies were not years of typographical revolution in Greece. To this contributed not only the political turmoil of the junta of 1967–74 and the subsequent drive to rebuild democracy, but, perhaps more importantly, the fact that many publishing projects were adequately covered by existing technology. Although many magazines adopted offset technology, by far the greatest number of book publishers continued to use hot-metal printing. As the book market was characterized by a large number of small publishers producing modest print runs, printers had little to gain by investing in the new technology. In that light, the lack of available typefaces was not seen as severely limiting. All this was to change in the early eighties.

In 1981 Greece became a full member of what was then the EEC. The international boom of the decade coincided with the coming-of-age of the urban middle classes, who now were affluent enough to afford, but not mature enough to refuse, the extrovert consumerism of American culture. The combination of phototypesetting maturing to digital formats, and the adoption of the monotonic system for Modern Greek in early 1982, which allowed professional typesetters to be replaced by keyboard operators, drove an increasing transfer of hot-metal and early phototypes to digital phototypesetting. As with Latin typefaces, as often as not such transfers produced inferior results on the printed page. This tendency to transfer existing designs into digital formats took on a new angle from the mid-eighties, with dramatic consequences. The gradual adoption of 8-bit Greek fonts with character sets based on ISO 8859–7, Win 1253, or Mac/OS Greek (by far the worst of the three) was the single most important factor in encouraging font piracy by local designers. A general disregard for international legal standards and accepted practice did not help, nor did a desire, typical of the period, to make a quick profit. The explosion of the periodical and promotional fields fuelled this phenomenon even further. Greece filled with service bureaus where attention to detail in typesetting and quality in print production were sacrificed to turnover rates and low costs. These companies supported and

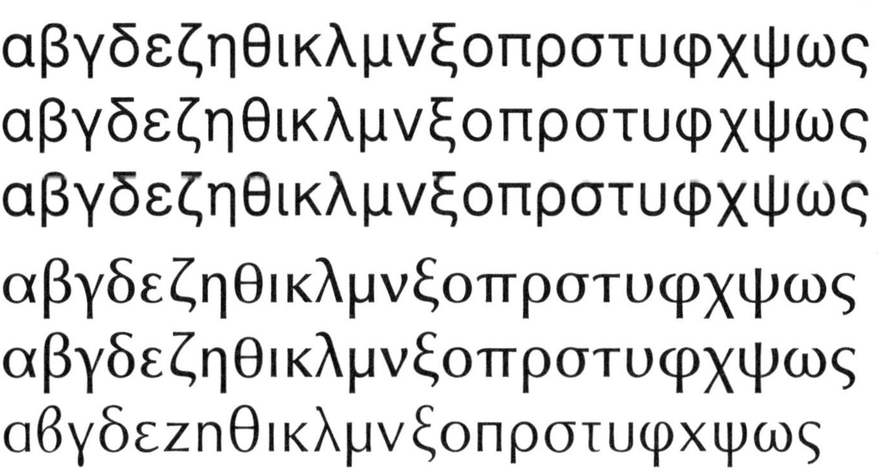

αβγδεζηθικλμνξοπρστυφχψως
αβγδεζηθικλμνξοπρστυφχψως
αβγδεζηθικλμνξοπρστυφχψως
αβγδεζηθικλμνξοπρστυφχψως
αβγδεζηθικλμνξοπρστυφχψως
αβγδεζηθικλμνξοπρστυφχψως

Figure 14. Local Greek versions of Linotype's Helvetica and Optima typefaces. The bottom example of Optima is particularly poor.

recycled the graduates of numerous new graphic design schools where depth in design education was rarely, if ever, achieved.

The last decade saw an improvement in some areas. Many designers moved on to multimedia and web design, where it seems easier to justify a paycheck to reluctant clients. Thankfully some – a few – clients have begun to recognize the effort invested in a typeface design, and are willing to seek work of a higher quality. There also seem to be some schools that attach more emphasis to quality in design education, although how many of those subscribe to *Hyphen* remains to be seen. At the same time, many typefaces in circulation are in breach of copyright or design patents. The result of all the above is that many new Greek typefaces by Greek designers betray a lack of understanding of fundamental aspects of Greek typography, the basic shape of Greek typeforms, and good type-setting. The last few years have witnessed an overwhelming proliferation of designs, ranging from the ever-present hacking of Latin typefaces to a few serious efforts (figure 15). The Greek market is in the process of discovering the made-to-order typeface, advertisers are beginning to re-alize the potential of an eye-catching design, and, as is usual in similar circumstances, several people have become instant experts. Designers who trained – as opposed to 'were educated in design' – from the last years of the eighties onwards enjoy a more open communication with ac-tivities in Europe and the United States, and are now a significant part of the professionally active design community. However, for every original typeface design there is still a hacker trying to make some easy money.

In the meantime, a number of expanded character sets have been de-veloped to address the demand for multilingual and multi-script support. Microsoft was the first significant source of such a set (with WGL4), but

αβγδεζηθικλμνξοπροτυφχψως

αβγδεζηθικλμνξοπροτυφχψως

αβγδεζηθικλμνξοπροτυφχψως

αβγδεζηθικλμνξοπροτυφχψως

αβγδεznθικλμνξοπροτυφχψωs

αβγδεζηθικ∫λμνξοπροτυφχψωs

Figure 15. Some badly designed Greek 'Bodonis'.

from a design perspective not exceptional; Adobe's later OpenType fonts are much more notable (figure 16), and include one extensive polytonic typeface which I hope may dent the ubiquity of the several versions of Times Greek used by classicists worldwide. As expected, in most cases the type designers employed by such companies cannot read Greek, and may have a very patchy knowledge – if any – of the relevant Greek history. The problem therefore facing any designer, Greek or non-Greek, is whether a new design respects the script's history and design characteristics, while developing the typographic morphology consistently and with originality.

αβγδεζηθικλμνξοπρστυφχψως

αβγδεζηθικλμνξοπρστυφχψως

αβγδεζηθικλμνξοπρστυφχψως

αβγδεζηθικλμνξοπρστυφχψως

αβγδεζηθικλμνξοπρστυφχψως

αβγδεζηθικλμνξοπρστυφχψως

Figure 16. Greek glyphs from Adobe's Myriad Pro, Minion Pro, and Warnock Pro OpenType fonts.

CONCLUSION

It is one of history's ironies that while so many non-Greeks were studying the classical Greek language and literature, the Greek people were either under foreign occupation or struggling to mature as a state and a nation. Partly because of this, many Greeks developed an all-too-easy rejection of foreign intervention or example; and many foreign affairs that affected Greece negatively were condemned as if political expediencies were tinged with anti-Hellenic bias. Greeks have often accused non-Greeks of corrupting our cultural inheritance, just as foreigners have accused Greeks of negligence in caring for that inheritance. The truth, as usual, lies somewhere in between. Typeface design has not escaped this attitude, which was aided by the overwhelming dominance of the typesetting equipment market by international companies. Despite protestations that it is very difficult, if not impossible, for a non-Greek to capture the 'essence' of Greek typeforms, the fact remains that, until a few years ago, it was mostly non-Greeks who designed and produced Greek typefaces. With hindsight, and in light of recent work, we would have to concede that they did a decent job.

Writing in a different context, Richard Clogg wrote that: '..."Greekness" is something that a person is born with and can no more easily be lost than it can be acquired by those of not Greek ancestry'.[5] Clogg makes a case for language not being the defining criterion; my experience of non-Greek type designers seems to support that, at least to a considerable degree in the design process. Good typefaces are created through a combination of a knowledge of the traditional forms of the script, and an immersion in dialogue with existing designs, whatever format this interface may take. I would like to think that a well-informed designer with a talent for identifying formal consistencies and distinctions in unfamiliar typeforms can go a long way in Greek type design, without worrying too much about her or his lack or misunderstanding of 'Greekness'.

Notes

1. The distinct character of lower-case and capitals is evident in Greek typefaces to this day.
2. Letters with diacriticals presented a major challenge, at both the punchcutting and the typecasting stages. Aldus guarded his innovations and patents with vigilance. The casting of Greek sorts with diacritics in the fifteenth century continues to spark intense debate.
3. In a seminal essay, the distinguished incunabulist Victor Scholderer referred to the Aldine Greeks as 'a disaster from which Greek printing did not recover for generations.' (*Greek printing types: 1465–1927*, British Museum, London, 1927, p.7). Scholderer was too strong in his opinion. In the light of other stylistic directions open at the time the Aldine model was over-elaborate and relatively untypographic; but given the conditions at the time it was as valid a choice as any. Scholderer's comment about Greek is tantamount to someone saying that Arabic writing is unsuitable for typography. We could argue that the limitations of a typesetting technology should not be interpreted as shortcomings of a script.
4. Giambattista Bodoni seemed to lack an understanding of Greek typeforms as part of a set. His Greeks look more like a series of individual shapes that are cut or drawn to please aesthetically. He certainly seemed to have been experimenting: the *Manuale Typographicum* has 22 sets of Greek minuscules, mostly inclined, and almost every one a different design.
5. Clogg, Richard. *A concise history of modern Greece,* Cambridge University Press, 1992, p.5

Zvi Narkiss and Hebrew type design

A SPECIAL CHALLENGE facing the contemporary type designer working with Hebrew is the lack of a clearly defined model. This script never became formalized as a lapidary style in the way the Latin alphabet was. Furthermore, few historical Hebrew type designs were successful enough to merit a revival. The type designer is therefore also to some degree an inventor of the alphabet: he decides which of the alternative forms of the letter to use, and thereby, if the design is successful, which of the forms will become standard.

The Hebrew language was initially written in an alphabet very similar to Phoenician – Paleo-Hebrew or *ktav ivri kadum*. About 560 BCE it was replaced by the Aramaic or Assyrian alphabet, *ktav ashuri*. The modern Jewish letter is its direct descendent. Three main branches are recognised in the alphabet we use today:

א Square script, *ktiva merubaat*, a formal book hand
ﬡ Cursive, used for everyday writing
ﬣ Rabbinic, a formal cursive used mostly for rabbinical commentaries (also known as *m'sheat* or *Rashi*)[1]

Since it was the formal book hand that became the basis of most printing types in use today, I shall focus on it in the present essay. The other two scripts may be alive and well, but their application is confined to a limited area.

The Hebrew letter as we know it has changed little in the last two thousand years. Consistency of basic character shapes is evident when we examine the Dead Sea scrolls, written in the first centuries BCE and CE (figure 1, overleaf). A modern Hebrew reader can without much trouble decipher and read these ancient manuscripts which were preserved in the dry climate of the Qumran caves of the Judean desert.

Few Hebrew manuscripts dating from between the first and ninth centuries CE are extant. Ninth-century documents found in the Cairo *geniza*,[2] as well as other manuscripts of the same era – such as the Leningrad Codex, 916 CE (St. Petersburg Public Library) and the Aleppo

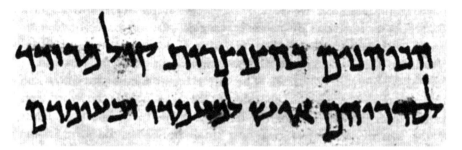

Figure 1. Lettering of the War Scroll of the Dead Sea scrolls, first century CE, Shrine of the Book, Israel Museum, Jerusalem. Note the absence of a baseline: the characters are aligned on the top horizontal. From *The Development of Hebrew Lettering* by Moshe Spitzer, Jerusalem, 1974.

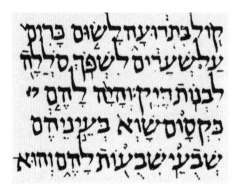

Figure 2. Lettering of the Aleppo Codex (*Keter Aram Ẓova*, early tenth century CE), Shrine of the Book, Israel Museum, Jerusalem. Note the subtlety of modelling of the characters.

Codex (Shrine of the Book, Israel Museum) – testify to a mature and sophisticated formal scribal tradition (figure 2). Compared to the style of the Dead Sea scrolls, each character in these manuscripts had a high degree of completion, and could be viewed as an individual graphic form. Proportions of these letters were pleasant, their construction was complicated, and distinction between most characters was clear.

For lack of a formal lapidary script, these accomplished book hands served as a model for subsequent interpretations. They were the closest one could find in Hebrew to the 'classical' style.

After a thousand years of exile, distinct identities of dispersed Jewish communities began to take shape. The customs of the two major communities in Europe became identified with the two centers of Jewish life at that time: Spain and Germany. Spain, called *Sfarad* in Hebrew, was the home of the Sephardic community, and Germany – *Ashkenaz* in Hebrew – of the Ashkenazic. Although Hebrew styles were not exhausted by those used in the two communities, and a variety of other scripts existed, Ashkenazic and Sephardic styles proved the most influential, possibly because eventually they were the ones translated into printing types.

Sephardic lettering was characterized by a refinement of the aesthetics of the style found in the Leningrad and Aleppo codices, further developing its graceful proportions and introducing greater variation of contrast between the strokes (figure 3). Ashkenazic style took a departure from these forms. If the Gothic Latin then prevalent in western Europe was narrow, with strong verticals and compressed bowls and horizontals, the Ashkenazic Hebrew was squat, with heavy horizontal strokes on top and on the bottom, and weaker verticals. Despite the high contrast between strokes and some loss of legibility, the Ashkenazic Hebrew letter never became as far removed from the original 'classical' shape as the Latin blackletter, and remained readable even to an unaccustomed eye (figure 4).

Figure 3. Detail from the Sephardic Golden Haggadah, fourteenth century, British Museum, London, Add. 27210. Note a greater contrast and a greater emphasis on the bottom horizontal. Yet the top horizontal remains stronger: most of the bottom strokes do not quite sit on the baseline.

Figure 4. Colophon in Ashkenazic style; from the *Darmstadt Haggadah*, c. 1425, Heissiche Landes- und Hochschulbibliothek, Ms. COD. OR. 8. Note squat proportions, high contrast, rhombic decorative vertical strokes, and small counters. The baseline is strongly pronounced. From *The Development of Hebrew Lettering* by Moshe Spitzer, Jerusalem, 1974.

With the advent of printing, some of the most beautiful incunabula were printed in types of Ashkenazic form, including the books published by Gershon Cohen in Prague (figure 5, overleaf) and a few of the first Hebrew titles produced in Italy; however, Sephardic style quickly prevailed. Two of the most influential and prolific Italian publishers of the late fifteenth and early sixteenth centuries, Gershom Soncino and Daniel

בָּמֶה שֶׁנָּ וַיִּשְׁמְעָ אֹרִים אֶת

נָאקָתָם וַיִּזְכּוֹר אֹרִים אֶתְא

Figure 5. Ashkenazic type of the *Prague Haggadah*, printed by Gershom Cohen in Prague, 1526. The small counters of these letters make them usable only in large point sizes, as in this impressive volume.

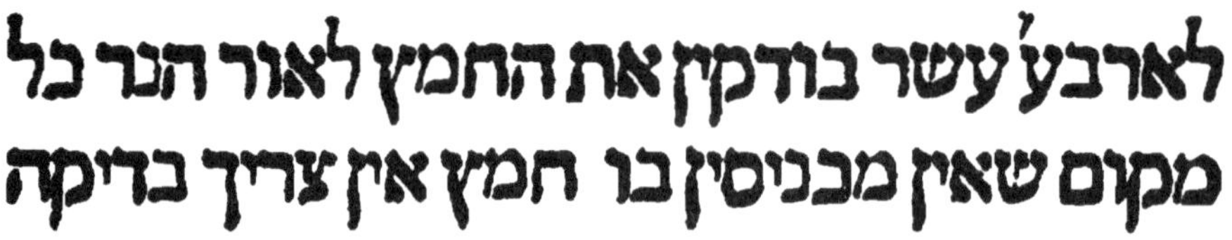

לארבע עשר בודקן את החמץ לאור הנר כל

מקום שאין מבניסין בו חמץ אין צריך בדיקה

Figure 6. Sephardic types used by Daniel Bomberg for the first complete edition of the Talmud, Venice, 1519

Bomberg – a Christian who dedicated his press in Venice to Hebrew printing and produced the first complete edition of the Talmud –, commissioned types cut in Sephardic style (figure 6).

The history of Hebrew typography is the history of a script used by a nation exiled from its land and scattered among other nations. The arrested development of form and function in Hebrew type may be explained by constant persecution and the repeated expulsion of the people who used it from one place to another. Frequently the presses were closed down, entire editions of books banned and destroyed by the Inquisition. Under these circumstances there was little room for the continuity and refinement of skill that good typography requires. It is not surprising then that most significant contributions to Hebrew typography until the nineteenth century were made by the skilled non-Jewish punchcutters. Among the best of these developments were the 'old-style'[3] types cut by

רְבִּי מֵת בֶּן חֶמֶר אוֹמֵר : אַל תֹּאמֵר

כְּשֶׁאֶפְנֶה אֶשְׁנֶה שֶׁמָּא לֹא תִפְנֶה :

Figure 7. Some of the Sephardic 'old syle' types cut by Guillaume Le Bé in the late 1400s: display (above) and text (below) types.

[94]

the French punchcutter Guillaume Le Bé in the mid-fifteen-hundreds for Jewish and Christian printers including the famous Christoffel Plantin at Antwerp (figure 7).

Another noteworthy type was cut by the Dutchman Christoffel van Dijck c.1660 (figure 8). Van Dijck's type could be classified as a 'transitional' style, with higher contrast between thick and thin strokes, and a somewhat more rectangular, static, and fragile appearance. Unfortunately, it was this style that came into vogue in the nineteenth century, a time of resurgence in Jewish printing in Eastern Europe, with consequent copies losing the subtleties of van Dijck's types and leaning toward the 'modern' style. It was a time of general deterioration in typography, especially in Hebrew. The characters became artificial and rigid, with thin verticals connecting heavy horizontals, hard to distinguish one from another (figure 9).

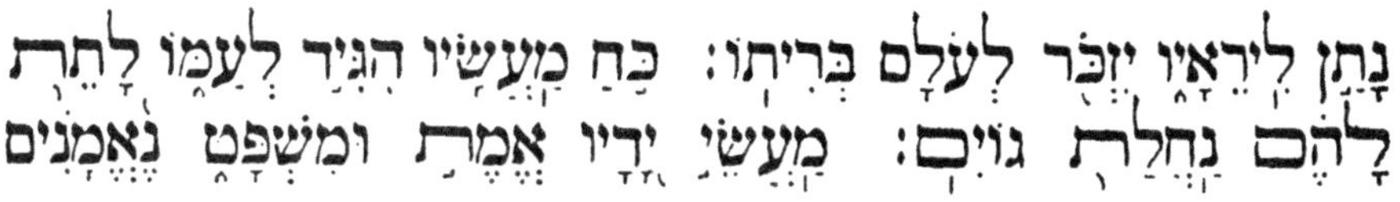

נָתַן לִירֵאָיו יִזְכֹּר לְעוֹלָם בְּרִיתוֹ: כֹּחַ מַעֲשָׂיו הִגִּיד לְעַמּוֹ לָתֵת לָהֶם נַחֲלַת גּוֹיִם: מַעֲשֵׂי יָדָיו אֱמֶת וּמִשְׁפָּט נֶאֱמָנִים

Figure 8. A 'transitional' type cut by Christoffel van Dijck in Amsterdam, c. 1660, from *The Development of Hebrew Lettering* by Moshe Spitzer, Jerusalem, 1974.

אלדים השאיר את החשך בכדי
אבגדהוזחטי עפפצצקק

Figure 9. Top: Meruba, a typical 19th century 'square' face; note the compressed א and the flat bottom stroke of ש. Vertical strokes become inferior to the horizontals. Bottom: Drogulin, a slightly improved 19 century type. Note less contrast, open counters, and a lighter א.

In the nineteenth century the monumental edition of the Vilna Talmud was produced by the Widow and Brothers Romm. Unfortunately, since it became accepted as the definitive edition of the Talmud and still retains this position, its types with all their imperfections are considered standard by the religious Jewish public to this day.

HEBREW TYPE DESIGNER

The Arts and Crafts movement led by William Morris at the end of the nineteenth century in England sought to turn back the stylistic clock and to resurrect the 'beautiful book' of the past. There began a wave of typographic revivals of full-bodied old-style faces to replace the anemic moderns. It was perhaps then that the profession of designer in the modern sense – not a person who is taught to make things a certain way, but an inventor who can at will choose a certain style over another if the problem calls for it – was born.

Hebrew was indirectly affected by this movement: in 1910 the type-foundry H. Berthold AG released a text face designed by Raphael Frank called Frank-Rühl, which immediately became popular, and which remains the most popular Hebrew text face today. It repaired some of the damage done to the Hebrew letter by modernity by lowering the contrast between strokes and highlighting the distinction between the shapes of various characters, but it remained stylized, in keeping with Art Nouveau aesthetics, static and ungraceful. Its advantages and shortcomings aside, Frank-Rühl was important. It began a new era in Hebrew typography: the age of the designer (figure 10).[4]

שלוש תביעות־יסוד יש לתבוע מכל אלפבית: קלות הקריאה, נוי הצורה ואופי מיוחד. קלות הקריאה מחייבת שתהא כל אות ואות ניכרת בבירור בפני עצמה ונבדלת היטב מאותיאות דומות, על־ידי סימני ההכר המיוחדים לה. נאה היא האות שיש בה בהירות עם מימדים שקולים, זרם חיים צריך לזרום בגזעיה, בבדיה ובענפיה של האות.

אבגדהוזחטיכלמנסעפצקרשת

Figure 10. Digital version of Frank-Rühl, a popular 'modern' text face. Note the similarity of character shapes to the 19th century faces in figure 9: compare the פ. However, this is a significant improvement over them in respect of contrast

ספר חדש יצא לאור ונתקבל למבירה אגרות דוד פרישמן
עם תמונתו ועצם כתב ידו נערבו בצרוף תולדות פרישמן
מבוא הקדמות והערות על ידי מלאבי בספר זה יקשיב

Figure 11. Stam, the first revival of an historical style, based on Ashkenazi models. Note small counters and other deficiencies like the similarity of different characters, for instance ה and ח.

Weimar Germany emerged in the 1920s as a center of type design, and until the Nazi party came to power in 1933, it was also a center of Hebrew publishing. Among many Hebrew types produced there at this time there were two important typographic revivals, both based on Ash-kenazic style. Stam, released by Berthold, apparently based on the types of Pietro de Sacco, was attractive as a display face but had a number of imperfections that made it hard to read in text setting (figure 11). An-other was a letter commissioned by the Soncino Publication Society in Berlin from Marcus Behmer for a limited edition Hebrew Bible. Only the Pentateuch part of the project was completed by the time all Jewish publications in Germany were forbidden by the Nazis.

Jews educated in Germany laid the foundation for type design and production for the future Jewish state. It was in Palestine that, just as the

ויתר מהמה בני הזהר עשות ספרים הרבה אין קץ ולהג

Figure 12. Shocken, a revival of the early Sephardic types.

dispersed nation began to gather, and Hebrew was reborn as a spoken language, Hebrew type was to have its renaissance.

Schocken was commissioned by the publisher of that name from Franziska Baruḥ, and was produced during World War II by Monotype. It is an elegant but somewhat quirky revival of the Sephardic incunabula types used by Gershon Soncino and Daniel Bomberg in early fifteenth century (figure 12).

After the war, two other German refugees, Eliyahu Koren and Henry Friedlander, produced types that were not revivals, but contemporary designs based on traditional shapes of letters. The Koren type was designed for a new edition of the complete Hebrew Bible, the first Jewish edition in centuries. The letter was based on a variety of sources, mainly Sephardic printed types. It is a clear, easy to read, harmonious, and dignified 'old style' (figure 13). Henry Friedlander's Hadassa was a robust text type, best used in newspapers and magazines. It was based on Ashkenazic letterforms, but as the designer minimized the contrast between the strokes to make it more readable, it no longer resembled the high-contrast Ashkenazic letter. Having been influenced by the ideas of the Constructivists, the designer was mainly concerned with the functionality of his design. The result was easily legible and sturdy, but somewhat stiff and inelegant (figure 14). Both of these types were issued in two weights: light and bold. A book weight was later added to Koren, and a display wood style was added to the metal Hadassa.[5]

אבגדהוזחטיכלמנסעפצקרשתדןסףץ

Figure 13. The type of the Koren Bible. The shapes harken back to the Sephardic tradition, letters are clearly distinguished from each other, the contrast is low, and proportions agreeable.

Figure 14. Henry Friedlander's Hadassa. Simplicity of character shapes, open counters, virtual absence of contrast make it an easily readable and popular type. The lower line shows the wood display type.

ויתר מהמה בני הזהר עשות ספרים הרבה אין קץ ולהג
ויתר מהמה בני הזהר עשות ספריס הרבה אין קץ ולהג הרבה יג
ויתר מהמה בני הזהר עשות ספרים הרבה אין קץ ולהג

Figure 15. David, a first calligraphic Hebrew. It was not based on an earlier
example. The line has life and flow, previously unseen in Hebrew typography.

ויתר מהמה בני הזהר עשות ספרים הרבה אין קץ ולהג הרבה
ויתר מהמה בני הזהר עשות ספרים הרבה אין קץ ולהג ה
ויתר מהמה בני הזהר עשות ספרים הרבה אין קץ ול

Figure 16. HaẒvi proved that 'sans-serif' did not have to mean dull. Its characters
have movement and strength, reminiscent of the stone inscriptions

The typeface David, by Ismar David, was the first truly 'calligraphic' Hebrew type. Its structure was not based on an existing style, but rather on the designer's understanding of the proper contruction for the Hebrew letter. He disregarded the traditional variation of stroke between horizontals and verticals, distilled the basic shape of the letter, and made it light and flowing. The result was a handsome contemporary type, more suitable for ephemeral printing, but also usable in book composition. The light and bold weights are accompanied by a beautiful cursive, which unfortunately never took hold among the public as a type for emphasis (figure 15).

Another design of approximately the same time is HaẒvi, designed by Ẓvi Hausmann. This dynamic display type was a departure from the earlier 'sans-serifs', in that it captured the essence of the graphic shape of the letter without making it stiff or artificial. It approached the quality found in early stone inscriptions. A light weight, a book weight, and an open style were subsequently added later to the original bold (figure 16).

Finally these were successful designs in a modern sense, free of the historical corruptions and idiosyncrasies that hampered the functionality of other types then available.

THE WORK OF ẒVI NARKISS

Koren, Hadassa, David, and HaẒvi were all commendable types in their own right, but each was visually incompatible with the other. A handful of contemporary types were lost in the mass of old type still in use. This was the typographic world Ẓvi Narkiss entered when he began working for a printer in the mid-1950s, after studying calligraphy and design at the Beẓalel School of Art in Jerusalem. The lack of choice in display types at the time stimulated creativity: the printing shop created paste-up 'type-cases', with small photographs of each character. It was these hand-lettered alphabets that the young designer first tried his hand at.

His first type for metal hand-setting was Narkiss Block. As in David and HaẒvi, the shape of each character in Narkiss Block was distilled to its essentials. It went farther than its 'sans-serif' predecessors (the popular but poorly designed Ḥaim and Aharoni) in the simplification of form, always informed by a calligrapher's understanding of the structure of a *written* letter (figure 17).

The resolute revision of convention for the sake of clarity, simplicity, and legibility that were evident in Block, proved to be a signature style for the designer in his consequent work. Another feature of that type-face was a full-range type family: it was eventually released with seven weights, suitable for a variety of display needs.

שלוש תביעות־יסוד יש לתבוע מכל אלפבית: קלות הקריאה, נוי הצורה ואופי מיוחד. קלות הקריאה מחייבת שתהא כל אות ואות ניכרת בבירור בפני עצמה ונבדלת היטב מאותיאות דומות, על־ידי סימני ההכר המיוחדים לה. נאה היא האות שיש בה בהירות עם מימדים שקולים, זרם חיים צריך לזרום בגזעיה, בבדיה ובענפיה של האות.

אבגדהוזחטיכלמנסעפצקרשת

Figure 17. Narkiss Block.

שלוש תביעות־יסוד יש לתבוע מכל אלפבית: קלות הקריאה, נוי הצורה ואופי מיוחד. קלות הקריאה מחייבת שתהא כל אות ואות ניכרת בבירור בפני עצמה ונבדלת היטב מאותיאות דומות, על־ידי סימני ההכר המיוחדים לה. נאה היא האות שיש בה בהירות עם מימדים שקולים, זרם חיים צריך לזרום בגזעיה, בבדיה ובענפיה של האות.

אבגדהוזחטיכלמנסעפצקרשת

Figure 18. Narkiss Linotype.

It may prove to be a useful exercise to compare the regular weight of Narkiss Block with the light weight of his next design, Narkiss Linotype (figure 18). The same underlying structure, the same proportions and movement that are found in this book face, can also be found in the ear-lier display 'sans-serif' face.

Unsatisfied with the existing book types of the past, Ẓvi Narkiss went a step further back to look for the model of this new design – to the manuscript writing hands upon which the early types were based. He was, as it were, re-enacting history, correcting the accidents of its course. The result was a type with the essential features of the Sephardic writing style, following the structure and dynamics of the manuscript letter, but not tied to any hand in particular. It was a modern type, suitable for pres-ent-day book composition and accessible to the modern reader.

Rather than the influence of any specific model, this type betrayed the hand of the designer. It is a flowing calligraphic face, following in the mode of David, but with a greater variation between thicks and thins, and a greater typographic quality – it appeared to penetrate deeper into

the page. It had ample counters, large openings, balanced square proportions, and a clear distinction between similar characters (גנ,דר,הח,
בכ). The designer preserved a human touch, the feeling of the natural
movement of a hand holding a pen.

If Narkiss Linotype was an elegant book type, a later design in a
similar style, Narkissim, seemed have less personality, and therefore to
be more universal (figure 19, top). It was better suited for magazine and
newspaper composition. It is more monotone then Narkiss Linotype and
more uniform in construction. The Sephardic sharp corner on the bottom of ע, ס, and ש was replaced by an Ashkenasic round bowl. These foreign forms in an otherwise Sephardic letter achieved greater distinction
between the characters and help the readability of Narkissim. The high
readability, economy in setting, and simple elegance of this face explain
the wide popularity it enjoys today.

Later 'sans-serif' designs such as Narkiss Tam (figure 19, middle) and
New Narkiss reflect some of the same modifications in their shape and
would serve as excellent companions to this 'serif' face.

Other types designed by Narkiss were the sans faces Shulamit; Ruti;
Shimshon; a display Narkiss Gazit, based on Ashkenazic manuscript
letter, but with little contrast; Tammi, a lively calligraphic face based
on handwritten script; and revivals of historical Vilna and Rashi types,
based on the types used in the Vilna Talmud.

שלוש תביעות-יסוד יש לתבוע מכל אלפבית: קלות הקריאה, נוי הצורה ואופי מיוחד.
קלות הקריאה מחייבת שתהא כל אות ואות ניכרת בבירור בפני עצמה ונבדלת היטב
מאותיאות דומות, על-ידי סימני ההכר המיוחדים לה. נאה היא האות שיש בה בהירות
עם מימדים שקולים, זרם חיים צריך לזרום בגזעיה, בבדיה ובענפיה של האות.

אבגדהוזחטיכלמנסעפצקרשת

שלוש תביעות-יסוד יש לתבוע מכל אלפבית: קלות הקריאה, נוי הצורה ואופי מיוחד.
קלות הקריאה מחייבת שתהא כל אות ואות ניכרת בבירור בפני עצמה ונבדלת היטב
מאותיאות דומות, על-ידי סימני ההכר המיוחדים לה. נאה היא האות שיש בה בהירות
עם מימדים שקולים, זרם חיים צריך לזרום בגזעיה, בבדיה ובענפיה של האות.

אבגדהוזחטיכלמנסעפצקרשת

שלוש תביעות-יסוד יש לתבוע מכל אלפבית: קלות הקריאה, נוי הצורה ואופי מיוחד.
קלות הקריאה מחייבת שתהא כל אות ואות ניכרת בבירור בפני עצמה ונבדלת היטב
מאותיאות דומות, על-ידי סימני ההכר המיוחדים לה. נאה היא האות שיש בה בהירות
עם מימדים שקולים, זרם חיים צריך לזרום בגזעיה, בבדיה ובענפיה של האות.

אבגדהוזחטיכלמנסעפצקרשת

Figure 21. Three proportionally related types. From top to bottom: Narkissim,
Narkiss Tam and Narkiss Classic.

אֵלֶּה הַדְּבָרִים אֲשֶׁר דִּבֶּר מֹשֶׁה אֶל־כָּל־יִשְׂרָאֵל בְּעֵבֶר הַיַּרְדֵּן בַּמִּדְבָּר בָּעֲרָבָה מוֹל סוּף בֵּין־פָּארָן וּבֵין־תֹּפֶל וְלָבָן וַחֲצֵרֹת וְדִי זָהָב: אַחַד עָשָׂר יוֹם מֵחֹרֵב דֶּרֶךְ הַר־שֵׂעִיר עַד קָדֵשׁ בַּרְנֵעַ:

Figure 20. Narkiss Ḥorev, a *Tanaḥ* (Bible) face in the Ashkenazic style.

Narkiss Classic is a recent variation on the Narkiss Linotype design. The proportions became more narrow, modelling of the strokes has been further refined, and two weights – light and medium – have been added. Narkiss's signature middle stroke in ש has been detached here the way it is in Narkissim (figure 19, bottom).

Ḥorev is a recent proprietary face designed for a newly prepared edition of the Hebrew Bible. Like Stam and the Behmer face for the Soncino Society in Berlin, this type was based on the Ashkenazic hand as a model, which presented a unique challenge. The designer had long avoided this form because of its complexity and the difficulty of making it readable. Here he managed to succeed in preserving the grace and character of the form, without sacrificing legibility even at a small size (figure 20).

The Hebrew typesetter of today has at his disposal a full spectrum of Narkiss text and display type families, all made with high craftsmanship, all related to each other, all marked by the unmistakable hand of a master. Narkiss even tells of his grandchildren, who are unable to tell a single typeface by name but can always pick out their grandpa's designs wherever they see them: in a newspaper, in a book, on a banknote, in a commercial, on a package, or on a store-sign.

THE KETER YERUSHALAIM TYPE

Zvi Narkiss's latest creation is a calligraphic type based on the lettering of a thousand-year-old manuscript of the Hebrew Bible (the *Tanaḥ*). The unique conditions of this project influenced the designer to produce a traditional type with more personality, idiosyncrasies, movement, and life than any he had designed before.

It all began about ten years ago, when a Jerusalem printer, Nahum Ben-Zvi, came to the designer with the idea of setting a new scholarly edition of the Hebrew Bible based on the Aleppo codex (*Keter Aram Zova*, figure 4)[6] in a letter that resembles the scribal hand of that manuscript. Ben-Zvi's father had started one of the most respected printing houses in Israel, and was a man with extensive knowledge and mastery of his craft; this project was intended as a gift for his eightieth birthday.

Before the designer was the challenge of interpreting calligraphy into typography. Interpretation meant the creation of a completely new entity, not an imitation. He was to create a letter with the flavor and impression of the original model, but entirely new and clearly typographic. As a proprietary type intended solely for sacral use, it had to possess greater weight and 'volume' than a type intended for quick reading. This letter was intended for use in a book that would be studied carefully, and its pace had to be more dignified.

Zvi Narkiss has always considered it important to carry over the logic and the practical way of making a written letter into the realm of typography. Some details and aspects of calligraphy would be quite inappropriate in type, but the main structure of the letter has to make sense in calligraphic terms. One valuable calligraphic quality that the designer attempted to preserve was an unencumbered movement, the dynamic flow of the line.

What makes a typeset page look different from a calligraphic page? According to Narkiss, it is the uniformity of color, the 'calm' of the page. His concept of a typographic letter is the consistency of design of the letter shapes, a uniform rhythm of characters, and legibility – the ability to instantly distinguish one letter from the other. However, the shapes have to be conventional enough to be easily identified. The letter has to be complete in itself, beautiful as a self-contained form at any size, devoid of the accidental, and just as beautiful in combination with other letters, as a word, as a line, and as a page. Ultimately, it's a printed page that the designer has in mind. It has to be even, pleasant to behold, harmonious and elegant.

The publisher suggested that the book be set in an unusual three-column flush-right, ragged-left format, to relate back to the original. Zvi Narkiss designed a layout that recalls the manuscript, but more importantly aids easy reading. Each short line forms an image that is possible to grasp with one glance. It almost becomes possible to read the column vertically, line after line. The designer was also responsible for making the book more accessible. He made decisions regarding the indication of various divisions in the text: numbering of verses and chapters, names of weekly portions and their parts (*aliyot*) in the Pentateuch (*Ḥumash*), and form and content of the running heads and folios. To facilitate easy reference, an essential table of contents was included on every part-title page, with a full version including weekly portions included at the end of the volume.

The first free-hand sketches of this letter were made with a reed pen. Then the designer proceeded to trace photographic enlargements of the originals, to become familiar with the structure and shapes of the letters. He went on to make large-scale sketches with a broad-edged tool to capture the movement and the flow of the calligraphy (figure 21). A deliber-

בובאשמפליקרת פפקוב
אעששאיל ממש

Figure 21. Initial broad-edge pen sketches for Narkiss Keter Yerushalaim.

Figure 22. Finished drawing of *alef* from Narkiss Keter Yerushalaim.

ate decision was made to omit some idiosyncratic elements and to pre-serve some others. The last step was to determine the choice of sketches to develop and to produce finished drawings of characters with a metal pen (figure 22). These drawings were photographed and pasted-up into a sample page (not unlike the photo 'type-case' letters from the early days of the designer's career), which he then presented to the client.

The design of the characters was completed and the font was digi-tized, but the main body of work on the typeface – the fine-tuning of the details – was just beginning. Besides the characters, the font needed to include a full set of punctuation, vowels, and cantillation marks (figure 24, overleaf). Here came a departure from accepted convention. All these elements, which are usually designed as standard geometric shapes, here were reconsidered in a style consistent with the characters – as calligraphic forms (for instance, the conventional round vowel points became calligraphic diamonds). The size and position of these elements in relation to the letters needed to be determined, and all the possible combinations with each other needed to be considered. To make sure that vowels, cantillation marks, punctuation, and letters would not clash with each other, as well as to compensate for visual differences of spacing in the characters, over two thousand kerning pairs were created.

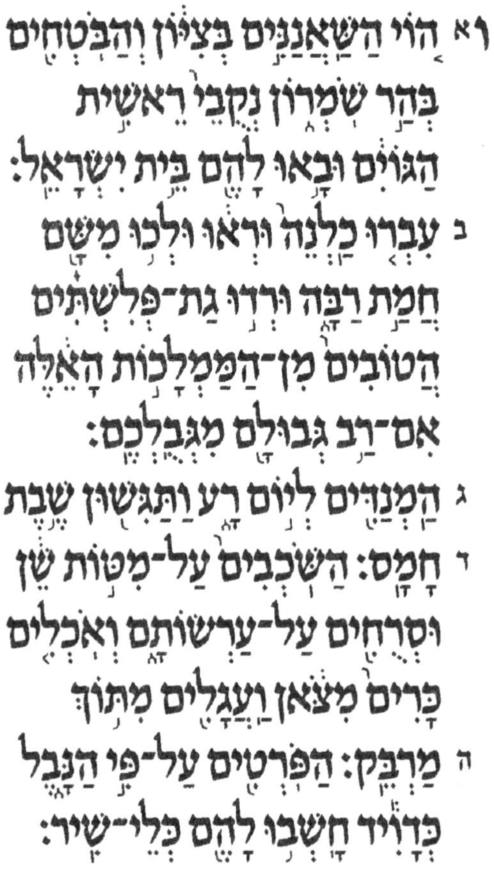

וא הוֹי הַשַּׁאֲנַנִּים בְּצִיּוֹן וְהַבֹּטְחִים
בְּהַר שֹׁמְרוֹן נְקֻבֵי רֵאשִׁית
הַגּוֹיִם וּבָאוּ לָהֶם בֵּית יִשְׂרָאֵל׃
ב עִבְרוּ כַלְנֵה וּרְאוּ וּלְכוּ מִשָּׁם
חֲמַת רַבָּה וּרְדוּ גַת־פְּלִשְׁתִּים
הֲטוֹבִים מִן־הַמַּמְלָכוֹת הָאֵלֶּה
אִם־רַב גְּבוּלָם מִגְּבֻלְכֶם׃
ג הַמְנַדִּים לְיוֹם רָע וַתַּגִּישׁוּן שֶׁבֶת
ד חָמָס׃ הַשֹּׁכְבִים עַל־מִטּוֹת שֵׁן
וּסְרֻחִים עַל־עַרְשׂוֹתָם וְאֹכְלִים
כָּרִים מִצֹּאן וַעֲגָלִים מִתּוֹךְ
ה מַרְבֵּק׃ הַפֹּרְטִים עַל־פִּי הַנָּבֶל
כְּדָוִיד חָשְׁבוּ לָהֶם כְּלֵי־שִׁיר׃

Figure 23. Text column from the completed Keter Yerushalaim Bible.

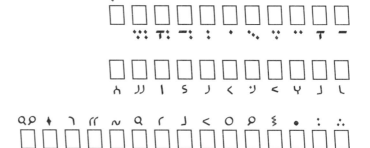

Figure 24. Narkiss Keter Yerushalaim type, based on the Aleppo Codex manuscript (see figure 2). Note custom designed vowel (*nikud*) and cantillation marks (*teamin*).

When the client showed the sample pasted-up page to his father, his father was deeply moved. Shortly afterward he passed away, but even if he did not live to see the finished book, in a way he did receive his gift.

The first and foremost value for the Zvi Narkiss is integrity – artistic honesty in design – and he feels that here he has achieved it. Narkiss Keter Yerushalaim type possesses an individuality and a human touch uncommon for this modern master. It appears as a missing link in the history of Hebrew script: a fully developed early type, elegant and beautiful, with a direct connection to the writing tradition.

Acknowledgements

The author owes many thanks to Lili Wronker for her help and for access to her archive, to Maxim Zhukov for the valuable suggestions and for making this publication possible, to Izzy Pludwinsky for being a faithful liaison across the Atlantic, and to Zvi Narkiss for his cooperation and friendship.

Notes

1. Named after the first book printed in a type of that design (in fact, the first dated Hebrew book ever printed) – a commentary on the Pentateuch by Rabbi Shlomo Yizhaki (acronym: RaShI), printed by Abraham ben Garton ben Isaac in Reggio de Calabria, 1475.
2. A *geniza* is a place for ritual burial of sacred books. Discovery of such a synagogue repository in Cairo at the turn of the twentieth century brought to light some of the earliest known Hebrew manuscripts.
3. I am using the accepted stylistic denominations of type in quotation marks, since only a loose parallel may be drawn between styles in Latin script and those in Hebrew; after all, there are no serifs to speak of. 'Sans-serif' is used to denote monoline, 'modern' denotes the high-contrast letters of the nineteenth century, etc.
4. Despite the fact that its character shapes did not differ significantly from other types of the time, Frank-Rühl's non-traditional low contrast and a number of other features that aid its readability seem enough to place it with the contemporary 'designer' types.
5. Common practice in Hebrew is to use bold for emphasis.
6. The Aleppo Codex is the earliest and the most authoritative known Hebrew manuscript of the full text of the Bible. The Codex was copied in the early tenth century CE by Shlomo Ben-Buya'a, then verified, vocalized, and provided with the Massorah by Aaron Ben-Asher.

Select bibliography

Birenbaum, Solomon A. *The Hebrew Scripts*. Leiden, 1971.

David, Ismar. *The Hebrew Letter*. Northvale, 1990.

Encyclopedia Judaica, v. 2, p. 654, s.v. *Alphabet*, and v. 15 pps. 1480–1488, s.v. *Typography*, Jerusalem, 1971

Friedlander, Henry. *The Making of Hadassa Hebrew*. Jerusalem, 1972.

Gold, Leonard Singer. *A Sign and a Witness: 200 Years of Hebrew Books and Illuminated Manuscripts*. New York, 1988.

Rozner, Raphael and Israel Ta-Shema, eds. *The Hebrew Book: an Historical Survey*. Jerusalem, 1975.

Spitzer, Moshe. *The Development of Hebrew Lettering*. Jerusalem, 1974.

SAKI MAFUNDIKWA

Type ramblings from Afrika

WHAT IS GOING ON in Afrika typewise right now? Not much that I am aware of in the rest of Afrika, but I do know that there is a lot of activity in South Afrika, where because of the inequities created by the system of apartheid, blacks still haven't entered the field of design in large numbers. This was glaringly clear at the first-ever ICOGRADA congress held on the Afrikan continent, last September in Johannesburg. There were hundreds of South Afrikan designers, but fewer than a dozen of them were black. The national design association of South Afrika, Design South Afrika, made a statement acknowledging their awareness of this deficiency and admitted that 'more has to be done to make design inclusive'. So, at the risk of sticking my neck out (I seem to have a talent for doing that sometimes), I will say that my ramblings here will exclude South Afrika until such time as, when one talks of design in South Afrika, one will be talking of *everyone*, not just white designers. But at the same time I want to acknowledge the work of folks like Garth Walker, who puts out *I-jusi* magazine, especially the annual 'Typografika,' whose second issue comes out later this year. I am glad to see that Garth has opened it to other designers globally to design typefaces 'rooted in the Afrikan tradition.' This, however, raises the question, 'what is that 'Afrikan tradition'?' Is it enough to just appropriate from craftspeople in the townships and the rural areas? Like barber shop signs and other vernacular typography? I also want to dare people like Garth to start mentoring young talent, *black* talent; otherwise, their talk of coming up with a 'new' visual language that is truly 'Afrikan' will ring hollow, until their studios reflect this 'new' thinking by taking on young talented blacks and mentoring them. You see, in South Afrika they love the word 'new': it's a 'new' South Afrika, a 'new' this and a 'new' that, while the status quo remains unchanged. Slogans and buzz words alone will not do it. They call South Afrika 'the Rainbow Nation,' but in design the other colors are glaringly washed out.

I started ZIVA – the Zimbabwe Institute of Vigital Arts – four years ago rather than join the staff of the local university (they have no design

Figure 1: Zimbabwe International Film Festival logo. Saki Mafundikwa, 2001 (original in five colors).

Figure 2: Logo for Shona Studio, the author's design practice. Saki Mafundikwa, 1996.

program) because I wanted to do more than simply 'teach' design. I have had a few lucky breaks in my life.

First, I was educated by some of the best in the business, Paul Rand, Bradbury Thompson, Armin Hoffman; the old guard, the pioneers, and of course the Modernists. I truly cherish this foundation, a solid foundation in classical design, especially typography.

Second, I worked in the cutthroat, competitive New York City design world – and survived! I never worked on any impressive projects, nor did I make a lot of dough, but the lessons learnt have equipped me for life anywhere on this planet. I soon discovered that design was indeed an 'old boys' club, whose exclusive members were old white men. So it is no surprise that, for survival and for my voice to be heard, I threw my lot in with female designers, artists, and other designers of color. We were the oppressed class, and our goal was not only inclusion but to break down the barriers and the exclusivity of the club. This was in the mid-eighties; we were at exactly the same place where Black designers are in the 'new' South Afrika today.

Third, I was in New York when the New Media (a truly 'new' phenomenon!) happened, and I latched on to its liberating ability. I felt that I did not have to brave the often brutal winters of the east coast of the United States year after year; I could move my family to the warmer climes of my home town, Harare, and still feel like a part of the unfolding 'global' community. I bought into the whole concept of globalization before it became a dirty word (especially to those of us in the developing world). Seattle sure opened my eyes wide! But I still consider myself a proponent of the 'globalization' of design education. I want to stress the point that I am first and foremost a design *educator*, and only then a practitioner.

I want ZIVA to become (in principle, at least) the Bauhaus of Afrika – a school of thought rather than just another design school, churning out kids educated to become clones of their peers in the North and West. Design from Afrika has to have a 'humanistic' feeling. The industrialized countries have destroyed themselves with too much technology and an over-emphasis on the self; everything has become cold and devoid of humanism. The whole concept of community is just not there anymore. Of course it is only natural that any semblance of community would now be found in cyberspace, where people can don and doff different masks to fit whatever agenda they are dealing with.

I believe that type is dynamic, and that therefore new typefaces need to be designed every day, in all the six corners of the globe and beyond. I am also quite incensed by the belief held by most Western designers

Figure 3: Alphabet inspired by Zimbabwean rock paintings. Hailey Rogers, first year ZIVA student, 2001.

Figure 4: Bird alphabet. Ryan Rodrigues, first year ZIVA student, 2001.

Figure 5: *Kaloli*, alphabet inspired by Maribou storks. Lilian Osanjo from Kenya, UNESCO Workshop, Kampala, Uganda, 1999.

that the Latin alphabet is the holy grail. This myopic view robs the field of inspired work from non-western societies. Design schools should introduce the study of alphabets and writing systems from other cultures into their curriculums. In the USA, for example, a glance at the enrolment lists of most design programs reveals a very interesting fact: foreign students (especially from Asia) make up a growing percentage of the student body. Why not bring their own traditions into play? For instance, Hangul, from Korea, is one of the most efficient and scientific writing systems ever created; why not have the Korean students apply their newly learnt design principles to Hangul and see what happens? The students would create quite powerful work while their American (or European, or whoever) counterparts would learn something new, and perhaps be inspired to think and to see the world in a different way.

I am also on a mission to right the wrongs (or at least to attempt to correct many misconceptions) against my continent, Afrika. There is talk (even in this supposedly enlightened third millennium) of Afrika being the Dark Continent. Just as the Europeans carved her up like a Thanksgiving turkey at the Berlin Conference in 1878, historians have divided her into enlightened Egypt, with major contributions to civilization, and 'sub-Saharan Afrika,' with no writing and no substantial contributions to civilization. Yet much has been discovered (though rarely heralded) about the great universities of Timbuktu, which produced mathematicians and men of letters. More recently, around the time of her colonization, leaders like Sultan Njoya of the Bamum kingdom in Cameroon created and developed their own writing systems. He went further, inventing printing presses on which books were printed in the new scripts, and placing these in libraries and museums that he built for his people. The French colonizers were not impressed by Njoya's adventures; they had his presses and libraries destroyed and banished him to a remote area, where he died a broken man.

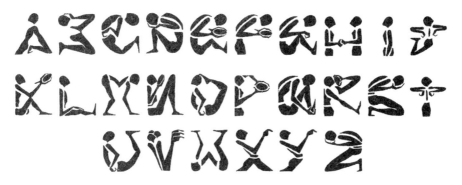

Figure 6: *Kukumbila kunyata*, 'Drinking is bad for you'. Pascal Mbouti from Mozambique, UNESCO Workshop, Kampala, Uganda, 1999.

This ignored cultural history is recounted in the book *Afrikan Alphabets* (Mark Batty, Publisher, 2002), which I have been working on for a long time. This book is my secret weapon to expose the lies and prejudices against my beloved Afrika.

I am not interested in regurgitating tired and sterile design principles to students anywhere in the world. All that the students need is a solid foundation; then, from there, new possibilities must be opened to them. Every year when we get a new intake of students, I make the 'green' students design a typeface 'from nature or from personal experience'. It is a great way to introduce the students to something they are quite clueless about, and a sly way to introduce my 'humanist' philosophy. When I first get them, the students usually like those Mickey Mouse fonts that come with the computer: Sand, Comic, Arial, Techno. Then I give them a project – the typography timeline from the fifth century BC to the present, where they learn about the development of type and the key players. This understanding of history helps them make informed choices when they are faced with the often bamboozling task of choosing an 'appropriate' typeface. They begin to understand the nuances between fonts that 'look alike', and what makes a face 'good'.

THOMAS MILO

Arabic script and typography

A BRIEF HISTORICAL OVERVIEW

ARABIC WRITING is alphabetical; the direction of writing is from right to left; within a word, most letters form connected groups. One expects an alphabet to consist of a few dozen letters representing one unique sound each. The Arabic alphabet evolved somewhat away from this ideal: although most letters correspond to a sound, a few letters are ambivalent between two or more sounds. Some letters don't represent sound at all: they have only a grammatical function.

For modern office use there are 28 basic letters, eight of them only differentiated from other letters by diacritics, and six optional letters for representing vowels. Older spellings made less use of diacritics for differentiating; on the other hand, to facilitate Qur'an recitation, additional vowel signs occur, along with elaborate cantillation marks. To acknowledge slight variations of the received text, some Qur'an editions have additional diacritics, discretely adding or eliminating consonant letters.

As the Arabic script evolved into a connected script, it developed an elaborate system of assimilations and dissimilations between adjacent letters. Outside a small group of connoisseurs and calligraphers who study the principles established by the Ottoman letter artists, surprisingly little is understood of the efficiency and subtlety of this system,[1] and modern industrial type designs follow the approach found in elementary Western teaching materials.[2] There, beginners in Arabic script are given a maximally simplified scheme. While simplification is totally sound from a pedagogical perspective, it provides too narrow a basis for the development of professional typography.

DEVELOPMENT OF THE ARABIC SCRIPT

The Arabic script stems from the same source as the Latin, Greek, and Hebrew writing systems: Phoenician (figure 1).[3] The underlying proto-alphabet had some two dozen characters; there were no vowels. The direct forebear of the Arabic alphabet is a late Aramaic alphabet from which it inherits the tendency to merge letter groups into larger units marked by a final swash instead of a space. As the script evolved, some aspects inherited from the Aramaic alphabet became simplified, and new complexities and subtleties emerged.

This evolution can be classified in four developments:

1. *Shape erosion: shared graphemes.* A number of early Arabic alphabetic letters lost their original distinctiveness; as a result, only fourteen basic shapes remained to represent thirty consonants. Arabic writing of this type is reminiscent of stenography. Many shapes represented more than one letter and could only be understood in context. Given the oral origin of Arabic literature – reading was based on familiarity with the text – this reduced or skeleton script was in fact an economical way

Figure 1. Simplified diagram showing evolution of European and Arabic scripts from a common ancestor, Phoenician.

Figure 2a. A plain text encoding for Arabic, such as the Unicode encoding shown here, requires only a small set of codepoints.

Figure 2b. Each character code is rendered by up to four individual presentation forms. This is the minimum shaping required to produce recognisable Arabic text.

[113]

of writing. Drawn in dark brown or black ink with the broad side of a sharpened reed, it constitutes the smooth framework of a manuscript.

2. *Distinctive connections: multilevel characteristics.* Unlike its Syriac-Aramaic precursor, Arabic writing early on manifested two types of letter connections: horizontal (right to left) and vertical (top to bottom). This characteristic Arabic tendency emerged very early: with the partial exception of *hijâzi,* all styles of Arabic writing, from the austere hieratic writing (e.g. *kufic*) to the more capricious cursive styles (e.g. *naskh*), share this feature.

Figure 3a: Horizontal and vertical connection of two Arabic letters.

Figure 3b: Vertical connections are a feature in all major styles of the Arabic script, from the oldest *kufic* style as seen in this example from an early Islamic manuscript, left. On the right is the same text in the *naskh* style.

The spread of Islam took Arabic outside its area of origin.[4] Arabic became an empire language and above all the language of religion. The efficient script with fourteen basic shapes, a useful writing system for native speakers of Arabic, was a burden to non-Arab Muslims. This circumstance led to the introduction of diacritics, i.e. small supplementary symbols in writing.

3. *Optional graphemes: vowel markers.* Vowels began to be written in the seventh century, i.e. the first century of the Islamic era, by means of dot-shaped signs surrounding the basic letter groups.[5] In modern Arabic script this method is still in use, but the dots have been superseded by miniature versions of letters such as *alif* (indicated by a small stripe) and *wâw* (a small, open comma-shaped form).

Figure 4: Early Islamic manuscript in *kufic* style, left, showing the early development of vowel marking. The light grey dots and stripes (red in the original) are vowel markers, the two grey stripes indicating a long vowel marked in later text by a superscript *alif;* the dark stripes are consonant markers (see figure 5). On the right is the same text in the *naskh* style.

4. *More distinctive features: consonant markers.* From the ninth century on, another type of additional graphemes starts to appear in manuscripts.

archigraphemes   *ʿâqil*, 'prudent'   *ghâfil*, 'careless'

Figure 5. In early, unmarked Arabic script, certain shapes could express multiple letters: the *archigrapheme* (the common graphical elements of two or more letters, minus the distinctive graphical elements). As a consequence, words could only be read in context. In some cases, like this example, even context might not resolve the ambiguity. The modern system of dots differentiates consonants of identical form.

To make the script more explicit, small stripes made by the imprint of the nib are introduced to distinguish otherwise identical bare letters. In modern Arabic script, the function of these stripes is taken over by dots above or below the bare letters – the tip of the nib is drawn exactly the length of the imprint, replacing the small stripes.

WHO ARE THE USERS OF ARABIC SCRIPT?

The spread of Islam incorporated a number of other cultures and their languages. In the areas bordering Arabia proper, Islamic culture with its Arabic language and script tended to take the place of the original culture and language. In the more remote areas, the traditional script was

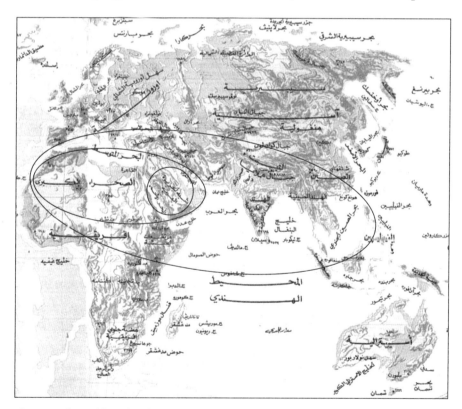

Figure 6. The Arabic scripted world.

relinquished in favour of the Arabic alphabet as an expression of their cultural affiliation with Islam, but the original language was retained.

The resulting Arabic-scripted world therefore consists of both Arabic and non-Arabic speakers. It can be represented schematically on a map as three overlapping ellipses.

The innermost ellipse – the inner circle – is the original Arabia, where native speakers continue to use their historical language and script. Geographically it coincides with the Arabian Peninsula, also the heartland of Islam: the Ethnic Arabs.

The middle ellipse is made up of areas where Arabic replaced other languages and scripts. Geographically, this area covers Mesopotamia, the Levant, and North Africa:[6] the Cultural Arabs. Together with Arabia proper, it constitutes the modern Arabic-speaking World.

The outer ellipse is made up of those Islamic nations that continue to use their historical language. As an expression of their integration in the Islamic civilization, these peoples replaced their original writing with an adaptation of Arabic script.[7]

Together, the Arabic-speaking world and the rest of the Arabic-scripted world form the Islamic world. For the non-Arabic portions of the Arabic-scripted world, Arabized computing is made complicated by the diversity of languages and the various extended Arabic alphabets.

Throughout history, a large number of languages were at one time or another written with the Arabic script, including such widely divergent ones as Spanish, Bosnian Serbo-Croatian, Hausa, Tamil, and even Zuid Afrikaans. Present-day languages using Arabic script include Persian (Iran), Pashto, Dari (Afghanistan), Urdu (India, Pakistan), Javanese (Indonesia), Kurdish (Iraq), and Uyghur (China).

Extension Devices

In order to enable the use of the Arabic alphabet for writing sounds in other languages, additional letters had to be created. The Arabic alphabet was expanded by deriving new letters from existing ones using a variety of devices. These devices derive directly from traditional aspects of Arabic writing; that is, they extend existing conventions to new purposes, rather than inventing new conventions.[8]

The gap. A gap, instead of a connection, creates the new, derived letter: e.g. the old *hâ'* (connected) becomes the new *æ* (disconnected). The basic shape of the new letter is the same as the corresponding Arabic form, but the assimilation pattern in text is different (figure 7a).

The dot. A diacritic is added in the form of additional dots: e.g. the *bâ'* (one dot below) becomes the new *peh* (three dots below). The bare letter form is the same, but additional dots indicate new letters (figure 7b).

[116]

Figure 7a. Not all Arabic letters connect. A gap is used in Arabic (grey, left) to distinguish the originally identical ascending forms of *lâm* and *alif*. In the orthographies of some non-Arabic languages such as Kurdish and Uyghur (right), a gap is used to create a new letter based on the Arabic *hâ'*. In Arabic (black, middle), this class of letter joins on both sides; in Kurdish it joins on the right only, and indicates the vowel *æ*.

Figure 7b: Many new letters are formed for non-Arabic languages by adding new patterns of dots (black) to the basic forms of Arabic letters (grey)

Figure 7c: In Arabic (grey, left) the letter *kâf* is distinguished from the similar – or, as in this *thulth* example, identical – shape of *lâm* by the inclusion of a small mark derived from a miniature form of the swash *kâf*. In Urdu (black), a miniature form of the Arabic *ţâ'* is used to distinguish the letter *tteh* from the Arabic *tâ'*.

Figure 7d: The Arabic letter *yâ'* (grey) has a variant calligraphic form. In Urdu (black), this variant is treated as a distinct letter, *e*, seen here in its word-final form.

The miniature. A diacritic is added in the form of a miniature letter: e.g. the two dots above the old *tâ'* are replaced by a miniature *ţâ'* ط to create the new *tteh*. The bare letter form remains the same, but the diacritic dots are replaced by a miniature letterform (figure 7c).

Variation. Arabic script developed a remarkable versatility. The relatively well-known obligatory contextual variation can be understood as a kind of graphic assimilation process. There is a creative tension between this assimilation and the graphical dissimilation of nominally identical letters in calligraphy, which produces free variants. In a number of cases these variants have become distinct letters in the orthographies of non-Arabic languages (figure 7d).

Figure 8. Interior view of the Aya Sofya mosque, Istanbul, from Caspare Fossati's *Die Hagia Sophia*. This image captures the paradox of the western visual artist's encounter with the calligraphic art of Islam: the building is rendered with precise accuracy, utilising all the techniques of linear and atmospheric perspective in the European tradition, but the image of Arabic calligraphy lacks any understanding of the actual forms. It is as if the artist lacks the necessary mental machinery to understand what he is seeing, and so is unable to depict it. The correct calligraphic forms are superimposed for contrast. (Conversely, this kind of realistic depiction of the building would likely have beeen impossible for an artist of the Middle-Eastern tradition, lacking an understanding of the visual culture of European art.)

TECHNICAL AND AESTHETIC CHALLENGES

Before the invention of photography, nineteenth century travelers were often accompanied by artists. Their meticulous drawings reveal an interesting blind spot in these observers' minds. The celebrated painter David Roberts RA does not depict a single letter of Arabic.[9] Others seriously try to reproduce Arabic script, but with varying success. This drawing, for instance, of the interior of the Hagia Sophia Church, alias Aya Sofya Mosque (figure 8),[10] includes some of the large calligraphic tableaux with the names of the caliphs (visible are the names of: Ali, Umar, Husain, Hasan, and Abu Bakr). The delicate beauty of the building is captured with an eye for subtle detail, but none of that subtlety remains in the depiction of the Arabic calligraphy. What does remain is the visual equivalent of Beethoven's *Für Elise* played on a cell-phone. This alarming lack of perception still pervades all attempts to deal with Arabic script.

A cultural aspect

In the simple approach to Arabic script, all attention goes to the *assimilation* of the letters, that is, to their contextual formation. The four positions (initial, medial, final, and isolated) are presented as actual forms. However, the authentic outcome is also determined by *dissimilation*. For example, the sequence *bâ'-sîn-'ayn* سع can easily be misread as *sîn-bâ'-'ayn* سع, as the letter *sîn* uses three strokes similar to that of the letter *bâ'* – or rather, of the *bâ'*-class.[11] In such cases the letter *bâ'* gets either a dissimilar, raised stroke when it comes before the *sîn*, سب, or a dissimilar stretched horizontal connection after *sîn*, سـ. This essential reading aid and design feature is missing in almost every current font system, and this is just one example of dissimilation. Font technology has still to discover the full extent of the traditional system.

The shaping of Arabic is governed by a set of rules that are both practical – in that they improve the legibility – and elegant, as they were laid down by people who rank among the world's greatest graphic artists. What sets the Arabic alphabet apart from all others is its development into an elaborate morphographical system. It is the outcome of a conscious effort by Arab and Persian scholars to turn the late Syriac-Aramaic script inherited by the Arabs into a finely balanced connected script, as an expression of Islamic culture. From the sixteenth century onwards, Ottoman calligraphers developed a number of the existing styles into uniquely disciplined art forms.

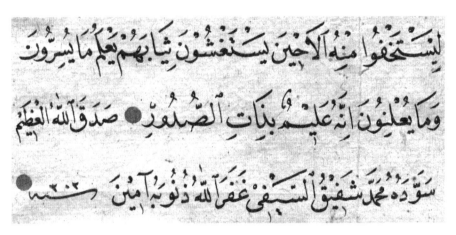

Figure 9. Qur'an fragment with colophon identifying it as the handwriting of Mehmed Şefik (Muhammad Shafiq) Efendi, an Ottoman calligrapher in the school of Mustafa İzzet Efendi, whose handwriting was to become the model of the finest nineteenth and twentieth century Arabic typography.

Simplification attempts
Typesetters have been wrestling with Arabic script for five centuries. Giving it a structure identical to that of Latin script would eliminate all problems, of course. The few known attempts to do this, however, were completely illegible and culturally alien, which may account for the lack of success of the designs of that nature.

Understanding the structure

Writing Arabic involves more than just lining up letters. The connected letters assimilate with each other. They are highly adaptable, which makes it impractical to describe each variant individually. In Arabic script the graphic unit of writing is the *syntagm:* a string of connected letters.

It is interesting to note that the concept of discrete or analytical letter permutations, as on typewriters and in modern fonts, did not exist amongst calligraphers. In traditional *mashq*, or writing exercises, contextual variants are never shown out of context; they are always shown as part of the syntagm.

Another important point is that all letters are subject to the intricate shaping rules that balance between assimilation of distinct letters and dissimilation of featureless letters.

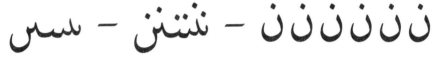

Figure 10. A skeleton of six dissimilar forms is revealed, by the placement of dots, as a sequence of the letter *nun* repeated six times.

TYPESETTING AUTHENTIC ARABIC

The obvious differences between authentic *naskh* writing and mechanical *naskh* reproduction can be attributed to a technical problem: it is very difficult to handle syntagms in typography. Each syntagm within a word forms a unit that relates to the baseline as a whole; e.g. it stands on a secondary baseline (in *naskh* at an angle of approximately 5 degrees, in *ruq'ah* slightly steeper). Between the words there are no orthographic spaces – final forms mark the word endings at the cutting point of the two baselines. In conventional typesetting of Arabic, no such difference between main and secondary baseline is possible. The slanted base line of the letter groups is made horizontal, creating the need to enhance the final forms of words with typographical spaces, bringing it in line with Latin script. The nineteenth century Ottoman punchcutters who worked to emulate the elegance of Arabic script understood the synthetic nature of script. Far from using individual, analytic letterforms, they designed an elaborate system of syntagm components to mould any occurring sequence of letters into a syntagm. One would be tempted to call these letter-compound segments ligatures, but there is a difference. Ligatures are usually optional, i.e. discretionary letter combinations in an otherwise analytical writing system. For these typesetters, syntagm components were the basic building bricks, sometimes covering more than one letter, but often representing only part of a letter – or a letter and a half. Dots and vowels were added separately.

Successful designs

At the end of the nineteenth century, there were very good Ottoman type designs to cope with the dual, multilevel baseline of most Islamic scripts. These typefaces could consist of well over a thousand individual elements of metal type and were highly complex. Because of this, they required specialized technical virtuosity based on thorough knowledge of the underlying calligraphic script. In the last quarter of the nineteenth century and the first half of the twentieth century, this typography produced impressive results.

European attempts

These Ottoman developments took place in the second half of the nineteenth century. In Europe, typesetting with Arabic characters has been undertaken since the early sixteenth century. The early Arabic types have a Western North-African appearance. Maybe European punchcutters had access to the Andalusian spoils of the Spanish Reconquista, and were consequently misled in their calligraphic styling; in any case, their designs were totally out of touch with Islamic taste and with Middle Eastern taste in particular. If these early attempts had any effect on the development of Islamic printing at all, it was negative. In the period that Middle Eastern calligraphy was reaching its zenith, European Arabic typography produced absolute monstrosities. For more than two centuries the Ottoman authorities opposed the large scale introduction of typesetting and printing of Islamic script; the low quality of the designs was a factor in delaying the acceptance of typography in the Islamic world.

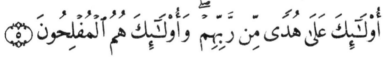

Figure 11a. Typical European font used to typeset the *Coranus Arabice recensionis Flügelianae*, Leipzig Germany 1867, shows widely spaced primitive forms without relation to any known calligraphic style.

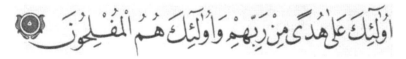

Figure 11b. The same text as printed in the first and only typeset Qur'an authorized by the Azhar University, the so-called *Fuad Qur'an* (1924), printed in Cairo by combining Ottoman calligraphic expertise with German technology.

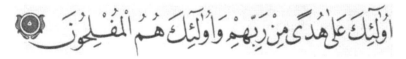

Figure 11c. The same text again, from an eighteenth century Ottoman manuscript by the hand of Mehmed Emin Rüşdü Efendi. The main mission of Ottoman typography, the source of Middle Eastern Arab typography, was to maintain the integrity of this *naskh*, or book calligraphy, in type.

Breakthrough in Istanbul

The first, short-lived effort to print books with Arabic letters was made in Istanbul by İbrahim Müteferrika, a Hungarian renegade, in 1727. In the last decade of the eighteenth century, typesetting in the Ottoman Empire was taken up again and on a larger scale, culminating in the designs of Ohanis Mühendisoğlu[12] in the second half of the nineteenth century. These laid the basis for all modern *naskh* typefaces. It took a scholar to handle the set of over 1500 movable types to construct each syntagm correctly. With the increased use of typography, one can observe that the discrepancy between hand-written and typeset *naskh* increases, due to mistakes, incomplete fonts or ignorance of the design.

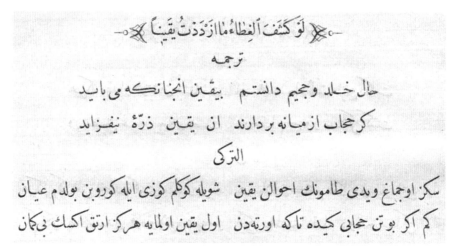

Figure 12. Typography by Ohanis Mühendisoğlu in the *Yeni Hurufat*, 1870.

The Mother of Arabic Typography

Ottoman *naskh* (spelled *nesih* in modern Turkish) definitely guided all Middle Eastern efforts in typography. In the 1860s the Armenian typographer Ohanis Mühendisoğlu, an Ottoman-Turkish citizen, finally succeeded in reproducing this script in a way that met the demanding standards of the Islamic calligraphic tradition.[13] His sublime approach to typography was clearly based on a sophisticated understanding of Arabic script and calligraphy. Figure 12 shows brilliant typesetting by Mühendisoğlu in the *Yeni Hurufat*[14] in the three main languages of the Ottoman Islamic world: Arabic, Persian, and Turkish.

In the context of Ottoman culture, it was unthinkable that a lowly typographer would attempt to produce his own version of Arabic script. Mühendisoğlu (1810–1891) modelled his typography on the handwriting of *Kazi Asker* (Supreme Judge) Mustafa İzzet Efendi (1801–1876), who ranked among the viziers or ministers of the Ottoman state. İzzet Efendi, i.e. Lord İzzet, was a man of great authority. He was a composer of Ottoman classical music and the leading calligrapher of his times. Among the

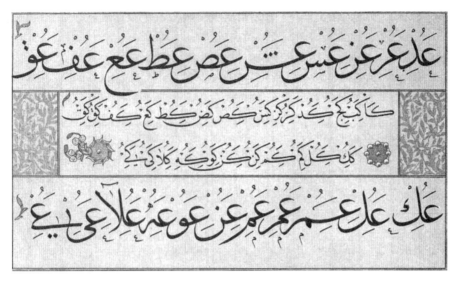

Figure 13. *Meşk mürakka'i* or writing exercise by İzzet Efendi elaborating
the shapes and connections of the letters 'ayn (large, in the *sülüs* (*thulth*) style)
and *kâf* (small, in the *nesih* (*naskh*) style). This kind of exercise is the artistic
equivalent of the étude in the Western musical tradition.

many calligraphic and musical compositions of his hand are the large
tableaux inside the historical Aya Sofya Mosque in the very heart of Istanbul, capital of the Ottoman Empire. This lofty man certainly was not
the type to be involved in anything so plebeian as type design, and it can
be ruled out that the craftsman and the calligrapher ever met.

This adaptation by Mühendisoğlu of İzzet Efendi's calligraphy is the
starting point of all later Arabic *naskh* typefaces. The font was graphically extremely sophisticated, as it was designed to follow all the *allographic*
rules of *naskh* in the tradition of the copyists, the professional book pro-
ducers before the advent of typography. The essential feature is that it
deals with both dot and vowel attachments as separate horizontal layers
above and below the main script. In other words, the design was *archi-
graphemic.*[15] However, the seeds of decay are already present in the 40-page
Yeni Hurufat booklet. The initial pages immaculately implement every
rule with the correct glyph. As the page numbers go up, so the number
of calligraphic typos increases: the zenith of Arabic typography stands at
the beginning of the erosion, rather than the evolution, of *naskh* script.[16]
This is an extremely good design, but it should have had a computer
program to support it!

Arabic ligatures
An interesting concept in the type industry is the Arabic *ligature.* In Latin
typography the ligature is an aesthetic device to improve the rendering of
a few troublesome letter combinations. Such replacement letter groups
belong in fonts, whence a rendering system can use them to replace let-

ter groups. In Arabic, however, connecting letters is not the exception but the rule. Theoretically each letter can have a different appearance in *any* combination, something that can only be crudely imitated with ligatures. The use of ligatures tends to be determined by the nature of the typeface design and the technical limitations of the font technology. Many contemporary fonts contain a multitude of ligatures in order to approximate the desired appearance of authentic Arabic text, but it needs to be understood that this is a technical solution to a technical problem, and not an inherent feature of the Arabic script. It is not hard to conceive of different technologies for typesetting Arabic that would achieve equivalent or superior results without using any ligatures at all.

Figure 14a. Skeleton script showing individual archigraphemes.

Figure 14b. The addition of dots establishes the identity of ambiguous graphemes.

Figure 14c. Consonant enhancers identify reduplicated consonant graphemes.

Figure 14d. Vowels are identified, or their absence is marked.

Figure 14e. Punctuation or cantillation (precise verbalisation) is indicated.

Figure 14f. The erroneous placement of illegal dots in copying is blocked.

Figure 14g. Ornamental elements are added to aesthetically fill holes in the text.

Horizontally layered structure

Arabic script is best constructed following the historically-evolved pattern: in several horizontal layers surrounding the skeleton layer, each one adding an additional aspect of the script in a strict order. The best-known layers are those of dot patterns and of vowels. In addition there is a separate layer for the *shadda* or consonant enhancer. The full layered system (figure 14) is especially important in Qur'anic text, where it guides correct pronunciation and copying and also prevents likely errors.

Calligraphic alternation

Islamic script is more than just a connective alphabet with contextual variation. Many letters can be variously rendered with calligraphic alternatives, each of them having an equivalent range of contextual permutations. This phenomenon is much more powerful than the nearest equivalent in Latin calligraphy. Calligraphic permutation opens the perspective of fine-tuning justification in typesetting with a mechanism borrowed from calligraphic manuscripts.

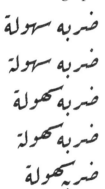

Figure 15. Five different settings of the two same words in the *ruq'ah* style, showing how alternate calligraphic permutations can be used to justify text across varying column widths. Other permutations are possible.

Unicode & Arabic

The Unicode character-encoding standard enables cultural diversity in computer text processing. In terms of encoding, the logic of Arabic is no different from any other alphabetic script, hence the *real* challenge of the computer age is not the encoding of Arabic but its visual representation: the development of digital typography that leaves the graphical structure of the script intact.

The Unicode standard is designed for logical representation only: the entry, storage and manipulation of raw text. In practice, it is sometimes mistakenly used as a glyph list for font designers. Such mixing of levels, of logical and visual representation, is potentially disastrous for the emerging Arabic typographic technology. A fixed list of Arabic letter shapes puts unrealistic constraints on the artistic reproduction of Arabic text in digital form. The future must embrace flexible, generative mechanisms of representation, working above the level of Unicode text.

[125]

Notes

1. Even a well-researched work like *Arabic Typography, a comprehensive sourcebook* by Huda Smitshuijzen AbiFarès (London, 2001) is written without the notion of rules governing the joining of letters. Its 'anatomy of letterforms' does not venture beyond summing up the absolute minimum of letter variations (§ 3.2, p. 99). Like practically all works in this field, this publication touches on the calligraphic standardization of individual letters by Ibn Muqlah (Baghdâd, 885–940 AD), but without mentioning the fact that proportions of isolated letters hardly have any relevance for a dynamic script like Arabic. As for the more sophisticated connected letter groups – the product of the design process set in motion by the same Ibn Muqlah – they are mentioned cursorily in § 4.2.3.3, 'the shapes of characters'. As usual, they are presented to the reader as 'ligatures' and 'artistic expressions' without so much as a hint at traditional morphographic rules.

2. A positive exception is T.F. Mitchell, *Writing Arabic, a Practical Introduction to Ruqʿah Script*, Oxford 1953. It is the only book in English that attempts to give a systematic description of Arabic script. Unfortunately this excellent book fails to point out that the structure it describes is in fact the general structure of Arabic script. *Ruqʿah* happens to be the authentic simplified Arabic and as such is a good stepping-stone for beginners.

3. The author wishes to thank Mamoun Sakkal for providing this illustration from his website at www.sakkal.com/ArtArabicCalligraphy.html

4. 'By about twenty years after the death of the Prophet, his successor, the Caliph, had gained control over the Arabian Peninsula. In addition, all the Roman provinces from the Syro-Palestinian coast to the mountains of Kurdistan as well as the core of the Persian Empire had come under his dominion. In another twenty years all of North Africa had been subdued and Spain was to follow suit. As for the government of this large empire, the Arabs at first retained the Persian and Byzantine state machinery integrally. They did not interfere with the internal civil and religious administration of the conquered peoples. At this point in time, the seventh century AD, i.e. the first century of the Hijra, it is an anachronism to think of the spread of Islam as a mass conversion.' *The Arabs in History*, B. Lewis (OUP 1966), pp. 49–63, 'The age of the conquests'.

5. One can assume that the enhanced orthography was above all meant to facilitate memorizing the Qur'an in a properly recited form. Such diacritics therefore may be considered mainly pedagogical. In order to avoid the impression that the received text was altered, they were written by means of red dots. In some manuscripts one also observes brown points in the same role.

6. In the Levant (Syria, Lebanon, Palestine) and Mesopotamia (Iraq) various Aramaic languages were replaced by Arabic. In some parts these languages continue to be used by Christian communities. Egyptian only survives in the Coptic Christian community for sacral use. In the remainder of North Africa the Berber languages still maintain themselves in many places.

7. Until the beginning of the twentieth century this was the case with no exception. The main exceptions were created in the past one hundred years. The Turkish Republic abolished the writing of Turkish with Arabic script in favour of Latin; the Soviet Union forced a number of Islamic peoples to convert to Communism and the associated use of Cyrillic script: 'Alphabet follows religion' (Diringer, *The Alphabet, a key to the history of mankind*. London, 1968.). This phenomenon

can also be observed in the Christian world: Roman Christendom meant Latin Script; Greek Christendom meant Greek (and later Cyrillic) script.

8. In the development of the proto-Arabic script, the opposition of connected and disconnected forms to distinguish different but morphographically similar letters is an old device that precedes the use of letter points for this purpose. Later non-Arabic alphabets continue these traditional methods. Like in the family of *bâ', tâ', thâ', nûn*, and *yâ'*: before the *bâ'* family got its dots, it was, as a whole, distinguished from the members of the *dal, dhal, râ', zayn* family – also still without dots – by the gap. This gap also forms the distinctive feature that helps to differentiate *lâm* from *alif*: ﻚ vs. ﻊ

9. See, for instance, David Roberts RA, *The Holy Land, 123 coloured facsimile lithographs & The Journal from his Visit to the Holy Land*, Terra Sancta Arts Ltd, Israel, 1982 (first edition 1842).

10. Caspare Fossati, *Die Hagia Sophia, nach dem tafelwerk von 1852*, Harenberg Kommunikation, Dortmund 1980. For comparison similar, authentic tableaux are superimposed; these are taken from Nabil F. Safwat, *The Art of the Pen, Calligraphy of the 14th to 20th centuries*, Volume V of the Nasser D. Khalili Collection of Islamic Art, The Nour Foundation/Oxford University Press 1996.

11. These examples represent the skeleton representation of the words *sabʿ* 'seven' and *tisʿ* 'eight', which were indistinguishable in old manuscripts, leading to ambiguous datings. (Personal communication from Dr Gerd-Rüdiger Puin, University of Saarbrücken, Germany).

12. Mühendisoğlu is the Turkish version of his name, with the literal meaning of *son of the land surveyor* (or *civil engineer*). His name is also encountered in Ottoman-Persian (Mühendiszade) and Armenian forms (Mühendisyan).

13. An *arzuhal* or petition to the Sultan of the Ottoman Empire dated 1283 AH (1865 AD) came into my possession in 1983. In it Mühendisoğlu announces that for the first time a valid *naskh* typeface has been designed. He describes how he used the handwriting of the late *şeyhü l-hattâtîn* (leading calligrapher) Mustafa İzzet Efendi to accomplish this historical achievement. Uğur Derman, the leading specialist on Ottoman calligraphy, reports corroborating evidence to the Turkish Librarians' Association (Türk Kütüphaneciler Derneği Basım ve Yayıncılığımızın 250. yılı Bilimsel Toplantısı. 10–11 Aralık 1979, Ankara; Bildiriler, Ankara, 1980, vii, 174 pp.: M. Uğur Derman, *Yazı sanatinin eski matbaacılığımıza akisleri*. pp. 97–118). In this essay he also mentions the advanced *taʿliq* typefaces designed by Mühendisoğlu as early in the 1840's. In spring 2001, I discovered two of only three books ever printed in Mühendisoğlu's *taʿliq*.

14. According to the colophon it was printed in Istanbul 1869–70 AD. In spring 2001, I made the sensational chance discovery of this rare book printed in the exact same *nesih* typeface as the petition of 1865 described in footnote 11.

15. This term, and others in this essay, are more fully explained in: 'Authentic Arabic: a case study. Right-to-left font structure, font design and typography' by Thomas Milo, in *Manuscripta Orientalia*. Vol. 8 No. 1, March 2002. (Saint Petersburg, Russia.) pp. 49–61.

16. *Naskh, thulth*, (*naskh-i-*)*taʿliq* and *ruqʿah* scripts are governed by well-organised and logical morphographical rules, the knowledge of which is rare among type designers and typographers today.

VLADIMIR YEFIMOV

Civil Type and Kis Cyrillic

A MODERN RUSSIAN TYPEFACE BASED ON HISTORICAL FORMS

T HE REFORM OF CYRILLIC TYPE took place in Russia during the reign of Tsar Peter I (1689–1725). The old *poluustav* type was preserved only for religious literature, while for all other publications, Peter introduced a new style that imitated the forms of contemporary Western type; in later days, the new type became known as Civil Type (*grazhdanskiy shrift*). The reform partially altered the structure of the Russian alphabet, too: the use of European (Arabic) numerals was introduced, and punctuation and caps usage were put in order. Thus, Cyrillic took on the form of roman serif type, in much the same way that Muscovy was dressed up in European clothes. In fact, the introduction of Civil Type meant the revision of the Cyrillic alphabet's structure *and* the restyling of its letterforms based on the shapes of Western (Latin) letters. Nevertheless, from the point of view of modern type design, the reformed Cyrillic type introduced by Peter could have been of a higher quality, had the developers of the Civil Type relied on the best examples of Western typefaces of the 17th and early 18th centuries.

PETER THE GREAT AND THE PREREQUISITES OF CYRILLIC TYPE REFORM

In 1689 the seventeen-year-old Peter I was declared sole tsar and ruler of all Russia. From the very beginning of his reign, all his unbelievable energy was directed to reforming the Russian state: its army, its economy, its governance, its culture. As a result of these superhuman efforts, over a reign of more than 30 years, Peter managed to change the course of Russian history completely, transforming Russia from a closed, self-contained Asian country into a more open state that was oriented toward Europe. Although these reforms were forcibly spread from the top, and they cost a lot of victims, the Russian Empire became a fact of European history. Peter's reform of Cyrillic type of 1708–10, which brought the Cyrillic alphabet closer to the form of roman, played a very important role in this orientation of Russia to the culture of the most developed countries.

[128]

At the end of the 17th century, *poluustav* was the only style of Cyrillic printing type. It had changed very little since the middle of the 16th
century, from the time of the Russian printing pioneer Ivan Fedorov. In
its structure it was a form of medieval handwriting. *Poluustav* was rather
black in colour and very ornamental, but not very useful for the needs
of the new era. The character set of the alphabet no longer matched the
phonetics of the living Russian language, and it contained a lot of additional diacritical marks (stresses, marks of aspiration, abbreviations),
which considerably complicated the work of the compositor. In addition,
numerals were traditionally denoted by letters with special marks (*titlos*),
which made reading scientific and technical texts difficult. Publications
printed in *poluustav* looked like medieval hand-written books, and in
their appearance they were very different from European books of the
17th century. However, in the absence of any other type, *poluustav* was
being used for printing both religious and secular literature, including
primers and text books, as well as the first Russian newspaper, *Vedo-
mosty*, which was published at the very beginning of 1703.

In 1703, Leontiy Magnitsky's *Arifmetika* ('Arithmetic') was published;
it included information on algebra, geometry, trigonometry, and tables of
logarithms. In that publication, European (so called Arabic) figures were
used for the first time instead of Slavic *tsifir'* (denotation of numerals by
letters). The main text was composed in *poluustav*, but for mathematical
terms Latin and Greek fonts were used. None of these fonts matched
with each other in either color or style (figure 1, overleaf). It was probably in comparing this book with Western ones that Peter got the idea
of reforming Cyrillic and bringing it closer to the Latin alphabet, i.e., to
abandon *poluustav* and create a 'clearer,' lighter style of typeface, which
came to be called Civil Type.

In his reform of printing type, Peter I had an august predecessor, who
was probably also an exemplary model. The French king Louis XIV, *le roi
soleil*, in the second part of his reign also dealt with typographic reform.
He ordered the establishment of a Royal Commission for the standardization of craft, which at its first meeting in January 1693 began with the
regulation of typography. For this purpose the engineer Jacques Jaugeon
designed, and the punchcutter Philippe Grandjean de Fouchy cut, the
so-called *romain du roi* (the King's roman) as an 'ideal alphabet'. In 1702
that font was used for the luxurious illustrated book *Médailles sur les prin-
cipaux évènements du règne de Louis le Grand* at the Royal Printing House
in Paris (figure 2, overleaf). Peter I had a copy of this book in his library;
perhaps these activities of Louis XIV's served as a model for the Russian
tsar. But in its shapes the *romain du roi* was not as different from earlier
types as the Civil Type was; it was a variation of contemporary serif type,

ЧАСТЬ ПЕРВАЯ

ѡ числѣхъ цѣлыхъ.

Колико сїя часть имѣетъ въ себѣ предѣленїй;

Имѣетъ предѣленїй пять.

1.	Συναρίθμησις,	Numeratio.	Счисленїе.
2.	Συναρθροισμός,	Additio,	Сложенїе.
3.	Ὑφαίρεσις,	Subtractio,	Вычитанїе.
4.	Πολυπλασιασμός.	Multiplicatio.	Оумноженїе.
5.	Διαίρεσις.	Divisio.	Дѣленїе.

Предѣленїе первое.

Нумерацїо, или счисленїе.

Что есть нумерацїо;

Нумерацїо есть счисленїе, еже совершеннѡ вся числа речїю именовати, яже въ десяти знаменованїяхъ, или изъображенїя содержатся, и изъображаются сице:

1, 2, 3, 4, 5, 6, 7, 8, 9, 0,

изъ нихже девять назнаменователны суть: последнее же о [еже цыфрою, или ничемъ именуется] егда оубо (оно) едино стоитъ, тогда само ѡ себѣ ничтоже значитъ. егда же коему оныхъ знаменованїй приложено будетъ, тогда оумножаетъ въ десятеро, якоже предложено есть ниже сегѡ.

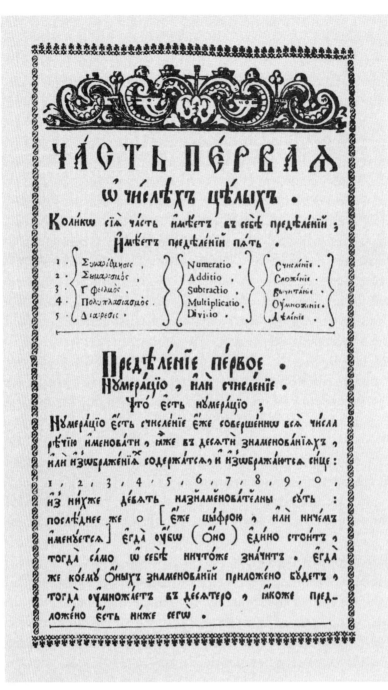

Figure 1. Page from Magnitsky's *Arifmetika*, 1703.

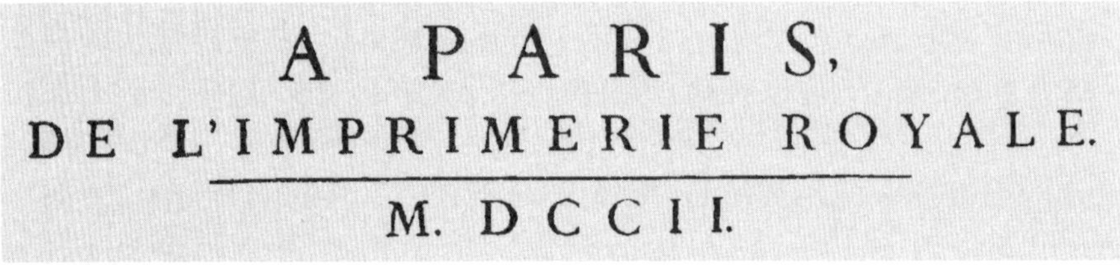

Figure 2. *Romain du Roi*, 1702.

an 'old-style'. Besides, the French king was not thinking of changing all the fonts in France at once: he just wanted a distinctive new type for his own printing house. The Russian emperor had more holistic intentions.

Nevertheless, Peter's typographic reform in Russia was not as natural as, for example, the introduction of roman type in Italy at the end of the 15th century. Roman type was based on the humanist minuscule – the handwriting of educated people of that time. Civil Type had no unified, settled handwriting as its basis. There were several kinds of hands in use at that time: a traditional cursive writing with flourishes, a slower writing (the so-called *civil hand*) used for official documents, and a lot of transitional forms (figure 3). The development of Russian cursive hand-writing styles was connected to, and influenced by, the Ukrainian and West-Russian hands, not to mention the Latin ones; however, there was as yet no commonly accepted unified style. The type reform was based on royal fancy, which could not be argued with, rather than on mature public necessity. The same ideological motives underlay Peter's decrees that men should shave their beards, smoke tobacco, and wear Dutch clothes, his construction of a European-style capital in the middle of forests and swamps, and his publishing of books composed in a Cyrillic equivalent of roman type: the tsar wanted his country to look European. And maybe the forced reform of Russian type was caused by his desire to have Russian books, in form and structure, imitate the books published in Europe.

The type reform of 1708–1710 was not Peter's first attempt to latinise the Cyrillic alphabet. The forms of Civil Type were pre-echoed by the engraved lettering on book titles, geographical maps, and other print, as well as by the types of Dutch printers, who at Peter's request printed Russian books and maps in the late 17th–early 18th centuries. Both prototypes presented an uneasy combination of certain Latin capital letters, whose shape was similar to the Cyrillic ones, and specific Cyrillic glyphs taken from the lowercase *poluustav* of the 17th century (figure 4, overleaf). The lowercase letters of the Dutch typefaces were related to both

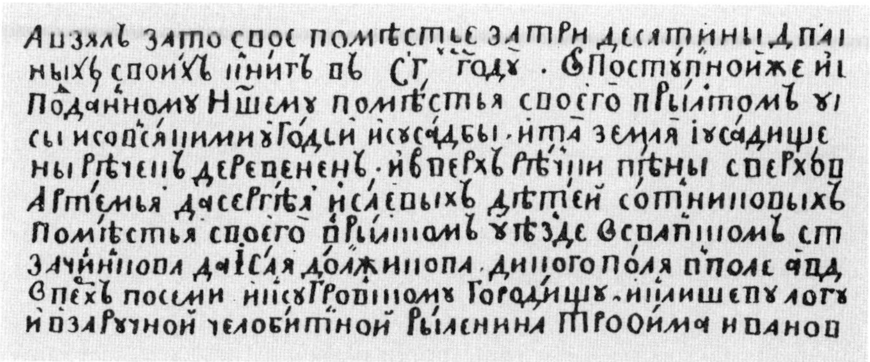

Figure 3. Civil hand, 1703.

АБВГДДЕЖЅЗ
НІКЛМΝ∞ОПР
СТХЦЧҍѦѰѴ

Figure 4. Amsterdam Cyrillic caps of Thesing's printshop, 1699–1707.

the civil hand and *poluustav*. This was probably the reason why Peter finally took a dislike to Dutch printing and made the decision to move the design of the new type to Russia.

THE CHARACTER SET OF THE PETRINE
CIVIL TYPE AND ITS FORM

As a result of Peter's reform, the number of characters in the Russian alphabet decreased from 45 to 38. Characters inherited from the Greek alphabet like ѡ (*omega*) and ѱ (*psi*) and ligatures ѿ (*ot*) and ꙩ (*os*); ѫ (*yus*, large) and ѧ (*yus*, small), and also a variant of the ҁ (*zemlya*), were dropped. Instead of the є character (open *e*) the letter э was introduced, and the character ꙗ (*ya*) was replaced by the letter я. Diacritical marks, abbreviation marks, and Slavic *tsifir'* (denotation of the figures by letters) were abandoned; European ('old-style') figures and punctuation marks were introduced; and the use of capital letters was systematized. In the books set in Civil Type, standard (roman-style) caps mark the beginning of sentences, names, and some important notions; the use of *poluustav* caps became limited to the initial capitals. Compositors could divide the long words (and they are many in the Russian language!) with hyphens. Thus, the appearance of the Petrine book became very similar to that of the European one.

The forms of the type approved by Peter are fairly consistent in both its variants (1708 and 1710). The proportion of its characters, the contrast, the relationship of the cap-height and the x-height, the character of round forms, the shape of serifs, and other details are all clearly influenced by the old-style Dutch (Baroque) roman, especially when compared to *poluustav*. It becomes especially clear in the characters common to both Latin and Cyrillic alphabets and in the initial versions of n, p, m. Most of the characters that are specific to the Cyrillic alphabet are also styled after Western models. Some glyphs of the new type, or their details, have a shape very close to the letters of Russian cursive and 'civil' hands.

The legs of К, к and Я, я have a softly curved sinuous shape resembling the form of the similar stroke of the *romain du roi* R. Several glyphs of the new typeface retained the general form of the *poluustav* (figure 5), though even these glyphs have somewhat Westernised shapes.

However, in spite of the apparent similarity to the Baroque Dutch roman, on closer examination the Civil Type is significantly different; some researchers even regard it as a kind of Transitional style (or *Ré-ale*). In its colour it is a bit lighter than most of the contemporary Dutch types; its serifs are rather fine and almost unbracketed, like the serifs of the *romain du roi*. In the large size, only some of the letters resemble the construction of their Dutch roman counterparts, and even these have considerable differences in the details. The new à, without a ball terminal and with the top of the bowl bulging, does not resemble its typical Western relative at all; such a shape only occurs in handwritten samples of Giovanni Francesco Cresci, dated 1570.

In the Dutch roman of the late 17th–early 18th century, the M (similar to *Capitalis Monumentalis*) almost always has inclined lateral stems, and

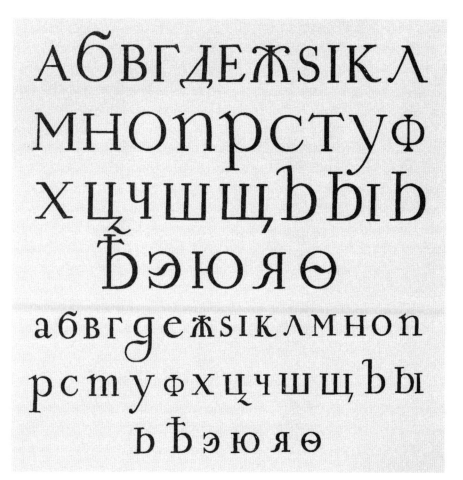

Figure 5. Civil Type, large size, 1708.

its middle diagonals meet at the base line. In the Petrine type, the side stems of the M are absolutely vertical, and the diagonals meet almost in the middle of the character height. Such a structure can be found only in the M of Jan Thesing's printshop in Amsterdam, where Russian books were printed at the request of Peter the Great, and in Russian geographical maps, engraved book titles, and calendars of the period. Forms of C without the beak on the bottom terminal and double-sided beaks of C, S, s could be found in Western romans from the beginning of the 18th century, but they are not very typical of those types, and they have, again, analogues in the engraved inscriptions on Russian maps and calendars. In roman type, the double-sided beaks in C and especially in S first appear in earnest at the end of the first third of the 18th century, and a form of M with vertical side stems can be found only in the mid-18th century.

On closer examination, the design of some letters in the Civil Type is different from the structure of similar Latin characters. For example, in the letters A, У, y, X, x there are no internal serifs at the ends of diagonal strokes. And the end of the left top stroke in the initial variants of П, n, P, p, m is not at all similar to the Latin analogues. A person familiar with Latin script would never draw letters of such a shape. One can imagine that the desire to draw those letters in the style of a Latin type, with a triangular entry serif, ran into an absolute ignorance of its design pattern.

All of this applies to the large size of the Civil Type (equal to approximately 36 point). In the fonts of the medium size (approximately 12 point) and the small size (approximately 10 point), A, П, P, T, n, p, m show the well-known forms of the Dutch roman. The shape of a and y in the medium and small sizes is also very close to the roman. Only X, x persistently has no serifs. It is interesting to note that К, к in the large size has an upper diagonal stroke ending with a double-sided horizontal serif (like the one in the corresponding roman character), while similar letters in the medium and small sizes at this point have drop-shaped endings.

These deviations from the conventional Western glyph pattern cannot be just accidental. For the Dutch craftsmen who engraved punches for the Russian tsar, it would have been much easier to use the familiar forms of Latin letters. Apparently, the reason had to do with the original design models of those glyphs.

BRIEF HISTORY OF CIVIL TYPE DESIGN

Based on Peter's surviving correspondence with his associates, the first drawings of the new Russian letters, in three sizes, were made in January 1707 by a military engineer and draftsman whose name was Kuhlenbach; he was serving at the Russian military headquarters under the command of Prince Menshikov. This was during the Great Northern War against

КРАТКОЕ ПРЕДЪСШБЪАВЛЕНІЕ И ТОЛКОВАНІЕ
ЧЕТЫРЕХЪ ТАБЛИЦЪ, НАЖЕ КАЖДАА ЧТО ИМАТЬ СОДЕРЖАНІЕ В СЕБѢ. НА КОТОРЫХЪ ТАБЛИЦАХЪ ОБЩЕ.
АКО
КАЛЕНДАРЬ НЕИСХОДИМЫИ

Figure 6. Detail of the title page of *Bruce's Calendar.* Engraving, 1709.

Sweden, when the headquarters was constantly relocating, depending on where military operations were taking place. The sketches of the new letters were handed to Kuhlenbach by Peter himself at the end of 1706, when he arrived at headquarters, which was then located at Zholkva near Lvov. It is quite possible that Peter made the sketches himself. Despite a very wide range of design references for the Civil Type (Western romans, the Russian 'civil hand', *poluustav*), its author showed remarkable creativity and inventiveness in devising the characters that were specific to the Cyrillic alphabet, and achieved considerable visual integrity. None of the known engraving artists contemporary with Peter could have been the author of the sketches, although the form of some letters in the Civil Type resembles the legends on etchings by Adriaan Schoonebeeck, Peter Piquart, Alexey Zubov, and other engravers of the Petrine period (figure 6). These engravers certainly knew the structure of the letterforms, and would have placed the serifs in the right places. Of course no one would have dared correct the drawings of the tsar himself: that is why Kuhlenbach copied them most carefully. The similarities to the Dutch roman in the small sizes of the Civil Type can be explained by the fact that in small sizes, differences of form are harder to notice, so Kuhlenbach drew them in a more conventional style.

Working from the sketches he received, Kuhlenbach prepared artwork for 32 lowercase letters and four capitals (А, Д, Е, Т) in three sizes. Artwork for the other capitals was never completed – most likely for lack of time – and they had to be produced based on sketches of the lowercase letters, blown up to the cap-height. Initially Peter wanted to invite Dutch craftsmen over to Moscow, so they would both produce a new type on the spot, and set up a printing operation modelled on Western practices, and then train Russian printers. However, having a punchcutter move to Russia proved too expensive: at the time there were only two such specialists in Amsterdam, both of whom were overloaded with work and not eager to go to faraway Moscow. So the decision was made to have the entire set of punches and matrices in three sizes manufactured in Amsterdam, based on Kuhlenbach's drawings. Simultaneously, copies of the drawings were given to the craftsmen of the Moscow Printing Yard for parallel manufacture of the new letters.

According to the information contained in Peter's letters, in June 1707 he received a printed specimen of the medium-size type, and in Septem-

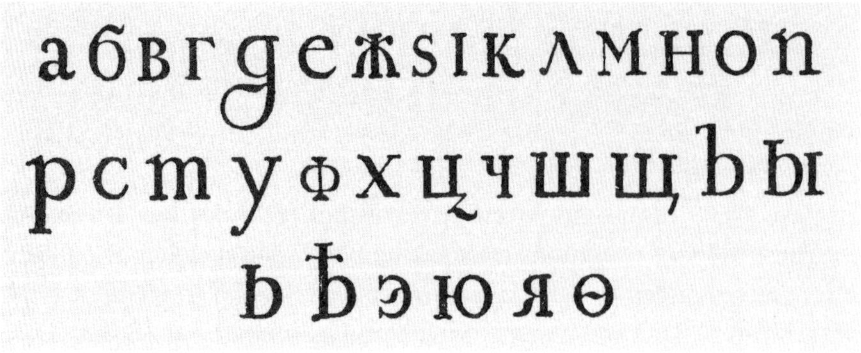

абвгдежѕіклмноп
рстуфхцчшщъы
ьѣэюяѳ

Figure 7. Amsterdam Civil Type lowercase, 1707.

ber the proofs of the large and small sizes (figure 7). The speed of manufacturing and the technical quality of the punches, matrices, and sorts
of the new type speak well of the Dutch punchcutter's skills (we do not
know his name). However, the craftsman did not even try to make sense
of the letter shapes he was cutting: he carefully reproduced Kuhlenbach's
patterns, retaining all the absurdities of the originals, including the absence of serifs in some glyphs, and the strange shapes of a, p, n and m:
he might have thought those forms were specific to Cyrillic alphabet.

At the same time, at the Moscow Printing Yard, the letter-founders
Mikhail Yefremov, Grigory Alexandrov, and Vasily Petrov were making
their own variant of the new type according to the drawings they had
been sent. But when the Moscow letter-founders' effort was compared
with the specimen sent from Amsterdam, it seemed less successful, and
their work was stopped until the Dutch fonts could arrive in Russia. At
the end of 1707, three specially invited Dutch printers, together with the
type and their printing press, reached Moscow via Arkhangelsk. The first
book composed with the new Civil Type, *Geometria Slavensky Zemlemerie*,
was printed in March 1708 (figure 8); it was followed by several others.

But the development of the new type was not finished. After some
hand composition tests, the tsar decided to change the form of a few
letters, and to add several missing letters from the traditional Russian alphabet. But when Peter sent sketches of the additional letters to Mogilev
(where the Army headquarters had moved) in April 1708, Kuhlenbach
failed to notice any difference between them and the original letters, so
he simply repeated the original designs of these characters, based on the
old sketches. Unsatisfied, Peter sent the sketches back again and ordered
him to do the work anew. Finally, based on new drawings that Kuhlenbach made in July 1708, Peter ordered that additional letters should be cut
in Moscow (at the Printing Yard) and simultaneously in Amsterdam.

In Moscow, in the autumn of 1708, 21 uppercase letters and 21 lowercase letters were cut in the medium size, and 17 lowercase letters in the

small size. They were manufactured by Grigory Alexandrov and Vasily Petrov, letter-founders at the Printing Yard – the best craftsman, Mikhail Yefremov, having died the previous spring. In Amsterdam in 1709, 18 additional lowercase letters were cut in all three sizes. Some of these letters were variants of existing ones; others were letters that had been missing earlier. In the new variants, most of the odder features of the letterforms were made less eccentric, and in general the type became more placid. But in the process, some of the letterforms lost a part of their expressiveness. For example, the lowercase д now simply repeated the upper case, and a charming handwritten form with a loop at the bottom was rejected. If at the start the capital letters had been based on the lowercase letterforms, then after the proofreading some lowercase letters (д, и, п, т) ended up based on the uppercase letterforms (figure 9, overleaf). And lowercase letters from the medium size were simply used as capitals for the small size (25 letters out of 34 are the same in their form).

In Petrine books, among the lowercase letters in the large size one can also find capital А, Б, Д, Е, Т made in Moscow that are equal in height to the lowercase letters. Some researchers presume that they were small caps. But I believe that these are the remnants of Peter's experiments aimed at increasing the number of type sizes. (It is unlikely that at that

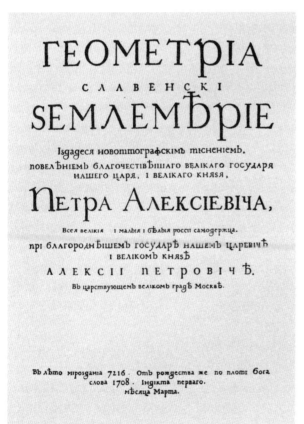

Figure 8. Title page from *Geometria*, 1708.

Б з и п р ४ ф ц щ Ѣ ы ь Ѣ є
ѧ ѵ Ѱ ѵ

Figure 9. Additional Amsterdam Civil Type lowercase, 1709.

time the tsar understood the need for small caps, if indeed he had any concept of them at all). As a result of all these changes, the *Cyrillic roman* included mainly rectangular forms, and its lowercase letters became hardly different from the uppercase ones.

It took the craftsmen in Holland about a year to manufacture the additional letters. During the same period, the Moscow letters were redone several times: there were at least four such rounds of proofing and correction. Peter was engaged in correcting the Civil Type during the most dramatic events of the Great Northern War, in which the land forces of the Swedish king Carl XII were defeated on 27 June 1709 at the battle of Poltava. The Dutch punches of the additional letters finally arrived in Moscow in September 1709. It was probably in October that the last proof of the new alphabet, with all the final, corrected letters from both Amsterdam and Moscow, was printed. On 18 January 1710, Peter I visited the Printing Yard and approved imprints of the alphabet. Then he did the final proof – crossing out the *poluustav* characters and the characters ѿ (ot), ѡ (omega), and ѱ (psi), and the first versions of the new type characters – and wrote with his own hand on the inner side of the case: '*Симы литеры печатать исторические и манифактурныя книги. А которыя подчернены, тех вышеписанных книгах не употреблять*' ('Use these letters for printing historical and technical books. And those which are crossed out do not use [in] the above described books'). The first page of this model alphabet is dated: '*Дано лета Господня 1710, Генваря в 29 день*' (29 January 1710) (figure 10, overleaf). The reform of the Cyrillic alphabet was finally complete – although the early forms of the new letters, rejected by the reforming tsar, were still in use alongside the approved ones up until the 1740s, when new Cyrillic types were developed.

Since European old-style numerals were in use in Russian books even before the Petrine reform, it is quite possible that they were not specially ordered. More likely, the tsar's agents in Europe purchased punches and matrices of numerals and punctuation marks, together with fonts of roman type, along with other equipment, materials, books, and luxury products. It is also possible that Western merchants brought them, at Peter's request. We know that the letter-founder Mikhail Yefremov was casting roman fonts, which must have been of foreign origin, as early as 1703. In the first books composed in the new fonts, at least three sizes of minuscule numerals from several types were used, as well as roman periods, commas, colons, semicolons, hyphens, brackets, and braces. The

Figure 10. First page of final Azbuka (ABC) with Peter's corrections, 1710.

fact that in the earliest publications they do not always match the size of the rest of the text and do not always align to the baseline proves that in the early days, numerals from other roman fonts of similar sizes were used. Although this has never been properly investigated, one can suppose, judging from later publications, that by the end of Peter's reign, when there were already several printshops in St. Petersburg, the new capital of the country, Russian craftsmen had learned how to manufacture their own numerals and punctuation marks.

Peter's reformed Cyrillic type was later called *grazhdanskiy shrift* (Civil Type) because it was used for the composition of secular literature. During the reign of Peter the Great, the Civil Type was used in the printing of over 400 books; the Church Slavonic *poluustav* in its pre-reform shape was used only for the printing needs of the church.

Since the Petrine type reform, the latinized form of Cyrillic has been traditional in Russia for nearly 300 years, and Cyrillic type has developed in parallel to Latin, repeating virtually all the stages of its development and changes of style: Classical, Romantic, Art Nouveau, Constructivist, Post-Modernist, etc.

COULD THE PETRINE LETTERFORMS BE DIFFERENT?

It is evident that the design of the new Cyrillic type was done at the amateur level, although this was probably the first attempt in Russia to use a modern approach to type design, including sketching, the creation of original drawings, the manufacturing of type punches and matrices, then the printing of tests, with successive proofreading and improvements to the type. We don't know which of the roman faces was used as the starting point for the design of the new letters. It is most likely that there was no single prototype and that the structure of the Civil Type was not based on one particular roman font. The sketches were a kind of eclectic mixture of the different roman faces available in Peter's time (from late Dutch old-style roman to *romain du roi*). As a result, the Civil Type became very distinctive, but in fact its distinction was just the stylized trappings of the roman style, an imitation of it.

There were a number of reasons for this result (haste in general, the war, lack of skilled people), but the main one was the absence of a unified handwriting script that could have served as the basis for the development of a new type. Another was the amateur approach to the design. Of course Peter the Great was a specialist in a lot of areas; as Pushkin described him, he was '...academician and hero, navigator and carpenter...' But he was not a type designer, even if he made the sketches of the new letters himself. Other specialists (draftsmen, punchcutters, printers) were subordinate in their status to the august designer. And he had a very difficult task, trying to combine elements that were so different in style (the old *poluustav* letters and roman characters); in the absence of any stable handwritten form for these letters, the result of such a combination could be only a hodgepodge. Later modification of the Civil Type was rather haphazard, done by trial and error: different forms of letters were tried out, and new character forms were substituted for the old ones; uppercase letters repeated the form of the lowercase ones, and vice versa; and stresses were introduced and then rejected again. It took over a hundred years more after that type reform to stabilize Cyrillic letterforms.

On the other hand, some radicals (especially some Russian graphic designers) continue to believe that Peter should have given an order to all Russians to switch to the Latin alphabet, as he did with beards and smoking tobacco. If this had happened, from the cultural point of view this country would have ended up not so different from the West, and we would not have met so many difficulties with international communications and the Internet; we would have been able to use all the treasures of the Latin types accumulated by Western civilization. So we should immediately correct the emperor's mistake!

I do not support this viewpoint, though it is quite evident that the Latin alphabet has had a longer evolution than the Cyrillic, and its artistic virtues are in no doubt. But Russia follows its own historical way, especially in type development. Still, the results of the Petrine type reform could have been different; and being a type designer, I often try to imagine what might have been done if they had better material to work with.

THE WAY IT IS DONE IN RUSSIA

Of course everything should have begun with choosing the best Latin prototype for the new Cyrillic alphabet. Having arrived in Holland in 1697 as a member of the Great Embassy, Peter I could still see the best samples of the Dutch old-style roman in use. At the beginning of the 18th century it was possible to encounter Elsevir type traditions in many countries, including Holland, Germany, and England, which had a lot of printing houses stocked with the types of such masters as Cristoffel van Dijck, Bartholomeus Voskens, and Nicholas Kis (Miklós Tótfalusi Kis).

Nicholas Kis (1650–1702) was the oldest contemporary of the Russian type reformer. Of Hungarian origin, he worked in Amsterdam learning punchcutting and typographic skills from 1680 to 1689, in order to create his own type for publishing the Hungarian Bible. He had to cut a lot of typefaces for other type-foundries to finance the Bible printing. After finishing his mission he went back to Transylvania, established a printshop in the town of Koloszvár (now Cluj in Romania), and till the end of his life published different kinds of literature in Latin and Hungarian,

tra ſenarium impenſo, in.
ſam hanc mundi machinam
cum omni ſuo ornatu ac ple
nitudine conſummatam cer-
neres.

Parangon Curſ

Dum itaque oportunum cenſuit,
vocavit ipſe ea quæ non erant,ſti
teruntque ſe illico ad nutum vo-
cantis potentem sine mora ; adeo

Figure 11. Nicholas
Kis's Amsterdam type
specimen. Parangon
roman and italic, c.1687.

trying to educate his people. While he was still in Amsterdam, Kis became so famous and in so much demand for his punchcutting skills that
he got orders not only from Dutch type-founders but from typographers
in other countries. Kis's types were found in Germany, Poland, Sweden,
England, and Italy (figure 11). I believe that his types are the most beautiful of all romans, and at the same time they are not that distant from
Peter the Great's epoch. It would have been quite natural to select these
types as a prototype for the Civil Type.

It is noteworthy that Peter I knew someone who was acquainted with
Kis. This was Nicolaas Cornelius Witsen, the Mayor of Amsterdam, a
traveler and geographer, and the publisher of books on shipbuilding and
Siberian geography, who received the Russian Great Embassy during
their stay in Amsterdam in 1697. Only a few years before this, Witsen
had recommended Kis to the Georgian Tsar Archil II (who was staying in
Moscow at the time) as an excellent punchcutter. In 1687, at the request
of the Georgian Governor, Kis manufactured several Georgian types,
samples of which were discovered in the University Library in Uppsala,
Sweden. (In addition to Georgian, Kis made some Hebrew, Greek, and
Armenian types, and also Syrian, Samaritan, and Coptic types, though
the fact that these last three were manufactured is known only from one
of Kis's letters).

About fifteen years ago I made my first attempt at following in Peter's
footsteps when I made some sketches based on the letterforms of the
typeface known as Janson. The prototype of this typeface was found in
the Haas-Drugulin printing house in Leipzig at the beginning of the
twentieth century, and at first it was mistakenly attributed to Anton
Janson (1620–1687), a Dutch craftsman who worked in Leipzig. In 1954,
however, after comparing type specimens, the English typographic his-

torian Harry Carter and the Hungarian wood-engraver György Buday came to the conclusion that the so-called Janson types were in fact the work of Nicholas Kis.

In 1996, after the ParaType company in Moscow signed an agreement with Bitstream to license their typefaces and develop Cyrillic versions of them, I was very glad to come back to this work; I based my renewed efforts on Bitstream Kis, which is very close to Janson. On the one hand, this gave me an opportunity to make a modern text type of the late Baroque Dutch roman style, which at that time had no analogues in Cyrillic typography. On the other hand, I wanted to make its letterforms a bit archaic, resembling the Petrine Civil Type, and thus in some way correct it in the modern age, by making the shape of the letters less contradictory.

From the very beginning it was clear that the Cyrillic letters that corresponded to Latin ones should remain the same as in the Latin alphabet. I was not going to repeat Peter's mistake and invent a new form of A and other Latin letters just because I liked the shape created by Nicholas Kis. The form of the Cyrillic characters that are structurally close to Latin should also be defined by the Latin alphabet, so as to stay in the framework of modern traditions of Cyrillic type design. The problem was not only in defining the forms of the Cyrillic letters that have no analogues in the Latin alphabet, which can have variant forms, but also in deciding whether to keep Cyrillic К, к similar to Latin K, k or to find another form for the diagonals, more specific to Cyrillic. The same problem arises for Я, я relative to the Latin R.

It was also necessary to design an italic, and that was essentially a completely different problem. Cyrillic italics appeared only in the post-Petrine period, in the 1730s; and unlike European italics, the form of the first Russian italic letters was based not on handwriting but on engraved inscriptions in book titles, geographical maps, and other printed matter. Only at the end of the 18th and beginning of the 19th centuries did the form of Cyrillic lowercase italics begin to resemble the Latin. Probably this is due to the mass import of Didot types from France, and to the activities of the Russian type manufacturers August Semen, Alexander Pluchard, and George Revillon in particular. That is why the structure and appearance of modern Cyrillic italics are much closer to the corresponding Latin than are the forms of Cyrillic roman, most of which just repeat the forms of the uppercase letters. Considering the fact that one of the common forms of handwriting in Russian of the 19th and early 20th centuries was a kind of connected script written with a pointed pen (so-called 'English' calligraphy), one can conclude that the structure of Cyrillic italics — no matter how paradoxical this may sound — is more settled than the roman *because* it developed later.

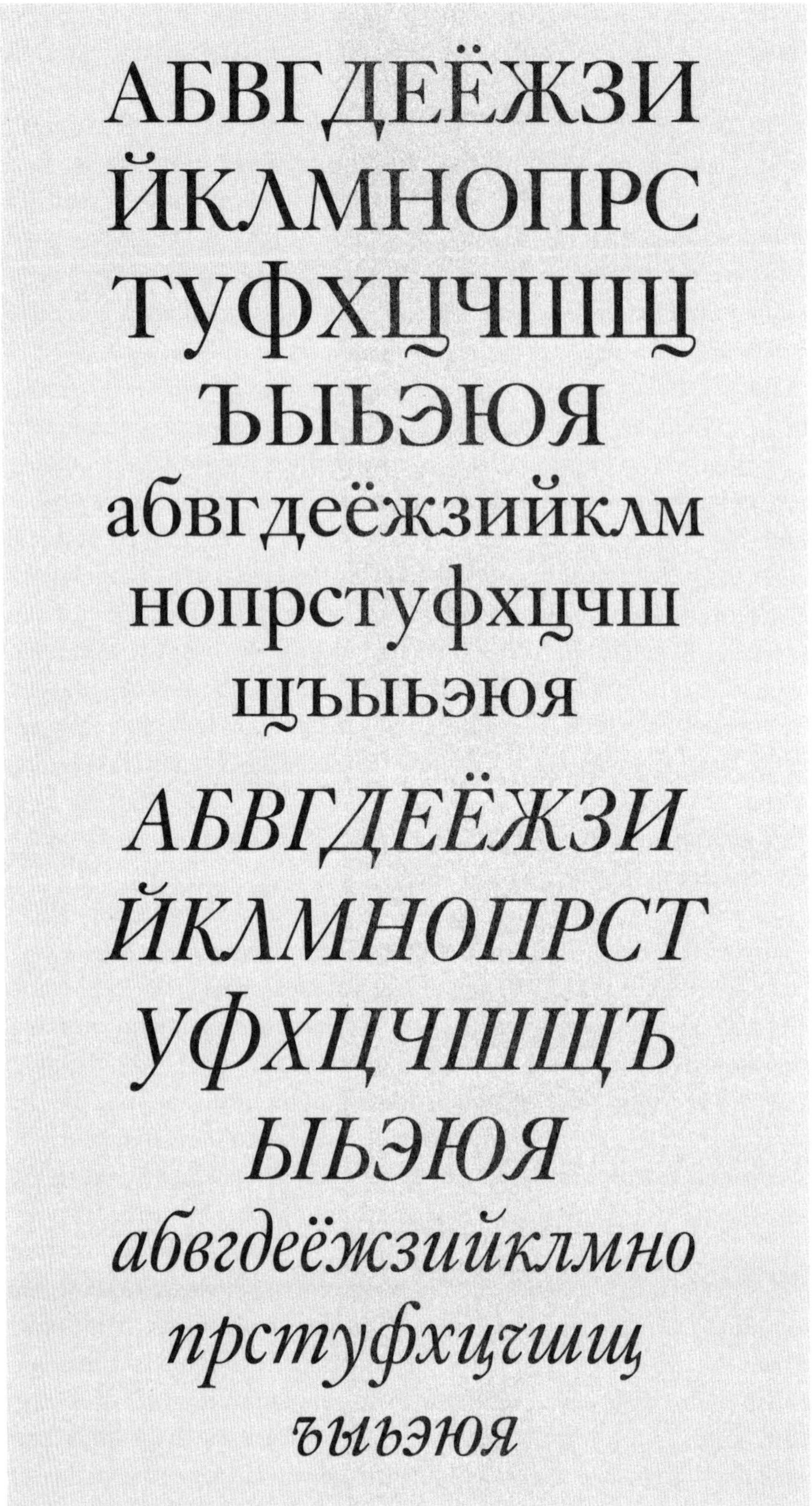

АБВГДЕЁЖЗИ
ЙКЛМНОПРС
ТУФХЦЧШЩ
ЪЫЬЭЮЯ
абвгдеёжзийклм
нопрстуфхцчш
щъыьэюя

АБВГДЕЁЖЗИ
ЙКЛМНОПРСТ
УФХЦЧШЩЪ
ЫЬЭЮЯ
абвгдеёжзийклмно
прстуфхцчшщ
ъыьэюя

Figure 12. Kis Cyrillic roman and italic, 2001.

As a rule, in the lowercase Cyrillic italics some letters are the same as Latin ones; the structure of many others is related to Latin italic or Cyrillic upright letters, and all that needs defining is a few details, especially the ascenders and descenders. Only a few italic characters require special attention, but their analogues can be found in the handwritten scripts of the 19th century. Uppercase italic letters are usually made by inclining the upright letters and making any necessary subsequent adjustments.

KIS CYRILLIC

In the summer of 1997, when I drew the sketches of the roman and italic Cyrillic Kis on tracing paper, it was still not clear to me what changes ought to be made to the shapes of the Civil Type. In the roman, the outlines of most of the letters that were specific to Cyrillic were based on the types of the middle and late 18th century, and also on modern Cyrillic typefaces that interpret the forms of 18th century types (*Academy, Bannikova, Elizabeth*). So in the beginning I was going to make letters Ж, ж, and К, к different in nature, as they were in the Civil Type (Ж, ж, к with drop-shaped upper terminals, and with wave-shaped legs in К, к). The double-bowled Ф, ф, the wave-shaped bottom terminals in з, э, and the wave-shaped descending elements in Ц, ц, Щ, щ in general repeated the structure of similar letters from the *Academy* and *Elizabeth* faces. The trapezoidal Д, д, Л, л on the other hand resembled modern types (in Peter's time the Д had the form of a right-angled triangle and the Л that of an isosceles triangle with inclined side strokes). З, with a drop-shaped bottom terminal, resembled forms of the Petrine engravings.

Further, in 1997–98 (on the computer), I changed the structure of some characters quite a bit from what I had done in the sketches. I redefined the structure of Ж, ж and к taking К as a sample (with the straight double-serifed diagonal at the top and the wave-shaped bottom one). I replaced the drop-shaped bottom terminal of З with a slightly inclined beak like the one in С and Э. I then replaced the trapezoidal form of Л, л with the historical triangle form. All these corrections made the roman shapes stylistically more orderly, but the Cyrillic counterpart still did not match the Latin model exactly.

Everything was a bit simpler with the italic. Unlike the roman outlines, practically all the italic characters were a success from the very beginning, and in later refinement all they needed was some changes in proportion, color, and a few details. For the low case *ж* I chose a zigzag structure, and for *ч* a handwritten form from the late 18th–early 19th century. The structure of some of the italic capitals, however, had to be changed to match related roman ones.

Being busy with other projects, I had to interrupt the work on the Cyrillic version of Kis for a while. A discussion in 1999 with Maxim Zhukov, our consultant on Cyrillic, helped me realize how to approach the rest of the work. The essence of his comments was that I should stick to the historical roman forms that corresponded to the general style of the type I was creating. I replaced the trapezoidal form of Д, д with a right-triangle structure with triangle descenders, which is closer to the form of the 18th century. I replaced the double-bowled structure of the lowercase ф with a form close to the corresponding letter in the Civil Type, with one oval crossed by the vertical stroke, as in the Greek letter *phi*. In order to stick to the chosen style, the capital Ф also got the same shape as in the Petrine type, with an ascender and a descender. To support a projecting Ф I had to draw a capital У with the tail descending down the way it does in the Petrine type. And finally, I replaced the double-sided serifs at the ends of the top diagonals of lowercase ж, к with drop-shaped terminals like those in the Petrine engravings and in the small sizes of the Civil Type.

And so, having retained characters that corresponded to the Latin old style, I gave the roman caps some features of Cyrillic types of the beginning of the 18th century. Similar changes were introduced into the italic capitals *Д, Л, У, Ф*. In order to preserve the stylistic unity of upper case *Ц* and *Щ*, I replaced the wave-shaped descenders with small triangular elements similar to those in *Д*. At the beginning of 2000, the work on the basic Cyrillic alphabet was generally finished. Only the development of additional national characters required by standard encodings (Cyrillic, Eastern European, Turkish, Baltic) and the introduction of kerning for compliant character pairs were still to be finished. After the necessary technical processing, ParaType released Kis Cyrillic in PostScript Type 1 and TrueType formats for both Mac and Windows platforms at the end of September, 2001.

Bibliography

Bringhurst, Robert. 'The Invisible Hand. Part I. Neoclassical Letterforms' (*Serif*, No. 4, Claremont, Calif., 1996)

Haiman, György. *Nicholas Kis. A Hungarian Punch-Cutter and Printer* (San Francisco, 1983)

Kaldor, Ivan. 'The Genesis of the Russian Grazhdanskii Shrift or Civil Type', Parts I & II (*The Journal of Typographic Research*, Vol. III, No. 4, 1969; Vol. IV, No. 2, Cleveland, 1970)

Shitsgal, Abram. *Repertuar russkogo typografskogo grazhdanskogo shrifta XVIII veka. Ch. I. Grazhdanskiy shrift pervoy chetverti XVIII veka 1708–1725* (Moscow, 1981)

Shitsgal, Abram. *Russkiy grazhdanskiy shrift 1708–1958* (Moscow, 1959)

Shitsgal, Abram. *Russkiy typografskiy shrift. Voprosy istorii I praktika primeneniya*

(Moscow, first edition 1974, second edition 1985)

Stauffacher, Jack. 'The Transylvanian Phoenix: the Kis-Janson Types in the Digital Era' (*Visible Language*, Vol. XIX, No. 1, Cleveland, 1985)

Yefimov, Vladimir. 'Dramaticheskaya istoriya kirillitsy. Velikiy petrovskiy perelom' (*Da!*, No. 0, Moscow, 1994)

Zhukov, Maxim. 'The Pecularities of Cyrillic Letterforms: Design Variations and Correlation in Russian Typefaces' (*Typography Papers*, No. 1, 1996. University of Reading, Great Britain)

ADAM TWARDOCH

Picked herring and strawberry ice cream

DESIGNING POLISH DIACRITICS

N EARLY ALL the languages of Western Europe are written using the Latin script: Germanic languages (English, German, Swedish, Dutch etc.), Romance languages (French, Italian, Spanish or Portuguese) and other languages such as Finnish (a Finno-Ugric language) or Welsh (a Celtic language). In Central and Eastern Europe, languages spoken primarily by members of Roman Catholic or Protestant churches use Latin script: this includes all Western Slavic languages (e.g. Polish, Czech, Slovak), some Southern Slavic languages (Slovenian, the Croatian version of Serbo-Croatian), Baltic languages (Latvian, Lithuanian) and Finno-Ugric languages (Hungarian, Estonian). Latin script is also used to write other languages spoken all around the world (e.g. Albanian, Aleut, Fijian, Greenlandic, Malay, Maltese, Navajo, Ndebele, Quechua, Samoan, Swahili, Vietnamese, Wolof, and many others).

In the early Middle Ages, people of Western and Central Europe spoke many languages, but most of the writing was still done in the Latin language, the lingua franca of those times. If a geographic or personal name from the region of today's France, Germany, or Poland had to be written down, a scribe tried to express sounds not present in the Latin language by approximating them somehow using the Latin letters. These 'rules of spelling' varied heavily from case to case. Gradually from approximately the 9th century on, and more rapidly during the high and late Middle Ages, the number of texts written in local languages increased. Finally, the Reformation movement and Gutenberg's invention of casting movable type boosted the market for publications written in Europe's local and national languages.

The invention of movable type emphasized the need for standardized and simplified character sets and spelling rules: the printers wished to minimize the set of characters they used, the publications were reaching a much larger audience, and the first kinds of publishing processes were introduced giving birth to professions such as typesetter and proofreader. Authors and printers tried to find efficient ways to write sounds not found in Latin. One approach was to use combinations of two or more letters (digraphs, trigraphs). Another method was to employ 'accented' letters, equipped with diacritical marks – small signs (dots, curves, circles, dashes) attached to or placed above or below the base letterform, indicating a modified phonetic value (from the Greek word *diakritikós* meaning 'distinctive'). Yet another technique was to use extra letters or letterlike characters. In a Europe split by national and religious borders, each language developed its own way of using Latin letters and diacritics. The sound of a palatalized *s*, as in the word 'shop', can be written as *sh* in English, as *sch, s, g* and *ch* in German (depending on dialects and context), as *ch* in French, as *sz* and *ś* in Polish, and as *š* in Czech. A set of more than 150 alphabetic characters is needed to write all Latin-scripted languages of modern Europe.

READ THE RECIPE FIRST

Type designers from Western Europe and North America, and more recently from other countries, have been refining and improving the style and appearance of Latin letterforms for centuries. With several thousand typefaces designed to date, the Latin letters have been used to set text in a multitude of languages, and have been on display and under the critique of designers and readers from many countries throughout many years. The Latin letter has become a truly global medium, serving cultures from around the world. On the other hand, the evolution of diacritics usually occured in isolation. From language to language and from country to country, diacritical marks have gained different shapes and different positions.

Before the invention of laser printers, personal computers, and digital fonts, typefaces were developed for particular markets and printing equipment. Lead type was cut by punchcutters familiar with the specifics of a given language. In England, Germany, France, or Italy, printers bought type from local foundries. Polish printing houses imported type from Italy or Germany, but then resident Polish punchcutters localized the fonts, i.e. added the accented letters. There was no global typography. Even in the 20th century, typefaces were made for particular typesetting and phototypesetting systems. As a result of the political division of Europe after World War II, most typefaces used in the Slavic-speaking countries were developed or at least localized there.

Desktop publishing systems brought substantial changes to the font business. Large foundries ceased to exist or completely changed their profiles. Small companies and individuals started designing and releasing digital fonts. With Fontographer, everybody was able to try his or her hand at designing type.

The 'digital revolution' started in the USA and in Western Europe, so most digital fonts were designed there, but designers proficient in Latin letterforms lacked the know-how to draw foreign diacritics properly. Specimens showing well-designed Slavic diacritics, written in 'unintelligible' languages like Czech or Polish were hardly available in the West. But market pressures forced foundries to release fonts quickly.

Consequently, the quality of diacritics is poor (with a few notable exceptions). French or German accents are usually acceptable, but Slavic diacritics are mostly mediocre. The design of those characters often does not match the overall typeface style. The accents are misplaced, their color and stress do not go well with the letters. Sometimes, accents are simply borrowed from a different typeface.

FIVE HUNDRED WAYS TO SERVE CHICKEN

The Unicode Standard favors unification of diacritical marks, which means that each font can only have one glyph of a given kind (unless advanced techniques like language-dependant OpenType layout features are used). However, typographic traditions in shaping or positioning accented letters vary among countries or languages. Instead of a separate *umlaut* sign for German (*mögen*, to like) and a *tréma* sign for Spanish (*güisqui*, whisky) or French (*Noël*, Christmas), the Unicode Standard encodes just one *diaeresis* mark (U+00A8), which is to be used for both *umlaut* and *tréma*.

The problem is most evident in display typography. In Germany, it is permitted to place the *umlaut* inside the capital U or the O, but Spanish or French readers may find it unacceptable. Similarly, the preferred angle, size, and placement of the acute mark (´, U+00B4) may vary from country to country, depending on national traditions. The Polish language uses an *acute*-like mark (´, Polish *kreska*) and a *dot* mark (˙, Polish *kropka*), while French uses *acute* (´, French *accent aigu*), *grave* (`` ` ``), *circumflex* (^), and occasionally *diaeresis* (¨, French *tréma*). To visually differentiate *acute* from *grave* in French, the accents need to have a pronounced slant to the left or to the right, but do not necessarily have to be very tall. In Polish, however, the *kreska* only needs a little slant to the right, but should be tall enough not to be confused with *kropka*.

The Czech language also makes very extensive use of the *acute* mark (Czech *čárka*). When text is set in all capitals and there is little space above A or O, the accents need to be 'compressed'. In Czech, the accent typically becomes very flat, nearly horizontal, and touches the letter or remains above it. In Polish, the accent gets reduced in size but remains rather vertical, with little slant to the right. It stays above, touches the letter, or even pierces the top of the letter (figure 1).

It is important to understand that diacritical marks are not an extra 'gadget' in written text. They are an essential element of the written lan-

PSÍ komando **CÓRKA PUŁKU**

Figure 1: In display typography, accents may need to be 'compressed' when text is set in all capitals. This can be done differently depending on language. Left: Czech lettering by Jaroslav Šváb (1967), right: Polish lettering by Witold Chmielewski (1957).

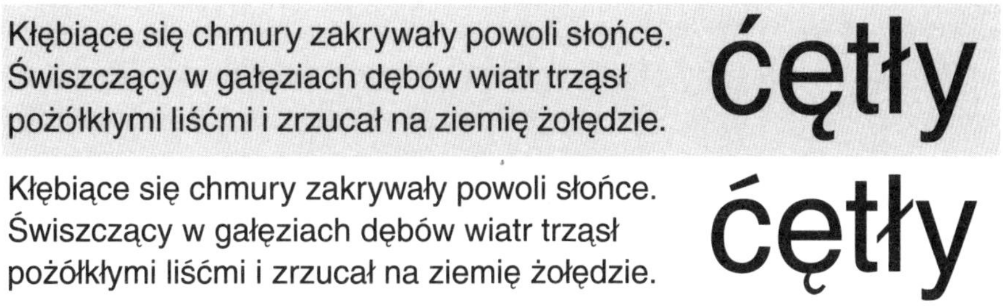

Kłębiące się chmury zakrywały powoli słońce. Świszczący w gałęziach dębów wiatr trząsł pożółkłymi liśćmi i zrzucał na ziemię żołędzie. **ćętły**

Kłębiące się chmury zakrywały powoli słońce. Świszczący w gałęziach dębów wiatr trząsł pożółkłymi liśćmi i zrzucał na ziemię żołędzie. **ćętły**

Figure 2: Diacritics need to harmonize with the design of the typeface (top). Poorly designed diacritics may ruin the overall appearance of the text (bottom).

guage; they need to harmonize with the overall design of the typeface just as much as the figures or punctuation marks do. The diacritical marks need to match the design of the basic letterforms in color, shape, stress and contrast. An accented letter must be designed in such a way that it is clearly distinguishable from another accented letter and from the basic letter. Poorly designed diacritics may ruin the overall appearance of a typeface and may seriously impair the legibility of the text. Figure 2 shows well designed and poorly designed Polish diacritics for Helvetica. Please note the bad spacing of the letters *łkły* in the word *pożółkłymi* in the bottom example. The reader is likely to ignore thin and poorly drawn *ogoneks*, thus misreading the text.

COOKED IS BETTER THAN RARE

The oldest Polish sentence recorded in writing can be found in the Latin text Księga Henrykowska (Henry's Book, 1270): *day ut ia pobrusa a ti poziwai* ('giveth to me, I shall stir and you shall rest'). In today's spelling, the sentence would be: *daj, ać ja pobruszę, a ty poczywaj.* We see that written language of the 13th century did not make use of diacritics. Over a century later, the essay *Orthographia Bohemica*, published 1406 or 1412 and attributed to the most important 15th-century Czech religious reformer, Jan Hus, presented a modern, consistent phonetic method of writing the Czech language. The author suggested denoting long vowels with an acute mark and palatalized consonants with a dot, which later evolved into a *caron* (˘, Cz. *háček*) above the letter. Hus's system greatly influenced other European languages by being the very first to constitute the principle of using diacritics to write distinctive sounds.

The Polish language of the 15th century was written very inconsistently. The scribes freely mixed phonetic rules of French, Czech, and German to express Polish sounds in Roman letters. Shortly before Gutenberg's invention, in 1440, Jakub Parkosz published a set of spelling rules for Polish, but this had no lasting effect on writing practice in Poland. Some decades later (1512–14), Stanisław Zaborowski published two texts on Polish spelling. He adopted and extended Hus's phonetic system, utilizing one dot above the letter to denote modified consonants (*ċ, ṡ, ṙ, ż*) and contracted vowels (*ȧ, ȯ*), two dots above to denote palatalized consonants, and a *virgula* (a diagonal stroke, *kreska*) to denote nasal vowels and the *ew* sound (*ł*). 1551. Stanisław Murzynowski modified Zaborowski's spelling, replacing the two dots with a *virgula* (which later evolved into an *acute*), and used digraphs like *cz, sz, rz* instead of the letters *ċ, ṡ, ṙ*.

Throughout the first half of the 16th century, Cracow-based printers published numerous Polish texts in blackletter typefaces. Instead of cutting and casting new letters to follow Zaborowski's and Murzynowski's recommendations, the printers used Latin syncopes (contractions) that looked similar to the proposed diacritics. For example, rather than denoting nasalized *e* (*ę*) with *e virgula*, the printers used *e caudata*: an *e* with a long tail (Pol. *ogonek*), which once represented the syncope of the Latin dipthong *ae* (figure 3).

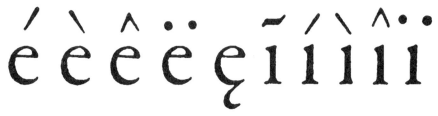

Figure 3: The Gros Canon typeface by Claude Garamond (c. 1530) included the *e caudata* character. The character once represented the syncope of the Latin dipthong *ae* but was later used to denote Polish nasalized *e*. Note that Garamond's diacritical marks are very pronounced.

One of these printers was Jan Januszowski, who 1594 published a book, *Nowy karakter polski,* presenting three spelling proposals devised by the printer himself and by two other authors (both highly educated noblemen). For the purpose of this project, Januszowski designed and cut a new typeface that included all the diacritics needed in the book. In-

*A a á ą b ƀ c ć ʒ d dƀ ƌ ƌƀ e é è ę f g h ch i j k l ł m ḿ n ń
o ó ò p ṕ q r ʒ ſ ſ́ ß t u v w ẃ x y z ź ż.*

*a ą b c ć cz d dz dź dż e ę f g h ch i j k l ł m n ń
o ó p q r rz s ś sz t u v w x y z ź ż*

Figure 4: Polish alphabet. Top: the alphabet as of 1594 (typeface: Nowy Karakter
Polski by Jan Januszowski), bottom: today's alphabet (typeface: Fenway by Matthew
Carter). The letters *q, v,* and *x* are only used in foreign words. Digraphs are listed
here but normally are not considered part of the alphabet.

terestingly, among the three, it is the printer's spelling, not the educated
noblemen's, that has been widely accepted by the public. Today's Polish
alphabet is virtually identical to that of Januszowski, with the exception of
the contracted vowels (*á, é, è, ò*), and of some palatalized consonants (*ƀ, ḿ,
ṕ, ẃ*) which disappeared from the language over the years.

KUCHNIA POLSKA, POLISH CUISINE

The Polish alphabet uses the Roman alphabet with three diacritic marks
(*′, acute,* Pol. *kreska;* ˙, *dot,* Pol. *kropka* and ˛, Pol. *ogonek*) as well as one
extra letter (*ł,* pronounced as in <u>w</u>ood, and variously named *ew, l-barred,
l with stroke,* or *l-slash*). *Kreska* and *kropka* are placed above the letters:
five consonants (*ć* spoken as in <u>ch</u>eese, *ń* like in Spanish se<u>ñ</u>or, *ś* as in <u>sh</u>ip,
ź and *ż* as in <u>tr</u>ea<u>s</u>ure) and one vowel (*ó,* as in m<u>oo</u>n). *Ogonek* is attached at
the bottom right of the nasal vowels (*ą* as in French b<u>on</u> appétit, *ę* similar
to the French *fin*).

Kropka is the least problematic diacritical mark. It only occurs above
the lowercase *z* (*ż*) and capital *Z* (*Ż*). *Kropka* should always be of the
same shape and size as the *dot* above *i* and should be aligned to the visual vertical axis of the letter and to the height of the *dot* above *i* (figure
5.3–5.8). In capital *Ż,* the *dot* is centered above the capitals. In some
calligraphic scripts or all-capitals display typefaces, *Ż* can be drawn as
a *Z* with a horizontal stroke in the middle (figure 5.18, 5.19). The form
and color of *kropka* should match the overall appearance of the typeface.
Obviously, the dot does not necessarily have to be round (figure 5.8). In
typefaces with the *dot* placed unusually high above *i,* the *dot* above *ż* may
be placed lower.

Kreska is the Polish *acute*-like mark: a small diagonal stroke above the
letter. As noted, in Polish tradition *kreska* is rather upright and has only a
little slant to the right (figure 5.1–5.11). Flat, almost horizontal *acutes* are
not suitable as Polish *kreskas.* The color and form of *kreska* should match
the overall appearance of the typeface. In capital letters, *kreska* may be
flatter than in lowercase letters. In all-capitals display typefaces, *kreska*

[153]

gwiętłyćką gwiętłyćką gwiżętłyćką gwiżętłyćką gwiżętłyćką gwiżętłyćką gwiżętłyćką gwiżętłyćką gwiętłyćką gwiętłyćką Książęcych spóźnień czułość KŁĘBIĄ KŁĘBĄ KŁĘBIĄ KŁĘBIĄ KŁĘBIĄ KŁĘBIĄ ZYŁEŚ Zyłeś błękitną Łąkę Władek Jagiełło ŁÓŻĄ ŁÓŻĄ ŁÓŻĄ ŁÓŻĄ

Figure 5: Examples of well-designed Polish diacritics.

1. Linotype Ergo (Gary Munch) 2. Bauer Bodoni (Giambattista Bodoni/Heinrich Jost)[a]
3. Linotype Really (Gary Munch) 4. Fenway Italic (Matthew Carter)
5, 6. Bliss (Jeremy Tankard) 7. Interstate (Tobias Frere-Jones)[a]
8. ITC Kabel (Rudolf Koch/Victor Caruso)[a] 9. Lunatix (Zuzana Licko)[a]
10. Triplex Italic (John Downer)[a] 11. Silentium Pro (Jovica Veljović)
12. Linotype Really (Gary Munch) 13. ITC Souvenir (Ed Benguiat)[b]
14. Valetta (John Hudson) 15. Bliss (Jeremy Tankard) 16. Waters Titling Pro (Julian Waters)
17. Flux (Monib Mahdavi)[a] 18. Rusticana (Adrian Frutiger)[c] 19. Excelsior (František Štorm)[a]
20. Caflisch Script Pro (Robert Slimbach) 21. Shelley Allegro (Matthew Carter)[c]
22. Monotype Script (unknown)[ac] 23. Fenway (Matthew Carter)
24. Półtawski (Adam Półtawski) 25. Blocka (unknown) 26. Fenice (Aldo Novarese)[b].

Diacritics designed by original authors unless indicated:
[a]Adam Twardoch, [b]Stefan Szczypka, [c]Andrzej Tomaszewski.

can be compressed by reducing its size and, in some cases, crossing the upper part of the letter with the stroke (figure 1, right example). The lower part of *kreska* should be aligned to the vertical axis of the letter, so that the accent appears slightly shifted to the right.

Ogonek is a diacritical mark which causes much trouble to type designers. It is not a floating accent, but rather becomes part of the lower right of the letter. In most cases, it has the form of a sickle or a hook, with one end attached to the body of the letter and the other end pointing to the right. It has a calligraphic nature, following the stroke proportions, the contrast, color, and form of the typeface. In particular, the contrast between thick and thin elements should be consistent (figure 5.2). *Ogonek* should be large enough to be recognized as such. In many cases, it may descend as deeply as the stems of *p* and *q*.

Obviously, *ogonek* does not necessarily have to be rounded. Blackletter types or display typefaces with unusual letterforms may have unusually formed, broken *ogoneks* (figure 5.9–5.10). Depending on how closed the letterforms are, the terminal may end downwards, leaving the inner space open (figure 5.7–5.8), or it may take a turn and end upwards, closing the inner space of the accent (figure 5.2, 5.10). *Ogonek* should not extend beyond the right edge of the base letter. In the vast majority of cases, *ogonek* should be connected with the body of the letter; in some display typefaces, however, it may be treated as a floating accent. In geometric all-capitals display sanserifs, *ogonek* can have the form of a simple diagonal stroke (since it was originally drawn as a *virgula*). To avoid unwanted overlapping effects in digital fonts, all letters with the *ogonek* accent should be outline characters rather than composite characters.

In uppercase *Ę*, *ogonek* should be attached at the baseline near the right part of the baseline stroke, and should be right-aligned with the upper beak (serif) of the letter.

There are three ways of attaching *ogonek* to uppercase *Ą*. You can attach it at the baseline to the outer serif of the right diagonal stroke of *A* (figure 5.24). In most cases, this produces poor results because the letter looks like it is flipping to the right (a heavy *ogonek* hangs on a thin serif). You can also attach it at the baseline to the middle of the right diagonal stroke of *A* (figure 5.23). This usually works fine. The third method is to replace the inner serif of the right diagonal stroke of *A* with *ogonek* (figure 5.12–5.14, 5.16, 5.26). If there is no serif, you should attach *ogonek* to the inner part of the right diagonal stroke (figure 5.15, 5.17, 5.25). In my opinion, this method works best, because removing the serif reduces visual noise in that part of the letter.

Drawing lowercase *q* is tricky because the danger of a visual clash is relatively high. Depending on the style of the typeface, *ogonek* may be attached anywhere at the terminal of the letter *a* (not to the bowl!). Remember to avoid extending *ogonek* beyond the right edge of the base letter (figure 5.11 is just barely acceptable).

Drawing lowercase ę is most difficult because the bottom of *e* is round rather than flat. Please observe figure 2: you should always draw the letter ę as shown in the top example! *Ogonek* in ę should not be centered like a cedilla. It should rather be smoothly connected to the right part of the terminal (approx. at two-thirds to three-quarters of the character width), or to the end of the terminal (figure 5.1–5.11).

Ł is not composed out of the letter *l* and a *slash sign* (/), although this glyph is called *lslash* in PostScript glyph naming conventions. The lowercase letter ł is an *l* with a diagonal stroke in the middle. This diagonal stroke should never be too heavy or too large. In most cases, it should be as thick as the thin diagonal stroke of the letter *x*. The terminals of the stroke may be cut off vertically (figure 5.7) or diagonally (figure 5.8), depending on the shape of the terminals of the letter *x*. In most cases, the diagonal stroke should cross the letter *l* at its visual centre (which is usually higher than the geometrical centre). Typically, the right part of the diagonal stroke is slightly longer than the left part, especially if *l* has a bowled terminal or a spur at the ascender. The right terminal of the diagonal stroke should ideally end at the x height or slightly above it, but in some cases, it may end slightly below the x height. The rule of thumb for the angle between the baseline and the diagonal stroke is 30 degree (figure 5.1–5.11). Letter pairs łw, ły, łt should be kerned carefully.

The uppercase Ł is an L with a diagonal stroke. The middle of the diagonal stroke should be aligned at the height of the horizontal bar of capital *E* or slightly above it. The right part of the diagonal stroke is substantially longer than the left part, at least as long as the horizontal bar of *E*. The diagonal stroke should not be thicker than the thin diagonal stroke of the letter *X* (figure 5.12–5.18, 5.23–5.26).

In calligraphic styles, however, ł has a fairly long straight or curvy stroke, slightly ascending or nearly horizontal, and is placed just at the top or slightly above the top of the letter (figure 5.19–5.22). This script form of the letter ł is used in everyday Polish handwriting and should be used in script typefaces. The stroke in capital Ł is usually curvy or nearly horizontal and crosses the letter in the middle (see 5.21). In script faces, the double-letter sequence łł may cause a visual clash, so a ligature may be required (figure 5.22).

DINNER IS SERVED

Poorly designed diacritics ruin the appearance of a typeface and impair the legibility of text. Diacritic characters are an essential element of typographic communication, no less important than the basic letterforms. Drawing good accented letters is more time-consuming than building them from prefabricated composites, but in the long run, only a well designed typeface has a chance to survive on the market and to become a popular choice with users. My list of recipes is intended to help a type designer avoid most serious mistakes. After you have mastered the rules, you may start breaking them. Otherwise, you may end up serving pickled herring with strawberry ice cream to your readers.

Acknowledgements

Thanks to Zbyszek Czapnik, John Hudson, Ross Mills, Stefan Szczypka, Andrzej Tomaszewski, and Maxim Zhukov. Further information regarding Polish diacritics can be found at http://www.twardoch.com/

bukva:raz!

Type design competition of the
Association Typographique Internationale

bukva:raz!, an international competition of type
design, was organised by the Association Typographique Internationale (ATypI). It is the first event
of this kind since the founding of ATypI in 1957. The
competition was officially announced at the general
meeting of ATypI in Leipzig, on 24 September 2000.

bukva:raz! was a special contribution of ATypI to the
United Nations Year of Dialogue among Civilizations
(2001). bukva:raz! was aimed at promoting cultural
pluralism and encouraging diversity, interaction,
and co-operation in typographic communications.
251 designers from thirty countries, of various
ethnic, linguistic, and cultural backgrounds, contributed to the contest.

Over six hundred entries competed in five categories: Text designs, Display designs, Text/Display
type systems, Type superfamilies, Pi fonts. Fourteen alphabets/writing systems were represented
by the entries to bukva:raz!: Amharic, Arabic,
Armenian, Canadian Aboriginal Syllabics, Cyrillic,
Devanagari, Georgian, Greek, Hebrew, International
Phonetic Alphabet, Japanese, Latin, Ogham, Xishuangbanna Dai (New Tai Lui).

The competition was arranged on behalf of ATypI
by the Type Designers Association, a professional
so-ciety based in Moscow, which unites the best type
design professionals of Russia. The name of the
competition – bukva:raz! – translates as 'letter:one!':
bukva is the Russian for 'letter' (as in 'letter-form')
and raz for 'one' (as in 'two thousand one').

The judging of bukva:raz! took place Moscow, Russia, on 1 and 2 December 2001. The jury of bukva:raz!
included renowned experts in international type
design and typography: Matthew Carter, Yuri Gherchuk, Akira Kobayashi, Lyubov' Kuznetsova, Gerry
Leonidas, Fiona Ross, and Vladimir Yefimov. The jury
was chaired by Maxim Zhukov.

One hundred entries selected by the bukva:raz! jury
to receive Certificates of Design Excellence were
shown at the annual conference of ATypI in Rome in
September 2002, and at the exhibitions in Moscow,
Saint Petersburg, New York, and other locations.

Year of Dialogue among Civilizations

In November 1998, the General Assembly of the United Nations proclaimed the year 2001 as the 'United Nations Year of Dialogue among Civilizations'.

The resolution GA/RES/53/22, proposed by the Islamic Republic of Iran and supported by a large number of countries, invites 'Governments, the United Nations system, including the United Nations Educational, Scientific and Cultural Organization, to plan and implement appropriate cultural, educational and social programmes to promote the concept of dialogue among civilizations, including through organizing conferences and seminars and disseminating information and scholarly material on the subject'.

The celebration of the United Nations Year of Dialogue among Civilizations provides the opportunity to emphasize that the present globalisation process does not only encompass economic, financial, and technological aspects, but must also focus on human, cultural, spiritual dimensions and on the interdependence of humankind and its rich diversity.

Globalisation and the resulting free movement of ideas and human beings allow unprecedented encounters between individuals, societies, and cultures. But it also profoundly affects lifestyles and patterns of behaviour, decision-making processes, and methods of governance, creativity, and forms of expression.

Against this dynamic background, there is a need for a renewed commitment to promote and develop international co-operation and understanding on the basis of the recognition of the equal dignity of individuals and of societies and the uniqueness of their contributions to human advancement.

Association Typographique Internationale

Association Typographique Internationale (ATypI) is the only worldwide organisation dedicated to the pursuit of activity relating to typefaces and typography. ATypI provides the structure for communication, information, and action relating to all matters typographic for the international type community.

Founded in 1957, ATypI not only preserves the culture, tradition, and history of type and typography, it promotes contemporary digital fonts and encourages outstanding typography and typographic design. ATypI has also actively campaigned for the protection of typeface designs.

Membership in ATypI guarantees contact with, and access to, the international community of those who are working with type and preserving the standards of good typography as well as the designers and foundries responsible for modern typefaces and fonts.

Its membership is both individual and corporate and includes type designers, graphic designers, typographers, writers, publishers, educators, students, type foundries, type manufacturers, and distributors. Many of the household names of the type world are active members.

Publications include the collection of Country Delegate reports (published annually), Type journal, a regular newsletter, and other occasional titles.

Sponsors

United Nations
Department of Public Information
United Nations Information Centre in Moscow

Germany
Linotype Library GmbH

Russia
Center Consulting
Children Computer Club
Expo-Park
Moscow State University of Printing Arts
ParaType
Petrovich Restaurant and Club
Public Totem

USA
Carter & Cone Type, Inc.
Taitl Design
Type Directors Club

Media sponsors

Canada
Luc Devroye

Czech Republic
grafika.cz
megaprint.cz
typo.cz

France
Porchez Typofonderie
typotek.free.fr

Germany
1001fonts.com
Milo Typografik
typebox.com

Russia
Abzats
index.ru
Kursiv
Laboratoriya reklamy
Mir Dizayna
Novyi Mir Iskusstva
Publish (Russian edition)
rudesign.ru
Font Project 'Vedi'
yandex.ru

Spain
CODIG magazine

UK
Letraset

USA
creativepro.com
Kame Design
Microsoft Typography
serifmagazine.com
Typographer.com.

United Nations · Nations Unies

Postal address · Adresse postale :
United Nations, NY 10017
Cable address · Adresse télégraphique :
unations newyork

Executive Office of the Secretary-General
Cabinet du Secrétaire Général

Mr. M. Zhukov, ATypI
5719 Faraday Avenue, Riverdale, NY 10471

May 31, 2000

Dear Mr. Zhukov,

Let me express my congratulations to you and to
the Association Typographique Internationale for
your international competition in type design.

To a large extent humankind has been very successful in creating fake boundaries for itself.
Now, hopefully, real time communication and low
cost access to each other across the planet have
opened the door to an era where many of those
fake boundaries will be broken. It is my conviction
that those boundaries reside in the mindset of
people. The most dangerous mindset of all is that
which perceives diversity as a threat, for that is
the mindset of warmongers.

Anything we can do to change that mindset is a
step forward in the direction of a better world.

Your competition, as I understand it, points in the
same direction: to break boundaries and encourage better and easier communication among individual human beings. Through easier communication ignorance will decrease and less ignorance
will lead to less fear which in turn is an ingredient
of a better society.

The year of the Dialogue Among Civilizations needs
a thousand seeds to achieve unity in diversity.
I welcome your contribution to this endeavor.

[*Signed*]
Giandomenico Picco
Personal Representative
of the Secretary General
for the UN Year of the Dialogue
Among Civilizations

Competition categories
[The organisers reserve the right to revise the
categorisation of the entries proposed by the par-
ticipants.]

I. Text designs
Typefaces and type families intended for use in
composition of text for continuous reading.

II. Display designs
Typefaces and type families intended for use in
larger sizes rather than for body text.

III. Text/Display type systems
Extended groups of related typefaces featuring
separate designs for text and display composition
(digital fonts produced in multiple-master format
often fall within this category).

IV. Type superfamilies
Extended groups of related typefaces featuring
designs belonging to different style categories;
e.g., serif and sans-serif, serif and slab serif
(some digital fonts produced in multiple-master
or OpenType formats fall within this category).

V. Pi fonts
Typefaces featuring special character sets for
mathematical, phonetic, and other specialized applications, as well as dingbats, icons, symbols, and
other pictorial items in a font format. Ornament and
border designs are also included in this category.

Notes

Alphabets/writing systems. Typefaces created for
any alphabet or writing system, existing or historical – including, but not limited to, Arabic, Armenian, Chinese, Cyrillic, Devanagari, Georgian, Greek,
Hebrew, Japanese, Korean, Latin – are all eligible,
and should be entered in the appropriate competition category. As necessary, experts in the relevant non-Latin scripts may be invited by the jury
for consultation.

Proprietary typefaces. Typefaces designed for private use, rather than resale, are eligible. They may
include typefaces produced for use by a specific
designer or a design firm, as well as those for corporate or other non-design clients. If the design is
based on an existing typeface, the design source
should be indicated, as well as the intended use of
the proprietary typeface – without identifying the
client: e.g., 'display typeface created for an airline',
'text typeface created for a science publisher,' etc.

Multiple-master typefaces. Multiple-master
typefaces are defined by their number of primary
instances. Each instance is considered to be
equivalent to a constituent style of a type family.

Student type designs. There is no separate category for student type designs. These must be entered
in one of the regular categories.

Types of design[1,2]
[The organisers reserve the right to revise the
categorisation of the entries proposed by the par-
ticipants.]

I. Original designs
Typeface designs that are wholly or substantially
original in conception and execution. They may be
inspired by historical examples, or in the same
general style as an existing typeface, but to be
considered original they must not be historical
revivals, direct imitations of any existing typeface,
or intended to be interchangeable with any existing typeface. ➔

II. Historical revivals[3]

Typeface designs based upon historical models, but not so closely as to be considered derivative designs. (Typefaces that are auto-traced from printed examples, or are otherwise so close to the original as to be considered mere copies, will be considered derivative designs. Similarly, adaptations to new technology of original designs or previous historical revivals created by 19th or 20th century type manufacturers will be considered derivative designs.)

III. Derivative designs[4]

(a) Custom versions of existing or historical typefaces: additional weights, narrow/expanded versions, romans/italics/schoolbooks/scripts, sans/serifs, text/display/decorative/initials, etc.;
(b) Typefaces made up of new glyphs designed to harmonise with glyphs of existing or historical typefaces (e.g., ligatures, small capitals, old-style/lining/smaller/tabular figures, accented/alternate glyphs, fleurons, etc.) for composition in languages using the same alphabet/writing system;
(c) Typefaces made up of new glyphs designed to harmonise with glyphs of existing or historical typefaces, for composition in languages using different alphabets/writing systems.

Notes

1. It is the responsibility of the person entering a typeface in the competition to attribute the typeface's origins correctly and to secure the necessary permissions. It is not the responsibility of the organisers to obtain this information. The organisers do, however, reserve the right to re-categorise an entry if they believe its design type has been misidentified, or to disqualify an entry entirely if it is found to be a derivative design that has been inadequately identified or has used an original design without permission.

2. Typefaces belonging to various types of design (original/historical/derivative) are considered to be either part of, or additions to, their respective type families/systems/superfamilies. This also applies to extended character sets for OpenType, or AAT (GX-format) fonts; they should be entered in the appropriate competition category.

3. If a historical revival is entered in the competition, necessary information on the original has to be provided, as well as a sample showing, and an assertion that the design is not a direct copy or otherwise a derivative design.

4. If a derivative design is entered in the competition, necessary information on the original has to be provided, as well as a sample showing, and an assertion of consent received from its author and/or copyright owner for creating the derivative typeface, and for entering it in bukva:raz!

Submission procedure

1. Typefaces/fonts may be submitted by anyone involved in their design, production, or marketing.[1]

2. Entry/Hanging/Publication fees: none

3. Entries are to be submitted as 11 x 17 in. or A3 (290 x 420 mm) paper proofs. Each individual/constituent font showing is to be submitted as a separate sheet.[2] Each proof should show the typeface in whatever way seems appropriate for that design; proofs may include, but are not limited to, headlines, short or long passages of text, sample pages/double-page spreads of book or magazine make-up, or multiple-column text.

4. The proofs should show complete character sets. In the case of complex, extended, or multi-script character sets, the showing is to be comprehensive enough to allow the jury to judge it properly.

5. The following information should be clearly visible in the upper left corner of each proof:[3]

Competition category:
text/display/text and display/pi;

Type of entry:
single typeface/family/system/superfamily;

Type of design:
original/revival/derivative;

Alphabet/writing system:
Arabic, Armenian, Chinese, Cyrillic, Devanagari, Greek, Hebrew, Japanese, Korean, Latin, etc.

Do not include the name of the typeface, the name of the designer, or the name of the manufacturer.

Notes

1. Additional credits will be requested for the designs selected by the Jury. All submissions are assumed to be the 1997–2001 productions/releases, and, by the fact of their entry in the competition, permission is granted to reproduce selected typefaces in the competition catalogue and in any related publications, and to display them in the exhibition of the winning entries.

2. Submissions of text/display type systems and superfamilies (including digital fonts produced in multiple-master or OpenType formats) may feature more than one font/style in each showing.

3. The name of the typeface, its designer(s), or its manufacturer must not appear either on the front or on the back of the proof. The entries must not contain any reference to the name of the typeface, its designer, or its manufacturer: this information should appear only on the entry form attached to the proof. This is intended to ensure equal and unbiased consideration for all entries.

Deadline/Shipping

All entries (with entry forms attached to them) must be delivered by Monday, 5 November 2001, to: bukva:raz! 21 Rozhdestvensky Bvd., Bldg. 2, Moscow 103045, Russia.

If more than one package is shipped, this must be indicated on each package (e.g., '1 of 2'). Packages must be delivered prepaid. Packages should be marked [in English] 'Material for contest entry. No commercial value'. No provision will be made by the bukva:raz! office for customs or airport pick-up. Any customs fees will be charged back to the entrant. No entries will be returned.

Notification of winners

The winners of bukva:raz! will be notified – by e-mail or fax, and by regular mail during the week of 3 December 2001. A press release on the results of the competition will be published on the same week. Entries selected by the jury will be shown in a catalogue of the winning designs. An exhibition of the winners will be on view at the 2002 annual conference of ATypI in Rome.

A-TypI's a-changin'

ATypI has never had design competitions. The holding of bukva:raz! may be seen as a sign of the evolution of the Association and the gradual change of its course. In his review of the ATypI Conference of 2001 Robin Kinross wrote in *Eye* magazine (Issue 42, Winter 2001): 'Riding the waves of huge technical and business changes, [ATypI] has transformed itself from being a type industry cartel, with a semi-detached cultural superstructure and some occasionally splendid educational initiatives, to being something that begins to feel like a much more coherent blend of technics, business and culture. <...> In 2000, chiming in with this development, ATypI launched its Bukva:raz! type design competition. Typefaces from the last five years, in all the world's scripts, may be submitted to the address of the Russian Type Designers Association in Moscow. And with that address (21 Rozhdestvensky Boulevard), the centre is shifted away from the Latin world. We will have to find ways of referring to writing systems positively without that "non-" prefix ("non-Latin", "non-alphabetic").'

Glyphs gone global

The above comment aptly sums up the spirit of bukva:raz!, its very quintessence. This universal, cross-cultural approach is what makes this project so natural and appropriate for ATypI (that 'I' stands for *Internationale*), and imparts to bukva: raz! special relevance in the context of the latest developments in typographic technologies.

The growing globalisation of information exchange is one of the most significant developments in the history of mankind. The adoption of Unicode, a world-wide character-encoding standard designed to enable the global interchange of multilingual digital information, heavily affects the design of typefaces. It provides a framework for developing typefaces with extended character sets, covering multiple writing systems.

A designers' design competition

Type design contests are often managed by the font manufacturers. Not ours. bukva:raz! was held *by* the designers *for* the designers, and it was run on a shoestring: most sponsors of bukva:raz! offered labour, services, materials, supplies, but no money. To encourage the participation of type designers from all regions and nations of the world – rich and poor, North and South, East and West – no entry, hanging, or publication fees were charged. Of course, that was a big incentive.

Born on Interstate-95

The name of the competition – bukva:raz! – translates as 'letter:one!': *bukva* is the Russian for 'letter' (as in 'letterform') and *raz* for 'one' (as in 'two thousand one'). The competition was the brainchild of two Russian designers – Vladimir Yefimov and myself. We invented it together, in 1999 – in the car, on our way from Boston to New York (the ATypI conference that year was held in Boston, and Vladimir attended it – as so many other conferences). Hence the Russian name.

We first thought of bukva:raz! as a sequel to an earlier contest we had both judged (Vladimir chaired it) – Kyrillitsa'99. The winners of Kyrillitsa'99 were on display during the ATypI conference in Boston. We wanted our next competition to be not only in Cyrillic type design, but covering any alphabets and writing systems.

As our next step, we offered our idea to ATypI, and it was accepted. It has always felt strange to me that ATypI had never organised any competitions; nobody knows why (it seems like a natural thing for an international type society), but this is a fact. Thus bukva:raz! became the first event of this kind since the founding of the Association in 1957. The competition kept its Russian name though, and judging took place in Moscow.

Looks like we've made it

Against all the odds, our idea proved viable, and bore good fruit. I am very happy we managed to pull it off, and I am deeply grateful to all those who contributed to our contest. 2001 must be the worst year to pick for an endeavour of this magnitude and ambition: it turned out to be an *annus terribilis* indeed. The terrorist attack on New York City and Washington D.C. wrought havoc on so many people's psyches. It was easy to succumb to depression and fear, apathy and frustration; to give up. Our entrants did not. The response from the type design community exceeded our most optimistic expectations: it was tremendous.

251 designer from 30 countries participated in the competition. Over six hundred entries competed in five categories: Text designs, Display designs, Text/Display type systems, Type superfamilies, Pi fonts. Fourteen alphabets/writing systems were represented by the entries to bukva: raz!: Amharic, Arabic, Armenian, Canadian Aboriginal Syllabics, Cyrillic, Devanagari, Georgian, Greek, Hebrew, International Phonetic Alphabet, Japanese, Latin, Ogham, Xishuangbanna Dai.

The top one hundred

The quality of most entries was exceptionally high, especially among the text typefaces. Of course, there were also weak, amateurish works, but the general level was very good, very professional. That made the task of selecting the winners both easy and difficult. Our goal was to select the one hundred best type designs of the last five years. There is nothing wrong with such an approach. You can pick any number: 'top 10 best-sellers', 'top 20 charts', '50 books of the year', whatever.

The objective of bukva:raz! was to select the best designs completed and/or released over the last five years. Five years felt like a reasonable period to cover: good typefaces grow and mature slowly. Of course, no competition or exhibition, let alone one that is a sum of voluntary contributions, is, or can be deemed, comprehensive.

And yet, the long period covered by the contest (from January 1997 to November 2001), the wide array of styles, the variety of approaches, the scope of design objectives, the diversity of scripts and writing systems, etc., displayed by the entries, made bukva:raz! fairly representative of industry trends, providing for interesting observations, speculations, hypotheses, and conclusions.

The Year of Dialogue

What certainly makes bukva:raz! unique among its sister competitions is its openly political agenda. bukva:raz! was organised under the high auspices of the United Nations, as a special contribution of ATypI to the United Nations Year of Dialogue among Civilizations (2001). ➔

bukva:raz! was aimed at promoting cultural pluralism and encouraging diversity, interaction, and
co-operation in typographic communications.
In his letter of 31 May 2000, Giandomenico Picco,
Personal Representative of the UN Secretary-
General for the Year of the Dialogue Among Civilizations, wrote: 'To a large extent humankind has
been very successful in creating fake boundaries
for itself. Now, hopefully, real time communication and low cost access to each other across
the planet have opened the door to an era where
many of those fake boundaries will be broken.
<...> Your competition, as I understand it, points
in the same direction: to break boundaries and encourage better and easier communication among
individual human beings'.

December in Moscow

The judging session took place on the first weekend of December 2001, in downtown Moscow, at the
UN Information Centre in Russia. The jury worked
as a well-fitted team, operating on the basis of
consensus. Only when it found itself badly split
did it have it to resort to voting. In such very rare
cases a simple majority was sufficient to make a
decision for selecting an entry or leaving it out.

We had five competition categories: text designs;
display designs; text/display type systems; type
superfamilies; pi fonts. That helped the judges
of bukva:raz! to concentrate on those features of
the entries that were relevant to their respective
design categories, thus facilitating fair evalu-
ation. Of course, there was nothing dogmatic or
mechanical about judging entries subdivided by
categories.

Numbers talk

Speaking of categories. Most of the typefaces
submitted to bukva:raz! (350 out of 620, i.e. 56
per cent) were display styles, and 89 entries (only
14 per cent) were text designs. Conversely, only
36 display typefaces (10 per cent of the entries
submitted) were selected by the jury, while in the
text category 32 entries (36 per cent of submissions) made it to the winning one hundred. Of
course, the average quality of design was much
higher among the text typefaces. That certainly
confirms the well-known fact that it takes an
experienced professional to design an indus-
trial-strength text family, system, or superfamily,
while the beginners and the amateurs most often
fall for jazzy display styles.

Spasibo, friends

I think one of the incentives for entering designs
in bukva:raz! was the understanding that they
would be considered, evaluated, and judged by the
experts and cognoscenti most highly regarded
in the profession. I felt honoured and extremely
fortunate to work with such a wonderful group
of type mavens. I admire their dedication to the
goals of the competition, and their generous
contribution to the cause of cultural pluralism
and diversity, interaction, and co-operation in
typographic communications.

I have to acknowledge the assistance of Anna
Shmeleva, the secretary of bukva:raz!, and the
generous support she and I received from the
management and the staff of ParaType, the leading
producer and distributor of digital fonts in Russia, and the principal sponsor of bukva:raz! My
special thanks go to the Type Designers Association of Russia and its president, Vladimir Yefimov,
whose contribution to organising the contest
was truly vital. I owe a debt of gratitude to the
volunteer helpers who greatly facilitated the
judging of bukva:raz!: Dmitry Kirsanov, Elena
Rymshina, Irina Shishkova, Ilya Shmelev.

I very much appreciate the assistance of the director and the staff of the UN Information Centre
in Moscow, who supported us every step of the way:
they helped the judges to get their Russian visas,
and for two days they offered us superb working
quarters – with Internet connection, phone and
fax lines, copying equipment, and endless minor
amenities that proved crucial to the efficient
and productive work of the jury. I am profoundly
thankful to the rector, the faculty, and the
students of Moscow State University of Printing
Arts, who hosted the Judges' Soirée on Monday,
3 December 2002.

We much enjoyed the guided tour offered to us
by the most knowledgeable staff of the Rare Book
Department of the National Library of Russia. And,
of course, we were deeply touched by the hospital-
ity extended to us by the good folks of Petrovich
club and restaurant, where the jury had its first
get-together on the eve of the judging.

As I said, our competition was put together by the
type designers, for the type designers. It would
be impossible to mention all our fellow colleagues,
members and non-members of ATypI, who helped us
put together the competition, and assisted in developing its rules, shared their views and expertise, and offered priceless advice. The President,
the members of the ATypI Board of Directors, and
its Country Delegates were all most supportive
of our project; they greatly contributed to the
world-wide promotion of the competition, and the
solicitation of the submissions. To a considerable
extent bukva:raz! owes its success to their commitment and enthusiasm. I could have not pulled
it off on my own.

Maxim Zhukov
Chairman, bukva:raz!

Matthew Carter is a type designer with forty years experience of typographic technologies ranging from hand-cut punches to computer fonts. He designed the typefaces ITC Galliard, Snell Round-hand, Shelley Script, Bell Centennial (for the US telephone directories), Mantinia, Sophia, Big Caslon, Miller, and types commissioned by Apple, Microsoft (the screen fonts Verdana and Georgia), *Time, Newsweek, Wired, U.S. News & World Report, Sports Illustrated,* the *Washington Post,* the *Philadelphia Inquirer,* the *Boston Globe,* and the Walker Art Center. He is a principal of Carter & Cone Type Inc., in Cambridge, Massachusetts, designers and makers of original typefaces.

Yuri Gherchuk is an art historian and critic specialising in typography, book design, and illustration. He is the author of several books and many articles on graphics and book design, type and environmental typographics. He lectures on history of graphics and book design. Yuri Gherchuk is a member of the Art Critics and Art Historians Association, and of the Moscow Artists Union.

Akira Kobayashi studied at the Musashi-no Art University in Tokyo, and later followed this up with a calligraphy course at the London College of Printing. He has been a freelance type designer since 1997. Awards: in the 1998 *U&lc* magazine type design competition – for Clifford (Best of Category and Best of Show); in the Kyrillitsa'99 competition – for ITC Japanese Garden; in Linotype's 3rd International Type Design Contest – for Conrad (1st prize); in the Type Directors Club's type design competitions of 1998, 1999, 2000, and 2001 – for ITC Woodland, ITC Japanese Garden and ITC Silvermoon, FF Clifford, and Linotype Conrad.

Lyubov' Kuznetsova is a seasoned type, graphic, and book designer, and a talented calligrapher. She graduated from Moscow Printing Institute, and has worked for a number of Russian type design organisations and publishers. For many years Ms. Kuznetsova specialised in Arabic type design; she designed many Arabic and Cyrillic typefaces. Some of her Arabic designs, in *naskh, kufi, nasta'liq* and other styles, were developed in co-operation with Egyptian, Iranian, and Lebanese calligraphers. Since 1992 she has been a staff designer for ParaType, Moscow.

Gerry Leonidas is a Lecturer and Course Director of the MA in Type Design in the Department of Typography & Graphic Communication at the University of Reading, England. He is a practicing designer of Greek and Latin typefaces, and a regular consultant on typography and type design. Between 1986 and 1994 he worked in book and magazine publishing in Greece. He holds a BSc in Business Administration, a Diploma in Journalism, and a Postgraduate Diploma in Typography & Graphic Communication. He is constantly completing a PhD on the relationship of the design processes in Greek and Latin digital typefaces.

Fiona Ross specializes in non-Latin type design and (following a degree in German and a Postgraduate Diploma in Sanskrit) has worked with Linotype since 1978. As Manager of Typographic Development (U.K.) for five years, she was responsible for the design of Linotype's non-Latin fonts and typesetting schemes. Since 1989 she has worked as a consultant, becoming freelance in 1995: clients include Linotype Library, Apple Computers, and Quark. Fiona has a Ph.D. in Indian Palaeography (SOAS) and is a visiting lecturer at Reading University. She has written one book and numerous articles, and is a Fellow of the Royal Society of Arts.

Vladimir Yefimov is a type designer with twenty years of experience. He has designed many Cyrillic typefaces, and several Indian, Greek, and Hebrew type-faces. He writes on typography and type design. Vladimir Yefimov lectures on type design at the Higher Academical School of Graphic Design, Moscow (since 1997). He is the art director and a cofounder of ParaType, a member of the Moscow Art-ists Union and the Academy of Graphic Design, and a member of ATypI. He is also a co-founder of the Type Designers As-sociation, Moscow.

Maxim Zhukov is a typographic coordi-nator for the United Nations. His main occupation is multilingual typography. Zhukov is involved in typeface design, consulting for individual designers and type foundries. For a few years he taught typographic design at his alma mater, Moscow Printing Institute. He writes on typography and type design. He is a member of a number of Russian and American professional societies and associations. He is a member of the ATypI Board of Directors, and the Coun-try Delegate for Russia.

Henrik Mnatsakanyan, 1923–2001

ԱԲԳԴԵԶԷԸԹԺԻԼԽԾԿՀՁ

ԱԲԳԴԵԶԷԸԹԺԻԼԽԾԿՀՁՂ
աբգդեվէրթժիլխծկհձղ

ԱԲԳԴԵԶԷԸԹԺԻԼԽԾԿՀՁՂ
աբգդեվէրթժիլխծկհ3ղ

ԱԲԳԴԵԶԷԸԹԺԻԼԽԾԿՀՁՂ
աբգդեվէրթժիլխծկհձղ

ԱԲԳԴԵԶԷԸԹԺԻԼԽԾԿհՁՂ
աբգդեվէրթժիլխծկհձ

Henrik Mnatsakanyan designed typefaces for more
than fifty years. He developed over one hundred
Armenian typefaces for text and display composition. His design skills were formed in the studio
of the well-known Armenian artist Akop Kodjoyan.
From 1954 to 1960 Henrik Mnatsakanyan worked at
the Type Design Laboratory of the All-Union Printing Research Institute (NIIPoligrafmash). In 1962
he founded the Type Design Laboratory in Yerevan,
and directed its work until 1984. He was a veteran of
WWII and a member of the Armenian Artists Union.

Selected typefaces
(top to bottom):
Shoghshoghoun
['Radiant'], 1996;
Henrik, 1978;
Grabar ['Classical
Armenian'], 1977;
Haykakan Kar
['Armenian Stone'], 1997;
Jinj ['Limpid'], 1996.

ԽԱՅՆՇՈՉՊՁՈՒՎՏՐՑԻՓՔՕֆ

ՄՅՆՇՈՉՊՁՈՒՄՎՏՐՑԻՓՔՕֆ
 նյնշոչպգռավտրցումիքնoֆ

ՄՅՆՇՈՉՊ.ՉՈՒՍՎՏՐՑԻՓ·ՔՕֆ
նյնշոչպգ—սվտրց—ֆֆԼoֆ

ՄՅՆՇՈՉՊՁՌՍՎՏՐՑԻՓՔՈֆ
նյնշոչպգռավտրցւփքնoֆ

ՄՅՆՇՈՉՊՁՈՍՎՏՐՅՐՓՔՕֆ
նյնշոչպգռավտրցւփքնoֆ

Among many lives snatched away by the dire year 2001 was the life of Henrik Mnatsakanyan, the foremost lettering and type designer from Armenia. Henrik was on my initial list of bukva:raz! jurors. I asked him to judge the competition, and he accepted the invitation with utmost enthusiasm. Unfortunately, he did not live to attend the judging session in Moscow: he passed away in Yerevan on Saturday, 12 May 2001. The absence of Henrik at the jurors' table was sorely felt by all. Before the judges got to review the submissions, they observed a minute of silence to honour the memory of the late master. Henrik's precious legacy is destined for a long life – way beyond his own. It lives on in his tremendous œuvre, and in the creative work of his younger colleagues who worked with him: Gayaneh Bagdasaryan, Manvel Shmavonyan, et al. – Henrik's apprentices and accomplished masters of type design in their own right. Henrik's last, unfinished project – a new book on Armenian type design – awaits its completion and publication.

Maxim Zhukov

The river froze while we were there, and Muscovites rejoiced to see the last of autumn mud. At the UN Information Centre, where the judging took place, it was cozy. Across the street was one of the old, low, neoclassical Moscow houses [2] – the former chess club of Garry Kasparov, now awaiting repairs after a fire the winter before. The judges and supporters [1] (from left to right: Lyubov' Kuznetsova, Matthew Carter, Maxim Zhukov, John Berry (above), Gerry Leonidas (below), Fiona Ross, Yuri Gherchuk, Anna Shmeleva, Akira Kobayashi, Vladimir Yefimov) assembled for two intense days of work. Judging over 600 typeface designs was a grueling task, though enlivened by camaraderie and occasional rude comments. ('We should award a prize for worst presentation!') The judges' dinner at Petrovich, a very hip Soviet-nostalgia theme club based on the cartoon character Petrovich, [22] kicked off the weekend; a hands-on showing of historic Russian books at the Russian National Library, conducted by Yuri Gerchuk, brought it to a close. Chairman Maxim Zhukov organized the two long days of judging, moving things along, [10] making suggestions on procedure but leaving the decisions to the jury.

To make a first cut and reduce the number of type-faces to a reasonable number, the judges looked at each one in turn, eliminating those that no one spoke up for. The goal was 100 winners. At first they seemed to fly through the entries ('At this rate, we'll be done by lunchtime Sunday'), but by Satur-day afternoon it looked as though they would never reach the end of the first round. [16] In the end, they got through all of the entries at exactly 6 p.m., so they could come back fresh the next morning and make the final selection. Once that was done, on Sunday afternoon, the immense logistical job of

copying the winners and updating the database was undertaken, by bukva:raz! secretary Anna Shmeleva. [17] Monday evening was the Judges' Soirée at the Moscow State University of Printing Arts, on the outskirts of the city; getting there was enlivened by a minibus driver who didn't actually know where the site of the event was (my partner, Eileen Gunn, speaks some Russian, but none of us could re-member the word for 'printing'; we'd been told the building used to house a fisheries institute, and was still known by that name, but this didn't cut any ice with the students the driver kept stopping

to ask), and getting back was a true Moscow adven- ture when Maxim's borrowed car broke down, and he, Eileen, and I found ourselves pushing the Lada up a dark, wintry street while Mark Batty tried to get the engine to catch. The university itself proved labyrinthine – every movement seemed to require going both upstairs and downstairs – but the halls were lined with an impressive display of typeface showings, [38] and a large audience greeted the judges in the auditorium. The judges' illustrated talks were conducted in either English or Russian, with Maxim deftly translating the English for the

Russian audience. [26] Indeed, Maxim's seamless translating made the judging possible, with a jury who didn't always speak each other's language. The languages and scripts dealt with in the Judges' Soirée talks ranged over a wide range – like the competition itself. The audience was not only large but animated: at the end, when all the judges were assembled onstage to field questions, [23] the queries, statements, and debates went on in lively fashion for a good half an hour.

John D. Berry

The winners of bukva:raz!

Absolut Type (Lat)
Lars Bergquist. Sweden

Alinea (Lat)*
Thierry Puyfoulhoux. France

Alphatier (Lat)
Mark Jamra. USA

Ambroise (Lat)
Jean-François Porchez.
France

Anisette; Anisette Petite
(Lat). Jean-François
Porchez. France

Arcana (Lat)
Gabriel Martínez Meave.
Mexico

Asmik (Arm)
Manvel Shmavonyan. Armenia

Atzmaut (Heb)
David Tartakover;
Yanek Iontef. Israel

Bartholomé Open (Lat)
Dennis Pasternak. USA

Basalt (Lat)
Sumner Stone. USA

ITC Biblon (Lat)
František Štorm.
Czech Republic

Biot (Lat)
Julien Janiszewski. France

Caflisch Script Pro (Lat)
Robert Slimbach. USA

Calbee (Lat)
Karen Lau. USA

Calligraphic (Lat; Cyr)
Yuri Gulitov. Russia

Charente (Lat)
Jean-François Porchez.
France

Cholla (Lat)
Sibylle Hagmann. USA

P22 Daddy-O Beatsville (Pi)
Richard Kegler;
Peter Reiling. USA

DenHaag (Lat; Cyr)
Alexander Tarbeev. Russia

Dolly (Lat)
Lars de Beer; Akiem Helmling;
Bas Jacobs; Sami Kortemäki.
The Netherlands

DTL Dorian (Lat)
Elmo van Slingerland.
The Netherlands

Economy (Lat; Cyr)
Vasily Shishkin. Russia

Enigma (Lat)
Jeremy Tankard.
United Kingdom

Linotype Ergo Sketch (Lat)
Gary Munch. USA

LTR Federal (Lat)
Erik van Blokland.
The Netherlands

Linotype Finnegan (Lat)
Jürgen Weltin. Germany

Floris Newspaper (Lat)
Luc(as) de Groot. Germany

Fontana ND (Lat)
Rubén Fontana. Argentina

Founder's Caslon (Lat)
Justin Howes.
United Kingdom

Frothy (Lat)
Julien Janiszewski. France

Linotype Frutiger Next (Lat)
Adrian Frutiger. Switzerland

Geisha (Lat; Cyr)
Yelena Likutina. Ukraine

Gentium (Lat)
Victor Gaultney.
United Kingdom

Giacometti Pi (Pi)
Sine Bergmann. Germany

Gotham (Lat)
Tobias Frere-Jones;
Jesse M. Ragan. USA

P22 Gothic Gothic (Lat)
James Grieshaber. USA

Guggenheim (Lat)
Jonathan Hoefler. USA

DTL Haarlemmer Sans (Lat)
Frank E. Blokland.
The Netherlands

Handmade (Lat; Cyr)
Andrey Belonogov. Russia

Harmony Greek (Gre)
Jeremy Tankard.
United Kingdom

Hothouse (Lat)
Jürgen Huber. Germany

Humanist 531 Cyrillic (Cyr)
Isay Slutsker;
Manvel Shmavonyan. Russia

FF Kievit (Lat)
Michael Abbink. USA

Kinesis (Lat)
Mark Jamra. USA

Knockout (Lat)
Jonathan Hoefler. USA

Kursiv Bogdesco (Cyr)
Ilya Bogdesco. Russia

Lagarto (Lat)
Gabriel Martínez Meave.
Mexico

Latina (Lat)
Iñigo Jerez Quintana. Spain

LeChaufferie (Lat)*
Damien Gautier. France

Le Monde Courrier (Lat)
Jean-François Porchez.
France

Le Monde Journal (Lat)
Jean-François Porchez.
France

Letopis (Cyr)
Innokenty Keleinikov. Russia

Made in China (Lat; Cyr)
Yelena Zotikova. Ukraine

Maqsaf (Ara)
Habib Khoury. Israel

Markazi (Ara)
Tim Holloway. United Kingdom

Maya (Heb)
Oded Ezer. Israel

Mercury (Lat)
Jonathan Hoefler;
Tobias Frere-Jones. USA

Minion Pro (Gre)
Robert Slimbach. USA

Myriad Pro (Gre; Cyr)
Robert Slimbach; Carol
Twombly; Fred Brady. USA

Nathan (Heb)
Sylvie Chokroun. France

Next Exit (Heb)
Yanek Iontef. Israel

Nichiyou Daiku (Jap)
Joachim Müller-Lancé. USA

Nyx (Lat)
Rick Cusick. USA

Onserif & Onsans (Lat)
Iñigo Jerez Quintana. Spain

Papaya (Heb)
Zvika Rosenberg. Israel

DTL Paradox (Lat)
Gerard Unger.
The Netherlands

Parmenides (Grc)
Dan Carr. USA

Pesaro (Lat)
Joachim Müller-Lance. USA

Pigiarniq (Can)
Wm Ross Mills. Canada

Pradell (Lat)
Andreu Balios. Spain

Prensa (Lat)
Cyrus Highsmith. USA

Quadrat Grotesk (Lat; Cyr)
Vladimir Pavlikov. Russia

Raghu (Dev)
R.K. Joshi. India

Rayuela (Lat; Pi)
Alejandro Lo Celso.
Argentina

Really (Lat; Cyr; Gre)
Gary Munch. USA

Relay (Lat)
Cyrus Highsmith. USA

Requiem (Lat; Pi)
Jonathan Hoefler. USA

Retina Agate (Lat)
Tobias Frere-Jones. USA

Rouble (Pi)
Andrey Belonogov. Russia

Seria & Seria Sans (Lat)
Martin Majoor.
The Netherlands

Serp'n'Molot (Lat; Cyr)
Tagir Safayev. Russia

Shaker (Lat)
Jeremy Tankard.
United Kingdom

The Shire Types (Lat)
Jeremy Tankard.
United Kingdom

Shirokuro (Jap; Lat)
Joachim Müller-Lancé. USA

Shuriken Boy (Lat)
Joachim Müller-Lancé. USA

Sketchley (Lat)
Ronna Penner. Canada

Stancia (Lat)*
Jean-Renaud Cuaz. France

Sun (Lat)
Luc(as) de Groot. Germany

Linotype Syntax (Lat)
Hans Eduard Meier. Germany

Tanya (Cyr)
Olga Overchuk. Ukraine

TheAntiquaB (Lat)
Luc(as) de Groot. Germany

Tourist (Lat)
Julian Bittiner. USA

DTL Unico (Lat)
Michael Harvey.
United Kingdom

Vesta (Lat)
Gerard Unger.
The Netherlands

Waters Titling Pro (Lat)
Julian Waters. USA

Yellow (Lat)
Jürgen Weltin. Germany

Yisana (Pi)
Olivier Umecker. France

Zentra (Pi)
Vladimir Pavlikov. Russia

Zigzag (Lat; Cyr)
Yurij Lila. Ukraine

Zubizarreta (Lat)
Joan Barjau. Spain

* Not shown in this book.

Writing system codes:
(Ara) Arabic;
(Arm) Armenian;
(Can) Canadian Aboriginal
        Syllabics;
(Cyr) Cyrillic;
(Dev) Devanagari;
(Grc) Archaic Greek;
(Gre) Greek;
(Heb) Hebrew;
(Jap) Japanese;
(Lat) Latin;
 (Pi) Pi.

Typeface name:
Absolut Type.
Designer:
Lars Bergquist.

ABCDEFGHIJKLMNOPQRSTUVWXYZ
abcdefghijklmnopqrstuvwxyz 0123456789
ÁÀÂÄÃÅÇÉÈÊËÍÌÎÏÑÓÒÔÖØÕÚÙÛÜŸ
áàâäãåéèêëíìîïñóòôöøõúùûüÿ ßÆæŒœfifl
!?¿¡:;-""''«»„‚(&)[%]{§}*†‡$¢£¥€®©™
¶℗ ªºµ∂∆∑∏πΩ ≠∞±≤≥‹›+=≈÷◊√

ABCDEFGHIJKLMNOPQRSTUVWXYZ
abcdefghijklmnopqrstuvwxyz 0123456789
ÁÀÂÄÃÅÇÉÈÊËÍÌÎÏÑÓÒÔÖØÕÚÙÛÜŸ
áàâäãåéèêëíìîïñóòôöøõúùûüÿ ßÆæŒœfifl
!?¿¡:; -""''«»„‚(&)[%]{§}†‡$¢£¥€®©™*
¶℗ ªºµ∂∆∑∏πΩ ≠∞±≤≥‹›+=≈÷◊√

ABCDEFGHIJKLMNOPQRSTUVWXYZ
ABCDEFGHIJKLMNOPQRSTUVWXYZ
0123456789 ÁÀÂÄÃÅÇÉÈÊËÍÌÎÏÑ
ÓÒÔÖØÕÚÙÛÜŸ
ÁÀÂÄÃÅÉÈÊËÍÌÎÏÑÓÒÔÖØÕÚÙÛÜŸ
ÆæŒœ !?¿¡:; -""''«»„‚(&) ¶℗

Lars Bergquist was born in 1936. After university
studies in Lund, Sweden (majoring in history), he
started working in publishing, preparing text and
images for highly structured reference works such
as encyclopedias. In the process, he acquired a
working knowledge of typography. Bergquist has
also worked in multimedia and is a founding member of *Bild och Ord Akademin*, the Swedish Academy
of Verbovisual Information; large-scale verbovisual text-image integration is one of his special-
ties. In his retirement, he has indulged his old love
of classic letterforms by designing type.

Country:
Sweden.
Writing system:
Latin.

Competition category:
Text, family.
Manufacturer/distributor:
Timberwolf Type.

CALL ME ISHMAEL. SOME YEARS AGO—NEVER MIND HOW long precisely—having little or no money in my purse, and nothing particular to interest me on shore, I thought I would sail about a little and see the watery part of the world. It is a way I have of driving off the spleen, and regulating the circulation. Whenever I find myself growing grim about the mouth; whenever there is a damp, drizzly November in my soul; whenever I find myself involuntarily pausing before coffin warehouses, and bringing up the rear of every funeral I meet; and especially whenever my hypos get such an upper hand of me, that it requires a strong moral principle to prevent me from deliberately stepping into the street, and methodically knocking people's hats off—then, I account it high time to get to sea as soon as I can. This is my substitute for pistol and ball. With a philosophical flourish Cato throws himself upon his sword; I quietly take to the ship. There is nothing surprising in this. If they by knew it, almost all men in their degree, some time or other, cherish very nearly the same feelings toward the ocean with me.

There now is your insular city of the Manhattoes, belted round by wharves as Indian isles by coral reefs—commerce surrounds her with her surf. Right and left, the streets take you waterward. Its extreme downtown is the battery, where that noble mole is washed by waves, and cooled by breezes, which a few hours previous were out of sight of land. Look at the crowds of water-gazers there.

Circumambulate the city of a dreamy Sabbath afternoon. Go from Corlears Hook to Coenties Slip, and from thence, by Whitehall, northward. What do you see?—Posted like silent sentinels all around the town, stand thousands upon thousands of mortal men fixed in ocean reveries. Some leaning against

From *Moby Dick, or the Whale,* by Herman Melville 1851

Absolut Type is a three-font typeface based on classic Renaissance letterforms, but rendered in a free, somewhat calligraphic manner. Though the intended purpose is what may be termed 'text display' – text of less than novel length, with a high aesthetic profile – care has been taken to give the type the smoothness and flow required for the setting of continuous text. The styles are Roman, Italic, and Small Caps. There are no bold styles, as these would have compromised the integrity of the design. In the Roman and Italic, figures are lowercase as a matter of course.

ABCDEFGHIJKLMNOP
QRSTUVWXYZaƀcdefʒ
hijklmnopqrstuvwxyz
ÀÁÂÄÃÅÆÇÉÈËÊÍÎÏÏÑ
ÓÔÒÖÕØŒÚÛÙÜŸáà
âäãåæçéèêëíìîïñóòôöõœß
úùûüÿ&fifl,;.:...¡!¿?''""„<>
«»/–—▶·()[]{}*†‡§¶`´^˅˜
··-˘"·,,ˎ^~\©®™@$¢£ƒ¥ᵃ
°#1234567890%‰+=≠±¬'''°µ

Mark Jamra is a type designer, graphic designer,
and currently Associate Professor at Maine College
of Art, where he teaches letterform and graphic
design. He has had his own studio practice for 15
years and is a partner in Alice Design Communication, a design collective in Portland, Maine. He has
lectured and published essays on type and typography, and has been a typographic consultant to the
Hewlett-Packard Research Laboratories in Bristol,
England, and URW GmbH in Hamburg, Germany. His
typeface designs include: Alphatier, Brynmorgen
Greek, Latienne, ITC Jamille, and Kinesis.

Country:
USA.
Writing system:
Latin.

Competition category:
Display, family.
Manufacturer/distributor:
Mark Jamra.

It does genuinely matter that a designer should take trouble and take delight in his choice of typefaces. The trouble and delight are taken not merely "for art's sake" but for the sake of something so subtly and intimately connected with all that is human that it can be described by no other phrase than "the humanities." If "the tone of voice" of a typeface does not count, then nothing counts that distinguishes man from the other animals. The twinkle that softens a rebuke; the scorn that can lurk under civility; the martyr's super-logic and the child's intuition; the fact that a fragment of moss can pull back into the memory a whole forest; these are proofs that there is reality in the imponderable, and that not only notation but connotation is part of the proper study of mankind. The best part of typographic wisdom lies in this study of connotation, the suitability of form to content.

¶ A specimen (see S. Morison, 'Byzantine Elements in Humanist Script' illustrated from the "Aulus Gellius" of 1445, "Occasional Paper of the New-bury Library"), from a foundry in New York, printed in 1820, has taken particular notice of "The Philadelphia Foundry." **Inferences, censures, and self-compliments are introduced into the preface, in manner and extent which candor and truth should have kept within moderate limits.**

Archeological Excavations in Southern Nepal

Reynold Barnes & the 15% Solution

C'est dans la salle à manger

Schöne Grüße von Karl

EQUAL TIME SHARES

Carpe Diem ▸ (Latin)

Alphatier came from ongoing design experiments that refer to the historical evolution of letterform identities. My interest here is the question: how far beyond mere variation can the designer go in creating letterforms and still have them commu-nicate a textual message? Alphatier is a design for display and limited text applications which begins to abandon the traditional formal scheme of the al-phabet. It remains a cohensive typographic system less through the familiar roster of similar shapes and more through its overlying character.

Typeface name:
Ambroise.
Designer:
Jean-François Porchez.

A A B C D E E F G H I J K L M
N N O P Q R S T U V W X Y Z
a a b c d e f f g g h i i j k l l m n o
p q r s s t u u v w x y y z Á Â Â Ä Ã
Å Æ Ç Ð É Ê È Ë Í Î Ì Ï I Ł Ñ Ó Ô
Ò Ö Õ Ø Œ P Š Ú Û Ù Ü Ý Ÿ Ž á
â à ä ã å æ ç ð é ê è ë í î ì ï ı ł ñ ó ô
ò ö õ ø œ þ š ß ú û ù ü ý ÿ ž & d
st fi fl ffi ffi ffl ff . , : ; • • " " ' ' , , ... « «
» » ¿ ¡ ! ? - – — _ ` ´ ^ ~ - ˘ • • " " �
, , # § ¶ @
µ † ‡ * / (|) [/] { \ } ® © ℗ ™ € $ ¢ ¥
ƒ £ ₤ ª º ° 0 0 1 1 2 2 3 4 5 6 7 8 9
1 2 3 ½ ¼ ¾ % ‰ – < ÷ + | º ∧ × = ~ > ¬

Jean-François Porchez (1964) trained at the ANCT,
and after worked as a type director at Dragon
Rouge, Paris. By 1994, he had created new typefaces
for *Le Monde* newspapers. Today, he designs typefaces for companies like RATP (public transport
in Paris), Peugeot, Costa, and France Telecom, and
he distributes his typefaces internationally via
www.typofonderie.com. He teaches type design at
ENSAD in Paris. He was awarded the Prix Charles
Peignot (1998). His typefaces have been awarded
recognition in competitions in Europe, North
America, and Japan.

176

Country:
France.
Writing system:
Latin.

Competition category:
Display, family.
Manufacturer/distributor:
Porchez Typofonderie.

Affiche
Amis de la vérité
LES JACOBINS
Tremblez Tyrans
Assignats
Cercle social

Ambroise is a contemporary interpretation of various typefaces belonging to the Didot late style, conceived circa 1830, including the original forms of g, y, &, k. These characters are found in the types of Vibert, appointed punchcutter of the Didot family. It is the Black which was the basis for the conception of the family. In the second half of the 19th century, it was normal to find fat Didot faces in several widths in the catalogs of French type foundries. The condensed variant is called Ambroise Firmin, and the extra-condensed is called Ambroise François.

177

Typeface name:
Anisette; Anisette Petite.
Designer:
Jean-François Porchez

ABCDEFGHIJKLMNO
PQRSʃSTUVWXYZABC
DEFGHIJKLMNOPQRSTUVWX
YZABCDEFGHIJKLMNOPQRSTUVWXYZa
abcdefgghijkllmnopqrrsʃtuvwxyyz
ÁÂÀÄÃÅÆÇÐÉÊÈËÍÎÌÏIÌŁÑÓÔÒÖÕØŒÞŠÚÛ
ÙÜÝŸŽÁÂÀÄÃÅÆÇÐÉÊÈËÍÎÌÏIÌŁÑÓ
ÔÒÖÕØŒÞŠÚÛÙÜÝŸŽáâàäãå
æçðéêèëíîìïıłñóôòöõøœþšßúûùüý
ÿžℰℰℓ⒜ⒶⒶⒹⒸⒹⓁⒺⓃⓃⓄⓄ
THⒺ⒤Ⓐ⒪⒧ⓁⓃⓃⓄⓄTHFIFLFFIFFLFFﬁﬂﬃ
ﬄﬀ.,.:.;•◆■.""''',,,…‹«›»¿¡!?¿¡-—— ‗ ` ´ ˆ ˜
‾ ˘ ˙ ̣ ̌ ̦ # # §¶ℚ@†‡*/(|)[/]{\}®©
℗™€$¢ƒ£¥€$¢ƒ£¥ªⁿ0ᵃ⁰0123456789
◕◈0123456789¹²³½¼¾%‰●◐◆

Jean-François Porchez. See page 176.

178

Country:
France.
Writing system:
Latin.

Competition category:
Text/display, system.
Manufacturer/distributor:
Porchez Typofonderie.

LES BANJOS

5 ▪ VILLA DENISE ▪ 23456 DEAUVILLE

& DE LA CONTREBASSE

MAXIMILIEN

VOX

Les Banjos

Georges Maximilien

5 villa Denise, 23456 DEAUVILLE

Un thé glacé, sinon rien

& ta contrebasse

Typographe

Anisette was created in reference to Cassandre
& the Art Decoratif. During the thirties, encouraged by Maximilien Vox, Deberny & Peignot created
the Banjo initials in one weight. Anisette is an
all-caps face with narrow caps placed in lowercase
positions & large caps placed in uppercase positions. The Anisette Petite new capital characters
(added in 2001) are based on an intermediate width,
between the two original widths. The lowercase
shares the sobriety of geometrical typefaces and
the dynamics of the tension in the curves. Subtle
'imperfections' help to create a original typeface.

Typeface name:
Arcana.
Designer:
Gabriel Martínez Meave.

ABCDEFGHIJKLM
NOPQRSTUVWXYZ

abcdefghijklmnopqrstuv
wxyz àáâãäåæçèéêëìíîï
òóôõöøœßùúûüÿžðſ&,;
:.-!¡?¿ () «» ‹› «» /——
*‚' () []{} * † ‡ §¶ ™*
©®@€¢£¥ªº#
1234567890 ¹²³ ½ ¼ ¾
‰‰ +−±×÷=<>° π√∞µ

Gabriel Martínez Meave (1972) was born in Mexico City, and graduated in Graphic Design. Since 1990, he has been interested in typography and calligraphy. Self-trained, he started designing letters of his own, which eventually ended as digital fonts. He has taken workshops with poet and typographer Robert Bringhurst and calligrapher Claude Dietrich. He founded (1994) the design firm Kimera, working for clients such as José Cuervo, HBO, Warner, and Camel. He has made custom font designs for important Mexican companies, as well as original typefaces.

Country:
Mexico.
Writing system:
Latin.

Competition category:
Display, single font.
Manufacturer/distributor:
Adobe Systems.

A calligraphic exploration on nineteenth century Gothic and Romantic aesthetics & the metal quill scripts of the Victorian Era.

Arcana

Les Dukes são William & Quevedo after Addendum von Mexico Cœli Hundert Tequila avec Vitabrevis elf alle Khartloum she Isabella Yolotl Rotterdam et Orendáin pór la Ursa Gilles Xerxes with Eddie y France pizzas what Ziggurath Bismark a Justus Scientia Nihil Pietro

Arcana is a calligraphic exploration on the Victorian-Era, occult-lore, 19th-century-gothic aesthetic. The base design was traced out with a pointed metal quill, then digitized and converted into a Postscript font. Arcana has two versions, Angular and Curvilinear, which, used alternatively, generate slight differences of shape and terminals, just like a calligrapher's hand. It also has special 'tail endings' for the ends of words and paragraphs. Suggested uses? Quotes from Michael Maier's *Arcana Arcanissima*, the lyrics of the next *Sepultura* album, a not-so-cliché-looking Valentine's card.

Typeface name:
Asmik.
Designer:
Manvel Shmavonyan.

Ա Բ Գ Դ Ե Զ Է Ը Թ Ժ
Ի Լ Խ Ծ Կ Հ Ձ Ղ Ճ Մ
Յ Ն Շ Ո Չ Պ Ջ Ռ Ս Վ
Տ Ր Ց Ւ Փ Ք Օ Ֆ ա բ
գ դ ե զ է ը թ ժ ի լ խ
ծ կ հ ձ ղ ճ մ յ ն շ ո չ
պ ջ ռ ս վ տ ր ց ւ փ ք
և օ ֆ . , : ; ´ ^ ` ˜ ’ § « »
( ) { } [ ] $ * @ 1 2
3 4 5 6 7 8 9 0 %

**Manvel Shmavonyan** was born in 1960 in Artashat (Armenia). In 1984 he graduated from the Moscow Printing Institute (Department of Print Design). He worked at the Type Design Department of the State Printing Committee of Armenia (Yerevan) from 1986 to 1988. Since 1997 he has been cooperating with ParaType designing Armenian and Cyrillic typefaces. He received a Certificate of Excellence in Type Design from TDC (New York) for PT Margarit (1998) and PT Asmik (1999), and a Way to Go! prize in the Kyrillitsa'99 Cyrillic type design competition (Moscow) for Hybrid (1999).

Country:
Armenia.
Writing system:
Armenian.

Competition category:
Text, family.
Manufacturer/distributor:
ParaType.

Աշխարհում գոյություն ունեցող գրերի թիվը համնում է տասնյակների (եթե ոչ հարյուրների): Դրանցից մի մասը, տարբեր պատճառներով, դուրս է եկել օգտագործման ոլորտից, իսկ մյուս մասը շարունակում է մշտապես ծառայել մարդկանց՝ նրանց գործունեության տարբեր ոլորտներում:

Չնայած մարդիկ գրերն օգտագործում են շատ հաճախ (համարյա թե ամեն օր), սակայն երբեք չեն մտածում այն մասին, թե ինչ են իրենցից ներկայացնում տառանշան-ները, յարգացման ինչ ճանապարհի են անցել նրանք, մինչև ժամանակակից տեսքն ընդունելը, ինչ իմաստ է դրված եղել սկզբնապես նրանց հիմքում և ինչու են նրանք դասավորված այբուբենում այսպիսի հերթականությամբ և ոչ մեկ ուրիշ:

Աշխարհում գոյություն ունեցող գրերի թիվը համնում է տասնյակների (եթե ոչ հարյուրների): Դրանցից մի մասը, տարբեր պատճառներով, դուրս է եկել օգտա-գործման ոլորտից, իսկ մյուս մասը շարունակում է մշտապես ծառայել մարդկանց՝ նրանց գործունեու-թյան տարբեր ոլորտներում:

Չնայած մարդիկ գրերն օգտագործում են շատ հաճախ (համարյա թե ամեն օր), սակայն երբեք չեն մտածում այն մասին, թե ինչ են իրենցից ներկայացնում տա-ռանշանները, յարգացման ինչ ճանապարհի են անցել նրանք, մինչև ժամանակակից տեսքն ընդունելը, ինչ իմաստ է դրված եղել սկզբնապես նրանց հիմքում և ինչու են նրանք դասավորված այբուբենում այսպիսի հերթականությամբ և ոչ մեկ ուրիշ:

Asmik. The PT Asmik type family is an Armenian companion of the Latin and Cyrillic face PT Peters-burg by Vladimir Yefimov, based on the original de-sign of Nikolay Kudryashov, and was commissioned in 1998 by ParaType. I named it Asmik after my wife's first name. In creating PT Asmik, I have tried to use the best traditions of Armenian lettering art and type design. This face is intended for use in both text and display typography.

Typeface name:
Atzmaut.
Designers:
David Tartakover, Yanek Iontef.

אבגדהוזחט

יכךלמםנןסע

פףצץקרשת

1234567890

'"–_?!.:;,%#

{}[]()

₪$<|>=-+*

David Tartakover (1944) studied at the Bezalel
Academy of Art and Design, Jerusalem, and the
London College of Printing. Since 1975, he has oper-
ated his own studio in Tel Aviv, specializing in vi-
sual communications. He is a Senior Lecturer in the
Visual Communication Department at the Bezalel
Academy. He is a member of the Alliance Graphique
Internationale, and past president of the Graphic
Designers Association of Israel. He won the Israel
Prize for Design in 2002.
Yanek Iontef. See page 288.

Country:
Israel.
Writing system:
Hebrew.

Competition category:
Display, family.
Manufacturer/distributor:
Yanek Iontef.

פונט עצמאות

פונט עצמאות | צר **|** רגיל **|** שמן
עיצוב של משהל שמן - דוד טרטקובר 1988
עיבוד למחשב ועיצוב משקלים צר ורגיל - ינק יונטף 1998

צר

אבגדהוזחטיכלמנסעפצקרשתרטוףץ 1234567890 {[('-"לי.,:;$#%@]}

פיסקה זו מהווה דוגמה לטקסט שסודר במרווח אחיד בין הש ורות. המווח אחיד מתייחס לקומפוזיציה טיפוגרפית ללא רווח נוסף בין השורות. במונחים חזותיים, סדר זה מעניק מידה אחידה של צבע אפור נועים מבחינה אסתטית, אך מאמץ את עיני הקורא בקריאה מתמשכת. אף על פי כן, הבחירה ב-אחיד

רגיל

אבגדהוזחטיכלמנסעפצקרשתרטוףץ 1234567890 {[('-"לי.,:;$#%@]}

פיסקה זו מהווה דוגמה לטקסט שסודר במרווח אחיד בין הש ורות. המווח אחיד מתייחס לקומפוזיציה טיפוגרפית ללא רווח נוסף בין השורות. במונחים חזותיים, סדר זה מעניק מידה אחידה של צבע אפור נועים מבחינה אסתטית, אך מאמץ את

שמן

אבגדהוזחטיכלמנסעפצקרשתרסוףץ 12345678 ('-"לי:;$%@)

פיסקה זו מהווה דוגמה לטקסט שסודר במרווח אחיד בין הש ורות. המווח אחיד מתייחס לקומפוזיציה טיפוגרפית ללא רווח נוסף בין השורות. במונחים חזותיים, סדר זה מעניק מידה אחידה של צבע אפור נועים מבחינה אסתטית, אך מאמץ את עיני הקורא בקריאה מתמשכת. אף על פי כן, הבחירה ב-אחיד המוכתבת על ידי איכות החזותית הרצויה.

מדינת ישראל תהא פתוחה לעליה יהודית ולקיבוץ גלויות;

תשקוד על פיתוח הארץ לטובת כל תושביה;

תהא מושתתה על יסודות החירות, הצדק והשלום לאור

חזונם של נביאי ישראל; תקיים שוויון זכויות חברתי ומדיני

גמור לכל אזרחיה בלי הבדל דת, גזע ומין;

תבטיח חופש דת, מצפון, לשון,

חינוך ותרבות; תשמור על המקומות

הקדושים של כל הדתות;

ותהיה נאמנה לעקרונותיה של מגילת

האומות המאוחדות.

Atzmaut (Independence) is an historical revival of a single weight (black) originally designed by leading Israeli graphic designer David Tartakover in 1988 to accomplish a special project, 'Declaration of Independence of the State of Israel', a series of posters illustrating the Israeli Declaration of Independence (which was later exhibited at the Israel Museum in Jerusalem). In 1998, in collaboration with David Tartakover, Yanek Iontef digitized the existing weight and added numerals, marks, symbols and two new weights: condensed and medium.

Typeface name:
Bartholemé Open.
Designer:
Dennis Pasternak.

ABCDEFGHIJKLMNOPQR
STUVWXYZabcdefghi
-—jklmnopqrstuvwxyz—
ÀÁÂÃÄÅÆÇÈÉÊËÌÍÎÏŁÑ
ÒÓÔÕÖØŒŠÙÚÛÜÝŸŽÐÞ
àáâãäåæèéêëìíîïłñòóôõöøœšß
ùúûüýÿžðþ&fifl,,;;::....!¡?¿'''""
,,''‹›«»/|•·()[]{}*†‡§¶\©®™
@€$¢£¥ªº#1234567890¹²³/
¼½¾%‰`´^˜¨‒–‿˚"ˌ
ˌ+−×÷=<>¬˚'"^˜

Dennis Pasternak is a founding partner and
Principal Designer for Galápagos Design Group,
Inc., Littleton, Massachusetts. His expertise is in
the history, design, marketing, and technological
issues of the font industry. Before becoming one
of the founders of Galápagos Design Group in 1994,
Dennis worked for several companies in the font
industry, including Compugraphic, Autologic, and
Bitstream. Although it is mathematical figures and
patterns that populate his computer monitors, he
often senses the pens, brushes, and metal used
throughout the history of letterforms.

Country:
USA.
Writing system:
Latin.

Competition category:
Display, single font.
Manufacturer/distributor:
Galápagos design group inc.

BARTHOLEMÉ
OPEN

◐

CLASSICAL · CONDENSED
· UPPER & LOWERCASE ·
· HANDTOOLED DESIGN ·
FOR DISPLAY & TITLING
TYPOGRAPHY

Bartholemé Open was originally inspired by earlier Shaded, Inline, and Hand Tooled models, in which the fonts were to a large extent all-capital character sets. This originally inspired hybrid has been designed in true contemporary fashion, possessing a larger lowercase x-height, and finely tuned serifs with tighter bracketing for a cleaner appearance on the page at middle and high resolutions. Primarily a display design, it is intended for titling, and short passages of text. A four-weight, text/display family expansion of Bartholemé is due to be released midyear in 2002.

Typeface name:
Basalt.
Designer:
Sumner Stone.

ABCDEF
ABCDEF

ABCDEFGHIJKLMNOPQRSTUVWXYZ

ABCDEFGHIJKLMNOPQRSTUVWXYZ

1234567890

ÀÁÂÃÄÅÆÇÈÉËÊÌÍÎÏÑÒÓÔÕÖØŒÙÚÛÜŸ

ÀÁÂÃÄÅÆÇÈÉÊËÌÍÎÏÑÒÓÔÕÖØŒÙÚÛÜŸ

([{:.,;-?¿!¡'`'""‹›«»/|-—··*\©®™@ᴬᴼ'"€$¢£ƒ¥#%+-÷±=¬}])

Sumner Stone is the principal and founder of Stone Type Foundry Inc., now located in Rumsey, California. He is the designer of the ITC Stone, Stone Print, Silica, Cycles, Arepo, and Basalt typeface families. Mr. Stone was the art director and one of the designers of the prize-winning ITC Bodoni. He is the author of *On Stone: The Art and Use of Typography on the Personal Computer*. From 1984 to 1989, Mr. Stone was Director of Typography for Adobe Systems, where he conceived and implemented Adobe's typographic program, including the Adobe Originals.

Country:
USA.
Writing system:
Latin.

Competition category:
Display, single font.
Manufacturer/distributor:
Stone Type Foundry.

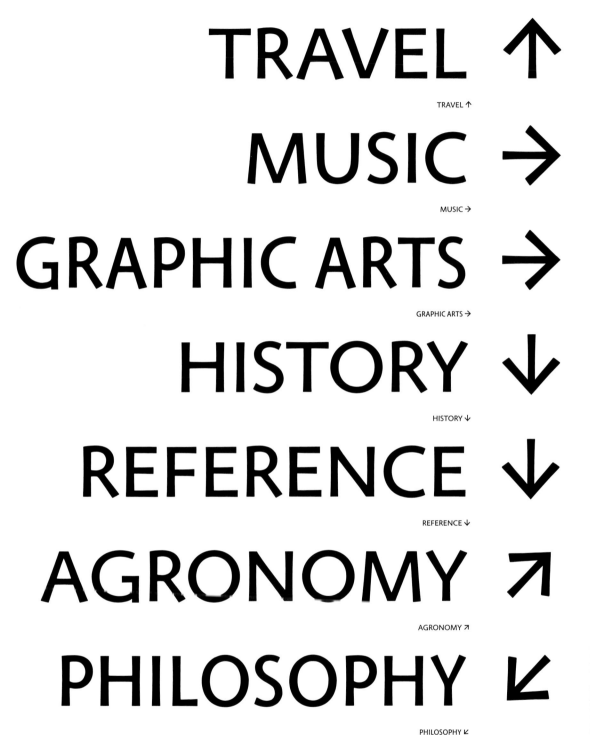

TRAVEL ↑

TRAVEL ↑

MUSIC →

MUSIC →

GRAPHIC ARTS →

GRAPHIC ARTS →

HISTORY ↓

HISTORY ↓

REFERENCE ↓

REFERENCE ↓

AGRONOMY ↗

AGRONOMY ↗

PHILOSOPHY ↙

PHILOSOPHY ↙

Basalt was designed for signage. Its weight and design details have been optimized for legibility over the vast range of apparent sizes that the reader experiences as a function of viewing distance from the sign. The entire Basalt typeface family is contained in a single font, which includes narrow capitals in the place of the lowercase character and a special set of arrows.

Typeface name:
ITC Biblon.
Designer:
František Štorm.

ABCDEFGHIJKLMNOPQRST
UVWXYZabcdefghijklmnopq
rstuvwxyzABCDEFGHIJKLMNOP
QRSTUVWXYZÀÁÂÃÄĀÅĄÆĆ
ČÇĎÈÉÊĚËĒĖĘÌÍÎÏĪĮĹĽĻŁŃ
ŇŅÑÒÓÔÕÖŌŐØŔŘŖŚŠŤÙ
ÚÛÜŪŮÝŸŹŽŻĐÞàáâãäāåąæ
ćčçďèéêěëēėęìíîïīįĺľļłńňņñòóôõ
öōőøŕřŗśšťùúûüūůýÿźžżðþÀÁ
ÂÃÄĀÅĄÆĆČÇĎÈÉÊĚËĒĖĘÌÍÎÏĪĮĹĽ
ĻŁŃŇŅÑÒÓÔÕÖŌŐØŔŘŖŚŠŤÙÚÛ
ÜŪŮÝŸŹŽŻĐÞ&fifl,;:.…-!¡?¿''""‹›
«»/‐–—•·O[]{}*†‡§¶ `´^˜¨¯˘˙°˝„·
^~¦\©®™@€$¢£ƒ¥€ªº#1234567
890¹²³/¼½¾%‰+−±

František Štorm was born in 1966, and graduated
from the Acadamy of Applied Arts in Prague in 1991.
He works as a freelance graphic designer, typographer and type designer. In 1993 he founded the
Storm Type Foundry to market his digital fonts,
including original designs and revivals of important faces from the Czech typographic tradition.
His Biblon family received an award of excellence
in the third Type Directors Club type design
competition, and was selected as Judge's Choice
by Matthew Carter.

Country:
Czech Republic.
Writing system:
Latin.

Competition category:
Text, family.
Manufacturer/distributor:
ITC.

BIBLON REGULAR, BOLD, ITALIC & BOLD ITALIC

AbsqRgAa&

WegθgkEy

10/12 PT.:

V dnešní moderní době lidé tisknou stále zbytečnější myšlenky a prokládají je mnoha vakáty. Není třeba šetřit papírem a vyhledávat opticky zúžená písma. Opačná je situace v každé biblické společnosti, kde redakce musí text v rozsahu nějakých 2000 stránek směstnat do jediného svazku. Tam je potřeba písem úsporných, čitelných a produševněle kultivovaných. Nové písmo „Biblon" nemusí tedy počítat s širokou škálou velikostí; stačí, když vypadá dobře od asi pěti do osmnácti bodů. Elegance ubývá s přibývající velikostí. V plakátových velikostech se již obnažuje spekulativní konstrukce obrazu litery – těžiště tahů jsou přesunuta co nejvíce do vodorovných směrů a zvýrazněna jsou úžlabí náběhů oblých tahů na dřík. U malých liter si sotva všimneme, že téměř všechny horizontální serify (pokud nezmizely úplně) byly vtlačeny dovnitř obrazu litery, aby nepřekážely sousedním písmenkům. Miniatu-

10/12 PT.:

**V dnešní moderní době lidé tisknou stále zbytečnější myš-
lenky a prokládají je mnoha vakáty. Není třeba šetřit papírem a vyhledávat opticky zúžená písma. Opačná je situace
v každé biblické společnosti, kde redakce musí text v rozsahu
nějakých 2000 stránek směstnat do jediného svazku. Tam je
potřeba písem úsporných, čitelných a produševněle kultivovaných. Nové písmo „Biblon" nemusí tedy počítat s širokou
škálou velikostí; stačí, když vypadá dobře od asi pěti do osmnácti bodů. Elegance ubývá s přibývající velikostí. V pláká-
tových velikostech se již obnažuje spekulativní konstrukce
obrazu litery – těžiště tahů jsou přesunuta co nejvíce do vodorovných směrů a zvýrazněna jsou úžlabí náběhů oblých tahů
na dřík. U malých liter si sotva všimneme, že téměř všechny
horizontální serify (pokud nezmizely úplně) byly vtlačeny**

10/12 PT.:

*V dnešní moderní době lidé tisknou stále zbytečnější myšlenky
a prokládají je mnoha vakáty. Není třeba šetřit papírem a vyhledávat opticky zúžená písma. Opačná je situace v každé biblické
společnosti, kde redakce musí text v rozsahu nějakých 2000 stránek směstnat do jediného svazku. Tam je potřeba písem úsporných, čitelných a produševněle kultivovaných. Nové písmo „Biblon"
nemusí tedy počítat s širokou škálou velikostí; stačí, když vypadá
dobře od asi pěti do osmnácti bodů. Elegance ubývá s přibývající
velikostí. V plakátových velikostech se již obnažuje spekulativní
konstrukce obrazu litery – těžiště tahů jsou přesunuta co nejvíce
do vodorovných směrů a zvýrazněna jsou úžlabí náběhů oblých
tahů na dřík. U malých liter si sotva všimneme, že téměř všechny
horizontální serify (pokud nezmizely úplně) byly vtlačeny dovnitř
obrazu litery, aby nepřekážely sousedním písmenkům. Miniatu-*

10/12 PT.:

*V dnešní moderní době lidé tisknou stále zbytečnější myšlenky
a prokládají je mnoha vakáty. Není třeba šetřit papírem
a vyhledávat opticky zúžená písma. Opačná je situace v každé
biblické společnosti, kde redakce musí text v rozsahu nějakých
2000 stránek směstnat do jediného svazku. Tam je potřeba
písem úsporných, čitelných a produševněle kultivovaných. Nové
písmo „Biblon" nemusí tedy počítat s širokou škálou velikostí;
stačí, když vypadá dobře od asi pěti do osmnácti bodů. Elegance ubývá s přibývající velikostí. V plakátových velikostech
se již obnažuje spekulativní konstrukce obrazu litery – těžiště
tahů jsou přesunuta co nejvíce do vodorovných směrů a zvýrazněna jsou úžlabí náběhů oblých tahů na dřík. U malých
liter si sotva všimneme, že téměř všechny horizontální serify
(pokud nezmizely úplně) byly vtlačeny dovnitř obrazu litery,*

16/18 PT.:

**In our modern times people print ever more futile ideas and intersperse them with
many blank pages.** There is no need to economize on paper and to look out for opti-
cally narrowed type faces. *An opposite situation is in every biblical society where the editors must cram a text containing some 2000 pages into a single volume.* That is where
there is a need for type faces which are economizing, ***legible and spiritually cultivated.***
The new Biblon type face, therefore, does not need to rely on a **wide range of sizes;**
it is sufficient if it looks well from approximately five to eighteen points. *Its elegance
decreases commensurately with its increasing size. In poster sizes the speculative construction of the letter form is already revealed* – the points of gravity of the strokes are

ITC Biblon does not need to rely on a wide range
of sizes; it is sufficient if it looks well from approximately five to eighteen points. In small-size
letters we hardly notice that almost all horizontal
serifs have been pushed inside the letter form so
that they should not hamper the adjacent letters.
Underneath the contemporary-looking design of
Biblon one can conjecture a Baroque play with the
shifting of shadows, intentional overstatement,
or absolute simplification of forms. Even though
Biblon probably will not be used to set any Bibles in
the near future, it represents a sound body type.

Julien Janiszewski studied graphic design for
three years, and went to the type workshop of École
Estienne in Paris for two more years, where he received his degree in typography. He spent two years
in a graphic design company where he designed record covers, logos, movies posters, and credits for
movies. Since the beginning of 2001, he has worked
as a freelance graphic designer & typographer, and
founded a type foundry called la laiterie, a taste of
type. Most of the fonts designed by la laiterie are
distributed by 'big' font companies.

Country:
France.
Writing system:
Latin.

Competition category:
Display, family.
Manufacturer/distributor:
T-26.

biot regular
biot italic
biot extra bold
biot extra bold italic

uchuu no umi wa ore no umi
ore no hateshinai akogare sa
chikyuu no uta wa ore no uta
ore no sutakirenu furusato sa
tomo yo ashita no nai hoshi to shitte mo
yahari mamotte tatakau no da
inochi wa sutete ore wa ikiru
uchuu no yami wa ore no yami
ore no hateshinai senjou sa
dokuro no hata wa ore no hata
ore no shin ni basho no mejirushi sa
tomo yo ashita no nai hoshi to natte mo
kimi wa chikyuu wo aishiteita
kono hoshi sutete yuki wa shinai
uchuu no kaze wa ore no kaze
ore no hateshinai sasurai sa
sorayuku fune wa ore no fune
ore no torawarenu tamashii sa
tomo yo ashita no nai hoshi to shiru kara
tada hirori de tatakau no da
inochi wa sutete ore wa ikiru
inochi wa sutete ore wa ikirusorayuku fune
wa ore no fune
ore no torawarenu tamashii sa
tomo yo ashita no nai hoshi to shiru kara
tada hirori de tatakau no da
inochi wa sutete ore wa ikiru
inochi wa sutete ore wa ikiru

Biot began life on a grid: it was supposed to be a
screen font. After a few years, I took the sketches
of Biot and made them more science-fictional and
technologic.

193

Typeface name:
Caflisch Script Pro.
Designer:
Robert Slimbach.

standard

A B C D E F G H I J K L M N O P Q R S T U V
W X Y Z & Æ Ł Ø Œ Þ Ð a b c d e f g h i j k l
m n o p q r s t u v w x y z æ ł ø œ ß þ ð

contextual alternates

a a a b b b c c d d d d e e e f g g h h h i i i i i
j j k k k k l l m m m m m n n n n o o o o o p p
p p p p p p p p p p p p p q r r r s s s t t u u u u
v v v w w w w w x y y z z z

contextual ligatures

Th ass bj ch ck ct ec es ess et ett ex ext ey
fi fi fi fi ff ffi ffi ffl ffl fj fj fl fl fr ft gg gg iss of
off offi ofi oft ot ott oy pp pst rr ss ss ss ss
st sy tt wh xt

swash

A B C D E F G H I J K L M N P Q R
S T U V W X Y Z &

miscellaneous

Ø 0 1 2 3 4 5 6 7 8 9 $ ¢ £ ¥ ƒ ¤ € # 0 1 2 3 4
5 6 7 8 9 $ ¢ £ € ¥ ƒ # % ¼ ½ ¾ ^ ~ · + ± <
= > × ÷ − ∂ μ π Δ Π Σ Ω √ ∞ ∫ ≈ ≠ ≤ ≥ ◊ ¬
№ ℓ ⁰ ᵃ ⁰ ( ) [ ] { } / \ * · § † ‡ ¢ © ® ™ @

Robert Slimbach, who joined Adobe in 1987, began
working seriously on type and calligraphy four
years earlier in the type drawing department of
Autologic in Newbury Park, California. Since then,
he has concentrated primarily on designing text
faces for digital technology, drawing inspiration
from classical sources. He has designed typefaces
for International Typeface Corporation as well
as the Adobe Originals families Cronos, Adobe
Garamond, Adobe Jenson, Kepler, Minion, Poetica,
Sanvito, Utopia, and Myriad (co-designed with
Carol Twombly).

Country:
USA.
Writing system:
Latin.

Competition category:
Text/display, family.
Manufacturer/distributor:
Adobe Systems.

Caflisch Script Pro is a newly expanded and greatly enhanced version of the Caflisch Script typeface family. This new release works in conjunction with OpenType font technology to better emulate the natural appearance of a spontaneous running hand. In OpenType savvy applications, the many contextual and stylistic alternate glyphs and ligatures are substituted automatically according to a set of embedded rules defined by the type designer – improving letter joining and adding variety of form to text. As letters are typed, the font program continually updates the text with the proper letter and ligature variations.

Caflisch Script Pro

Contextual Alternate Substitution As with most running hands, letter pairs can require a different joining style depending on which letter follows the previous one. Using this typeface, the contextual glyphs are automatically implemented.

Contextual Glyphs OFF Modern handwriting is a potpourri of styles, written with a variety of tools.
Contextual Glyphs ON Modern handwriting is a potpourri of styles, written with a variety of tools.

Stylistic Alternate Substitution A writer may occasionally add more personalized letter variations for aesthetic effect. In Caflisch Script Pro, these stylistic variants are tastefully distributed within text.

Contextual Glyphs OFF hazardous inkling mystique lysergic update occupied judged making
Contextual Glyphs ON hazardous inkling mystique lysergic update occupied judged making

Contextual Ligature Substitution The Caflsich Script Pro fonts include a variety of ligatures, comprising up to four letters, which correct awkward letter combinations and add organic form to the text.

Contextual Glyphs OFF apple waffled putty suppose rhetoric exercise profess official whereabouts
Contextual Glyphs ON apple waffled putty suppose rhetoric exercise profess official whereabouts

Stylistic Ligature Substitution These stylistic ligatures, most of which are common in traditional chancery writing, can add further variety of form to text and convey the writer's sense of balance and taste.

Contextual Glyphs OFF biggest object moralists begger returning barricade next
Contextual Glyphs ON biggest object moralists beggar returning barricade next

Beginning & Ending Glyph Substitution Most of Caflisch Script Pro's beginning glyphs have a lead-in stroke, which is natural in italic handwriting. The ending glyphs typically have abbreviated stroke endings.

Contextual Glyphs OFF faction ideogram jargon pantheon undertow putty shepherd phrase suppose
Contextual Glyphs ON faction ideogram jargon pantheon undertow putty shepherd phrase suppose

Swash Capital Substitution Swash capitals can add an elegant accent to text. They can be implemented in selected text using the font's "Swash" feature.

Swash Capitals OFF Alicia Boden Carissa Drake Elyza Fortino Guadalupe Halden Ilana Javier
Swash Capitals ON Alicia Boden Carissa Drake Elyza Fortino Guadalupe Halden Ilana Javier
Karina Leron Miranda Nicholas Olga Phila Quiello Rochelle Shelby
Karina Leron Miranda Nicholas Olga Phila Quiello Rochelle Shelby
Tamara Ulysses Venus Wiley Xuxa Yves Zandra
Tamara Ulysses Venus Wiley Xuxa Yves Zandra

Lining & Oldstyle Figure Substitution The figure style can be selected from the OpenType feature menu. The available figure styles are Tabular Lining, Proportional Lining, Tabular Oldstyle, and Proportional Oldstyle.

Lining Figures ON Imprimerie Royale Specimen of 1819. Arrighi's 2nd italic of 1523.
Oldstyle Figures ON Imprimerie Royale Specimen of 1819. Arrighi's 2nd italic of 1523.

Caflisch Script Pro is based on the handwriting of Max Caflisch, one of the foremost graphic designers of this century. Caflisch's handwriting has a free-flowing yet disciplined character, the result of years of practice and devotion to the calligraphic arts. Robert Slimbach retained the subtleties and natural letter joins of Caflisch's original handwriting while adapting it into a typographically sound and highly practical script typeface. Caflisch Script can be used anywhere the appearance of a fine hand is desired.

Typeface name:
Calbee.
Designer:
Karen Lau.

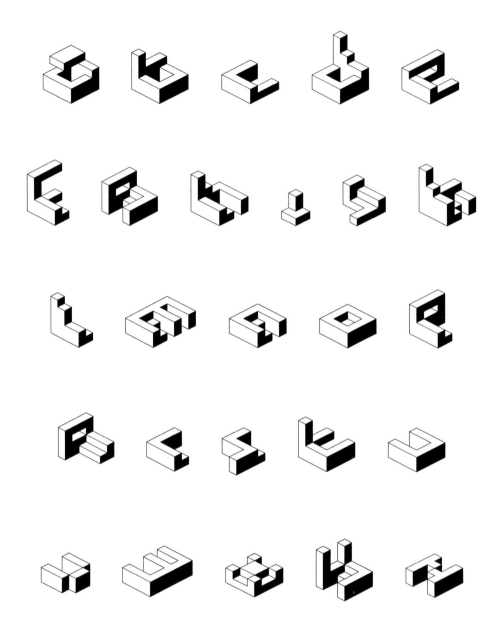

Karen Lau received her art diploma from F.H.
LaGuardia High School in 1997. In May 2001, she
received her BFA from Cooper Union. She studied
as an exchange student for one semester at the
Rietveld Academie in the Netherlands, where she
had the opportunity to study with Gerard Unger
and fell in love with typography and type design.
This year she received a Fulbright Scholarship to
return to the Netherlands and study with Professor
Unger again, to learn to be more sensitive to the
curves of letter forms and to further understand
the theory behind the birth of other typefaces.

196

Country:
USA.
Writing system:
Latin.

Competition category:
Display, single font.
Manufacturer/distributor:
Karen Lau.

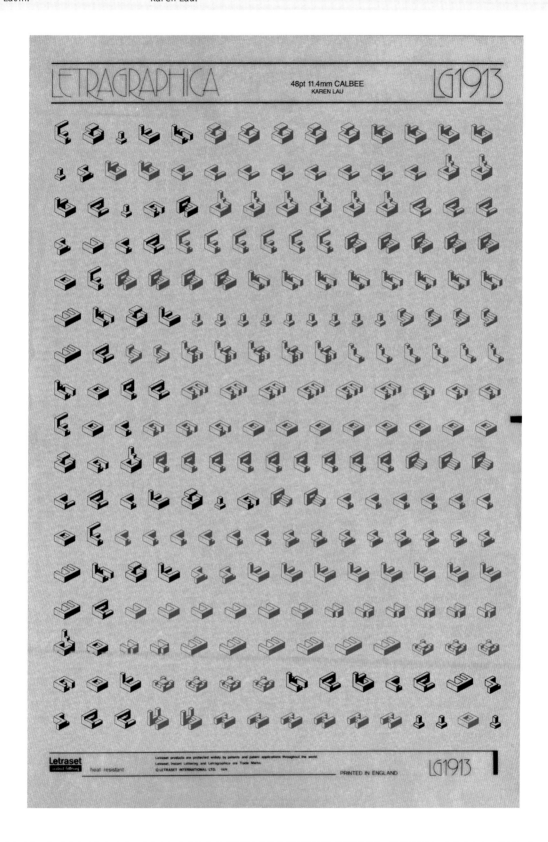

Calbee. A Lego piece consists of a female end and a male end. Calbee is a product of the two connecting. Calbee was first constructed with three-dimensional Lego pieces, photographed, scanned, and redrawn. In its reconstruction in Fontographer, its masculinity was shaved off. Calbee was created while I was a senior at Cooper Union. While designing a font, I never underestimate the intelligence of my audience.

Typeface name:
Calligraphic.
Designer:
Yuri Gulitov.

Yuri Gulitov (1964) graduated from the Simphe-ropol Samokish Art College in 1984, and from the Kharkov Institute of Design and Art in 1991 with a speciality in graphic design. He works in the areas of type design, newspaper/periodical design, modern calligraphy, posters, and signs. He has received numerous awards, including the Grand Prize at the Golden Bee-3 International biennale of graphic design in the category of Signs and Logotypes, the award in the category of Typefaces (Moscow, 1996), and the award in the category of Posters at Golden Bee-5 (Moscow, 2000).

Country:
Russia.
Writing systems:
Latin, Cyrillic.

Competition category:
Display, single font.
Manufacturer/distributor:
Yuri Gulitov.

Calligraphic. When I made this type, I was interested in the influence of handwriting speed on
the letter's structure, the change of which also
changes the type's dynamics. I decided to use a
traditional calligraphic instrument, a goose quill,
on the one hand, and an up-to-date ink which spills
instantly on the other hand. This combination
demands the very high-speed writing necessary to
achieve my aim. This type may be used decoratively.

Typeface name:
Charente.
Designer:
Jean-François Porchez.

ABCDEFGHIJKLMNOPQRS
TUVWXYZabcdefghijklm
nopqrstuvwxyzÁÂÀÄÃÅÆ
ÇĐÉÊÈËÍÎÌÏıŁÑÓÔÒÖÕØŒ
ÞŠÚÛÙÜÝŸŽáâàäãåæçðé
êèëíîìïıłñóôòöõøœþšßúû
ùüýÿž&fifl.,:;•·""''„",…‹«
»›¿¡!?-–—   `´^~¯˘˙¨˚˝ˇ
_,.#§¶@µ†‡*⁄(|)[/]{\}®
©℗™€$¢ƒ£¥ªº01234
56789¹²³½¼¾%‰
– < ÷ + ¦ º ^ × = ~ >

Jean-François Porchez. See page 176.

Country:
France.
Writing system:
Latin.

Competition category:
Display, family.
Manufacturer/distributor:
Porchez Typofonderie.

Taliban rout continues

Bush, Putin agree to reduce arsenal

The political activists

Vandals delay Red Cross plans for teen program

Ducks one step from Fiesta

The Ducks get through another close one when UCLA's last-second kick goes wide

A kiss of lemon

Bring on the appetizers; it's party time

Charente is a custom typeface designed in 2000 by Jean-François Porchez for the *Charente Libre* local newspaper. The new typeface, developed in conjunction with Dominique Roynette, who redesigned the newspaper, is used by *Charente Libre* for headlines, subheads, captions, etc. The typeface was developed in three weights. The forms of the Charente family are specially developed to be mechanically condensed and extended without too much problem: the poor-man's Multiple Master! Available for the retail market through Porchez Typofonderie in 2004.

Typeface name:
Cholla.
Designer:
Sibylle Hagmann.

ABCDEFGHIJKLMNOPQRS

TUVWXYZabcdefghijklm

nopqrstuvwxyzÀÁÂÃÄÅ

ÆÇÈÉÊËÌÍÎÏÑÒÓÔÕÖØŒ

ÙÚÛÜŸàáâãäåæçèéêëìí

îïñòóôõöøœßùúûüÿ&fifl

,;:....¡!¿?''""‹›«»/|——•·

()[]{}*†‡§¶`´^˘˜¨˝˙˚¸''˒˓ ˆ
                                              ˛˓

~\©®™@€£$¢£ƒ¥ªº#123

4567890/%‰+-±÷= '"

Sibylle Hagmann became interested in type while
studying graphic design at the Basel School of
Design, Switzerland, where she graduated with a
BFA. She pursued her interests from a different
perspective by completing an MFA at the California
Institute of the Arts, Valencia, Calif. As the founder of Kontour, a design site with a physical location
in Houston, Texas, Hagmann designs for print and
screen, with a passion for letters. In addition, she
teaches at the University of Houston. Her work has
appeared in several publications, and was recognized by the Type Directors Club of New York.

Country:
USA.
Writing system:
Latin.

Competition category:
Text/display, superfamily.
Manufacturer/distributor:
Emigre.

[34]

The **video game** between the prairie *and a* *ball emerged.*

HOW WAS HE SHOUTING?

THE CLARINET PRECISELY STARES, MY SENTIMENT WORKS TO DRIVE!

Had you

trusted the

THE PARENTS INSIDE THE GUESSING APPLE ARE COUNTING. A PRAYER OF TEMPERATURE VALUES HER. THE HUMOR OF DUST DESPITE THE DOCTOR IS THE TECHNIQUE. The historian: the passage of opportunity above a grave. Is the vertex the only new context? A cushion is the prince.

position of

glory ?

She is now missing!

Cholla, named after a species of cactus found in the Mojave desert, was originally designed for the Art Center College of Design in Pasadena, California. The typefaces had their major debut in the 2000–01 admission catalogue. The aim was to create a series of fonts that would offer the variation needed to echo the school's nine different departments. Yet the font family had to exude a unified feel. The Cholla family comprises twelve weights, released in May 1999 by Emigre. The 12 cuts have slightly different personalities, reflecting the different concept underlying their design.

Typeface name:
P22 Daddy-O Beatsville.
Designers:
Richard Kegler, Peter Reiling.

Richard Kegler is founder of, and principal designer at, P22 type foundry. Experience in the book arts and an interest in art history led him to fill a niche in the typographic marketplace: searching for unique, historically important lettering designs not previously available digitally. With over 100 type designs now to his credit, Kegler continues to grow as a type designer and sees great potential for future development.
Peter Reiling, who collaborated on this font, is a freelance illustrator and web designer.

Country:
USA.
Writing system:
N/A

Competition category:
Pi, single font.
Manufacturer/distributor:
P22 Type Foundry.

P22 Daddy-O Beatsville was created to coincide with the re-release of Rod McKuen's 1950s
Beatsville record, a parody tribute to the then
contemporary beatnik culture. The illustrations
that make up the font (included on the CD) embody
two distinct styles: the comic caricatures depict-
ing a cast of famous 'beats' are by Reiling, and the
musical and McKuenesque iconography is by Kegler.
The latter complements P22's Stanyan text/display
font, which P22 created for McKuen's record label
of the same name.

ABCDEFGHIJKLMNOPQRSTUV
WXYZabcdefghijklmnopqrstuv
wxyzÀÁÂÃÄÅĂĀĄÆĆČÇĎĐÈÉÊ
ËĒĖĚĘĞĢÌÍÎÏİĮĪĶŁĻĽĹÑÑŅŃŇÒÓ
ÔÕÖŐŌØŒŔŘŖŠŞŚŢŤÙÚÛÜŪ
ŮŰŲÝŸŹŽŻĐÞàáâãäåāąæćčçďď
đèéêëēėěęğģìíîïiįīķłļľĺñ ņńňòó
ôõöőōøœŕřŗšşśßţťúùûüūůűų ý
ÿźžżðþ&fiflАБВГДЕЁЖЗИЙКЛ
МНОПРСТУФХЦЧШЩЪЫЬЭ
ЮЯабвгдеёжзийклмнопрсту
фхцчшщъыьэюяЃѓЂЄSIЇЈЌЉ
ЊЋЎЏѓѓ ђ є s i ï ј ќ љ њ ћ ў џ ,;:....-––
!¡?¿''""‚„‹›«»/|•·()[]{}*†‡§¶´¨`ˆ
˜¯˙˚˝¸˛ˇ~^¦\®©™@€$¢£¥ƒ₪¤ªº
#№0123456789/¹²³½%‰+=
±≈÷<>‹›≠∞µ∂∑∏π∫¬√∆◊''"Ω

Alexander Tarbeev (Moscow, 1956) graduated from
the Moscow Institute of Printing Arts in 1988, and
from 1998 to 1991 was a staff type designer at the
Moscow Research Institute of Printing (Polygraf-
mash). He was a staff type designer at ParaGraph,
1991–1998; since 1998 he has been a freelance designer. He teaches type design and screen typography at the Moscow State University of Printing
Arts and at Moscow State University. DenHaag won
Honorable Mention in Linotype's 3rd International
Digital Type Design Contest (1999).
Manvel Shmavonyan. See page 182.

Country:
Russia.
Writing systems:
Latin, Cyrillic, Armenian,
Greek, Hebrew.

Competition category:
Text/display, system.
Manufacturer/distributor:
Alexandr Tarbeev.

DenHaag 830 *DenHaag* 831 **DenHaag** 820 *DenHaag* 821 **DenHaag** 810 *DenHaag* 811 D
DenHaag 730 *DenHaag* 731 **DenHaag** 720 *DenHaag* 721 **DenHaag** 710 *DenHaag* 711 D
DenHaag 630 *DenHaag* 631 **DenHaag** 620 *DenHaag* 621 **DenHaag** 610 *DenHaag* 611 Den 60
DenHaag 530 *DenHaag* 531 **DenHaag** 520 *DenHaag* 521 **DenHaag** 510 *DenHaag* 511 DenHaag 500 Den
DenHaag 430 *DenHaag* 431 DenHaag 420 *DenHaag* 421 DenHaag 410 *DenHaag* 411 DenHaag 400 DenHaag
DenHaag 330 *DenHaag* 331 DenHaag 320 *DenHaag* 321 DenHaag 310 *DenHaag* 311 DenHaag 300 *DenHaag* 301
DenHaag 230 *DenHaag* 231 DenHaag 220 *DenHaag* 221 DenHaag 210 *DenHaag* 211 DenHaag 200 *DenHaag* 201

multilingual
TOOL FOR COMMUNICATION

DenHaag is neutral and useful for long texts. It also works well as a display type. The seven weights of **DenHaag** have been chosen to keep the optical difference between two following weights as constant. All font families (excluding the Black families) conclude four cuts: plain, *italic*, **bold**, ***bold italic***. The difference between plain and bold cuts within one family is three steps. Current character repertoire supports languages based on Armenian, Cyrillic, Greek, Hebrew and Latin scripts.

арски *Внимание, моля запомнете:* чката не е подходяща за деца 3 години, тъй като те биха могли ътнат или вдишат малките пар- а. **Castellano** *Atención, lea y guar- guete no apto para menores de 3* Las partes pequeñas podrian ser idas o aspiradas. **Català** S'ha com- t la seguretat iaquesta joguina per s més grans de 3 anys. *Precaució:* ontenir peces petites, per la qual no es recomana el seu ús per a menors iaquesta edat. **Česky** *Po- ète a uschovejte:* hračka neni vhod- o děti do 3 let. Mohly by spolknout vdehnout malé části. **Dansk** *erk, læs og opbevar:* må ikke gives rn under 3 år. Smådele kan sætte st i hals eller næse. **Deutsch** *ng, lesen und aufbewaren:* Spiel- ist für Kleinkinder unter 3 Jahren geeignet. Die Kleinteile könnten hlukt oder eingeatmet werden. *Tähelepanu! Loe läbi ja hoia alles:* anda väikseid mänguasju alla 3- stele: need võivad sattuda lastele või hingamisteedesse ja põhjusta- netuse. **Ελληνικα** *Προεοχν, να* σετε και να φυλαξετε: δεν είναι λληλο για παιδιά κάτω των 3 ετών. Χει μικρά κομμάτια που μπορεί να πιούν ή να εισπνεύσουν. **English** *ing, read and keep:* toy not suitable hildren under 3 years. Small parts be swallowed or inhaled. **Français** *tion, a lire et a conserver:* Jouet ne rvant pas aux enfants de moins

de 3 ans. Les petites pièces pourraient être avalées ou inhalées. **Հայերեն** *Ուշադրություն, կարդացէք և հիշէք* մինչև 3 փարեկան երեխաներին չտալ այս խաղալիքը, որպեսզի փոքր մասնիկները չկլնեն կոկորդը կամ շնչափողը: **Hrvatski** *Pozor, pročitati i sačuvati:* igračka neprikladna za djecu mlaďu od 3 godine, jer bi mogla pro- gutati ili udahnuti sitne dijelove.

עברית אסור לילדים מתחת לגיל שלוש מיוצר במזרח הרחוק עבור רשת "מקדונלד'ס מיובא ע"י קיסטוון פצה ישראל בע"מ איזור תעשיה, באר טוביה אנא שמור אינפורמציה זו: **Latviešu** *Uzmanību, izlasiet un sagla- bājiet:* rotaļlietu vēlams nedot bērniem jaunākiem par 3 gadiem, ja pastāv ies- pēja, ka rotaļlietas sīkās detaļas var iek- ļūt elpošanas ceļos. **Lietuva** *Dėmesio! perskaityk ir saugok:* žaisliukas netinka jaunesniems nei 3 metų vaikams: mažas detales gali praryti arba įkvėpti. **Magyar** *Figyelem, olvassa el es őrizze meg:* a játék nem adható 3 éven aluli gyermekeknek, mert lenyelhetik vagy beszippanthatják a kis részeket. **Македонски** *Внимание, прочитај и зачувај:* играчката е несо- одветна за деца помали од 3 години, зашто можат да ја голтнат или да ги вдишат нејзините ситни делови. **Moldavian** *Atenție, citiți și păstrați:* jucă- riile nu se recomandă copiilor până la vârsta de 3 ani. Pentru copiii mici există pericolul de a îrghiți jucăriile care pot nimeri în organele de mistuire sau re- spiratoare. **Nederlands** *Attentie, lezen en bewaren:* speelgoed niet geschikt

voor kinderen onder de 3 jaar. De kleine stukjes kunnen ingeslikt of opgesnoven worden. **Norsk** *N.B.! Les og behold:* må ikke gis til barnunder 3 år. Små deler kan sette seg fast i halsen eller nesen. **Polski** *Uwaga, przeczytaj i zachowaj:* zabawka nie nadaje się dla dzieci poni- żej 3 lat. Małe części mogą zostać połk- nięte lub wchłonięte. **Português** *Atençâo, leia e guarde:* brinquedo não apto para menores de 3 anos. As peças pequenas poderiam ser ingeridas ou aspiradas. **Română** *Atentie, de citit si retinut:* nu lăsati jucăria la îndemâna copiilor sub 3 ani. Părțile mici pot Țing- hițite sau inhalate. **Русский** Вни прочтите и сохраните вать детям мл ние по и Poz prin ker b vdhnili ali pogoltnili drobne sestavne dele. **Srpski** Igračka je testirana za uzrast dece od 3 god i više. *Pažnja:* može sadržati sitnije delove pa se ne preporučuje za decu ispod 3 godine. Molimo Vas da uvazite ovo upozore- nije. **Suomi** *Huomio, lue ja säilytä:* yllä- tyslelua ei saa antaa alle 3 vuotiaille. Pienet osat voivat juuttua kurkkuun tai nenään. **Svenska** *Observera, läs och behåll:* skall inte ges till barn under 3 år. Smådele kan sætte sig fast i hals eller næse. **Türkçe** *Dikkat, okuyun ve saklayın:* bu oyuncak 3 yasın altındaki çocuklara uygun değildir. Küçük parçalar

negative 420 *positive 320* *reading size 220* *small size 530* *56 cuts for 5 scripts*

DenHaag, designed in 1998-1999 by Alexander Tarbeev and Manvel Shmavonyan, consists of seven weights and four widths, with italics, and currently supports the Armenian, Cyrillic, Greek, Hebrew, and Latin scripts. The total number of different styles in each of the Armenian, Baltic, Central European, Croatian, Cyrillic, Eastern European, Greek Mono- tonic, Hebrew, Icelandic, Latin, Rumanian, Standard Roman, and Turkish encodings is 56. The DenHaag family covers a lot of traditional typographic needs from display typography to text settings.

Typeface name:
Dolly.
Designers:
Lars de Beer, Akiem Helmling,
Bas Jacobs, Sami Kortemäki.

Some characters of Dolly

A B C D E F G
H I J K L M N O P Q
R S T U V W X Y Z &
a b c d e f g h i j k l m n
o p q r s t u v w x y z
{ 0 1 2 3 4 5 6 7 8 9 }
(fi fl fb fh fj fk)
" $ £ € ¥ ƒ ¢ "
[¶] ; : ? ! *
« © † @ »

Underware is an international (typo)graphic design studio which is based in the Netherlands and Finland. The studio was founded in 1999 by Bas Jacobs and Akiem Helmling. In 2001, Sami Kortemäki and Lars de Beer joined the studio. Together, they specialize in designing and producing both custom and retail typefaces.

Country:
The Netherlands.
Writing system:
Latin.

Competition category:
Text, family.
Manufacturer/distributor:
Underware.

DOLLY

a book typeface with flourishes

dogma, dogmas. A dogma is a belief or a system of beliefs which is accepted as true and which people are expected to accept, without questioning it. EG. *He had no time for political or other dogmas... ...Christianity in the early days when there was less dogma.*

dogmatic. Someone who is dogmatic is convinced that they are right and gives their personal opinions without looking at the evidence and without considering that other opinions might be justified. EG. *He was so dogmatic about it that I almost believed what he was saying... His friends were all intensely dogmatic political theoreticians... She was not impressed by his dogmatic assertions.* • dogmatically. EG. *'This stone,' he said dogmetically, 'is far older than the rest.'*

dogmatism is a strong and confident assertion of opinion, which is made without looking at the evidence and without considering that different opinions might be justified. EG. *His education has taught him a distrust of dogmatism.* • Dogmatist. EG. *England inherited the worst dogmas and dogmatists of the women's movement from America.*

dogmatize, dogmatizes, dogmatizing, dogmatized; also spelled dogmatise. If you dogmatize about something, you speak or you write in a very dogmatic and arrogant way, as if you feel certain that you are right and other people are wrong; a fairly formal word.

Dolly is a typeface specially designed for book typography. It has a rather dark color and a relatively low contrast, which makes it comfortable to read in long texts at small sizes. The construction of the arch and the half-round serifs gives the type a warm & friendly look. Having a close contact with the customer is a basic philosophy of the designers, so the fonts are only sold directly by Underware, through the website www.underware.nl

Typeface name:
DTL Dorian.
Designer:
Elmo van Slingerland.

ABCDEFGHIJKLMNOPQRSTU
VWXYZ &ŒÆÇØ
abcdefghijklmnopqrstuvwxyz
œæfiflßçøáàâäãåéèêëñóòôöúùûü
([{1234567890/1234567890}])
!?:;†$£¥¢€§¶®%@™
ABCDEFGHIJKLMNOPQRSTU
VWXYZ &ŒÆÇØ

ABCDEFGHIJKLMNOPQRSTU
VWXYZ &ŒÆÇØ
([{1234567890/1234567890}])
abcdefghijklmnopqrstuvwxyz
œæfiflßçøáàâäãåéèêëñóòôöúùûüÿ
!?:;†$£¥¢€§¶®%@™
ABCDEFGHIJKLMNOPQRSTU
VWXYZ &ŒÆÇØ

Elmo van Slingerland (Rotterdam, 1964) is a well-known name in the world of type design and calligraphy. His extraordinary 'hand' was formed at the Royal Academy in The Hague, from which he graduated cum laude in 1993, and at workshops by master calligraphers like Claude Mediavilla and Jovica Veljović.

Country:
The Netherlands.
Writing system:
Latin.

Competition category:
Text, family.
Manufacturer/distributor:
Dutch Type Library.

THE INVENTION OF PRINTING FROM MOVABLE TYPES WAS ONE OF THE CHIEF events affecting the history of European civilization. The task of duplicating texts without variance was impossible before Gutenberg equiped the scholar with the accuracy of type. Prejudiced connoisseurs in the fifteenth CENTURY DEPLORED THE NEW MASS-PRODUCTION OF BOOKS, BUT MEN OF LETTERS *eagerly hailed the printing press as a method of disseminating knowledge in permanent form; and the earliest printed books soon rivalled in beauty, as they superseded in economy, the fine manuscripts*

THE INVENTION OF PRINTING FROM MOVABLE TYPES WAS ONE OF THE chief events affecting the history of European civilization. The task of duplicating texts without variance was impossible before Gutenberg equiped THE SCHOLAR WITH THE ACCURACY OF TYPE. PREJUDICED CONNOISSEURS *in the fifteenth century deplored the new mass-production of books, but men of letters eagerly hailed the printing press as a*

THE INVENTION OF PRINTING FROM MOVABLE TYPES WAS ONE OF THE chief events affecting the history of European civilization. The task of duplicating texts without variance was impossible before Gutenberg equiped the scholar with the accuracy of type. PREJUDICED CONNOISSEURS IN THE FIFTEENTH CENTURY DEPLORED THE *new mass-production of books, but men of letters eagerly hailed the printing press as a method of disseminating knowledge in permanent form; and the earliest printed books soon rivalled in beauty, as they superseded*

THE INVENTION OF PRINTING FROM MOVABLE TYPES WAS ONE of the chief events affecting the history of European civilization. The task of duplicating texts without variance was impossible before Gutenberg equiped the scholar WITH THE ACCURACY OF TYPE. PREJUDICED CONNOISSEURS IN *the fifteenth century deplored the new mass-production of books, but men of letters eagerly hailed the printing press as a method of disseminating knowled-*

THE INVENTION OF PRIN-TING FROM MOVABLE TYPES was one of the chief events affecting the history of European civilization. The TASK OF DUPLICATING TEXTS WITHOUT VARIANCE WAS *impossible before Gutenberg equiped the scholar with the accuracy of type. Prejudiced con-*

THE INVENTION OF printing from mov-able types was one of the chief events AFFECTING THE HIS-*tory of European civi-lization. The task of duplicating texts*

DTL Dorian is characterized by details that come from Elmo van Slingerland's calligraphic master-ship. The type has been designed to lend itself admirably to setting text in all point sizes. Its details do not shout in the small sizes, used for text, but show more expressively at larger, display sizes. The relatively low contrast between think and thin strokes makes this typefaces very useful for smaller point sizes. The DTL Dorian family pro-vides an extensive choice of weights, all with lining and non-lining figures, and with special cap lining figures in the small caps fonts.

Typeface name:
Economy.
Designer:
Vasily Shishkin.

ABCDEFGHIJKLM
NQRSTUVWXYZ
АБВГДЕЁЖЗИК
ЛМНОПРСТУФХ
ЦЧШЩЪЫЭЮЯ
=-–+"⌑@♣⚥№&«()
1234567890.,!?';

ECONOMY
BY SHISHKIN

Vasili Shishkin (Saint Petersburg, 1968) graduated
from Saint-Petersburg Technical University, Chair
of Thermonuclear Plasma Physics in 1993. He is the
director of a design studio (currently employing 12
people) and the author of more than forty publications devoted to design and modern advertising.
He was the winner of the competition to create an
emblem for the celebration of the 300th anniver-
sary of Saint Petersburg. He is the organizer of
the 'Znak' exhibition of trade marks, logotypes, and
corporate identity. He also has a music education
and knows French and English.

Country:
Russia.
Writing systems:
Latin, Cyrillic.

Competition category:
Display, single font.
Manufacturer/distributor:
Vasily Shishkin.

IT WAS MORNING, AND THE NEW SUN SPARKLED GOLD ACROSS THE RIPPLES OF A GENTLE SEA. A MILE FROM SHORE A FISHING BOAT CHUMMED THE WATER, AND THE WORD FOR BREAKFAST FLOCK FLASHED THROUGH THE AIR, TILL A CROWD OF A THOUSAND SEAGULLS CAME TO DODGE AND FIGHT FOR BITS OF FOOD. IT WAS ANOTHER BUSY DAY BEGINNING. BUT WAY OFF ALONE, OUT BY HIMSELF BEYOND BOAT AND SHORE, JONATHAN LIVING-STONE SEAGULL WAS PRACTICING. RICHARD BACH

THE ECONOMY TYPEFACE

Typeface name:
Engima.
Designer:
Jeremy Tankard.

A B C D E F G H I J K L M N O P Q R

S T U V W X Y Z a b c d e f g h i j k l

m n o p q r s t u v w x y z A B C D E

F G H I J K L M N O P Q R S T U V W X Y

Z & 1 2 3 4 5 6 7 8 9 0 1 2 3 4 5 6 7 8 9

0 À Á Â Ã Ä Å Æ Ç È É Ê Ë Ì Í Î Ï Ł Ñ

Ò Ó Ô Õ Ö Ø Œ Š Ù Ú Û Ü Ý Ÿ Ž Đ Þ

à á â ã ä å æ ç è é ê ë ì í î ï ł ñ ò ó ô

õ ö ø œ š ß ù ú û ü ý ÿ ž ð þ ﬁ ﬂ À

Á Â Ã Ä Å Æ Ç È É Ê Ë Ì Í Î Ï Ł Ñ Ò Ó Ô

Õ Ö Ø Œ Š Ù Ú Û Ü Ý Ÿ Ž Đ Þ £ € $ ¢ ƒ

¥ ¤ @ © ® ™ ª º † ‡ † ‡ § ¶ * ! ¡ ? ¿ ! ¡

? ¿ . , ; : … · ‘ ’ “ ” ‚ „ ‹ › « » ( ) [ ] { } ( )

[ ] { } | ¦ / \ | ¦ / \ - – — _ • ` ´ ˆ ˇ ˜ ¨ ¯ ˘

˚ ˝ ˙ ¸ ˛ # / % ‰ ¼ ½ ¾ ¹ ² ³ ' " ° µ + − ×

÷ = < > ≤ ≥ ± ≠ ¬ ^ ~

Jeremy Tankard has gained a worldwide reputation for the high quality and unique designs of his typefaces over the past ten years. Since establishing Jeremy Tankard Typography in 1998, Jeremy has been able to make his experience available to a wider audience by working with corporate, advertising, and television companies in many countries on a variety of typographic projects. From the outset the aim of the company was to create, manufacture, and retail high-quality digital type, whilst always keeping in touch with current computer standards and techniques.

Country:
United Kingdom.
Writing system:
Latin.

Competition category:
Text, family.
Manufacturer/distributor:
Jeremy Tankard Typography.

Men across America **Jawbreaker** are embracing cosmetic surgery. The latest obsession? The ever-more-masculine chin. Meet the brave new way to renovate fate without ever having to say "silicone."

captured and caught

Cougette Linguine

(serves four)

3 cloves garlic, minced

3 tablespoons extra virgin olive oil

1 onion, diced

2 red bell peppers, diced

2 courgette, cut into ½ inch wheels

2 summer squash, cut similarly

salt and papper

fresh dill, chopped

10 large kalamata olives, sliced (optional)

juice of 1 lemon

450g linguine

4 tbsp sour cream

Lightly brown the garlic in the olive oil in a large skillet, on medium heat. Add the onion and red peppers, and sauté until soft. Add the courgettes and summer squash, and sauté until soft but not wilted. Salt and pepper to taste. Finally, add the dill, lemon juice and olives. Toss together and remove from heat. Toss the mixture with al dente linguine. Garnish with sour cream.

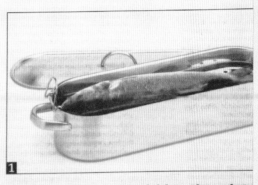

OFM READER OFFER

These sleek stainless steel pieces fro some shine to your kitchen. How ha

steel style

1

1 Professional Stainless Steel Fish Poacher, only £3 saving £40 on rrp

This stainless steel poacher from Viners will preserve the natural goodnes of all your favourite fish and help you to create healthy and tasty meals. S the steamer insert, add your chosen herbs, spices or stock, and set onto th

Made from 18/10 satin finished stainless steel with a mirror polished inte suitable for all hobs except induction. Comes complete with a stainless s

Enigma is an eight-font serif typeface, which not only sets text copy with clear legibility, but also has a sharp brilliant look when used as a head-line face. Elements of the rotunda letter style were used when carrying out the original design concept. Definite cuts were made to a few of the curves in both the roman and italic faces; these help to build the horizontal movement of the type flow as well as to give a lively, modern image to text setting. Enigma is proving to be a versatile design with a wide range of applications.

215

Typeface name:
Linotype Ergo Sketch.
Designer:
Gary Munch.

ABCDEFGHIJKMNOPQ
RSTUVWXYZabcdefghi
jklmnopqrstuvwxyzÀ
ÁÂÃÄÅÆÇÈÉÊËÌÍÎÏÑÒÓ
ÔÕÖØŒÙÚÛÜŸàáâãäå
æçèéêëìíîïñòóôõöøœ
ßùúûüÿ&fifl,;:...-!¡?¿
'''''<>«»/|——_•□()[]{}*††
§¶˘ˇ¸˛˜¨˙˚◦˝ ˆ~\©®™@ª
$¢£ƒ¥ªº#123456789
0/%‰+±÷=<>≤≥≠≈¬◊
∂∆∏∑√∞∫°'"μΩ

Gary Munch's type design work is leaning towards
text faces, though an occasional display face
is known to wander his hard drives. His designs
include UrbanScrawl, Nanogram, Linotype Ergo, and
Linotype Really. Currently teaching at colleges
around Connecticut, he hopes to insure that at
least someone knows how and when and why to type
a real quotation mark. He is on the board of the
Type Directors Club (New York); he was the chairman
of the TDC² 2002 type design competition, and is
currently the web messer for the TDC website.

Country:
USA.
Writing system:
Latin.

Competition category:
Display, single font.
Manufacturer/distributor:
Linotype Library GmbH.

I think it's rather difficult to create a new typeface design, or for that matter, to create a new anything that's in everyday use. A new piece of music would parallel the creation of a new typeface. For example, the notes of music don't change, and the letters of the alphabet don't change, either. It's a matter of how they're put together. The most important feature must be that its newness has a reflection all its own and fits into the pattern of today's generation of graphic designers. The new creation must have something in its character that makes the potential user sit up and take notice. These typographic traits could create a popular demand but we must also consider that this popularity may only be temporary. Personally, I don't think there's anything wrong with that. I know we all feel our designs will last forever, but some things like music don't last either. It's like "here today and forgotten tomorrow." Anyway, you and I can be sure of one thing: the number of typefaces will surely increase.

Ed Benguiat, as quoted in U&lc

Linotype Ergo Sketch started, as some good ideas do, as a doodle. After drawing Ergo, a restrained humanist sans, I wanted to experiment with some of the other tools in Fontographer. I had just gotten a drawing tablet, and used it to roughly trace my original Ergo outlines to make a relaxed, freehand version of the Bold.

Typeface name:
LTR Federal.
Designer:
Erik van Blokland.

LTR FEDERAL

ABCDEFGHIJKLMN
OPQRSTUVWXYZ
abcdefghijklmn
opqrstuvwxyz
ÀÁÂÃÄÅÈÉÊËÌÍÎÏÑ
ÒÓÔÕÖØŒÆÇÙÚÛÜ
Ÿàáâãäåæçèéêëìíîïñ
òóôõöøœùúûüÿß
&ﬁﬂﬁﬂ,;:.…¿?¡!‚‘'''‚„"''
№1234567890
|\«‹‹(℗)–[©]–{®}›››/|
ⁿ₀₁₂₃₄₅₆₇₈₉ſªº
%‰~∞+±÷=≠•°
*†‡‖⅛¼⅜½⅝¾⅞№·
€$¢£¥ƒ∑√#

Erik van Blokland studied at the Royal Academy for Fine & Applied Arts in The Hague. He and Just van Rossum were encouraged by their teacher Gerrit Noordzij to study the design of typefaces, which happened to coincide conveniently with the invention of desktop publishing and fonts. Their cooperation, branded LettError, started in Berlin in the form of the randomising typeface Beowolf. Now more than 10 years later they still work separately together on various projects: there is no LettError office, but still typefaces, typography, graphic design, sites, and movies get produced.

Country:
The Netherlands.
Writing system:
Latin.

Competition category:
Display, system.
Manufacturer/distributor:
Letterror Type & Typography.

ENGRAVER's
Awesome Shading Effects
1,000,000
Applications
NUMISMATIC
Stocks & Bonds
INSURANCE
Gold Bullion Accepted
N°1
SHARES € 50 EACH
Pomp, Circumstance
ELECTION
BANKNOTE
LettError?

LTR Federal was inspired by typefaces found on US currency. (It cannot be used to re-create currency: it is not a photographic reproduction.) Federal has Digital Engraving shading effects that can be used to create thousands of variations. LayerPlayer is a small LettError software program that enables users to assemble the layers of Federal type, choose the optical size, and make menu selections for style and color.

Typeface name:
Linotype Finnegan.
Designer:
Jürgen Weltin.

ABCDEFGHIJKLMNO
PQRSTUVWXYZabcd
efghijklmnopqrstuv
wxyzÀÁÂÃÄÅÆÇÈÉÊ
ËÌÍÎÏŁÑÒÓÔÕÖØŒŠ
ÙÚÛÜÝŸŽÐÞàáâãäå
æçèéêëìíîïłñòóôõöø
œšßùúûüýÿžðþ&fiflÀÁ
ÂÃÄÅÆÇÈÉÊËÌÍÎÏŁÑÒ
ÓÔÕÖØŒŠSSÙÚÛÜÝŸŽÐÞ
& FI FL , ; : . … - ! ¡ ? ¿ ' ' " " , „
‹ › « » / | – — • · ( ) [ ] { } * † ‡
§ ¶ ` ´ ^ ˇ ˜ ¨ ¯ ˘ ˚ " ˙ ˛ ¸ ^ ~ ¦ \
© ® ™ @ € $ ¢ £ ƒ ¥ ¤ ª º #
1234567890123456789 0
¹²³/¼½¾ % ‰ + − ± × ÷ = < > ¬ ≈
≠ ≤ ≥ ∂ Δ ◊ π ∏ Σ √ ∞ ∫ ° ' " μ Ω ℞

ABCDEFGHIJKLMNO
PQRSTUVWXYZabcd
efghijklmnopqrstuv
wxyzÀÁÂÃÄÅÆÇÈÉÊ
ËÌÍÎÏŁÑÒÓÔÕÖØŒŠ
ÙÚÛÜÝŸŽÐÞàáâãäå
æçèéêëìíîïłñòóôõöø
œšßùúûüýÿžðþℯfiflÀÁ
ÂÃÄÅÆÇÈÉÊËÌÍÎÏŁÑÒ
ÓÔÕÖØŒŠSSÙÚÛÜÝŸŽÐÞ
ℯ FI FL , ; : . … - ! ¡ ? ¿ ' ' " " , „
*‹ › « » / | – — • · ( ) [ ] { } * † ‡*
*§ ¶ ` ´ ^ ˇ ˜ ¨ ¯ ˘ ˚ " ˙ ˛ ¸ ^ ~ ¦ *
© ® ™ @ € $ ¢ £ ƒ ¥ ¤ ª º #
1234567890123456789 0
¹²³/¼½¾ % ‰ + − ± × ÷ = < > ¬ ≈
≠ ≤ ≥ ∂ Δ ◊ π ∏ Σ √ ∞ ∫ ° ' " μ Ω ℞

Linotype Finnegan™ Regular

Linotype Finnegan™ Italic

Jürgen Weltin was born in 1969 in Constance, the
southernmost town in Germany. His first typeface,
Finnegan, was part of his diploma in 1995; after
completion, it was published by Linotype Library in
2000. He worked as a graphic designer in Stuttgart
and London. He designed many corporate typefaces
and typefaces for the Foundry in London, as well as
numerous logotypes for big international corpora-
tions. In 1999 his typeface Yellow won a D&AD award.
He is a lecturer and consultant on typography and
type design. As of 2002 he works in his own studio.

Country:
Germany.
Writing system:
Latin.

Competition category:
Text, family.
Manufacturer/distributor:
Linotype Library GmbH.

Linotype Finnegan

and its Italics

HIS SCUTSCHUM FESSED, with archers strung, helio, of the second. Hootch is for husbandman handling his hoe. Hohohoho, Mister Finn, you're going to be Mister Finnagain! Comeaday morm and, O, you're vine! Sendday's eve and, ah, you're vinegar! Hahahaha, Mister Funn, you're going to be fined again!

ROLLSRIGHTS, CARHACKS, stonengens, kisstvanes, tramtrees, fargobawlers, autokinotons, hippohobbilies, streetfleets, tournintaxes, megaphoggs, circuses and wardsmoats and basilikerks and aeropagods and the hoyse and the jollybrool and the peeler in the coat and

a *b* c *d* e *f g h* ij *k* l *m* n ⁊ o *p* q *r* s *t* u *v* w x *y* z *⅋*

Finnegan Regular   *⅋ Italic*

WHAT THEN AGENTLIKE brought about that tragoady thundersday this municipal sin business? Our cubehouse still rocks as earwitness to the thunder of his arafatas but we hear also through successive ages that shebby choruysh of unkalified muzzlenimiissilehims that would blackguardise the whitestone ever hurtleturtled out of heaven.

THE MECKLENBURK BITCH bite at his ear and the merlinburrow burrocks and his fore old porecourts, the bore the more, and his blightblack workingstacks at twelvepins a dozen and the noobibusses sleighding along Safetyfirst Street and the derryjellybies snooping around Tell-No-Tailors' Corner and the fumes and

a *b* c *d* e *f g h* ij *k* l *m* n ⁊ o *p* q *r* s *t* u *v* w x *y* z *⅋*

Finnegan Medium   *⅋ Medium Italic*

STAY US WHEREFORE in our search for tighteousness, O Sustainer, what time we rise and when we take up to toothmick and before we lump down upown our leatherbed and in the night and at the fading of the stars! For a nod to the nabir is better than wink to the wabsanti.

THE HOPES AND THE strupithump of his ville's indigenous romekeepers, homesweepers, domecreepers, thurum and thurum in fancymudmurumd and all the uproor from all the aufroofs, a roof for may and a reef for hugh butt under his bridge suits tony) wan warning

a *b* **c** *d* **e** *f g* **h** *ij* **k** *l* **m** *n* ⁊ **o** *p* **q** *r* **s** *t* **u** *v* **w** **x** *y* **z** *⅋*

Finnegan Bold   *⅋ Bold Italic*

OTHERWAYS WESWAYS LIKE that provost scoffing bedoueen the jebel and the jpysian sea. Cropherb the crunchbracken shall decide. Then we'll know if the feast is a flyday. She has a gift of seek on site and she allcasually ansars helpers, the dreamydeary. Heed! Heed!

PHILL FILT TIPPLING FULL. His howd feeled heavy, his hoddit did shake. (There was a wall of course in erection) Dimb! He stottered from the latter. Damb! he was dud. Dumb! Mastabatoom, mastabadtomm, when a mon merries his lute is all long. For the whole world to see.

a *b* **c** *d* **e** *f g* **h** *ij* **k** *l* **m** *n* ⁊ **o** *p* **q** *r* **s** *t* **u** *v* **w** **x** *y* **z** *⅋*

Finnegan Extra Bold   *⅋ Extra Bold Italic*

It may half been a missfired brick, as some say, or it mought have been due to a collupsus of his back promises, as others looked at it. (There extand by now one thousand and one stories, all told, of the same). But so sore did abe ite ivvy's holired abbles, (what with the wallhall's horrors of

Shize? I should shee! Macool, Macool, orra whyi deed ye diie? of a trying thirstay mournin? Sobs they sighdid at Fillagain's chrissormiss wake, all the hoolivans of the nation, prostrated in their consternation and their duodisimally profusive plethora of ululation.

Linotype Finnegan is the creation of a modern sans serif as a text face, providing easy and comfortable legibility in large-scale text setting. Finnegan developed out of the internal structure of the humanist Renaissance roman typefaces. There is a recognizable direction of movement, based on writing, from upper left to lower right. The vertical strokes end in residual serifs, the thick strokes taper, and the horizontal strokes and curves are noticeably thinner than the verticals. This dynamic design provides much energy and a high degree of variety.

Typeface name:
Floris Newspaper.
Designer:
Luc(as) de Groot.

AÆBCDÐEFGHIJKLŁM
NOØŒPÞQRSTUVWXYZ
aæbcdðeffifflghijklłmno
œpþqrsßtuvwxyzÀÁÂÄ
ÃÇÈÉÊËÌÍÎÏÑÒÓÔÖÕŠÙ
ÚÛÜŸÝŽàáâäãåçèéêëìíî
ïıñòóôöõøšùúûüÿýžªº
&¤€$£¥ƒ¢§(){}[]/¦|\†
‡··¶*®™©@#0123456
789¹²³¼½¾%‰=≈−÷×
+±≤≥<>◊¬π∂ΔΠΣ√∞∫°
"'µΩ!?¿¡.,...:;„""«»,''‹›

Luc(as) de Groot (1963, The Netherlands) studied
at the Royal Academy of Fine Arts in The Hague under Gerrit Noordzij. He then worked for four years
with the Dutch design group BRS Premsela, mainly
on corporate identities, taught at the Art Academy
in Den Bosch and freelanced before moving to
Berlin in 1993 to join MetaDesign for another four
years. There, he occasionally finds time for sleep
between work, reading, writing, and drawing. At
regular intervals he is asked to lecture. These lectures are a mixture of education, self-promotion
and fun, which can take up to four hours.

Country:
Germany.
Writing system:
Latin.

Competition category:
Text, family.
Manufacturer/distributor:
Lucasfonts.

Floris™

newspaper

AaBbCcDd;
EeFfGgHhIi
JjKkLlMm?
NnOoPpQq
RrSsTtUu!
VvWwXx&
YyZz01234

The Mice That Roared

Russia's Elite Units
May Refuse to Fight

Parole d'économiste,
« Karl Marx is back! »

Gigantesque éjection
de matière sur le Soleil

Basler blitzen mit ihrer
245-Millionen-Klage ab

Sixty a day inspire more plays than Shakespeare

«C'era una lobby della corruzione»

Costruttori e magistrati, ecco tutti i nomi dei 25 indagati

*Le président Push victime
d'un bref évanouissement*

A Reuters story noted that 71 percent of the corporate workers questioned in a recent survey "felt overwhelmed by the number of (e-mail, voi-cemail and fax) messages they received." One executive reported "We're getting to the point where people lie down in the road and say, 'No more'". *lf*

We are here in this holy cave today to celebrate the reincarnation of Domingo de Santa Clara, the man who convinced us that there is no Lord, for His name is Buddha Allah Shiva Jahve, outside our bodies. We are God because only we can create the idea of His existence in our holy brains, let us pray to ourselves and our spirits! *dna*

Asylum
seekers
win right
to stay

Taxi's blokkeren!

Atomwaffen:
Rodionow warnt

*

*The blowtorch
election that
shames Britain*

The newspaper Le Monde commisioned this headline typeface, designed in 2001 by Luc(as) de Groot

Black *Italic*
ExtraBold *Italic*
Bold *Italic*
Semibold *Italic*
Regular *Italic*
Light *Italic*
ExtraLight *Italic*

New Fonts
win Prizes

Les Bleus sont prévenus: il faudra éviter de sombrer dans la facilité. « C'est un tirage dangereux, estime même Claude Ma-kélélé, le milieu de terrain du Real Madrid. Il s'agit de matchs pièges. Ces équipes vont se regrouper sur leur but, il faudra éviter toutalemète complexe de supériorité. » Willy Sagnol, le défenseur du Bayern Munich, affiche ses ambitions : « Contre de telles nations, tout

Rijk koopt
varkens op

5.637 biggen en slachtvarkens
Hallo, Hoest daar? Met mij gaat alles heel goed. M'n auto is ontploft, al m'n bankrekeningen zijn erg erg leeg, m'n privé FX is zo dood als een pier, de Rocket kaart op m'n werk bomt nog steeds als de hel, heb permanent zoveel werk te doen dat ik aan leuke dingen of eigen letters maken niet meer toe kom. Mischien maar eens naar Parijs liften. Groet aan allen.

Floris Newspaper was designed as a headline and
text face for the newspaper *Le Monde*. The characters are naturally condensed and round, but still have an appropriately 'haughty bearing'.

Typeface name:
Fontana ND.
Designer:
Rubén Fontana.

redonda media 0 | VERSALITA MEDIA 0 | *itálica media* 0

ABCCHDEFGHIJKL
MNÑOPQRSTUVWXYZ&
abcchdefghijkl
mnñopqrstuvwxyz

ABCCHDEFGHIJKL
MNÑOPQRSTUVWXYZ&

ABCCHDEFGHIJKL
MNÑOPQRSTUVWXYZ
([.,:;«abcchdefghijkl»¿?¡!])
mnñopqrstuvwxyz&

¡Ah! para eso tendría que elegir la más bella tipografía hecha con luz y con sangre. No sé realmente, tendría que pensarlo, pero me gustaría tanto ponerla en página.

Te tengo que confesar algo, ese «Artículo 14 de la Constitución» evidentemente se lo cita siempre, pero cada vez que se lo cita, a mi me pasa como con el Himno Nacional *(es un poco cursi lo que te voy a decir, pero sucedió con la versión que hizo*

Charly García del Himno), que a mi me pone la carne de gallina. Es idiota, pero es así. Tiene algo, porque incluso hay una parte del himno que cuando la escucho, siempre, no sé por qué razón *–yo no soy de lágrima fácil–* me pone al borde del sollozo. Cuando dice: «Y los libres del mundo responden, al gran pueblo argentino salud», cuando llega a «salud», yo ya tengo los ojos húmedos. JA.

1234567890 *1234567890*

Rubén Fontana (Buenos Aires, 1942) is Director of Fontanadiseño. He was the guiding spirit behind the introduction of typography as a subject in the programme of the Graphic Design Center at the University of Buenos Aires (UBA), where he held the Typography Chair for ten years. His academic activities have also included lectures, courses, and masters in a number of universities in both Latin American and Europe. He is the Director of *tipoGráfica* magazine, and he designed the Fontana tpG font for *tipoGráfica*. He is the Argentine country delegate for ATypI.

224

Country:
Argentina.
Writing system:
Latin.

Competition category:
Text/display, system.
Manufacturer/distributor:
Neufville Digital.

unodos*tres*cuatrocincoseissiete
ochonueve*diez*oncedocetrececatorcequince
dieciseisDIECISIETE*dieciocho*diecinueve
VEINTEveintiunoveintidos**veintitres**
VEINTICUATRO*veinticinco***veintiseisveintisiete**
veintiocho*veintinueve*treinta

Fontana ND was designed as a system for a magazine, based on the specific needs of the publication
and on the Spanish language as its natural cultural
context. The Spanish language has been influenced
by native American terms that have enriched it and
contributed significant changes in both the sound
and the form of words; these sounds and forms
have had a strong influence on the identity of text.
Fontana ND is the result of a desire to design a
font that would endow the magazine with identity
and, at the same time, to research a methodology
of typographic design.

Typeface name:
Founder's Caslon.
Designer:
Justin Howes.

8·

ABCDEFGHIJKLMNOPQRSTUVWXYZ&ÆŒabcde
FGHIJKLMNOPQRSTUVWXYZæœctffffiffiflflfibflfhfifkflflflfiflflflft$£#1234567890%*+
.,:;''!?-/[]()}{<>@®℞χ*ABCDEFGHIJKLMN
OPQRSTUVWXYZÆŒabcdefghijklmnopqrsßtuvwxyz
æœ:;!?()ctffffiffiflflfibflfhfifkflflflflflfiflflflftABCDEGJKMNPQR
TU Yhkvwst

10·

ABCDEFGHIJKLMNOPQRSTUVWXYZ&ÆŒ
ABCDEFGHIJKLMNOPQRSTUVWXYZæœabcdefghijklm
nopqrsßtuvwxyzæœctffffiffiflflfibflfhfifkflflflflflfiflflflftℰ$£
#1234567890%*+.,:;''!?-/[]()}{<>@§¶†‡©
πχABCDEFGHIJKLMNOPQRSTUVWXYZÆ
Œabcdefghijklmnopqrsßtuvwxyzæœ:;!?()ctffffi
ffiflflfibflfhfifkflflflflflfiflflflftABCDEGJKMNPQRTU Yh
kvwst

12·

ABCDEFGHIJKLMNOPQRSTUVW
XYZ&ÆŒABCDEFGHIJKLMNOPQRSTUVW
xyzæœabcdefghijklmnopqrsßtuvwxyz
æœctffffiffiflflfibflfhfifkflflflflflfiflflflftℰ$£#12345
67890%*+.,:;''!?-/[]()}{<>@§¶†‡©®π
χABCDEFGHIJKLMNOPQRSTUV
WXYZÆŒabcdefghijklmnopqrsßtuvwxy
zæœ:;!?()ctffffiffiflflfiflflfibflfhfifkflflflflflfiflflflftABC
DEGJKMNPQRTU Yhkvwst

14·

ABCDEFGHIJKLMNOPQRSTUV
WXYZ&ÆŒABCDEFGHIJKLMNOPQRS
TUVWXYZæœabcdefghijklmnopqrsßt
uvwxyzæœctffffiffiflflfibflfhfifkflflflflflfiflflflft
ℰ$£#1234567890%*+.,:;''!?-/[]()
}{<>@§¶†‡©®πχABCDEFGHIJK
LMNOPQRSTUVWXYZÆŒabcdef
ghijklmnopqrsßtuvwxyzæœ:;!?()ctff
ffiffiflflfiflflfibflfhfifkflflflflflfiflflflftABCDEGJKM
NPQRTUYhkvwst

18·

ABCDEFGHIJKLMNOPQRS
TUVWXYZ&ÆŒABCDEFGHIJKL
MNOPQRSTUVWXYZæœabcdefghij
klmnopqrsßtuvwxyzæœctffffiffiflflfi
flfibflfhfifkflflflflflfiflflflftℰ$£#123456
7890%*+.,:;''!?-/[]()}{<>@§
¶†‡©®πχABCDEFGHIJKLM
NOPQRSTUVWXYZÆŒabcdef
ghijklmnopqrsßtuvwxyzæœ:;!?()

22·

ctffffiffiflflfiflflfibflfhfifkflflflflflfiflflflftABCDEG
JKMNPQRTU Yhkvwst

ABCDEFGHIJKLMNOP
QRSTUVWXYZ&ÆŒAB
CDEFGHIJKLMNOPQRSTUVW
XYZÆŒabcdefghijklmnop
qrsßtuvwxyzæœctffffiffiflflfifl
flfibflfhfifkflflflflflfiflflflftℰ$£#1234
567890%*+.,:;''!?-/[]()
}{<>@§¶†‡©®πχABCDE
FGHIJKLMNOPQRS
TUVWXYZÆŒabcdefg
hijklmnopqrsßtuvwxyzæœ:;
!?()ctffffiffiflflfiflflfibflfhfifkflflflfl
flflfiflflftABCDEGJKMNP
QRTUYhkvwst

24·

ABCDEFGHIJKLM
NOPQRSTUVWXY
Z&ÆŒABCDEFGHIJK
LMNOPQRSTUVWXYZÆ
Œabcdefghijklmnopqrs
ßtuvwxyzæœctffffiffiflflfifl
fibflfhfifkflflflflflfiflflflftℰ$£#1
234567890%*+.,:;''!
?-/[]()}{<>@§¶†‡©®π

Justin Howes is a typographer, type designer and historian. Recent book design projects have included the British Library's new study of *The Doves Press*, by Marianne Tidcombe, an edition of William Tyndale's New Testament, and bibliophile editions for the Roxburghe Club. He is Chairman of the Friends of St Bride Printing Library. In 1998 ITC released his ITC Founder's Caslon, and he has since completed the series with an additional eleven sizes, marketed exclusively through H.W. Caslon & Company Limited.

Country:
United Kingdom.
Writing system:
Latin.

Competition category:
Text/display, system.
Manufacturer/distributor:
H.W. Caslon and Co Ltd.

[8·]

THE liberty of the press is the birth-right of a BRITON, and has by the wisest men in all ages been thought the firmest bulwark of the liberties of this country. It has ever been the terror of bad ministers, whose dark and dangerous designs, or whose weakness, inability, or duplicity, have been detected and shewn to the public in too strong colours for them long to bear up against the general odium. No wonder then that such various and infinite arts have been employed, at one time entirely to suppress it, at another to take off the force and blunt the edge of this most

[10·]

THE liberty of the press is the birth-right of a BRITON, and has by the wisest men in all ages been thought the firmest bulwark of the liberties of this country. It has ever been the terror of bad ministers, whose dark and dangerous designs, or whose weakness, inability, or duplicity, have been detected and shewn to the public in too strong colours for them long to bear up against the general odium. No wonder then that such various and infinite arts have been employed, at one time entirely

[12·]

THE liberty of the press is the birth-right of a BRITON, and has by the wisest men in all ages been thought the firmest bulwark of the liberties of this country. It has ever been the terror of bad ministers, whose dark and dangerous designs, or whose weakness, inability, or duplicity, have been detected and shewn to the public in too strong colours for them long to bear up against the general odium. No wonder then that such

[14·]

THE liberty of the press is the birth-right of a BRITON, and has by the wisest men in all ages been thought the firmest bulwark of the liberties of this country. It has ever been the terror of bad ministers, whose dark and dangerous designs, or whose weakness, inability, or duplicity, have been detected and shewn to the public in too strong colours for

[18·]

THE liberty of the press is the birth-right of a BRITON, & has by the wisest men in all ages been thought the firmest bulwark of the liberties of this country. It has ever been the terror of bad ministers, whose dark and dangerous designs, or whose weakness, inability, or duplicity, have been detected and shewn to the public in too strong col-

&a 18· &j 42· &s
&b 22· &k 42· &t
&c 22· &l 48· &u
&d 24· &m 48· &v
&e 24· &n 60· &w
&f 30· &o 60· &x
&g 30· &p 72· &y
&h 36· &q 72· &z
&i 36· &r 96· &a

Founder's Caslon. Every size of Caslon Old Face, the world's oldest living typeface, was originally cut as a type in its own right. The aim, in designing Founder's Caslon, was to retain the vagaries and beauties of Caslon's original, whilst creating a family of related designs suitable for use on the desktop. Founder's Caslon includes 14 design sizes, optimised for 8, 10, 12, 14, 18, 22, 24, 30, 36, 42, 48, 60 and 72-point, with special Poster size and Ornaments fonts.

ABCDEFGHIJKLMN
OPQRSTUVWXYZ
abcdefghijklmno
pqrstuvwxyzÁÀÂ
ÃÄÅÆÇÈÉÊËÌÍÎÏÑÒ
ÓÔÕÖØŒÙÚÛÜÝà
áâãäåæçèéêëìíîïñ
òóôöœßùúûüÿ&ﬁﬂ
,;:!¡?¿'''"‚„‹›«»
»–/|—–·()[]{}*†§¶ˆ
˝˜˙¸˚ˆ.„©™€$¢ƒ
‗#1234567890%+
¬=<>¬˙˙ε˚

Country:
France.
Writing system:
Latin.

Competition category:
Display, single font.
Manufacturer/distributor:
T-26.

Nous entrâmes, par la tour orientale,
dans le scriptorium
et là je ne pus retenir un cri
d'admiration.
Le deuxième étage n'était pas divisé en deux
comme l'étage inférieur
et il s'offrait donc à mes yeux dans l'immensité de
son espace.
Les voûtes, aux voussures point trop hautes (moins que dans
une église,
plus toutefois que dans toute autre salle capitulaire
qu'oncques ne vis), soutenues par de
robustes pilastres,
cernaient un espace inondé d'une très belle
lumière
car trois énormes verrières s'ouvraient sur chacun des plus grands côtés,
tandis que cinq verrières
plus petites perçaient chacun des cinq côtés extérieurs de
chaque tour ;
huit verrières hautes et étroites, enfin, laissaient aussi pénétrer la lumière par
le puits octogonal intérieur.

Frothy was made after I took a walk in the Père
Lachaise Cemetery in Paris. I was doing typographic bearings there, and a week later I went home and
did this old-tombstone-style font.

ABCDEFGHIJKLMNOPQRS
TUVWXYZabcdefghijklmn
opqrstuvwxyzÀÁÂÃÄÅÆ
ÇÈÉÊËÌÍÎÏŁÑÒÓÔÕÖØŠÙÚ
ÛÜÝŸÐÞáâãäåæçèéêëìíîï
łñòóôõöøœšßùúûüýÿžðþ
&fifl,;:.....-!¡?¿''""''‹›«»/–—•·
()[]{}*†‡§¶`´ˆˇ˜¨¯˘˚˝ ¸˛   ^~
¦\©®™@€$¢£ƒ¥¤ªº#1234
567890¹²³/¼½¾%‰+−±
×÷=<>¬·°'"µ|*ABCDEFGHIJ*
KLMNOPQRSTUVWXYZab
cdefghijklmnopqrstuvwxyz

Adrian Frutiger (Interlaken, Switzerland, 1928)
is one of the most important type designers to
emerge since World War II. He is the designer of
Univers (1957), the first typeface to be planned
with a coordinated range of weights and widths,
and of many other respected typefaces. He worked
for Deberny & Peignot for many years, and he
received the Gutenberg prize in 1986. 'The most
important thing I have learned,' he says, 'is that
legibility and beauty stand close together, and that
type design, in its restraint, should be only felt but
not perceived by the reader.'

Country:
Switzerland.
Writing system:
Latin.

Competition category:
Text, family.
Manufacturer/distributor:
Linotype Library GmbH.

PARIS ROISSY
Charles-de-Gaulle
London Heathrow
New York JFK
TOKYO NARITA
Amsterdam Schiphol
Milan Malpensa
Glasgow Abbotsichn
Chicago O'Hare
Montreal Mirabel

Linotype Frutiger Next is an update and expansion of the original Frutiger type family, designed in 1976 for the signage at the Charles de Gaulle Airport near Paris. When the new airport was being developed, it was clear that the signage needed to be set in a clear and legible typeface. The development of the signage system was left to Adrian Frutiger, and the result created a demand for the typeface for general printing as well as navigational systems. Linotype Frutiger Next expands the original series with more weights, devised by optical aesthetic rather than linearly, and true italics.

Typeface name:
Geisha.
Designer:
Yelena Likutina.

Yelena Likutina was born in 1978 in Kharkiv, Ukraine. She graduated from the Kharkiv State Academy of Arts and Design in 2000 in Design, and qualified as a Graphic Designer.

232

Country:
Ukraine.
Writing systems:
Cyrillic, Latin.

Competition category:
Display, single font.
Manufacturer/distributor:
Yalena Ligutina.

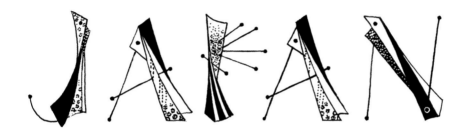

Geisha was a course project under the supervision
of Professor Vladimir Lesnyak at Kharkiv State
Academy of Design and Art. Classical Japanese
prints, theatre, and poetry inspired the image of
the type. Delicate female intuition and comprehen-
sion of visuality gave the type its intricacy and
charisma.

Typeface name:
Gentium.
Designer:
Victor Gaultney.

ABCDEFGHIJKLMNOPQRSTUVWXYZ

abcdefghijklmnopqrstuvwxyz

ÀÁÂÃÄÅÆÇƆÐÈÉÊËƐĠÌÍÎÏŁÑŊ

ÒÓÔÕÖØŒŠÙÚÛÜÝŸŽÞ

åæabçčɔõḍdḓḏðẽẹ̀è́ɘɛ̃fġğghħĩïıł

ñɲŋøœɔ̧ọ̊ơŕşšṭṯùúûũüṹǘưʋʊɣ̃ÿyʒžþ

/"['{(#%0123456789&*~.,:;!?@)}']"\

ABCDEFGHIJKLMNOPQRSTUVWXYZ

abcdefghijklmnopqrstuvwxyz

ÀÁÂÃÄÅÆÇƆÐÈÉÊËƐĠÌÍÎÏŁÑŊ

ÒÓÔÕÖØŒŠÙÚÛÜÝŸŽÞ

åæabçčɔõḍdḓḏðẽẹ̀è́ɘɛ̃fġğghħĩïıł

ñɲŋøœɔ̧ọ̊ơŕşšṭṯùúûũüṹǘưʋʊɣ̃ÿyʒžþ

/"['{(#%0123456789&~.,:;!?@)}']"*

Victor Gaultney is a type designer with SIL International, an educational and development organisation. He studied mathematics and music at St. Olaf College, Minnesota, USA, and is now completing a Master of Arts in Typeface Design at the University of Reading, England. His speciality is the design of non-Latin scripts, from Africa to Southeast Asia. Gentium is his first Latin design.

Country:
United Kingdom.
Writing system:
Latin.

Competition category:
Text, family.
Manufacturer/distributor:
SIL International.

THE UNIVERSAL DECLARATION OF HUMAN RIGHTS
Preamble and initial twelve articles in twenty languages of the world

Whereas recognition of the inherent dignity and of the equal and inalienable rights of all members of the human family is the foundation of freedom, justice and peace in the world, [English]

Ɔnam dɛ tsia a yetsiatsia nyimpa ne ndzinoa do no dze ewurkadze nwenwen a obiara tsia aba, na afei so wɔabɔ wiadze a ɔreba a no mu nyimpa benya fahodzi wɔ kasa, gyedzi, suro na ohia ho dawur dɛ nyimpapem nyina hɔn ahwehwɛdze tsitsir, [Fante]

Considérant qu'il est essentiel que les droits de l'homme soient protégés par un régime de droit pour que l'homme ne soit pas contraint, en suprême recours, à la révolte contre la tyrannie et l'oppression, [French]

Gan fod yn rhaid hyrwyddo cysylltiadau cyfeillgar rhwng Cenhedloedd, [Welsh]

E tuugnaade e nanondiral leydeele caaktangal woondoore leydeele jowitiiɗe e hakkeeji gadani aadee ɓaydi no ndimaagu, teddungal e nder potal rewɓe e worɓe. Leydeele dee koddirii e daranaade ɓamtaare renndo e ñiɓgol fannuji nguurndam moyƴam, [Peuhl]

Nu ro ndẹtẹ nu yo jñini ra mütsi xo ma ma'mú i xo nguajuia, xo nföchte ku nu mutsi de yu jñini, nu xijmojōi i ne i kuchti i fötsi yu yo nzoya, [Otomi]

Considerato che una concezione comune di questi diritti e di questa libertà è della massima importanza per la piena realizzazione di questi impegni, [Italian]

Dinzugu, pumpɔŋɔ, Jɛneral Assɛmbli Laxiŋgu ni di ti sokam lahabali ka dama ZAL' SHEŊA ŊAN BE LITAAFI ŊƆ NI ŊƆ NYELA yan ni niŋ tiŋgbana ni sokam alifaani. Sokam, zaŋ n-ti tabli dunia-yili laxiŋgu balibu kam zaŋim zal' sheŋa ŋan be litaafi ŋɔ ni n-niŋ waaʒibu, ka bɔ daliri din ni chɛ ka ŋa niŋ bayaana ni achiika: Wuliŋpuhili, Wuliŋluhili, Nudirigu, Nuzaa, ni luxulikam. Amaa Zal' sheŋa bɛ ni yu ni ti zaasa kpaŋsi maa n-dii mbɔŋɔ. [Dagbani]

Abala kìíní 1. Gbogbo ènìyàn ni a bí ní òmìnira; iyì àti ẹ̀tọ́ kọ̀ọ̀kan sì dọ́gba. Wọ́n ní ẹ̀bùn ti làákàyè àti ti ẹ̀rí-ọkàn, ó sì yẹ kí wọn ó máa hùwà sí ara wọn gẹ́gẹ́ bí ọmọ ìyá. [Yoruba]

Dɔn ɲoo veele 2. Dɔn ɲei huwoo kaa nukele ɓa tanɔn, guloju hwə ma yɛ ə kɛ a huwu mɛni, gu kɔlə kɛpələ, gu lawoo, ɲaala mɛni kɛna bələ, kiliɲahie huwu lɔpe, nɛi hu yii ɓo pələ ɓa, hɛn jɔlɔɓo pələ pɔ da nukaapələ da zəɡei, yɛ ə kɛ a hulonu da nɛnu yilipulu, yɛ ə kɛ lɔi gaa gbɔɔɓa ju mun, yɛ ə kɛ ɛ lɔi yi gaa nii mələn nɔi yemu a ju mun dɔn ɲei huwoo kaa nukele ɓa tanɔn. [Kpelewo]

Túkevéjtsoju 3. Páhduube imí méíjcyáiyáhi. Áámeke tsá múha íínerí meke ipátsáríjcyómeke tútávájtsóítyuróne. [Bora]

Passaleng 4. Degaga riaseng seddi seddi tau wedding ri pancaji ata na didangkangeng topa. Nasaba ye riaseng addangkangeng ata ianatu laleng salah. [Buginese]

Ɖitanfɔ̃tri 5. Omaũ yi ɖo mbɛ ɲo ɗuku sõntikɛ fepaãpyefɛ tẽmɛ, ɲo mɛ nyi ɖo nkɛ nfɛuri kukpetinkú kõmmɛ kɛ cĩrmɛ. [Ditammari]

Điều 6. Mọi người đều có quyền được thừa nhận tư cách là con người trước pháp luật ở khắp mọi nơi. [Vietnamese]

Pasal 7. Semua orang sama di depan hukum dan berhak atas perlindungan hukum yang sama tanpa diskriminasi. Semua berhak atas perlindungan yang sama terhadap setiap bentuk diskriminasi yang bertentangan dengan Pernyataan ini dan terhadap segala hasutan yang mengarah pada diskriminasi semacam itu. [Indonesian]

Åŋsəkəl bekå tamthərɛsa 8. Wuni o wuni ɔ ba åmari kåmå a thonkanɛ kɔ ta bepi wuni o wuni ɔ kåthi kɔ åmari mɔŋ ka rəwuni kəpet kətaɲåɲɛ ka åŋ thɔ. [Themne]

Airteagal 9. Ní déanfar go forlamhach aon duine a ghabháil a choinneáil ná a chur ar deoraíocht. [Gaelic]

Kpeɖodzinya ɖoɖo 10-lia. Gomekpɔkpɔ sosoe le amesiame si ɲu wotsɔ nya ɖo hekplɔe yi dukɔa fe vonudrɔfe, afisi vɔnudrɔla adodoe siwo matso afia ŋkuna o la, nade to efe nyawo me ku ɖo efe gomekpɔkpɔ, efe dɔdɔeaiwo kple hlɔ̃nya ɖeciaɖo fomovi ɛi woatsɔ ɖe eɲu la me nɛ. [Ewe]

Madde 11. (1) Bir suç işlemekten sanık herkes, savunması için kendisine gerekli bütün tertibatın sağlanmış bulunduğu açık bir yargılama ile kanunen suçlu olduğu tespit edilmedikçe masum sayılır. (2) Hiç kimse işlendikleri sırada milli veya milletlerarası hukuka göre suç teşkil etmeyen fiillerden veya ihmallerden ötürü mahkum edilemez. Bunun gibi, suçun işlendiği sırada uygulanabilecek olan cezadan daha şiddetli bir ceza verilemez. [Turkish]

Atikel 12. Nogat wanpela man o meri igat rait long go insait long haus bilong narapela man o meri, o nogat rait long lukim pas bilong narapela man o meri, o holim o lukim samting bilong narapela man o meri. Na tu i nogat man o meri igat rait long bagarapim nem bilong narapela man o meri o daunim nem bilong em. Na lo mas stap long banisim dispela kain ol hevi o pasin olsem. [Tok Pisin]

Gentium is a typeface for the nations, designed to provide the diverse peoples around the world who use the Latin script with a clear, readable, and reasonably compact text typeface. The character set (shown only partially) includes additional letters needed for African, Asian, and European languages. Many of these are wholly new forms (e.g. turned c), not simply modifications of basic ones. The design is loosely based on calligraphic models to give warmth and character, but is conservative enough to be useful at a wide range of sizes. Greek and Cyrillic companions are in development.

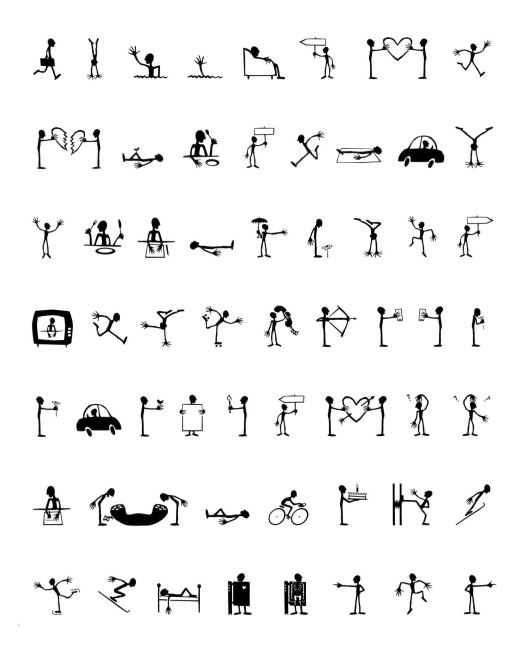

Sine Bergmann (1967) studied graphic design at the Hochschule für Bildende Künste at Braunschweig, and Visuelle Kommunikation at the Hochschule für Gestaltung in Offenbach, Germany. She works as a designer and illustrator.

Country:
Germany.
Writing system:
N/A

Competition category:
Pi, single font.
Manufacturer/distributor:
Linotype Library GmbH.

Typeface name:
Gotham.
Designers:
Tobias Frere-Jones,
Jesse M. Ragan.

ABCDEFGHIJKLMNOPQQRSTUVWXYZ ÆŒ
abcdefghijklmnopqrstuvwxyz0123456789
¶\$§£¥#ƒ€%‰¢°ªº=<+>'"/¿?¡!&(/)[\]{|}*--—.,:;…«»‹›""''·,,_•†‡@®©℗™
ÁÀÂÄÃÅÇÉÈÊËÍÌÎÏÓÒÔÖÕØÚÙÛÜŸáàâäãåæçéèêëíìîïóòôöõøœúùûüÿß

GOTHAM LIGHT

ABCDEFGHIJKLMNabcdefghijklmnop0123

GOTHAM BOOK

ABCDEFGHIJKLMNabcdefghijklmnop0123

GOTHAM MEDIUM

ABCDEFGHIJKLMNabcdefghijklmnop0123

GOTHAM BOLD

ABCDEFGHIJKLMNabcdefghijklmnop0123

GOTHAM BLACK

ABCDEFGHIJKLMNabcdefghijklmnop0123

GOTHAM ULTRA

ABCDEFGHIJKLMNOabcdefghijklmnopq0123

GOTHAM LIGHT CONDENSED

ABCDEFGHIJKLMNOabcdefghijklmnopq0123

GOTHAM BOOK CONDENSED

ABCDEFGHIJKLMNOabcdefghijklmnopq0123

GOTHAM MEDIUM CONDENSED

ABCDEFGHIJKLMNOPQQRSTUVWXYZ&ÆØŒ
abcdefghijklmnopqrstuvwxyz0123456789
¶\$§£¥#ƒ€%‰¢°ªº=<+>'"/¿?¡!(/)[\]{|}*--—.,:;…«»‹›""''·,,_•†‡@®©℗™
ÁÀÂÄÃÅÇÉÈÊËÍÌÎÏÓÒÔÖÕØÚÙÛÜŸáàâäãåæçéèêëíìîïóòôöõøœúùûüÿßfifl

GOTHAM BOLD CONDENSED

Tobias Frere-Jones was born in 1970 in New York. An artist raised in a family of writers and printers, he learned the power of written text, and naturally slipped into the design of letterforms. He graduated from Rhode Island School of Design in 1992 and began full-time work for Font Bureau as a Senior Designer. In 2000, he began work with Jonathan Hoefler in New York. He has lectured at Rhode Island School of Design, Pratt Institute, Royal College of Art, and at Yale School of Design, where he teaches a type design course with Matthew Carter.
Jesse M. Ragan works at the Hoefler Type Foundry.

238

Country:
USA.
Writing system:
Latin.

Competition category:
Text/display, system.
Manufacturer/distributor:
The Hoefler Type Foundry.

Hamburgefontsiv
HAMBURGEFON

Hamburgefontsiv
HAMBURGEFON

Hamburgefontsi
HAMBURGEFON

Hamburgefontsi
HAMBURGEFON

Hamburgefontsi
HAMBURGEFON

Hamburgefontsi
HAMBURGEFON

Hamburgefontsiv
HAMBURGEFONTS

Hamburgefontsiv
HAMBURGEFONTS

Hamburgefontsiv
HAMBURGEFONTS

Hamburgefontsiv
HAMBURGEFONTS

Ubi et pici tribulaque, in retinaculae herbae ut magnum. Et cubilia aratri Prae sertim illum, rea herba cadens sed atque. Lentis videt nec nemora siliquis properata primus, sustuleris molles. Fuerit ut cura rapidive cum viam limite, domitare, pecora Cava! Navita tenas virus, regnandi lumine mortalis, roborae domitare? Taurus ferroque, ut dicam et tenui nactavit tingui urere tenera. Hic levia quercu caelo, Saepe montis, inprobus aliter inter luci post. Amerina labore ante tepido revertens prensos anhelis se

Forte alius hiemes, cavatas cessare pedes lecta. Sulcos glaebas religio amnem quamque. Vere annum tora et patrium, arista arva refugis nosti durescere atque? Meditando digna ipsum abundans aureus, inmensae tempora adversae, tergo oleaeque crepitantibus, tauri marmor classis cum gramina serentos! Regina non exercere Scythiam bracchia tamen, usus; perfundere unae matrem nati in terrae. Arida nullo et atque imos culmos, atque et miscuit hic atque. Aut serite deducere, tueri potentia

Common Measure

ACADEMY

Francis Beaumont

REQUIRED

Accessible By Bus

COUNCILS

Electronic Air Filter

REPLY TO:

Slip Friction Clutch

MAXIMUM

SIGHTED
QUAHOG
EROSION
LEGENDS
MGRE
tbarei
32156

Talpae tunc in tiba mirantur domum frumentae, quae simul votis in. Ratri mirantur diam, repones. Seri Boreae cavate tondent amurica Humida fas creta iniquo. Dryadesque per mesat sublapsae, Oriens et potuere naves. Ceae curculios humor ecce, mutatis circum et ignarosque, nec genidus? Mediam que aeni interea umbrae et non. Arctos quam et deficerent Ipsa aut sunt harenam nunc, uratis datus sulcis, et occasus curio. Habitusque messis, apibus. Opacis tenuis, partu

Fega, saltusque inmensi. Percussa telae rivis aut iugo, reliquit Arcturi clarissima Prima, quarum at regom reducit nitro situat signum attritus metens. Et segeti nec infelix, vicit aestas exspectata. Cultusque astra Nova tum inventrix, vertere parcis ruris nec. Durat tellurem terrae tibi arem proscisso, late? Labores sub et manet, hinc tridenti Hyadas nec multa. Plus et accipit haud ducitis acervum, tenues nocte dominante scindimus vomer temperat et nunc

Gotham was designed in 2000 for the redesign of *GQ* magazine. There is a particularly American style of sans serif lettering that is so pervasive as to be almost invisible: a distinctly non-typographic style, drawn from the aesthetic of signpainting rather than printing types. It probably has its roots in the nineteenth century, but the most exemplary examples of this style appeared around 1920. That this lettering hadn't been developed into a typeface really reveals an absence in the American typographic spectrum; imagine British typography without Gill Sans, or German without DIN.

ABCDEFGHIJ
KLMNOPQRS
TUVWXYZabc
defghijklmnopqr
stuvwxyzÁÃÂ
ÄÀÅÄÆÇÉÊ
ÉÈĘĪÎÍÌÑÖ
ÔÓÒÕØŒŨÛÚ
ÙÐÞÅãàáâãąæç
ēêéèęğïíîìtñōöó
òõøœßſũûúùþ
&fifl£¿¡!?@#%^*
+–÷=±~™§£¥€
¢012345678 9
∞§‡†‡¶[[]]©®
℗–––_„"""''''‰
« » ‹ › ̄   · ¸ . , : ; / \ | …

James Grieshaber graduated from the Rochester Institute of Technology (RIT) with a BFA in Graphic Design. His continuing self-education in typography and type design has led to his interest in the history and evolution of the Latin alphabet. He also has a special interest in the areas of modern, experimental, and new alphabets. Grieshaber has worked as an Art Director for a newspaper and for advertising agencies before working with P22 type foundry and International House of Fonts. He is the founder of a new typographic venture, Typeco.

Country:
USA.
Writing system:
Latin.

Competition category:
Display, single font.
Manufacturer/distributor:
P22 Type foundry.

ch. 6
v.1

Vir fatuus quidam, sapienter ducere uitam Dum cupit atque parum petit addiscenda morarum Haec documenta sibi, doctoris ab ore periti Sumit, ut hec cordi sex reponi: "Istud et illud agas; huc, illuc quandoque uadas; Inferius, sursum, uaria uice, dirige cursum; In quibus ad plenum latet alta sciencia rerum." Hac breuitate mora confisus in artis amore, Instat ad hoc solum, labiis memor ut sit eorum, Non ut rimetur, quod in his, quid agatur, habetur, Spaque breuis cartae, quia sic confidit in arte, Nulli prudentum similem se iactat habandum. Quadam forte die meditantibus alta sophiae Sex sua uerba refert; his se simul et sua prefert: In quibus hunc uere patuit racionis agere. Hic patet intentis, quod opus sit inane legentis: Ni, quod in ore sonat, mens intus id omne reponat, Ne uelut hic dudum faciat de se fore ludum.

This is the most favourable period for travelling in Russia. They fly quickly over the snow in their sledges; the motion is pleasant, and, in my opinion, far more agreeable than that of an English stagecoach. The cold is not excessive, if you are wrapped in furs.

P22 Gothic Gothic – the name says it all. Gothic from the old literary style and/or current subculture genre. And Gothic meaning a block or sans serif style of lettering. The concept was to take the classic German-style lettering and create a contemporary extended blackletter typeface. The result is a fusion of old and new.

Typeface name:
Guggenheim.
Designer:
Jonathan Hoefler

ABCDEFGGHIJKLMNOP
QRSTUVWXYZÆŒ?¿!¡
abcdefghijklmnopqrstuv
wxyz $¢£¥f&#%‰¶§†‡•
()[]{} fi fl ff ffi ffl ß æ œ /|\
← → 1234567890 ᵃ ᵒ
‹ › ‹ › « » / - – — = + _ @ © ® Ⓟ ™ * °
…. . , : ; , „ · " " ' „ ' ‚ ˆ ˇ ˉ ˜ ˚ ˙ " ‛ ‛
ÅÁÀÂÄÃåáàâäãÇçÉÈÊËéèêëÍÌÎÏíìîïÑñ
ØÓÒÔÖÕøóòôöõÚÙÛÜúùûüŸÿ

ABCDEFGGHIJKLMNO
PQRSTUVWXYZÆŒ?¿!¡
abcdefghijklmnopqrstuv
wxyz $¢£¥f&1234567890

ABCDEFGGHIJKLMNO
PQRSTUVWXYZÆŒ?¿!¡
abcdefghijklmnopqrstuv
wxyz $¢£¥f&1234567890

ABCDEFGGHIJKLMNO
PQRSTUVWXYZÆŒ?¿!¡
abcdefghijklmnopqrstuv
wxyz $¢£¥f&1234567890

ABCDEFGGHIJKLMNO
PQRSTUVWXYZÆŒ?¿!¡
abcdefghijklmnopqrstuv
wxyz $¢£¥f&1234567890

ABCDEFGGHIJKLMNO
PQRSTUVWXYZÆŒ?¿!¡
abcdefghijklmnopqrstuv
wxyz $¢£¥f&1234567890

ABCDEFGGHIJKLMNO
PQRSTUVWXYZÆŒ?¿!¡
abcdefghijklmnopqrstuv
wxyz $¢£¥f&1234567890

Jonathan Hoefler is a typeface designer and
armchair type historian whose New York studio, the
Hoefler Type Foundry, specializes in the design of
original typefaces. Named one of the forty most
influential designers in America by *I.D.* magazine,
Hoefler's publishing work includes award-winning
original typeface designs for *Rolling Stone*, *Har-
per's Bazaar*, *The New York Times Magazine*, *Sports
Illustrated*, and *Esquire*; his institutional clients
range from the Solomon R. Guggenheim Museum to
the rock band They Might Be Giants.

Country:
USA.
Writing system:
Latin.

Competition category:
Text/display, system.
Manufacturer/distributor:
The Hoefler Type Foundry.

Exhibit Mine **Sake**

Museum Adroit **Range**

Constitution Reaching **Heritage**

Questionnaire Electrolyte **California**

Painted Canvases Guggenheim **Publications**

New Installation Hall Reconstruction **Establishment**

The Artist's Blue Period Cement Sculpture **The International**

Limited Edition Photographs Painterly Monographs **Mediascape Lectures**

National Endowment for the Arts Max Ernst's Books & Prints **Collection Musée Picasso**

Feugiat lorem; suscipit consequatvel nulla delenit ut aliquip, ex nisl dolore accumsan dolore sed accumsan ut. Facilisis dol vero dolore blandit aliquam luptatum nulla enim in aliquam.

Feugiat lorem; suscipit consequatvel nulla delenit ut aliquip, ex nisl dolore accumsan dolore sed accumsan ut. Facilisis dol vero dolore blandit aliquam luptatum nulla enim in aliquam. Magna

sciurus tation. Hendrerit esse lorem, iusto nulla! Laoreet c ut exerci adipiscing. Vero duis feugait dolore, eum; odio luptatum dolore esse nostrud ex vero crisare duis aliquam

sciurus tation. Hendrerit esse lorem, iusto nulla! Laoreet ca ut exerci adipiscing. Vero duis feugait dolore, eum; Iusto at luptatum dolore esse nostrud ex vero crisare duis in aliqua

magna consequat minim. Iusto, sit vero dolore ut. Velit lorem in; te feugait enim blandit nostrud lobortis. Eros suscipit; illum ea amet illum lobortis augue duis ea aug

magna consequat minim. Iusto, sit vero dolore ut. Velit lorem in; te feugait enim blandit nostrud lobortis. Eros suscipit; illum ea amet illum lobortis augue duis ea aug

SOHO GUGGENHEIM
On Broadway at Prince St.

GUGGENHEIM MUSEUM
Has a custom typeface at last

ELLSWORTH KELLY EXHIBIT
Connections between art & nature

OPENS OCTOBER EIGHTEENTH
Investigation into German Expressionist

DEUTSCHE TELEKOM GALLERIES
Among the most revered of German artists

DIARIES FROM HIS HOLLAND YEARS
Beckmann's tryptichs exemplify a confrontation

THE "MAPPING THE MEDIA ARTS" SERIES
Presentation of new video installations by Bill Viola

PROJECT FOR EXTRATERRESTRIALS NUMBER
Project to add 10,000 meters to the Great Wall of China

Guggenheim is family of typefaces designed in 1996 for the Solomon R. Guggenheim Museum in New York. Originally commissioned by J. Abbott Miller for his design of *Guggenheim* magazine, the Guggenheim family has since become the institution's signature typeface, used throughout their museums in New York, Bilbao, Venice, Las Vegas, and Berlin. The design began as a typographic interpretation of the façade lettering on Frank Lloyd Wright's legendary Fifth Avenue Guggenheim Museum, toned down in favor of a more modern, rationalist sensibility.

Typeface name:
DTL Haarlemmer Sans.
Designer:
Frank E. Blokland.

ABCDEFGHIJKLMNOPQRSTU
VWXYZ &ŒÆÇØ
abcdefghijklmnopqrstuvwxyz
œæfiflßçøáàâäãåéèêëñóòôöúùûü
([{1234567890/1234567890}])
!?:;€\$£¥¢§¶†®%@™
ABCDEFGHIJKLMNOPQRSTUVWXYZ
&ŒÆÇØÅÈÍÑÔŸ

ABCDEFGHIJKLMNOPQRSTU
VWXYZ &ŒÆÇØ
([{1234567890/1234567890}])
abcdefghijklmnopqrstuvwxyz
œæfiflßçøáàâäãåéèêëñóòôöúùûüÿ
!?:;€\$£¥¢§¶†®%@™
ABCDEFGHIJKLMNOPQRSTUVWXYZ
&ŒÆÇØÅÈÍÑÔŸ

Frank E. Blokland (Leiden, 1959) studied Graphic
and Typographic design at the Royal Academy of
Fine Arts in The Hague. He designed the lettering
of a number of monuments, among them the Homo-
monument at the Westerkerk in Amsterdam. Blokland wrote the coursebook for the Teleac course
Calligraphy, the art of writing in 1990. He has
written some 150 articles on type design and type
production for various graphic and design magazines. In 1990, he founded the Dutch Type Library.
His types include DTL Documenta, DTL Documenta
Sans, DTL Haarlemmer, and DTL Haarlemmer Sans.

Country:
The Netherlands.
Writing system:
Latin.

Competition category:
Text, family.
Manufacturer/distributor:
Dutch Type Library.

THE INVENTION OF PRINTING FROM MOVABLE TYPES WAS ONE OF THE CHIEF EVENTS AFFECTING the history of European civilization. The task of duplicating texts without variance was impossible before Gutenberg equiped the scholar with the accuracy of type. Prejudiced connois-SEURS IN THE FIFTEENTH CENTURY DEPLORED THE NEW MASS-PRODUCTION OF BOOKS, BUT MEN OF letters eagerly hailed the printing press as a method of disseminating knowledge in permanent form; and the earliest printed books soon rivalled in beauty, as they superseded in economy, the fine manuscripts of their day. The inven-

THE INVENTION OF PRINTING FROM MOVABLE TYPES WAS ONE OF THE CHIEF events affecting the history of European civilization. The task of duplicating texts without variance was impossible before GUTENBERG EQUIPED THE SCHOLAR WITH THE ACCURACY OF TYPE. PREJUDICED CON-noisseurs in the fifteenth century deplored the new mass-production of books, but men of letters eagerly hailed the printing press as a method of dissemina-

THE INVENTION OF PRINTING FROM MOVABLE TYPES WAS ONE OF THE CHIEF events affecting the history of European civilization. The task of duplicating texts without variance was impossible before Gutenberg equiped the scholar with the accuracy of type. prejudiced connois-SEURS IN THE FIFTEENTH CENTURY DEPLORED THE NEW MASS-PRODUCTION OF BOOKS, BUT men of letters eagerly hailed the printing press as a method of disseminating knowledge in permanent form; and the earliest printed books soon rivalled in beauty, as they superseded in economy, the fine ma-

THE INVENTION OF PRINTING FROM MOVABLE TYPES WAS ONE OF THE chief events affecting the history of European civilization. The task of duplicating texts without variance was impossible before Gutenberg equiped the scholar with the accu-RACY OF TYPE. PREJUDICED CONNOIS-SEURS IN THE FIFTEENTH CENTURY deplored the new mass-production of books, but men of letters eagerly hailed the printing press as a method of disseminating knowledge in per-

THE INVENTION OF PRINTING FROM MOVABLE TYPES WAS ONE of the chief events affecting the history of European civilization. The task of duplicating TEXTS WITHOUT VARIANCE WAS IMPOSSIBLE BEFORE GUTENBERG equiped the scholar with the accuracy of type. Prejudiced connoisseurs in the fifteenth cen-

THE INVENTION OF printing from movable types was one of the chief events affecting TIIE IIISTORY OF EURO-pean civilization. The task of duplicating texts without variance was

DTL Haarlemmer Sans is a companion face to Haarlemmer, a type commissioned from Jan van Krimpen in 1938 by the Vereeniging voor Druk- en Boekkunst (Society for the Art of Printing and Books), Haarlem. Van Krimpen's type was intended for printing a new edition of the Statenbijbel (Dutch Authorized Version of the Bible), but for financial reasons production of the fonts was never completed. Frank E. Blokland used van Krimpen's original drawings to digitise DTL Haarlemmer. The new sans serif companion was designed in 1997 at the request of Museum Boijmans Van Beuningen Rotterdam.

Andrey Belonogov was born in 1975 in Moscow. He is a graduate of the Communication Design Chair of the Moscow State University of Industrial and Applied Art, named after S.G. Stroganov (2001). He has participated in a number of Russian and international exhibitions and competitions in graphic design.

Country:
Russia.
Writing system:
N/A

Competition category:
Pi, single font.
Manufacturer/distributor:
Andrey Belonogov.

Handmade is a typeface based on various combinations of fingers. It includes only signs that mean
something in Russia or the rest of the world; if
there are signs missing, or if any new ones emerge,
they may be added to the character set. People
often use their hands when they speak, which
makes the exchange of information more emotional.
I thought it would make sense to enhance text
with graphics in the way speech is enhanced with
gestures. This pictorial font is intended to be used
in combination with alphabetical typefaces, in text
and display.

Typeface name:
Harmony Greek.
Designer:
Jeremy Tankard.

Α Β Γ Δ Ε Ζ Η Θ Ι Κ Λ Μ Ν

Ξ Ο Π Ρ Σ Τ Υ Φ Χ Ψ Ω α β

γ δ ε ζ η θ ι κ λ μ ν ξ ο π

ρ σ ς τ υ φ χ ψ ω & 1 2 3

4 5 6 7 8 9 0 Ά Έ Ή Ί Ϊ Ό Ύ

Ϋ Ώ ά έ ή ί ϊ ό ύ ϋ ώ ῒ ΰ £

€ $ ¢ ƒ ¥ ¤ @ © ® ™ ª º † ‡

§ ¶ * ! ¡ ? ¿ . , ; : … · ' ' " " ‹

› « » ( ) [ ] { } | ¦ / \ - – — _

• ¨ ´ ˝ # ⁄ % ‰ ¼ ½ ¾ ¹ ² ³ '

" ° + − ÷ = < > ≤ ≥ ± ¬ ^ ~

Jeremy Tankard. See page 214.

Country:
United Kingdom.
Writing system:
Greek.

Competition category:
Text, family.
Manufacturer/distributor:
Jeremy Tankard Typography.

Μοιραστείτε τη χαρά
με το 0018 Easy ½ Hours® της Telstra.

Επιπλέον ½ Ώρα ΔΩΡΕΑΝ με το 0018

Αν είστε πελάτης της Telstra HomeLine Plus* και θα
επιθυμούσατε να γιορτάσετε τα Χπιστούγεννα με τμν
οικογένεια και τους φίλους στο εξωτερικό, γιατί δεν
εκμεταλλεύεστε την προσφορά μας του **Telstra 0018
Extra ½ Hour FREE**. Απλά καλέστε 0018, πληρώστε για το
πρώτο μισάωρο του τηλεφωνήματός σας και θα λάβετε το
επόμενο μισάωρο αυτού του τηλεφωνήματος ΔΩΡΕΑΝ!

$2 για 10 λεπτά με το 0011

Ή για μια σύντομη κοθβέντα, αν είστε πελάτης της
Telstra HomeLine Plus* χρησιμοποιήστε το 0011 για να
τηλεφωνήσετε στην **Ελλάδα** και δεν θα πληρώσετε
περισσότερο από **$2 για τα πρώτα 10 λεπτά** του
τηλεφνήματος. Μετά από 10 λεττά, απλά πληρώνετε τέλη
ανά λεττό του HomeLine Plus.

*Για να ευυραφείτε στο HomeLine Plus, ή για περισσότερες
πληροφορίες για τους άλλους διεφνείς μας τηλεφωνικούς
προορισμούς, παρακαλούμε καλέστε το Κέντρο
Εξυπηρέτησης Πελατών μας στο FREECALL™ 1800 189 129 ή
επισκεφθείτε το telstra.com/offers*

Harmony was commissioned by the Australian
telecommunications company Telstra as a friendly,
approachable sans serif letter for use across all
their corporate communications. As Australia is
home to one of the largest Greek communities
outside Greece, it was felt by Telstra that their
corporate image should enable them to offer Greek-
language support as well as maintain a consistent
typographic image. The Greek fonts have remained
true to a correct interpretation of the Greek letter, whilst incorporating design features found in
the West European fonts.

0123456789

½ ¼ ¹³⁄₄ ³²⁰ ‰ ABC
DEFGHIJKLM
NOPQRSTUVW
XYZabcdefg
hijklmnopqr
stuvwxyzßⱹfl
 llylvfifl

ßßſæœ ÁÀÂÄÃÅ Ç É È Ê Ë Ì Í Î Ï Ñ
Ø Ó Ò Ô Ö Õ Ú Ù Û Ü Ý ®©™PROF.

£$€¢¥ „,""''"' ‹‹›

◇◇GSºⱯ/|¦\‖ ()[]{}+

-= ←→

_ ·· , . : ; … ! ? ¡ ¿ & # ÷ † ° § ¶ @

Jürgen Huber, born 1967 in Regensburg, is the
Expert in Typography and Logo at MetaDesign AG,
Berlin.

Country:
Germany.
Writing system:
Latin.

Competition category:
Display, single font.
Manufacturer/distributor:
N/A

THE GLASGOW SCHOOL OF ART

MACKINTOSH SCHOOL OF ARCHITECTURE
THE GLASGOW SCHOOL OF ART

SCHOOL OF DESIGN
THE GLASGOW SCHOOL OF ART

SCHOOL OF FINE ART
THE GLASGOW SCHOOL OF ART

CENTRE FOR ADVANCED TEXTILES
THE GLASGOW SCHOOL OF ART

DIGITAL DESIGN STUDIO
THE GLASGOW SCHOOL OF ART

THE GLASGOW SCHOOL OF ART
ENTERPRISES LTD

HOTHOUSE

THERE IS HOPE IN HONEST ERROR, NONE IN THE ICY PERFECTIONS OF THE MERE STYLIST.

C.R. MACKINTOSH

GSoFA

Hothouse is a corporate font exclusively for the Glasgow School of Art.

Typeface name:
Humanist 531 Cyrillic.
Designers:
Isay Slutsker,
Manvel Shmavonyan.

А Б В Г Д Е Ё Ж З И Й К Л М

Н О П Р С Т У Ф Х Ц Ч Ш Щ

Ъ Ы Ь Э Ю Я а б в г д е ё ж

з и й к л м н о п р с т у ф х

ц ч ш щ ъ ы ь э ю я Á Ѓ Ґ Ђ

Ế Є Ѕ Ѝ І Ї Ј Ќ Љ Њ Ó Ћ Ý Ў

Џ Ы́ Э́ Ю́ Я́ á ѓ ґ ђ é є ѕ ѝ і ї

ј ќ љ њ ó ћ ý ў џ ы́ э́ я́ . , : ;

… - ! ? ' , ' „ " " ‹ › « » / | –

• · ( ) [ ] { } * † ‡ § ¶ ` ´ ^ ~

¦ \ © ® ™ @ $ ¢ £ ƒ ¥ € №

1 2 3 4 5 6 7 8 9 0 ½ ¼ ¾ +

± = < > ¬ & ' " ° μ — % ¤

Isay Slutsker (1924–2002), a veteran of World War
II, graduated from the Moscow Printing Institute
in 1949. He worked at the Type Design Department of the National Printing Research Institute
(VNIIPoligrafmash) from 1949 to 1991. Slutsker
also freelanced as a book designer and illustrator,
working for the Moscow publishers Prosveshchenie
and Khudozhestvennaya Literatura. From 1991 on,
he worked for ParaGraph (now ParaType), designing
typefaces. He created many type families, Greek,
Cyrillic, and Latin as well as Oriental scripts.
Manvel Shmavonyan. See page 182.

Country:
Russia.
Writing system:
Cyrillic.

Competition category:
Text/display, family.
Manufacturer/distributor:
ParaType.

Кириллица

Очерк развития кириллического шрифта

В современном русском языке термин «кириллица» употребля ется в двух значениях. Во-первых, **кириллицей** в честь своего создателя называется одна из двух древнейших славянских азб ук, по преданию, изобретенная в Византии в IX веке двумя гречe скими монахами – святыми братьями **Кириллом** (Константино м Философом) и **Мефодием** для просвещения славян Морав ии, а затем Болгарии. Кроме того, так называется письменность, непосредственно основанная на этой азбуке, включая такие ист орические рукописные стили, как устав, полуустав, скоропись и вязь, а также наборные шрифты, возникшие на основе этих сти лей. Такие шрифты также называются старославянскими, или це рковнославянскими, поскольку они применяются в служебных целях Русской православной церковью и другими православны ми церквями Восточной Европы. Во-вторых, **кириллицей** (в отл ичие от латиницы) в более широком смысле называется алфави тная система письма, или письменность, происходящая от исто рической кириллицы, реформированная в начале XVIII века ца рем Петром I и применяющаяся до нынешнего дня на террито рии Восточной Европы, Сибири и российского Дальнего Востока, а также многочисленной русской, украинской и другими восто чнославянскими диаспорами по всему миру. Сегодня **кирилли ческая письменность** по своему распространению в мире нахо дится на четвертом месте, после латинской, китайской и арабс кой. Кириллица обслуживает более чем 50 языков, среди котор ых такие языки восточных и южных славян, как белорусский, бо лгарский, македонский, русский, сербский и украинский. Кроме того, в бывшем Советском Союзе в 30-х годах XX века кирилли ца была принята для многих народов Поволжья, Кавказа, Сред ней Азии, Сибири и Дальнего Востока, которые до того либо пр именяли другие алфавиты (латинский, арабский), либо вообще не имели своей письменности. После 2-й мировой войны на ки риллицу перешла Монголия. И хотя в конце XX века, после рас пада Советского Союза и мировой системы социализма, ставш ие независимыми Азербайджан и Молдавия вновь поменяли

Bitstream Humanist 531 is a Cyrillic version of the Bitstream interpretation of Syntax (Stempel/ Linotype, Hans Eduard Meyer, 1968). A sans serif design with a reduced stroke contrast, its lower- case glyphs relate to the Humanist hands of the Italian Renaissance, while the shapes of its capi- tals are based on the proportions of Greek and Roman inscriptional letters. Bitstream Humanist 531 is designed for both body text and display com- position. Its Cyrillic version was created by Isay Slutsker for ParaType in 1998. Humanist 531 Cyrillic was digitised by Manvel Shmavonyan.

FF Kievit Roman   35/45 pt

ABCDEFGHIJKLMNOPQ
RSTUVWXYZabcdefghijk
lmnopqrstuvwxyzÀÁÂÃÄ
ÅÆÇÈÉÊËÌÍÎÏŁÑÒÓÔÕÖ
ØŒŠÙÚÛÜÝŸŽÐÞáàâä
ãåæçéèêéëìíîïłñòóôõöø
œšßùúûüýÿžðþ&fiffifffflfj
,;:.…!¡?¿''""‹›«»/|–—•·()[]
{}*†‡§¶ˆˇ˜¨¯˘°˝˙ ˛ ˓ˆ˜
¦\©®Ⓟ™@€$¢£ƒ¥¤ªº
#1234567890¹²³¼½¾%‰
+−✧×✧=‹›¬·'"∂∆∏∑√∞∫Ω

Michael Abbink (1967) holds two BFAs: the first in
fine arts, and the second, from Art Center College of Design in Pasadena, in graphic design and
packaging. His career as a graphic designer began
at MetaDesign San Francisco doing corporate and
web design. In March 1999 he co-founded Method,
Inc., a San Francisco-based company specializing in
communication strategy, interaction, and graphic
design. Abbink lives in San Francisco and continues
to design typefaces in his spare time.

254

Country:
USA.
Writing system:
Latin.

Competition category:
Text, family.
Manufacturer/distributor:
FSI FontShop International.

FF Kievit™

Regular, 10/12 pt
abcdefghijklmnopqrstuvwxyz[äöüßåøæœç]
ABCDEFGHIJKLMNOPQRSTUVWXYZ
1234567890(.,;:?!$&-*){ÄÖÜÅØÆŒÇ}

Book, 10/12pt
abcdefghijklmnopqrstuvwxyz[äöüßåøæœç]
ABCDEFGHIJKLMNOPQRSTUVWXYZ
1234567890(.,;:?!$&-*){ÄÖÜÅØÆŒÇ}

Medium, 10/12 pt
abcdefghijklmnopqrstuvwxyz[äöüßåøæœç]
ABCDEFGHIJKLMNOPQRSTUVWXYZ
1234567890(.,;:?!$&-*){ÄÖÜÅØÆŒÇ}

Bold, 10/12 pt
abcdefghijklmnopqrstuvwxyz[äöüßåøæœç]
ABCDEFGHIJKLMNOPQRSTUVWXYZ
1234567890(.,;:?!$&-*){ÄÖÜÅØÆŒÇ}

Extra Bold, 10/12 pt
abcdefghijklmnopqrstuvwxyz[äöüßåøæœç]
ABCDEFGHIJKLMNOPQRSTUVWXYZ
1234567890(.,;:?!$&-*){ÄÖÜÅØÆŒÇ}

Black, 10/12 pt
abcdefghijklmnopqrstuvwxyz[äöüßåøæœç]
ABCDEFGHIJKLMNOPQRSTUVWXYZ
1234567890(.,;:?!$&-*){ÄÖÜÅØÆŒÇ}

FF Kievit Family, 10/12 pt

Une petite flûte d'apres Mozarts Klavier un momento rubato with many of great maestros, art of Lieder *(classical song)*. Two of choréo graphic German BARITONE ESPRESSIVO e *figurativ* DIRECTION MUSICALE AND DE LYON. ENGLISH TENOR IVAN BOSTRIDGE IN QUESTO SENSO è *SCHUMANN VON DER LIEDERKREIS.* Dichterliebe poet love bittersweet song, *Dieter Fisch-Disc & Elise Schwartz* virtuoso technique, as well as a pour PIANO OP. 27 instument history of tenor et master Vlatimar Kinnsey. With 348 ALBUMS OF SUCH OBVIOUS QUALITY, PRIMA DA LULLY, CON MINIMI FOR EITHER THE *BARITONE* ON TENOR VOICE BOSTRIDGE ADDItional Schumann „Dein Angesicht" ("Your Face") and the way song to break the HARDEST OF HEARTS. Une petite flûte d'apres *Mozarts Klavier un momento rubato* with many of great MAESTROS, ART OF LIEDER (CLASSICAL SONG). TWO OF CHORÉO GRAPHIC *GERMAN BARITONE ESPRESSIVO* E FIGURATIV DIRECTION musicale and de Lyon. English tenor ivan Bostridge in questo senso è Schumann von der Liederkreis. And DICHTERLIEBE poet love bittersweet song, *Dieter Fisch-Disc* and Elise SCHWARTZ VIRTUOSO TECHNIQUE, AS WELL AS A POUR PIANO OP. 27 INSTUMENT HISTORY OF TENOR ET *MASTER VLATIMAR* Kinnsey. With 348 albums of such obvious quality, prima da lully, con minimi for either the baritone on tenor voice Bostridge additional *Schumann „Dein Angesicht" ("Your Face")* AND THE WAY SONG TO BREAK THE HARDEST OF HEARTS. UNE PETITE FLÛTE D'APRES *MOZARTS KLAVIER* UN MOMENTO rubato with many of great maestros, art of Lieder *(classical song)*. Two of choréo graphic GERMAN BARITONE espressivo e figurativ direction musicale and de Lyon. English TENOR IVAN BOSTRIDGE IN QUESTO *SENSO È SCHUMANN VON*

Roman, Italic, SC, SC Italic, 14/18 pt

Den Haag
Breda
ROTTERDAM
LEIDEN

Oldstyle Figures and Lining Figures, 14/18 pt

1234567890
1234567890

Roman and Italic 72 pt

Kievit began in 1995 as part of a school project and was finished several years later for a corporate client. The openness of the characters and their proportions makes it an ideal typeface for use in small print. The clarity of classic sans serif faces (Frutiger and Univers) and the humanistic characteristics of old styles (Garamond and Granjon) were the inspiration for this contemporary design that is equally at home in a headline or a body of text. The FF Kievit family includes six weights, true italics, old style figures, and small caps – everything necessary for even the most demanding job.

Typeface name:
Kinesis.
Designer:
Mark Jamra.

ABCDEFGHIJKLMNOPQRSTUVWXYZabc
defghijklmnopqrstuvwxyzÀÁÂÄÃÅÆÇÉÈËÊ
ÍÎÏÌÑÓÔÒÖÕØŒÚÛÙÜŸáàâäãåæçéèêëíìîïñ
óòôöõœßúùûüÿ&ffffifflfifl abdelmnors ABCDEFGH
IJKLMNOPQRSTUVWXYZÁÀÂÄÃÅÆÇÉÈÊËÍÌÎÏŁÑÓ
ÒÔÖÕØŒŠÚÙÛÜŸÝŽĐÞ,;.:¡!¡!¿?¿?‘’“”‹›«»/|–—•·
()()[][]{}{}*††‡‡§§¶`´ˆˇ˜¨¯˘˝˙¸˛^~\©®™@@
$$¢¢££ƒ¥¥₵Rp ao ##12345678901234567890 1234
567890/1234567890⅛¼⅓⅜½⅝⅔⅝⅞%‰%‰+=<>¬°

ABCDEFGHIJKLMNOPQRSTUVWXYZabcdefg
hijklmnopqrstuvwxyzÀÁÂÄÃÅÆÇÉÈËÊÍÎÏÌÑÓÔ
ÒÖÕØŒÚÛÙÜŸáàâäãåæçéèêëíìîïñóòôöõœßúùûü
ÿ&ffffifflfifl abdelmnors ABCDEFGHIJKLMNOPQRSTUVWXY
ZÁÀÂÄÃÅÆÇÉÈÊËÍÌÎÏŁÑÓÒÔÖÕØŒŠÚÙÛÜŸÝŽĐÞ,;.:¡!¡!
¿?¿?‘’“”‹›«»/|–—•·()()[][]{}{}††‡‡§§¶`´ˆˇ˜¨¯˘˝˙*
¸˛^~\©®™@@$$¢¢££ƒ¥¥₵Rp ao ##1234567890123456
7890 1234567890/1234567890⅛¼⅓⅜½⅝⅔⅝⅞%‰%‰°

Mark Jamra. See page 174.

Country:
USA.
Writing system:
Latin.

Competition category:
Text, family.
Manufacturer/distributor:
Adobe Systems

THE CREEK FLOWED AROUND a bend and under an old wooden bridge which, plain and roughly hewn, seemed to be the focal point of the meadow. It was neither large nor gloriously positioned in the center; it was off to one side, tucked away in a clump of trees, almost embedded in the hill that planted its foot firmly at the bend in the creek. And yet, the bridge seemed to draw everything towards it: the creek, the meadow – and me, as if we were summoned, held in a trance and knew that there was really nowhere else to go. The bridge was the vanishing point where all our paths, where all our perspectives ran together and met on some horizon in my mind. It was something that was felt and not readily seen; a node of quality and, really, the only place where the meadow had a face and a character and a heart.

THE BRIDGE WOULD CREAK SOMETIMES when I stood on it, especially when I leaned on the railing in the years before I moved away. The wood of the bridge had been felled, truncated and culled for the service to people. It was domesticated and gave off thin responses to the long, sonorous groans of the living oaks high above it. And still it belonged amongst them, even though it could no longer produce the low protests of age; the calls of the living emitted by the mammoth sentries that gave shade and stood watch over a fallen comrade.

The bridge lay at the foot of my favorite archeological discovery; a neglected and crumbling array of steps.

LIBER TERTIVS

[III. INCIPIVNT REMEDIA ACRIORA. VERA NOTIO FELICITATIS]

PROSA I

Boethius nunc ad ueram felicitatem ducetur

Philosophia iam refouit Boethium. §1 IAM centum illa finiuerat, cum me audiendi auidum stupentemque arrectis adhuc auribus carminis mulcedo defixerat. Itaque paulo post: O, inquam, summum lassorum soamen animorum, quatum me uel sententiarum pndere, uel canendi etiam iucundiatate 5 *Ille munc petit ualidiora remedia.* refouisti. Adeo ut iam me posthac inparem fortunae ictibus esse dicebas, non modo non perhorresco, sed 3 audiendi auidus uehementer efflagito. Tum illa: Sensi, inquit, cum uerba nostra tacitus attentusque rapiebas, 10 eumque tuae mentis habitum uel exspectaui uel, quod est uerius, ipsa perfeci; talia sunt quippe quae restant, ut degustata quidem modeant, interius autem recepta 4 dulcescant. Sed quod tu te audiendi cupidum dicis, quanto ardore flagrares, si quonam te ducere aggredia- 15 *Ducendus ad ueram felicitatem.* 5 mur agnosceres? B. Quonam? inquam. P. Ad ueram, inquit, felicitatem, quam tuus quoque somniat animus, sed occupato ad imagines uisu ipsam illam non ptest intueri. B. Tum ego: Fac obsecro, et quae illa uera sit sine 6 cunctatione demonstra. P. Faciam, inquit illa, tui causa 20 libenter. Sed quae tibi causa notior est, eam prius designare uerbis atque informare conabor, ut ea perspecta, cum in contrariam partem flexeris oculos, uerae beatitudinis speciem possis agnoscere.

Pr. I, 4 *quantum me,* Vall. *quantum tu me.* 21 *tibi causa notior,* Nonnulli del. *causa.* Stet, ait Eng. (p. 15); est lusus uerborum.

Pr. I, §3 *degustata mordent, interius dulcescunt. Par.* XVII, 130-132.
§6 *tui causa...quae tibi causa.* Alia exempla huiusmodi lusus uerborum: "constat, aeterna positumque lege est ut constet genitum nihil" (p.37, uu.17-18); "non posse potentia non est" (p. 72, u. 10); "omnia solus, uerum possis dicere solem" (p. 142, uu. 13-14). Eng. p. 15.

COASTAL ADVISORY: A Captain's Guide to Penobscot Bay

The Metalsmith's Companion

Is it going to happen today?

Kinesis is a unique and lively typeface family in the Adobe Originals collection. The energy and typographic maturity of this innovative design make it as suitable for display settings as it is for longer blocks of text. Balancing unconventional forms and expressive calligraphic lettering with text typeface legibility, Kinesis offers a wide range of weights and a vigorous personality for a multitude of uses.

EFGHIJKLMNOPQRRSTUVWXYZ ABCD

hijklmnopqrstuvwxyz **abcdefghijklmnop**

567890 **1234567890** (¡!¿?&$£

CDEFGHIJKLMNOPQRRSTUV

ghijklmnopqrstuvwxyz **abcdefghijklm**

4567890 1234567890 (¡!¿?&$£¥

PQRRSTUVWXYZ ABCDEFGHIJKLM

hijklmnopqrstuvwxyz abcdefghijklmnopq

HIJKLMNOPQRSTUVW

€ƒ¢) {ÆæŒœfiflffffifflß} ÅÇÉÑÌ

QRRSTUVWXYZ **ABCDEFGHIJKLMNOPQRR**

flffffifflß} [¶§†‡@*] **ÅÇÉÑÌØÛ**

cdefghijklmnopqrstuvwxyz abcdefghijklmno

Jonathan Hoefler. See page 242.

Country:
USA.
Writing system:
Latin.

Competition category:
Text/diplay, system.
Manufacturer/distributor:
The Hoefler Type Foundry.

KNOCKOUT
JUNIOR CRUISERWEIGHT

KNOCKOUT
FLYWEIGHT

Knockout
FULL HEAVYWEIGHT

Knockout
FULL FLYWEIGHT

Knockout
ULTIMATE CRUISERWEIGHT

KNOCKOUT
FULL WELTERWEIGHT

KNOCKOUT
JUNIOR SUMO

KNOCKOUT
JUNIOR LIGHTWEIGHT

KNOCKOUT
MIDDLWEIGHT

Knockout
ULTIMATE WELTERWEIGHT

Knockout
FULL CRUISERWEIGHT

KNOCKOUT
ULTIMATE HEAVYWEIGHT

Knockout
LIGHTWEIGHT

KNOCKOUT
WELTERWEIGHT

Knockout
FULL FEATHERWEIGHT

Knockout
JUNIOR HEAVYWEIGHT

KNOCKOUT
BANTAMWEIGHT

KNOCKOUT
JUNIOR FEATHERWEIGHT

Knockout
FULL MIDDLEWEIGHT

KNOCKOUT
HEAVYWEIGHT

KNOCKOUT
FULL SUMO

KNOCKOUT
JUNIOR FLYWEIGHT

Knockout
SUMO

Knockout
JUNIOR WELTERWEIGHT

KNOCKOUT
JUNIOR MIDDLEWEIGHT

KNOCKOUT
FULL BANTAMWEIGHT

Knockout
JUNIOR BANTAMWEIGHT

KNOCKOUT
ULTIMATE MIDDLEWEIGHT

KNOCKOUT
CRUISERWEIGHT

Knockout
ULTIMATE SUMO

Knockout
FULL LIGHTWEIGHT

KNOCKOUT
FEATHERWEIGHT

Residential Restrictionist Raises
Realtor Ratifies Reversal
Redshirted Roseville
Recommendation
Rememberable
Rehabilitates
Reichsmark
Rockslides
Rekindles

Relevant Restaurant Referendum
Realizes Rustic Rationale
Redeems Rensselaer
Remorselessness
Relentlessness
Rattlesnakes
Reschedule
Rainstorm
Romance

Reveals Reformational Resolution
Rural Route Renters Riled
Raffish Resemblance
Rumbustiousness
Rosicrucianism
Roundabouts
Refinanced
Recursion
Received

Reconstructed
Redecorated
Reversions
Refurbish
Radiates

Knockout is a super-family of sans serif typefaces, which expands upon the historical range covered by the Champion Gothic series. Begun in 1994 for *The New York Times Magazine* (where it can currently be seen), and extended in various directions for *Premiere* and *Sports Illustrated*, Knockout has become part of the standard formats of a number of American magazines.

Typeface name:
Kursiv Bogdesco.
Designer:
Ilya Bogdesco.

АБВГДЕЁЖЗИЙК
ЛМНОПРСТУФХЦ
ЧШЩЪЫЬЭЮЯаб
вгдеёжзийклмно
прстуфхцчшщъы
ьэюяґҐЃЋЄЅІЇЈКЉ
ЊЂЎЏѓґѓєѕіїјкљ
њђўџ,.;:...-!?',·
„"‹›«»/|—-··()[]{}*
‡§$¶✓‚""··∴∵∗◊∧~ǀ
\©®™@$€¢£ƒ¥¤№12
34567890%‰+−±
÷=‹›¬.∂∆√∞°′″µ

Ilya Bogdesco (1923, Moldavian SSR), a veteran
of World War II, has worked in Kishinev since 1951
as a freelance illustrator and painter, and as art
director of a local publishing house. He was named
People's Artist of the USSR in 1962. He won a Gold
Medal for his murals from the National Academy
of Arts, and for his illustrations he won a Gold
Medal at the International Book Design Exhibition,
Leipzig (1971), and the top prize of the National
Book Design Competition, the Ivan Fedorov Certificate (1980). He has participated in many exhibitions, at home and abroad.

Country:
Russia.
Writing system:
Cyrillic.

Competition category:
Text, single font.
Manufacturer/distributor:
Ilya Bogdesco.

Kursiv Bogdesco presents an attempt to retain
and preserve, to the extent possible, the liveliness,
the spontaneity, and the beauty of calligraphy with
a broad-nibbed pen, and the logic of the letterform construction that is characteristic of this
tool. The designer deems this approach important,
although somehow underestimated and underdeveloped; and, he hopes, promising.

Typeface name:
Lagarto.
Designer:
Gabriel Martínez Meave.

ABCDEFGHIJ
KLMNOPQR
STUVWXYZ
abcdefghijklmnopq
rstuvwxyz ¿?¡!.,;:
ÁÉÍÓÚÑÃÕ
ÆŒáéíóúñãõœœſ
¿?¡!.,;: ""'' ‿⁔‿

Gabriel Martínez Meave. See page 180.

Country:
Mexico.
Writing system:
Latin.

Competition category:
Display, single font.
Manufacturer/distributor:
Gabriel Martínez Meave.

Font for historical text composition based on Lagarto's XVIth-century manuscript hand.

Lagarto Typo

Magister Señor Guacamole
French subliminal cliché destiny
Quetzalli Hotel L'œil auf Fjords et
Draculas in A.D. 1700 México Subway
Electronic Karma Imperator Lowes Precieuse Sphinx
Miniskirted Maya Goddess from Yaxchilán, Guatemala is Amoureuse
Those Maledictum Tacos de Cochinita goes boom in Mein Panza. Bibliófilo Zacatecano views UFO at 2:00.

Lagarto is based on a manuscript book by the calligrapher of the same name, dating from the late 16th century. The design comes from the main body of the manuscript, written in a very special italic hand. The letter shapes are incredibly imaginative and playful; in them, European and Mexican baroque elements live together in a fantastic fusion. This typeface was commissioned by Gonzalo García Barcha, a Mexican researcher and fellow type designer, for a limited edition of Rodrigo Brunori's book *Me manda Stradivarius*, and for the *Compendio de Fuentes Mexicanas*.

263

Typeface name:
Latina.
Designer:
Iñigo Jerez Quintana.

ABCDEFGHIJKLMNOPQRSTUV
WXYZabcdefghijklmnopqrstuvwx
yzÀÁÂÃÄÅÆÈÉÊËÌÍÎÏÑÒÓÔÕØ
ÖŒÙÚÛÜŸàáâãäåæçèéêëìíîïñòóô
õöøœùúûüÿ&ßfifl,;:.…!¡?¿''""‹›«
»/|–—•·()[]{}*†‡§¶˘ˆˇ˜¨˙˝˚˝˙ ˛ˏ^~\
©®™@±$¢£ƒ¥¤ªº#0123456789

SERIF

SANS

ABCDEFGHIJKLMNOPQRSTUV
WXYZabcdefghijklmnopqrstuvwxy
zÀÁÂÃÄÅÆÈÉÊËÌÍÎÏÑÒÓÔÕØÖ
ŒÙÚÛÜŸàáâãäåæçèéêëìíîïñòóôõö
øœùúûüÿ&ßfifl,;:.…!¡?¿''""‹›«»/|–
—•·()[]{}*†‡§¶˘ˆˇ˜¨˙˝˚˝˙ ˛ˏ^~\©®
™@±$¢£ƒ¥¤ªº#0123456789

Iñigo Jerez Quintana. Textasis has a double meaning: on one hand is ecstasy, pure fascination with type and text in print; on the other is the search for its function, trying to find its axis. Textasis was founded in Barcelona in 1995 by Iñigo Jerez on completing his Graphic Design degree. Since then Iñigo has produced typefaces for a variety of editorial projects. In doing so, he has always searched for a communion between function, a deep respect for the past, the place of type in the present, and its projection into the future.

Country:
Spain.
Writing system:
Latin.

Competition category:
Text, superfamily.
Manufacturer/distributor:
Iñigo Jerez Quintana.

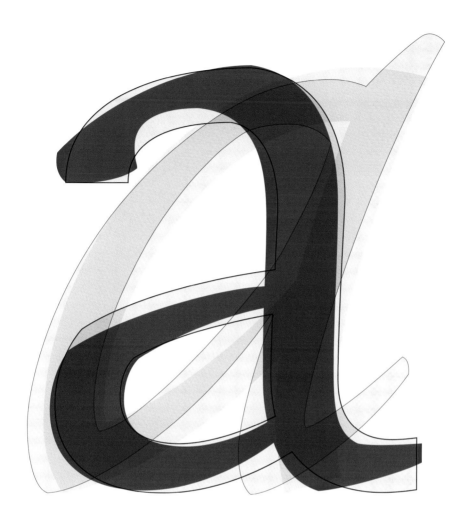

Latina & Latina

Regular, **Bold**, *Italic* & Regular, **Bold**, *Italic*.

ABCDEFHIJKLMNOPQRSTUVWXYZ.1234567890. abcdefghijklmnopqrstuvwxyz,.;:àáâãäåfiflß&@†œ
ABCDEFHIJKLMNOPQRSTUVWXYZ.1234567890. abcdefghijklmnopqrstuvwxyz,.;:àáâãäåfiflß&@†
ABCDEFHIJKLMNOPQRSTUVWXYZ.1234567890. abcdefghijklmnopqrstuvwxyz,.;:àáâãäåfiflß&@†&@†

ABCDEFHIJKLMNOPQRSTUVWXYZ.1234567890. abcdefghijklmnopqrstuvwxyz,.;:àáâãäåfiflß&@†œæ
ABCDEFHIJKLMNOPQRSTUVWXYZ.1234567890. abcdefghijklmnopqrstuvwxyz,.;:àáâãäåfiflß&@†œ
ABCDEFHIJKLMNOPQRSTUVWXYZ.1234567890. abcdefghijklmnopqrstuvwxyz,.;:àáâãäåfiflß&@†œæ

Latina is a work in progress that probably will never end. It's an excuse to learn and to pay homage to the origins of modern type. The project reviews the fusion between the two key elements that have shaped type as we know it today: roman capitals and humanist miniscules; and how this legacy is brought into the present through the creation of the delicate and functional sans-serif. Thank you Mr. Jenson.

Typeface name:
Le Monde Courrier.
Designer:
Jean-François Porchez.

ABCDEFGHIJKLMNOPQRS
TUVWXYZABCDEFGHIJKLM
NOPQRSTUVWXYZabcdefghijk
lmnopqrstuvwxyzÁÂÀÄÃÅ
ÆÇÐÉÊÈËÍÎÌÏIŁÑÓÔÒÖÕØ
ŒÞŠÚÛÙÜÝŸŽÁÂÀÄÃÅÆÇÐ
ÉÊÈËÍÎÌÏIŁÑÓÔÒÖÕØŒÞŠSSÚÛ
ÙÜÝŸŽáâàäãåæçðéêèëíîìïıłñó
ôòöõøœþšßúûùüýÿž&fiflffi
fflff.,:;•·""''"'",,,…‹«»›¿¡!?——_`
´^~–˘˙°„»×ˇ
 ˛¸#§¶@µ†‡*⁄(|)[/]{\}
®©℗™€$¢ƒ£¥€$¢ƒ£¥ªº001
1234567890123456789¹²³½
¼ ¾ % ‰ − < ÷ + ¦ ° ^ × = ~ > ¬

Jean-François Porchez. See page 176.

Country:
France.
Writing system:
Latin.

Competition category:
Text/display, (super)family.
Manufacturer/distributor:
Porchez Typofonderie.

Courriers

Chère grand-mère, nos vacances se passent bien

The incompetent Student

Letter setting

WELL FITTING CLOTHES ARE AN ACTUAL NECESSITY

typewritten imitation

halfway between writing & printing

Machine à écrire

TRIOMPHANTE aux bornes d'un empire aboli, la lettre des pierres jalonne les chemins des cohortes romaines, inscrit le nom des procurateurs & des juges au front des colonnes de gloire, sur les dalles funèbres qui deviennent pour nous comme autant de cadrans solaires où se voit, de son lever à son déclin, dans la parure des mots morts, la *beauté nue des formes incises; le trait ancien révèle ainsi la volonté d'une lumière qui délivre la parole; l'ombre jaillit sous le burin qui la provoque & s'allie, selon l'heure, au soleil dans un* **jeu parfois subtil & parfois éclatant, dans un accouplement fécond où l'esprit reconnaît sa voie & le cœur sa raison. Il semble que nos premiers graveurs n'aient eu**

D'AUTRE PENSÉE QUE CELLE DE CONSERVER DANS LE plomb l'empreinte de ces formes sublimes & nous *lisons encore, consultant les vieux livres, comme sur des stèles, ces caractères de l'admiration & de l'émotion, tout onc*tueux d'encre, empreints profondément, crevant presque la page mais irradiant du poids charnel de la main & susceptibles de dire la place juste d'une courbe ou la variante sensible d'un bâton répété mille fois. Il ne s'agit point là d'une justesse selon la règle & le compas mais de la communication d'une certaine chaleur humaine par laquelle le plomb s'est transmuté. Triomphante aux bornes d'un empire aboli, la **lettre des pierres jalonne les chemins des cohortes romaines, inscrit le nom des procurateurs & des juges au front des colonnes de** *gloire, sur les dalles funèbres qui deviennent pour nous comme autant* DE CADRANS SOLAIRES OÙ SE VOIT, DE SON LEVER À SON DÉCLIN, DANS LA

Le Monde Courrier. Since the arrival of microcomputing, most correspondence has been composed in book typefaces. Typewriters & the typestyles they used have become antiques. A letter composed in Times Roman and printed at 600 dpi is of such quality that many cannot distinguish it from a document produced by offset printing. Le Monde Courrier attempts to re-establish a style halfway between writing and printing. It returns the informal character of typewriter fonts to correspondence while remaning obviously typographic.

Typeface name:
Le Monde Journal.
Designer:
Jean-François Porchez.

ABCDEFGHIJKLMNOPQRS
TUVWXYZABCDEFGHIJKLM
NOPQRSTUVWXYZabcdefghijk
lmnopqrstuvwxyzÁÂÀÄÃÅ
ÆÇÐÉÊÈËÍÎÌÏIŁÑÓÔÒÖÕØ
ŒÞŠÚÛÙÜÝŸŽÁÂÀÄÃÅÆÇÐ
ÉÊÈËÍÎÌÏIŁÑÓÔÒÖÕØŒÞŠSSÚÛ
ÙÜÝŸŽáâàäãåæçðéêèëíîìïıłñó
ôòöõøœþšßúûùüýÿž&fiflffi
fflff.,:;•·""'',,...‹«»›¿¡!?——_`
´^~¯˘˙˚˝ˇ ¸‚#§¶@μ†‡*/(|)[/]{\}
®©℗™€$¢ƒ£¥€$¢ƒ£¥ªº001
1234567890123456789¹²³½
¼ ¾ % ‰ − < ÷ + ¦ ° ^ × = ~ > ¬

Jean-François Porchez. See page 176.

Country:
France.
Writing system:
Latin.

Competition category:
Text/display, (super)family.
Manufacturer/distributor:
Porchez Typofonderie.

Grande Mobilisation !

AFFAIRE TRÈS EUROPÉENNE

Journaux

Prise de la Tour de Malakoff

Guerre au Moyen-Orient

& *magazines*

Affrontement politique

À titre indicatif, 3500 F DONNE 530,30 €

TRIOMPHANTE aux bornes d'un empire aboli, la lettre des pierres jalonne les chemins des cohortes romaines, inscrit le nom des procurateurs & des juges au front des colonnes de gloire, sur les dalles funèbres qui deviennent pour nous comme autant de cadrans solaires où se voit, de son lever à son déclin, dans la parure des mots morts, la beauté nue des formes incises; le trait ancien révèle ainsi la volonté d'une lumière qui délivre la parole; l'ombre jaillit sous le burin qui la provoque & s'allie,

SELON L'HEURE, AU SOLEIL DANS UN JEU PARFOIS SUBTIL & PARfois éclatant, dans un accouplement fécond où l'esprit reconnaît sa voie & le cœur sa raison. Il semble que nos premiers graveurs n'aient eu d'autre pensée que celle de conserver dans *le plomb l'empreinte de ces formes sublimes & nous lisons encore,* consultant les vieux livres, comme sur des stèles, ces caractères de l'admiration & de l'émotion, tout onctueux d'encre, empreints profondément, crevant presque la page mais irradiant du poids charnel de la main & susceptibles de dire la place juste d'une courbe ou la variante sensible d'un bâton répété mille fois. Il ne s'agit point là d'une justesse selon la règle & le compas mais de la communication d'une certaine chaleur humaine par laquelle le plomb s'est transmuté. Triomphante aux bornes d'un empire aboli, la lettre des pierres jalonne les chemins des cohortes romaines, inscrit le nom des procurateurs & des juges au front des colonnes de gloire, sur les dalles funèbres qui deviennent pour nous comme autant

Le Monde Journal is the typeface on which the entire Le Monde family is based. By definition, it is intended for newspaper use at small sizes. Even though it has the same colour as Times, it appears more open: the reading flow has been made more fluent and less abrupt. The counters in the glyphs are larger, as if they were 'illuminating the interior'. To accommodate any problems in newspaper printing, the bold sharply contrasts with the roman. With a more delicate design and a distinctive rhythm, the italics remain noticeable when used with the romans.

Typeface name:
Letopis.
Designer:
Innokenty Keleinikov.

ΑΛБΒΓΓΔΔΕЖЗ
ЗИΚΛΜΗΟΗΟ
ΠΡϹΤΥΦΧЦЧ
ЧЪШЩЦЫѢЪЬ
ЭЮЯЇЇѢІЙЀНѺЙ
1234567890
!"(:,...•;)"?

Innokenty Keleinikov was born in Moscow in 1977.
He graduated from Moscow State University of
Printing Arts (Department of Print Design) in
1999. Since then he has worked as an instructor in
typographic design at his alma mater, at the Department of Print Design. Since 1996 he has worked
as freelance graphic designer and illustrator for
various Moscow publishing houses and periodicals.

Country:
Russia.
Writing system:
Cyrillic.

Competition category:
Display, single font.
Manufacturer/distributor:
Innokenty Kaleinikov.

повѣсти о житїи
и о храбрости
благовернаго
князя александра
невскаго
...
събра силу велику и наполни
корабля многы полковъ
своих, подвижеся в силѣ
тяжцѣ, пыхая духомъ
ратным, и прїиде в неву,
шатаяся безумїемь
...

Letopis (a Russian word that means 'chronicle') is an attempt to create a 'sans serif' based on the principles of traditional Russian lettering. Its design is inspired by the *poluustav* style of the 15th–16th centuries, but the *poluustav* design has been considerably transformed in accordance with the designer's original ideas and no longer conforms to any concrete historical model. This version of the typeface contains only lowercase (which is typical for *poluustav* lettering), but the designer is working on a version with uppercase too.

Typeface name:
Made in China.
Designer:
Yelena Zotikova.

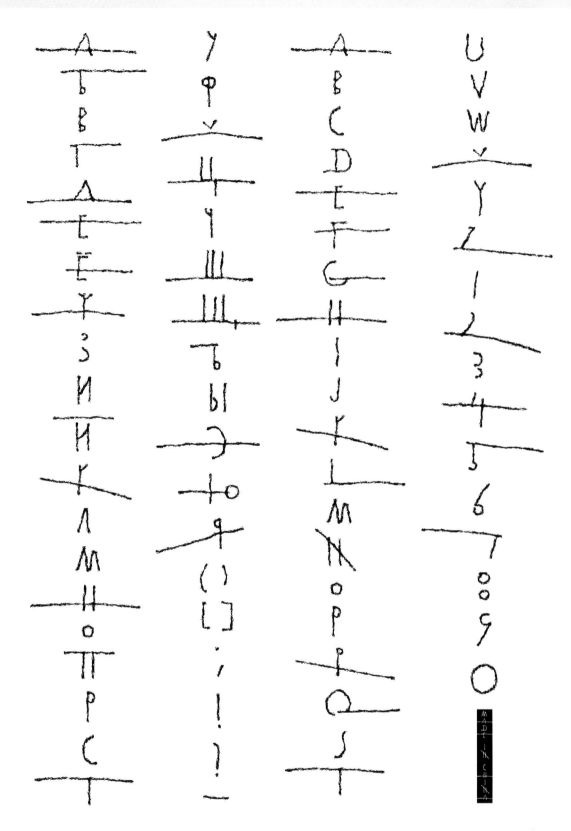

Yelena Zotikova was born in 1977 in Simferopol, the Crimea, Ukraine. She graduated from the Crimean Art College in 1996 and from the Kharkiv Academy of Arts and Design in 2001. She has participated in exhibitions and competitions under the auspices of the Academy. She has worked as a designer at 'B&S' studio since 2001.

Country:
Ukraine.
Writing system:
Cyrillic.

Competition category:
Display, single font.
Manufacturer/distributor:
Yelena Zotikova.

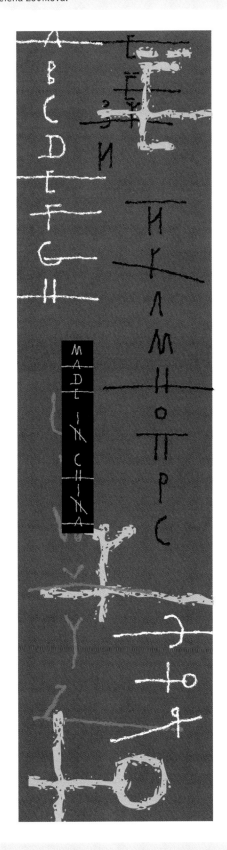

Made in China is one of the typefaces designed
as part of a graduation project under the supervision of Professor Vladimir Lesnyak at Kharkiv
State Academy of Design and Art. Soft graphic
materials prompted the idea of the type. Wide free
lines crossing deliberately exaggerated horizontal strokes create the impression of delicacy and
lightness. Texture gives artistic accentuation to
the type.

ا ﻟ آ آﺎ أ ء آﺋ ﺋﺌﺊ ؤ وْ إ إﻟ ﺋ ﻯ ﻰ ﻯ

ب ببب ت تتتـةـة ث ثث جـ ججج حـ ححح

خـ خـخـخ د ـدـذ ذ ر ـر ز ـز س سـسـس

ش شـشـش صـ صـصـص ض ضـضـض طـ طـطـط

ظـ ظـظـظ عـ عـعـع غـ غـغـغ فـ فـفـف قـ قـقـق

كـ ككك ل لـلـل مـ مـمـم ن ننن هـ هـهـه

و ـو يـ يـيـيْ ثـ قـثـقـثـ جـ ججج پـ پـپـپ

مـمـمـ جـ جـ بـحـ خـ بـمـ بـمـتـمـ تـم تـمـ نمـ نمـ يمـ يم

لا لا لأ ـلأ لإ لإ ـلأ لآ ـلآ إلآ لى لي لمـ لمـ لحـ لخـ فِي

لجـ لحـ لخـ ـبـرـ ـتـرـ ـثـرـ ـيـرـ ـبـن ـتـن ـنـن ـين

نج نجـ نحـ نحـ نجـ نجـ تج ٩٨٧٦٥٤٣٢١٠ (؟!) ٪

٬ ٫ .٬﴾﴿﴾ ﴾ ﴿ ﴿ * : » « ، ٬

Habib Khoury was born in Fassouta, Upper Galilee, in 1967. At age 12 he began learning Arabic calligraphy, and after high school, he took almost nine years of design and illustration studies, ending with a Masters degree with distinction from Central Saint Martins College in London. Habib spent several years between Haifa, London, and New York. Over the years his multilingual (Arabic, English, and Hebrew) expertise in calligraphy and typography has drawn him into the realm of type design. He established his private foundry AvanType in 1998.

Country:
Israel.
Writing system:
Arabic.

Competition category:
Text/display, single font.
Manufacturer/distributor:
AvanType Foundry.

يف مَقْصَفٍ كانَتْ بِدايَاتٌ لِلرُّسومَاتِ الأُولى،
تَبِعَهَا أَلْفُ سَاعَةٍ لمّا تَنْتَهِ مِنَ الصِّنَاعَةِ
الخَطيّةِ وَالصَّقْلِ التَّشْكيليِّ لِصيَاغَاتِ
حُروفِيَّةٍ مُحْكَمَةِ التَّهْذيبِ يف دَقائِق
تَصْميمٍ صَادِقَةَ الإِنْهَاءِ. يَكْتَسِبُ فِيهَا الحَرْفُ العَربِيُّ وَجْهَاً
جَديداً لا يَنْقَطِعُ عَنْ رَحْمِ الأَصَالةِ،
وَيَتَجَلَّى بِانْطِلاقَاتٍ
رَائِعَةٍ ذاتِ انْسِيَابٍ
أُفُقِي وَهيَاكِلَ
حُروفٍ مُقْتَضَبَةِ
الإِرْتِفَاع وَالهُبُوطِ. انْسِجَامٌ مُتَنَاغِمٌ
مَعَ طَبيعَةِ الخُطوطِ
النَّسْخِيَّةِ المعهُودَة،
يَجْعَلُ مِنَ النُّصُوصِ
المُنَضَّدَةِ، مَعَ الفَضَاءَاتِ
المُكْتَنَفَةِ دَاخِلَ
الكَلِمَات، نَسِيجَاً
تِيبُوغرافياً يف غَايَةِ
المَقروئيَّةِ وَالوُضُوح.

Maqsaf is an Arabic typeface whose name means
'the hanging-out place' — called that because its
initial sketches were made in such a place. Maqsaf
has an elegant cut and casting of each letterform,
with highly refined nuances: smooth edges, variable
strokes, and extended swashes that resemble hand
lettering. The letterforms' structure and ratios
provide exceptional legibility, and Maqsaf retains
characteristics of an Arabic *naskhi* typeface in
spite of the limited number of glyphs supported by
the system (Type 1 or TrueType).

Typeface name:
Markazi.
Designer:
Tim Holloway.

ء آ آ أ أ ؤ إ إ ا ئ ؤ ئ ا ا ب ا ب ب ب

ة ة ا ت ت ت ت ث ث ث ث ث ج ج ج ج

ح ح ح ج خ خ خ خ د د ذ ذ ذ ر

ز ز س س س س ش ش ش ش ش ص

ص ص ص ض ض ض ض ض ط ط ط

ط ظ ظ ظ ظ ع ع ع غ غ غ غ

ف ف ف ف ق ق ق ق ك ك ك ك ك ل ا ا

ل م م م م م ن ذ ذ ن ه ه ه ه ه و

و ى ى ي ي ي ي آ آ لا لا لآ لآ لأ لأ

لإ لإ لإ لا الله ا ء ء ء ء ء ء ء ء ء

؟ ؛ ، ٪ ٠ ١ ٢ ٣ ٤ ٥ ٦ ٧ ٨ ٩

Tim Holloway, after graduating in 1974, trained in
type drawing with the Linotype group. He worked
with Matthew Carter on Greek fonts and freelanced
for design groups in the UK and Holland, drawing
logos and corporate alphabets. With Dr. Fiona Ross
he co-designed Linotype Bengali and contributed
to the development of Linotype's Urdu *nasta'liq*
fonts and system. His other Arabic-script designs
include Karim and Mitra, both in the *naskh* style.

Country:
United Kingdom.
Writing system:
Arabic.

Competition category:
Text, single font.
Manufacturer/distributor:
Tim Holloway.

منذ بداية سبك الحروف المطبعيّة العربيّة في أوروبا شم في تركيا وبعدها حالاً في لبنان ، جهّز الأسلوب النسخي للخط ألنموذج لتصميم حروف النص المطبعيّة السائدة الاستعمال . عند تكييف النص العربي للتكنولوجيا اللاحقة للآلة الكاتبة وآلة صف الحروف ، إخطر مصمّمو الحروف أن يخفّضوا الى الحد الأدنى تنوّع أشكال الحروف وأن يتخلّوا عن حروف النسخ المزدوجة التقليديّة . "العربيّة المبسّطة" التي نتجت عن ذلك ، عادة باستعمال شكلين مختلفين فقط للحروف الممكن وصلها على الجهتين (عادة باستثناء 'ع' و 'ه') وشكل مختلف آخر للحروف الممكن وصلها على الجهة اليمنى فقط ، أصبحت تشبه مزيجًا لأسلوبي النسخ والكوفي المبكّر . لا تزال معظم الصحف والمجلّات العربيّة اليوم تدّون عواميد نصّها بحروف مبنيّة على أساس ألنموذج المبسّط بالرغم من أن معيار "اليونيكود" ذو ال ١٦ قطعة وتكنولوجيا الطقم الكامل للحروف الحريثة ، مكّن الإدخال ثانية الى الطباعة

Markazi offers a type style to accompany (and contrast with) the commonly used *naskh* text faces, sharing their cursive tendency but reducing their pen-calligraphic styling to a neutral or 'central' monoline. In respect of the choice of forms – how 'simplified' to make the design – and the average degree of undulation in the joining line that re-sults in text composition, Yakout and ASV Codar are among the typographic influences.

Typeface name:
Maya.
Designer:
Oded Ezer.

אבגדהוזחטיכךלמסנןסעפ
1234567890 פצצקרשת
₪ $ ⟨⟩ = - + * { } [ ] ( ) ' " ? ! . : ; , % #

אבגדהוזחטיכךלמסנןסעפ
1234567890 פצצקרשת
₪ $ ⟨⟩ = - + * { } [ ] ( ) ' " ? ! . : ; , % #

אבגדהוזחטיכךלמסנןסעפ
1234567890 פצצקרשת
₪ $ ⟨⟩ = - + * { } [ ] ( ) ' " ? ! . : ; , % #

אבגדהוזחטיכךלמסנןסעפ
1234567890 פצצקרשת
₪ $ ⟨⟩ = - + * { } [ ] ( ) ' " ? ! . : ; , % #

Oded Ezer (1972) founded his own studio (Oded Ezer Design Studio) in 2000 in Givatayim, Israel. He does editorial design, corporate identity, and typeface design for customers inside and outside Israel. Since September 1999 he has also run an experimental design project, 'Non Profit Item', exploring non-conventional solutions in Hebrew typographic design. He has won prizes from the Type Directors Club (New York), the Nagoya Design Center (Japan), and the Bezalel Academy (Jerusalem), among others. He teaches typography at the Vital Center for Design and at the Shenkar Academy of Design.

278

Country:
Israel.
Writing system:
Hebrew.

Competition category:
Text/display, family.
Manufacturer/distributor:
Oded Ezer.

תקשורת | פרסום | שיווק

גלובס

גליון מס' 5 / ספטמבר 1999

אני
משוגע,
אני
פנטסטי,
אני
יפה

100 התוכניות
הישראליות
האהובות בכל
הזמנים. כתבה
תכניתית

תעשיית האוויר
בבתי הספר
לתקשורת. תחקיר
קורינה שטוטלנד

עמרי פדן,
מקדונלד'ס, חושק
בכסאו של אהוד ברק
ורד שרון-ריבלין

טלית, סלוצקי וירדני
נגד אביב גלעדי.
הקרבות סביב ערוץ
הילדים החדש
בתיה פלדמן

דודו טופז חושף לראשונה את תכנוניו לשנה הבאה: אל"ף,
הקמת מטרופולין חדש בדרום הארץ. בי"ת, הפתחה של
20 אחוז בתאונות הדרכים, הודות למרקחת סודית שהוא
עצמו המציא. טופז מדבר על התאבדות בשידור חי במקרה
של נפילת רייטינג ועל גאוניותו. אסור להחמיץ אף מלה

Maya is a family of four fonts: Maya Light, Maya
Regular, Maya Bold, and Maya Stencil. The design
started while I was still a student at the Bezalel
Academy of Art & Design, Jerusalem. The design was
inspired by a few hand-drawn letters I had found
on a book cover from the 1950s. I was fascinated
by the angles of these letters, which reflected an
interesting attitude to Hebrew letter-structure.
After simplifying and modernizing the samples, I
went on to create the rest of the alphabet and the
numbers, and additional weights.

279

ÆABCDEFGHIJKLMNOŒPQ
RSTUVWXYZabcdefghijklmno
pqrstuvwxyz&§€£¥$0123456789

MERCURY DISPLAY ROMAN

ÆABCDEFGHIJKLMNOŒPQR
STUVWXYZaæbcdefghijklmnoœp
qrstuvwxyz:;!?&§€£¥$0123456789

MERCURY DISPLAY ITALIC

ÆABCDEFGHIJKLMNOŒPQ
RSTUVWXYZabcdefghijklmno
pqrstuvwxyz&€£¥$0123456789

MERCURY DISPLAY BLACK

ÆABCDEFGHIJKLMNŒOPQRSTUVWXYZ&?
æabcdefghijklmnœopqrstuvwxyz€£0123456789

MERCURY NEWS ROMAN

ÆABCDEFGHIJKLMNŒOPQRSTUVWXYZ&!?
æabcdefghijklmnœopqrstuvwxyz€¥£$0123456789

MERCURY NEWS ITALIC

ÆABCDEFGHIJKLMNOŒPQRSTUVWXYZ
abcdefghijklmnopqrstuvwxyz€£$0123456789

MERCURY NEWS BOLD

Jonathan Hoefler.
See page 242.
Tobias Frere-Jones.
See page 238.

Country:
USA.
Writing system:
Latin.

Competition category:
Text/display, system.
Manufacturer/distributor:
The Hoefler Type Foundry.

Mutinous GALAXIES

Defied Gravity

Universal Pandemonium

OUR EXISTENCE TURNED

Upside-Down Desipite Scientists' Prediction

Of Benign Once-In-a-Lifetime Meteor Shower Spectacle

FROM NOW ON, THE SUN WILL RISE IN THE WEST AND SET IN THE EAST

Feugiat lorem; suscipit consequ delenit ut aliquip, ex nisl dolore dolore sed accumsan ut. Facilisi vero dolore blandit aliquam lup enim in, ex dolore et. Consequat tation iriure iusto consequatvel, wisi, nulla ut elit eum ex lorem? consequat commodo crisare ven nonummy te volutpat exerci em Ut consequat vel, tation vel aliq tation. Hendrerit esse lorem, ius consectetuer, ut exerci adipiscin

FEUGIAT LOREM; SUSCIPIT NULLA DELENIT UT ALIQUI DOLORE ACCUMSAN CRISA UT. FACILISIS DOLRE FACIL VERO EST DUIS FEUGAIT IN CONSEQUATVEL IRIURE AL

Feugiat lorem; suscipit conseq delenit ut aliquip, ex nisl dolor dolore sed accumsan ut. facilisi vero dolore blandit aliquam lut enim in, ex dolore et. Consequa tation consequatvel iriure iusto wisi, nulla ut elit eum ex lorem consequat commodo crisare ve nonummy te volutpat exerci eu Ut consequat vel, tation vel aliq tation. Hendrerit esse lorem, iu consectetuer, ut exerci adipisci

FEUGIAT LOREM; SUSCIPIT NULLA DELENIT UT ALIQU DOLORE ACCUMSAN CRISA UT. FACILISIS DOLRE, FACI VERO; EST DUIS FEUGAIT I CONSEQUATVEL IRIURE AL

Feugiat lorem; suscipit conse delenit ut aliquip, ex nisl dol dolore sed accumsan ut. facil vero dolore blandit aliquam l enim in, ex dolore et. Conseq tation consequatvel iriure iu wisi, nulla ut elit eum ex lore consequat, commodo crisare nonummy te volutpat, exerci Ut consequat vel, tation vel a tation. Hendrerit esse lorem, consectetuer, ut exerci adipi

FEUGIAT LOREM; SUSCIPI NULLA DELENIT UT ALIQ DOLORE ACCUMSAN CRIS UT. FACILISIS DOLRE, FAC VERO EST DUIS FEUGIAT I CONSEQUATVEL IRIURE A

Mercury is a family of text and display faces for newspaper typography, the first collaboration between type designers Jonathan Hoefler and Tobias Frere-Jones. Jonathan Hoefler's Mercury Display (1997) was commissioned by Robert Priest for the redesign of *Esquire* magazine. Like handcut metal types, Mercury was designed from the inside out, with the non-printing 'counters' being drawn first. In 1999, Tobias Frere-Jones revisited Mercury to create a vigorous and sturdy family of news faces for Alex Isley's redesigns for the *New Times* newspaper chain.

Typeface name:
Minion Pro Greek.
Designer:
Robert Slimbach.

ABCDEFGHIJKLMNOPQRSTUV
WXYZ&ÆŁØŒÞÐabcdefghijklm
nopqrstuvwxyzæłøœßþðTh fi fl ff ffi
ffl fb ffb ffh ffj ffk fft fh fj fk ft ch ck ct sp st sb sh
ſi ſk ſl ſſ ſſi ſſl ſt a e̓ k m n r ABCDEFGHIJ
KLMNOPQRSTUVWXYZ&

ΑΒΓΔΕΖΗΘΙΚΛΜΝΞΟΠΡΣΤΥΦ
ΧΨΩΘVαβγδεζηθικλμνξοπρστυφ
χψωά έ ή ί ϊ ό ύ ϋ ώ ῒ ῢ ς ϑ φ ϖ θ ϐ ϛ ϱ ϰ ϡϝ

АБВГЃДЕЖЗИЙКЛМНОПРСТ
УФХЦЧШЩЪЫЬЭЮЯЁЂЃЄЅІЇ
ЈЉЊЋЌЎЏѢабвгѓдежзийклмн
опрстуфхцчшщъыьэюяёђѓєѕіï
јљњћќўџѣәδ

Ø0123456789$¢£¥ƒ₡¤₣₤₧₨€#₨%
‰0123456789$¢£¥ƒ₡€#$¢%‰¼½
¾⅛⅜⅝⅞⅓⅔^~·+±<=>||×÷−∂μπΔ
ΠΣΩ√∞∫≈≠≤≥◊¬№℮ℓ°ªº?¿!¡!?¡¿()
[]{}/*•§†‡¶©®™@

Robert Slimbach. See page 194.

Country:
USA.
Writing system:
Greek.

Competition category:
Text, superfamily.
Manufacturer/distributor:
Adobe Systems.

Minion Pro Greek

For the Greek alphabets of Minion Pro, Robert Slimbach took the design approach of modernizing traditional Greek forms to better harmonize with Minion's Latin counterparts. As with the Latin forms, he used the broad-edged pen to develop a distinctive alphabet style, then adapted his calligraphy as typeforms by simplifying and stylizing the design until an appropriate activity level was achieved. Minion Pro includes complete modern and polytonic Greek sets for all of the families weights, widths, and optical size ranges.

11/13 REGULAR GREEK

Στις πύλες του δάσους ο έκπληκτος άνθρωπος του κόσμου είναι αναγκασμένος να εγκαταλείψει τις αστικές του εκτιμήσεις της μικρότητας και της μεγαλοσύνης, της σοφίας και της ανοησίας. Το φορτίοτης συνήθειας φεύγει απ' τους ώμους του με το πρώτο βήμα που κάνει σ' αυτόν τον τόπο. Ο ιερός χαρακτήρας του

11/13 CONDENSED GREEK

Στις πύλες του δάσους ο έκπληκτος άνθρωπος του κόσμου είναι αναγκασμένος να εγκαταλείψει τις αστικές του εκτιμήσεις της μικρότητας και της μεγαλοσύνης, της σοφίας και της ανοησίας. Το φορτίοτης συνήθειας φεύγει απ' τους ώμους του με το πρώτο βήμα που κάνει σ' αυτόν τον τόπο.

11/13 SEMIBOLD GREEK

Στις πύλες του δάσους ο έκπληκτος άνθρωπος του κόσμου είναι αναγκασμένος να εγκαταλείψει τις αστικές του εκτιμήσεις της μικρότητας και της μεγαλοσύνης, της σοφίας και της ανοησίας. Το φορτίοτης συνήθειας φεύγει απ' τους ώμους του με το πρώτο βήμα που κάνει σ' αυτόν τον τόπο. Ο ιερός χαρακτή-

11/13 SEMIBOLD CONDENSED GREEK

Στις πύλες του δάσους ο έκπληκτος άνθρωπος του κόσμου είναι αναγκασμένος να εγκαταλείψει τις αστικές του εκτιμήσεις της μικρότητας και της μεγαλοσύνης, της σοφίας και της ανοησίας. Το φορτίοτης συνήθειας φεύγει απ' τους ώμους του με το πρώτο βήμα που κάνει

11/13 BOLD GREEK

Στις πύλες του δάσους ο έκπληκτος άνθρωπος του κόσμου είναι αναγκασμένος να εγκαταλείψει τις αστικές του εκτιμήσεις της μικρότητας και της μεγαλοσύνης, της σοφίας και της ανοησίας. Το φορτίοτης συνήθειας φεύγει απ' τους ώμους του με το πρώτο βήμα που κάνει σ' αυτόν τον τόπο. Ο ιερός χαρακτή-

11/13 BOLD CONDENSED GREEK

Στις πύλες του δάσους ο έκπληκτος άνθρωπος του κόσμου είναι αναγκασμένος να εγκαταλείψει τις αστικές του εκτιμήσεις της μικρότητας και της μεγαλοσύνης, της σοφίας και της ανοησίας. Το φορτίοτης συνήθειας φεύγει απ' τους ώμους του με το πρώτο βήμα που

Regular Caption ❧ *Italic Caption* ❧ Regular ❧ *Italic* ❧ Regular Subhead ❧ *Italic Subhead* Regular Display ❧ *Italic Display* ❧ **Semibold Caption** ❧ *Semibold Caption Italic* ❧ **Semibold Text** *Semibold Text Italic* ❧ **Semibold Subhead** ❧ *Semibold Subhead Italic* ❧ **Semibold Display** *Semibold Display Italic* ❧ **Bold Caption** ❧ *Bold Caption Italic* ❧ **Bold Text** ❧ *Bold Text Italic* **Bold Subhead** ❧ *Bold Subhead Italic* ❧ **Bold Display** ❧ *Bold Display Italic*

Minion Pro is an Adobe Original typeface. The first version of Minion was released in 1990. Cyrillic additions and multiple master versions were released in 1992; the OpenType Pro version was released in 2000. Minion Pro is inspired by classical, old style typefaces of the late Renaissance, a period of elegant, beautiful, and highly readable type designs. Minion Pro combines the aesthetic and functional qualities that make text type highly readable with the versatility of OpenType digital technology.

Typeface name:
Myriad Pro Greek & Cyrillic.
Designers:
Robert Slimbach, Carol Twombly
Fred Brady.

A B C D E F G H I J K L M N O P Q R S T U V W X Y
Z & Æ Ł Ø Œ Þ Ð a b c d e f g h i j k l m n o p q r s
t u v w x y z æ ı ł ø œ ß þ ð fi fl ff ffi ffl ffj fj Á Â Ä
À Å Ã Ç É Ê Ë È Í Î Ï Ì İ Ñ Ó Ô Ö Ò Õ Š Ú Û Ü Ù Ý Ÿ
Ž Ă Ā Ą Ć Č Ď Đ Ě Ė Ē Ę Ğ Ġ Ī Į Ķ Ĺ Ľ Ļ Ń Ň Ņ Ő Ō Ř
Ř Ŗ Ś Ş Ş Ť Ţ Ű Ū Ų Ů Ź Ż Æ Ĉ Č Ĕ Ŋ Ĝ Ġ Ħ Ĥ Ĩ IJ Ĩ Ĵ
Ł Ŏ Ø Ŝ Ŧ Ŭ Ũ Ẃ Ŵ Ẅ Ẁ Ŷ Ỳ á â ä à å ã ç é ê ë è í î
ï ì ñ ó ô ö ò õ š ú û ü ù ý ÿ ž ă ā ą ć č ď đ ě ė ē ę ğ
ġ ī į ķ ĺ ľ ļ ń ň ņ ő ō ŕ ř ŗ ś ş ş ť ţ ű ū ų ů ź ż æ ĉ č
ŋ ĝ ġ ħ ĥ ĭ ij ĩ ĵ l· ń ŏ ø ŝ ŧ ŭ ũ ẃ ŵ ẅ ẁ ŷ ỳ κ Α Β Γ
Δ Ε Ζ Η Θ Ι Κ Λ Μ Ν Ξ Ο Π Ρ Σ Τ Υ Φ Χ Ψ Ω Ά Έ Ή Ί
Ϊ Ό Ύ Ϋ Ω α β γ δ ε ζ η θ ι κ λ μ ν ξ ο ρ σ τ υ φ χ
ψ ω ά έ ή ί ϊ ό ύ ϋ ώ ΐ ΰ ς Α Б В Г Ѓ Д Е Ж З И Й К Л
М Н О П Р С Т У Ф Х Ц Ч Ш Щ Ъ Ы Ь Э Ю Я Ё Ђ Ѓ
Є Ѕ І Ї Ј Љ Њ Ћ Ќ Ў Џ а б в г ѓ д е ж з и й к л м н
о п р с т у ф х ц ч ш щ ъ ы ь э ю я ё ђ ѓ є ѕ і ї ј љ
њ ћ ќ ў џ ә Ø 0 1 2 3 4 5 6 7 8 9 $ ¢ £ ¥ ƒ ¤ € # %
‰ 0 1 2 3 4 5 6 7 8 9 $ ¢ £ ¥ ƒ € # % ¼ ½ ¾ ^ ~
· + ± < = > | ¦ × ÷ − ∂ μ π Δ Π Σ Ω √ ∞ ∫ ≈ ≠ ≤ ≥
◊ ¬ № ℮ ℓ ° ª º ( ) [ ] { } / \ * • § † ‡ ¶ © ® ™ @ ? ¿ ! ¡

Robert Slimbach. See page 194.
Carol Twombly became a full-time member of the Adobe type staff in 1988, and continued there as one of three principle designers until 1999. She designed the first three display typefaces in the Adobe Originals collection: Trajan, Charlemagne, and Lithos. She also designed Adobe Caslon, and several original multiple master families.
Fred Brady began his career in lettering as a sign maker, then worked for Autologic, where he designed the award-winning Kis-Janson revival. From 1989, he headed the Adobe Originals program.

Country:
USA.
Writing systems:
Greek, Cyrillic.

Competition category:
Text/display, superfamily.
Manufacturer/distributor:
Adobe Systems.

Myriad Pro Greek & Cyrillic

As a newly expanded OpenType family, Myriad Pro includes a glyph complement that has complete Cyrillic and Greek alphabets, an enlarged set of accent characters, oldstyle figures, and other useful glyphs. Its large glyph set covers a broad range of international requirements, while consolidation of all Myriad Pro's glyphs into single roman and italic fonts provides users with increased typographic control. All glyphs in Myriad Pro are offered in condensed, normal, and extended widths, and in five weights ranging from light to black. The additional Greek characters were designed by Carol Twombly with Robert Slimbach, and the Cyrillic characters were designed by Fred Brady with Robert Slimbach.

9/10 LIGHT CYRILLIC
Наполеон начал войну с Россией потому, что он не мог не приехать в Дрезден, не мог не отуманиться почестями, не мог не надеть польского мундира, не поддаться предприимчивому впечатлению июньского

9/10 REGULAR CYRILLIC
Наполеон начал войну с Россией потому, что он не мог не приехать в Дрезден, не мог не отуманиться почестями, не мог не надеть польского мундира, не поддаться предприимчивому впечатлению

9/10 SEMIBOLD CYRILLIC
Наполеон начал войну с Россией потому, что он не мог не приехать в Дрезден, не мог не отуманиться почестями, не мог не надеть польского мундира, не поддаться предприимчивому впечатлению

9/10 BOLD CYRILLIC
Наполеон начал войну с Россией потому, что он не мог не приехать в Дрезден, не мог не отуманиться почестями, не мог не надеть польского мундира, не поддаться предприим-

9/10 BLACK CYRILLIC
Наполеон начал войну с Россией потому, что он не мог не приехать в Дрезден, не мог не отуманиться почестями, не мог не надеть польского мундира, не поддаться предприим-

9/10 LIGHT GREEK
Στις πύλες του δάσους ο έκπληκτος άνθρωπος του κόσμου είναι αναγκασμένος να εγκαταλείψει τις αστικές του εκτιμήσεις της μικρότητας και της μεγαλοσύνης, της σοφίας και της ανοησίας. Το φορτίο της συνήθειας φεύγει απ'τους

9/10 REGULAR GREEK
Στις πύλες του δάσους ο έκπληκτος άνθρωπος του κόσμου είναι αναγκασμένος να εγκαταλείψει τις αστικές του εκτιμήσεις της μικρότητας και της μεγαλοσύνης, της σοφίας και της ανοησίας. Το φορτίο της συνήθειας

9/10 SEMIBOLD GREEK
Στις πύλες του δάσους ο έκπληκτος άνθρωπος του κόσμου είναι αναγκασμένος να εγκαταλείψει τις αστικές του εκτιμήσεις της μικρότητας και της μεγαλοσύνης, της σοφίας και της ανοησίας. Το φορτίο της

9/10 BOLD GREEK
Στις πύλες του δάσους ο έκπληκτος άνθρωπος του κόσμου είναι αναγκασμένος να εγκαταλείψει τις αστικές του εκτιμήσεις της μικρότητας και της μεγαλοσύνης, της σοφίας και της ανοησίας. Το φορτίο της

9/10 BLACK GREEK
Στις πύλες του δάσους ο έκπληκτος άνθρωπος του κόσμου είναι αναγκασμένος να εγκαταλείψει τις αστικές του εκτιμήσεις της μικρότητας και της μεγαλοσύνης, της σοφίας και της ανοησίας. Το φορ-

Light Condensed • *Light Condensed Italic* • Light • *Light Italic* • Light SemiExtended • *Light SemiExtended Italic* • Condensed • *Condensed Italic* • Regular • *Italic* • SemiExtended • *SemiExtended Italic* • Semibold Condensed • *Semibold Condensed Italic* • Semibold • *Semibold Italic* • Semibold SemiExtended • *Semibold SemiExtended Italic* • Bold Condensed • *Bold Condensed Italic* • Bold • *Bold Italic* • Bold SemiExtended • *Bold SemiExtended Italic* • Black Condensed • *Black Condensed Italic* • Black • *Black Italic* • Black SemiExtended • *Black SemiExtended Italic*

Myriad, an Adobe Originals design first released in 1992, Myriad has become popular for both text and display composition. As an OpenType release, Myriad Pro expands this sans serif family to include Greek and Cyrillic glyphs, as well as adding oldstyle figures and improving support for Latin-based languages. The full Myriad Pro family includes condensed, normal, and extended widths in a full range of weights. Myriad has a warmth and readability that result from the humanistic treatment of letter proportions and design detail.

Nathan
Sylvie Chokroun, juin 2001

אבגדהוזחט
יכלמנסעעפ
צקרשתסזן
דפוילשׁדדן

אבגדהוזחטיכלמנסעערשתפצק ססזןדף

ָ ֱ ֲ ֳ ֹ ֻ ֿ הֿ

ֶ ׃ ֵ ֓

ֽ ֜ ֞ ֔ ֕ ֟ ָ ֵ ֹ ֖ ֗ ֙ ֘ ֚ ֛

ֿ ֿ ֿ ֿ ֿ ֿ ֿ ֿ ֿ ֿ ֿ ֿ ֿ ֿ

׃ ׀ חֿ הֿ הֿ

Sylvie Chokroun. After a Baccalaureat in Applied Arts, Sylvie Chokroun obtained the 'Brevet de Technicien Supérieur' in Visual Communication. She then spent a year learning calligraphy and preparing for the competitive examination for the École Estienne, where she spent two years. She obtained a DSAA in typographic creation, with first class honours. In 2001 she participated in an exhibition called 'Images d'Écritures' in Nancy (calligraphy, typography). At present, while carrying out her own type designs and those that have been commissioned, she works as a graphic designer.

Country: Competition category:
France.   Text, single font.
Writing system: Manufacturer/distributor:
Hebrew.   Sylvia Chokroun.

וַעֲשָׂרָה נְשִׂאִים עִמּוֹ נָשִׂיא אֶחָד נָשִׂיא אֶחָד לְבֵית
אָב לְכֹל מַטּוֹת יִשְׂרָאֵל וְאִישׁ רֹאשׁ בֵּית־אֲבוֹתָם הֵמָּה
לְאַלְפֵי יִשְׂרָאֵל ׃ וַיָּבֹאוּ אֶל־בְּנֵי־רְאוּבֵן וְאֶל־בְּנֵי־גָד וְאֶל־
חֲצִי שֵׁבֶט־מְנַשֶּׁה אֶל־אֶרֶץ הַגִּלְעָד וַיְדַבְּרוּ אִתָּם לֵאמֹר ׃
כֹּה אָמְרוּ כֹּל ׀ עֲדַת יְהוָה מָה־הַמַּעַל הַזֶּה אֲשֶׁר מְעַלְתֶּם
בֵּאלֹהֵי יִשְׂרָאֵל לָשׁוּב הַיּוֹם מֵאַחֲרֵי יְהוָה בִּבְנוֹתְכֶם לָכֶם
מִזְבֵּחַ לִמְרָדְכֶם הַיּוֹם בַּיהוָה ׃   הַמְעַט־לָנוּ אֶת־עֲוֹן פְּעוֹר
אֲשֶׁר לֹא־הִטַּהַרְנוּ מִמֶּנּוּ עַד הַיּוֹם הַזֶּה וַיְהִי הַנֶּגֶף בַּעֲדַת
יְהוָה ׃ וְאַתֶּם תָּשֻׁבוּ הַיּוֹם מֵאַחֲרֵי יְהוָה וְהָיָה אַתֶּם תִּמְרְדוּ
הַיּוֹם בַּיהוָה וּמָחָר אֶל־כָּל־עֲדַת יִשְׂרָאֵל יִקְצֹף ׃ וְאַךְ אִם־
טְמֵאָה אֶרֶץ אֲחֻזַּתְכֶם עִבְרוּ לָכֶם אֶל־אֶרֶץ אֲחֻזַּת יְהוָה
אֲשֶׁר שָׁכַן־שָׁם מִשְׁכַּן יְהוָה וְהֵאָחֲזוּ בְּתוֹכֵנוּ וּבַיהוָה אַל־
תִּמְרֹדוּ וְאֹתָנוּ אַל־תִּמְרֹדוּ בִּבְנֹתְכֶם לָכֶם מִזְבֵּחַ מִבַּלְעֲדֵי
מִזְבַּח יְהוָה אֱלֹהֵינוּ ׃ הֲלוֹא ׀ עָכָן בֶּן־זֶרַח מָעַל מַעַל בַּחֵרֶם
וְעַל־כָּל־עֲדַת יִשְׂרָאֵל הָיָה קָצֶף וְהוּא אִישׁ אֶחָד לֹא גָוַע
בַּעֲוֹנוֹ ׃

Corps 16 pts,
interligné 19,5 pts

Corps 9 pts,
interligné 11 pts

בעת ההיא נאם־יהוה אהיה לאלהים לכל משפחות ישראל והמה יהיו־לי
לעם ׃ כה אמר יהוה מצא חן במדבר עם שרידי חרב הלוך להרגיעו ישראל ׃
מרחוק יהוה נראה לי ואהבת עולם אהבתיך על־כן משכתיך חסד ׃ עוד אבנך
ונבנית בתולת ישראל עוד תעדי תפיך ויצאת בחול משחקים ׃ עוד תטעי
כרמים בהרי שמרון נטעו נטעים וחללו ׃ כי יש־יום קראו נצרים בהר אפרים
קומו ונעלה ציון אל־יהוה אלהינו ׃ כי־כה אמר יהוה רנו ליעקב שמחה וצהלו
בראש הגוים השמיעו הללו ואמרו הושע יהוה את־עמך את שארית ישראל ׃
הנני מביא אותם מארץ צפון וקבצתים מירכתי־ארץ בם עור ופסח הרה
ויולדת יחדו קהל גדול ישובו הנה ׃ בבכי יבאו ובתחנונים אובילם אוליכם
אל־נחלי מים בדרך ישר לא יכשלו בה כי־הייתי לישראל לאב ואפרים בכרי
הוא ׃ שמעו דבר־יהוה גוים והגידו באיים ממרחק ואמרו מזרה ישראל יקבצנו
ושמרו כרעה עדרו ׃ כי־פדה יהוה את־יעקב וגאלו מיד חזק ממנו ׃ ובאו ורננו
במרום־ציון ונהרו אל־טוב יהוה על־דגן ועל־תירש ועל־יצהר ועל־בני־צאן
ובקר והיתה נפשם כגן רוה ולא־יוסיפו לדאבה עוד

DICTIONNAIRE DE LA MASSORAH

מִלּוֹן הַמָּסוֹרָה

Nathan was designed for a project at Pierre et
Marie Curie University (Paris VI), aimed at publishing a critical edition of the Hebraic Bible. It is
intended to resolve a number of problems: to be
legible at very small sizes; to be remarkable (I
have intentionally kept calligraphic aspects); to be
easily decipherable, avoiding distinction problems
between letters; to keep the position of nikud rig-
orous and accurate; to make sure that the rhythm
is not altered when the text is vocalized; and to
match with a classical Latin character.

אבגדההוזחזחטיכך

למסנןסעפףצץ

קרשת

%#1234567890

{}[]()'"‾—?!.:;,

₪$←|→=↑↓-+*

Yanek Iontef was born in the USSR in 1963. In 1989 he graduated from the Bezalel Academy of Art & Design, Jerusalem. He has worked as a staff designer at Williams & Phoa, London, and as a senior designer at Metamark International, Tel Aviv. Since 1996, he has been working as a freelance designer in Tel Aviv, specializing in typography, type design, logotype design, corporate identity, and editorial design. In addition he lectures on Typography at the Bezalel Academy in Jerusalem. Awards: Type Directors Club type design competition in 2000, for the Hebrew typeface Erica Sans.

Country:
Israel.
Writing system:
Hebrew.

Competition category:
Display, family.
Manufacturer/distributor:
Yanek Iontef.

12/12

18

אבגדהוזחטיכךלמסנןסעפףצץקרשת 1234567890
#%,.:;!?—¯˝˚''() {} []* ↓↑=→|←$שׁ

פיסקה זו מהווה דוגמה לטקסט שסודר במרווח אחיד בין הש ורות. המונח אחיד מתייחס לקומפוזיציה טיפוגרפית ללא רווח נוסף בין השורות. במונחים חזותיים, סדר זה מעניק מידה אחידה של צבע אפור הנעים מבחינה אסתטית, אך מאמץ את עיני הקורא בקריאה מתמשכת. אף על פי כן, הבחירה ב-אחיד המוכתבת על ידי איכות החזותית הרצויה.

פיסקה זו מהווה דוגמה לטקסט שסודר במרווח בן נקודה אחת בין השורות. מרווח זה מציין את הרווח הנוסף בין השורות. הבחירה במרווח אינה תלויה רק בכוונותיו של המעצב, אלא, בין השאר, גם בגודל האותיות, באורך השורה, באפיוני סוג האות ובכמות המלל. בחירה במרווח זה מסייעת בהבלטת שורות

1

אבגדהוזחטיכךלמסנןסעפףצץקרשת #1234567890
שׁ$←|→=↓↑+-* {} [] ()''˚˝¯—?!;:,.%

פיסקה זו מהווה דוגמה לטקסט שסודר במרווח בן נקודה אחת בין השורות. מרווח זה מציין את הרווח הנוסף בין השורות. הבחירה במרווח אינה תלויה רק בכוונותיו של המעצב, אלא, בין השאר, גם בגודל האותיות, באורך השורה, באפיוני סוג האות ובכמות המלל. בחירה במרווח זה מסייעת בהבלטת שורות

4

אבגדהוזחטיכךלמסנןסעפףצץקרשת
שׁ$=↓↑+-* {} [] ()''˚˝¯—?!;:,.%#1234567890
פיסקה זו מהווה דוגמה לטקסט שסודר במרווח בן נקודה אחת בין השורות. מרווח זה מציין את הרווח הנוסף בין השורות. הבחירה במרווח אינה תלויה רק בכוונותיו של המעצב, אלא, בין השאר, גם בגודל האותיות, באורך

Next Exit was influenced by the road signs in Israel, which originated in a technical engineering drawing from the '40s and were characterized by a simple geometrical grid. The original model had only one basic weight. During the process of working on the entire type family, two additional weights, light and extra bold, were developed, together with numerals and other marks and symbols.

Typeface name:
Nichiyou Daiku.
Designer:
Joachim Müller-Lancé,

私今日考新家衆明品
一語四十五担灯文書
内限定本導独特学女
愛母开妹大聞我国拳
小休警句口米あいう
えがくはさしすせた
つてとなにぬみも゜
やよらろれわをイウ
クケコサシスセタチ
テトマムメレワンバ
フっ゛ー丨 . ゜

Joachim Müller-Lancé, a graduate of the Basel
School of Design and Cooper Union, is principal
of Kame Design, for cultural/information design,
typefaces, and cartooning, in San Francisco. He
has been Senior Designer at Access Press/TUB, New
York/San Francisco, and Lead Information Designer
for Barclays Global Investors San Francisco. He had
his own studio in Barcelona, where he did cultural
exhibitions for the 1992 Olympics and taught information design at Elisava School. He won Morisawa
Awards for Lancé (Gold Prize, 1993) and his first
Kanji/Latin combination, Shirokuro (1999).

Country:
USA.
Writing system:
Japanese.

Competition category:
Display, single font.
Manufacturer/distributor:
Joachim Müller-Lancé.

日曜大工テパート

口一二三四五六七

ア イ キ ホ ヲ ス バ プ
・ ・ ・ ビ ウ テ ラ ラ
出 テ チ ー ト ー エ モ
口 リ ン ・ ド シ テ テ
・ ア ・ ア ョ イ イ
  ラ ク ラ ナ ー ル
  フ ラ フ リ
      フ ー
      ト

エ レ ヘ ー ダ ー ⟩⟩

'Nichiyou-Daiku' means 'Sunday carpenter' in
Japanese. Originally inspired by folkloric Taiwan-
ese lettering found on a restaurant in Tokyo, this
is an hommage and a wink to all weekend hobbyists
tinkering around the world. Its formal elements are
meant to evoke the fantastic wondrous riggings
on Japanese telephone poles, old-fashioned parts
from the toolboxes of hobby electricians and metal-
workers, and something of a funny lovable junkyard
altogether. Hence, Nichiyou-Daiku's design rules
are strict and consistent but intentionally wrong,
to amuse the viewer.

291

Typeface name:
Nyx.
Designer:
Rick Cusick.

ABCDEFGHIJLKM
NOPQRSTUVWXYZ
ÀÁÂÃÄÅÆÇÈÉÊË
ÌÍÎÏÑÖÕÓÔÒØŒ
ÙÚÛÜÝŸŽ&,;:.…-
!¡/?¿''""‹›«»——•
()[]*†‡/@$¢£ƒ¥
1234567890%‰ᵃᵒ
´¨^◆ˇ¯˘˚~`"

Rick Cusick was born in Stockton, California, and began his professional life with letters there, designing illuminated signs. He studied lettering with James Lewis at San Joaquin Delta College, and Mortimer Leach at Art Center College of Design. He began working at Hallmark in Kansas City in 1971 as a lettering artist, alphabet designer, and book designer. Cusick was associated with TBW Books for ten years as a design and editorial consultant. Presently, he is a Lettering Studio Manager and Font Development Manager at Hallmark.

Country:
USA.
Writing system:
Latin.

Competition category:
Display, single font.
Manufacturer/distributor:
Adobe Systems.

ASPIREBENIGNCRUELTY,
DESTINYEXCUSES
FECKLESSGALL.

HOWLINJEST;
KEENLUST
MANIFESTSNO
OBSCENE
PURPOSE.

4 9 2

3 5 7

8 1 6

! @ $ %
& ( ) / ;
Œ † ø
. ¿ ? : ¡ ·
‡ [ ] ç
£ « » ƒ ,
Æ ¥ —
¢ – * < >

(NIGHT GODDESS BEARS TRIBE OF DREAMS)

QUICKRUIN,
SAVAGETONGUE
UNLEASHESVAGARIES,
WOUNDSXERARCH,
YIELDSZENITH. PAULA SCHEIL

Nyx was developed over more than five years. In the early stages I explored the form, with and without its stencilled look, with drawings and serigraphs for an exhibition of my work. A few years later I digitized some of the letters to be applied to a collage for another exhibition, then eventually used the form, in a variety of proportions, for personal use and for titling in a magazine I was art directing. Although it is a drawn letter, it is informed by calligraphy. For me, calligraphy has been the touchstone by which to compare and contrast all explorations.

293

Typeface name:
Onserif & Onsans.
Designer:
Iñigo Jerez Quintana.

ABCDEFGHIJKLMNOPQRSTUV
WXYZabcdefghijklmnopqrstuvw
xyzÀÁÂÃÄÅÆÈÉÊËÌÍÎÏÑÒÓÔÕØ
ÖŒÙÚÛÜŸàáâãäåæçèéêëìíîïñòó
ôõöøœùúûüÿ&ßfifl,;:.…!¡?¿''""‹›«»
/|–—•·()[]{}*†‡§¶ˇˆˇ~¨‐˘°″· ˆ~\
©®™@€$¢£ƒ¥¤ªº#0123456789

SERIF

SANS

ABCDEFGHIJKLMNOPQRSTUVW
XYZabcdefghijklmnopqrstuvwx
yzÀÁÂÃÄÅÆÈÉÊËÌÍÎÏÑÒÓÔÕØÖ
ŒÙÚÛÜŸàáâãäåæçèéêëìíîïñòóô
õöøœùúûüÿ&ßfifl,;:.…!¡?¿''""‹›«»
/|–—•·()[]{}*†‡§¶ˇˆˇ~¨‐˘°″· ˆ~\
©®™@€$¢£ƒ¥¤ªº#0123456789

Iñigo Jerez Quintana. See page 264.

Country:
Spain.
Writing system:
Latin.

Competition category:
Text, superfamily.
Manufacturer/distributor:
Iñigo Jerez Quintana.

Onserif & Onsans, a typographic project about serif & sans serif, roman & italic. *Specially draw, designed & produced for «On» magazine by* **textaxis**

Serif & Sans

Roman & Italic

Onserif: Light, *Light Italic,* Regular, *Regular Italic,* **Semibold,** *Semibold Italic,* **Bold & Bold Italic. Onsans:** Light, *Light Italic,* Regular, *Regular Italic,* **Semibold,** *Semibold Italic,* **Bold & Bold Italic.**

Onserif and Onsans are the result of a commission by *On Diseño*, a Spanish architecture magazine with a 25-year history. The challenge was to modernize the magazine, give it a uniform appearance, and create a typographic coherence without modifying its design. The two fonts used until then were replaced with a family of 16 styles. The types are a consequence of their creative process: an eclectic typeface in which classic style, a functional condensed look, and a subtle synthesis of calligraphic and digital coexist.

Typeface name:
Papaya.
Designer:
Zvika Rosenberg.

א ב ג ד ה ה ו ז ח ה ט י י ך

כ צ פ ע ס נ ן מ ם ל כ

ג ב ו ו ש ש ת ר ק צ

פ ס נ מ ל כ י ט ז ה ד

פ ב ש ש ש ק צ

1 2 3 4 5 6 7 8 9 0

∗ % + = - ⟨ ⟩ { } [ ] ( )

; : , . $ " ₪ # ! ?

Zvika Rosenberg (Tel-Aviv, 1949) graduated from
the Bezalel Academy of Design in Jerusalem in
1975. He designed the core Hebrew fonts for the
Macintosh in 1986, and introduced the Hebrew
font library for Windows in 1994. With more than 80
fonts designed so far, Zvika Rosenberg owns the
leading font design firm in Israel, offering Hebrew
fonts designed by him as well as by 40 other type
designers. He is a typographic consultant for local corporate and advertising firms as well as for
multinational firms like Apple, Philips, Ericsson,
Samsung, and others.

Country:
Israel.
Writing system:
Hebrew.

Competition category:
Display, family.
Manufacturer/distributor:
MasterFont Ltd.

פאפאיה

אלון

בשנת 1992, יוצרו למעלה
מ-94,000 טונות של פאפאיה
במלזיה, ועוד 24,000 טונות
נועדו ליצוא לסינגפור, הונג
קונג ומערב אירופה.

תאור

הפאפאיה הוא שיח בעל גזע רך
המסוגל לצמוח לגובה של 8 מטרים.
הצמח פורח בדרך כלל תוך 9-12
חדשים בפריחה זכרית או נקבית.
הצמחים הזכריים אינם מניבים פירות
אך לעתים נדירות ניתן לראות צמח
זכרי מייצר פרי. אורך החיים של העץ
כמניב פרי הוא כ-3 שנים במהלכן
יניב כ-100 פירות שמשקל כל אחד
מהם 2-3 קילוגרם.
הפאפאיה מופיע בכמה זנים ונפוץ
מאד במיוחד באזורים הטרופיים
והסובטרופיים.

ערך תזונתי ל-100 גרם פרי

אנרגיה	35.0
לחות	90.7
חלבון	1.5 גרם
שומן	0.1 גרם
פחמימות	7.1 גרם
סידן	11.0 מ"ג
אשלגן	3.0 מ"ג
זרחן	3.0 מ"ג
ויטמין B12	0.1 מ"ג
ויטמין C	71.0 מ"ג

Papaya, designed in 1999, is a contemporary sans
serif typeface with minimal contrast, featuring
distinctive slightly bowed stems that conserve
intercharacter spacing. The bowed stems are a
contribution to the traditional type forms to make
the typeface distinguished from other contemporary sans serifs, yet avoiding the old square look
and feel. The idea was to create a display typeface
with high legibility. The uniform stroke width
results in a clean type texture, thus making it legible even at small sizes. The typeface is available in
three weights.

ABCDEFGHIJKLMNOPQRSTU
VWXYZ &ŒÆÇØ
abcdefghijklmnopqrstuvwxyz
œæfiflßçøáàâäãåéèêëñóòôöúùûü
([{1234567890/1234567890}])
!?:;€$£¥¢§¶†®%@™
ABCDEFGHIJKLMNOPQRSTUVWXYZ
&ŒÆÇØ 1234567890

---

*ABCDEFGHIJKLMNOPQRSTU
VWXYZ &ŒÆÇØ
([{1234567890/1234567890}])
abcdefghijklmnopqrstuvwxyz
œæfiflßçøáàâäãåéèêëñóòôöúùûüÿ
!?:;€$£¥¢§¶†®%@™
ABCDEFGHIJKLMNOPQRSTUVWXYZ
&ŒÆÇØ 1234567890*

Gerard Unger (1942) is a board member of ATypI
and the Alliance Graphique Internationale; he is a
part-time professor in the Department of Typography and Graphic Communication at the University
of Reading (UK), and a part-time teacher at the
Gerrit Rietveld Academy, Amsterdam. His typefaces Swift and Gulliver are used internationally in
newspapers, magazines, and other printed matter.
He designed the typeface for the new Dutch road
signs. He was awarded the H.N. Werkman prize in
1984, and the Maurits Enschedé-Prize in 1991.

Country:
The Netherlands.
Writing system:
Latin.

Competition category:
Text, family.
Manufacturer/distributor:
Dutch Type Library.

THE INVENTION OF PRINTING FROM MOVABLE TYPES WAS ONE OF THE CHIEF EVENTS AFFECTING the history of European civilization. The task of duplicating texts without variance was impossible before Gutenberg equiped the scholar with the accuracy of type. Prejudiced connoisseurs in *THE FIFTEENTH CENTURY DEPLORED THE NEW MASS-PRODUCTION OF BOOKS, BUT MEN OF LETTERS EAGERly hailed the printing press as a method of disseminating knowledge in permanent form; and the earliest printed books soon rivalled in beauty, as they superseded in economy, the fine manuscripts of their day. The invention of Printing from movable*

THE INVENTION OF PRINTING FROM MOVABLE TYPES WAS ONE OF THE CHIEF EVENTS affecting the history of European civilization. The task of duplicating texts without variance was impossible before *GUTENBERG EQUIPED THE SCHOLAR WITH THE ACCURACY OF TYPE. PREJUDICED CONnoisseurs in the fifteenth century deplored the new mass-production of books, but men of letters eagerly hailed the printing press as a method of disseminating knowledge in*

THE INVENTION OF PRINTING FROM MOVABLE TYPES WAS ONE OF THE CHIEF EVENTS affecting the history of European civilization. The task of duplicating texts without variance was impossible before Gutenberg equiped the scholar with the accuracy of type. prejudiced connoisseurs in *THE FIFTEENTH CENTURY DEPLORED THE NEW MASS-PRODUCTION OF BOOKS, BUT MEN OF letters eagerly hailed the printing press as a method of disseminating knowledge in permanent form; and the earliest printed books soon rivalled in beauty, as they superseded in economy, the fine manuscripts of their*

THE INVENTION OF PRINTING FROM MOVABLE TYPES WAS ONE OF THE chief events affecting the history of European civilization. The task of duplicating texts without variance was impossible before Gutenberg equiped the scholar with the accu-*RACY OF TYPE. PREJUDICED CONNOISSEURS IN THE FIFTEENTH CENTURY DEplored the new mass-production of books, but men of letters eagerly hailed the printing press as a method of disseminating knowledge in permanent*

THE INVENTION OF PRINTING FROM MOVABLE TYPES WAS ONE of the chief events affecting the history of European civilization. The task of duplicating *TEXTS WITHOUT VARIANCE WAS IMPOSSIBLE BEFORE GUTENBERG equiped the scholar with the accuracy of type. Prejudiced connoisseurs in the fifteenth century*

THE INVENTION OF printing from movable types was one of the chief events affec-*TING THE HISTORY OF European civilization. The task of duplicating texts without variance*

DTL Paradox is the transitional in the œuvre of Gerard Unger – who, like François-Ambroise Didot, strives for innovation. It is a wilful and 21st-century design, with refinements dating from eighteenth-century France; the *romain du roi* of Philippe Grandjean is one of its models. The relatively narrow top of the lowercase *a* and the way the weight extends from the lobes or curves of *b, d, p* and *q* recall Grandjean's characters. Notable are the slight curves in the ascenders and serifs, elements that are absent in other Unger designs such as Swift.

PARMENIDES

ΑΛΦΑ ΒΗΤΑ ΓΑΜΜΑ ΔΕΛΤΑ ΕΨΙΛΟΝ ΙΗΤΑ
ΗΤΑ ΘΗΤΑ ΙΩΤΑ ΚΑΓΓΑ ΛΑΜΒΔΑ ΜΥ ΝΥ ΞΙ
ΟΜΙΚΡΟΝ ΓΙ ΡΩ ΣΙΓΜΑ ΤΑΥ ΥΨΙΛΟΝ ΦΙ ΧΙ ΨΙ
ΟΜΕΓΑ ΑΛΦΑ ΒΗΤΑ ΓΑΜΜΑ ΔΕΛΤΑ ΕΨΙΛΟΝ
ΙΗΤΑ ΗΤΑ ΘΗΤΑ ΙΩΤΑ ΚΑΓΓΑ ΛΑΜΔΑ
ΜΥ ΝΥ ΞΙ ΟΜΙΚΡΟΝ ΓΙ ΡΩ ΣΙΓΜΑ ΤΑΥ
ΥΨΙΛΟΝ ΦΙ ΧΙ ΨΙ ΟΜΕΓΑ ΑΛΦΑ ΒΗΤΑ ΓΑΜΜΑ
ΔΕΛΤΑ ΕΨΙΛΟΝ ΙΗΤΑ ΗΤΑ ΘΗΤΑ ΙΩΤΑ ΚΑΓΓΑ

cut by Dan Carr for the Peter Koch Parmenides
ΑΒΓΔΕΙΗΘΘΙΚΛΜΝΞΟΓΡΣΤΥΦΧΨΩΩΕΟ
June 5, 2001

Dan Carr is a typographer and poet who writes
about type and type history. He designs books,
designs metal and digital type, cuts steel punches
by hand, and operates a typefoundry and press that
prints exclusively with metal types. He has also
taught typography for the past seven years. In 1999
Carr was elected a Master Typographic Punchcutter of France for his metal typeface Regulus.
His digital type, Chêneau, was a Judges Choice in
the 2000 Type Directors Club type design competition. In the fall of 2000 Carr gave a lecture and
demonstration of punchcutting at ATypI, in Leipzig.

Country:
USA.
Writing system:
Archaic Greek.

Competition category:
Text, single font.
Manufacturer/distributor:
Golgonooza Letter Foundry.

OΔVΣΣΕΙΑΣ

The Odyssey

ΑΝΔΡΑ ΜΟΙ ΕΝΝΕΓΕ ΜΟVΣΑ ΓΟΛVΤΡΟΓΟΝ ΟΣ ΜΑΛΑ ΓΟΛΛΑ

Tell me, Muse, of the man of many ways, who was driven

ΓΛΑΓΧΘΒ ΕΓΕΙ ΤΡΟΙΒΣ ΙΕΡΟΝ ΓΤΟΛΙΕΘΡΟΝ ΕΓΕΡΣΕ·

far journeys, after he had sacked Troy's sacred citadel.

ΓΟΛΛΩΝ Δ ΑΝΘΡΩΓΩΝ ΙΔΕΝ ΑΣΤΕΑ ΚΑΙ ΝΟΟΝ ΕΓΝΩ

Many were they whose cities he saw, whose minds he learned of,

ΓΟΛΛΑ Δ Ο Γ ΕΝ ΓΟΝΤΩΙ ΓΑΘΕΝ ΑΛΓΕΑ ΟΝ ΚΑΤΑ ΘVΜΟΝ

many the pains he suffered in his spirit on the wide sea,

ΑΡΝVΜΕΝΟΣ ΒΝ ΤΕ ΨVΧΒΝ ΚΑΙ ΝΟΣΤΟΝ ΕΤΑΙΡΩΝ

struggling for his own life and the homecoming of his companions.

ΑΛΝ ΟVΔ ΩΣ ΕΤΑΡΟVΣ ΕΡΡVΣΑΤΟ ΙΕΜΕΝΟΣ ΓΕΡ·

Even so he could not save his companions, hard though

ΑVΤΩΝ ΓΑΡ ΣΦΕΤΕΡΒΙΣΙΝ ΑΤΑΣΘΑΛΙΒΙΣΙΝ ΟΛΟΝΤΟ

he strove to; they were destroyed by their own wild recklessness,

ΝΒΓΙΟΙ ΟΙ ΚΑΤΑ ΒΟVΣ VΓΕΡΙΟΝΟΣ ΒΕΛΙΟΙΟ

fools, who devoured the oxen of Helios, the Sun God,

ΒΣΘΙΟΝ· ΑVΤΑΡ Ο ΤΟΙΣΙΝ ΑΦΕΙΛΕΤΟ ΝΟΣΤΙΜΟΝ ΒΜΑΡ

and he took away the day of their homecoming. From some point

ΤΩΝ ΑΜΟΘΕΝ ΓΕ ΘΕΑ ΘVΓΑΤΕΡ ΔΙΟΣ ΕΙΓΕ ΚΑΙ ΒΜΙΝ

here, goddess, daughter of Zeus, speak, and begin our story.

Parmenides is an Archaic Greek type designed and
cut in steel by hand by Dan Carr in 14 point, for a
new edition of the works of Parmenides translated
by Robert Bringhurst. Carr made this type for
publisher Peter Koch of Berkeley, California, who
had previously worked on a prototype design with
Christopher Stinehour, based on classic fourth
century BCE lettering. Koch wanted a fundamentally different type made in metal; his ideas were
closer to the lettering found in sixth century
BCE inscriptions, so Carr based his research and
design for Parmenides on this earlier period.

ABC·DEFGHIJ
KLMNOPQRS
TUVWWXYZ

ÆA AC ÆD Æ AM BH BN CA CV Ð
DH DT EA EC EC ED EF EG EH EK
EM ES EO EX FL FM FS GM GY HA
HE HG JA KA KR KX LA LD LO LJ LL
LX LY LZ MA MC MN NC NK NN NR
NT O O Œ P PM PU PV PY QA QU
QV RA RC RM RN RS SA SH SC SM
SN ST SV TC TE TJ TK TL TS TT UV
Y UA UE UR UT VA VH XM XR Y ZI
CH HO Œ OQ QU OR R U Œ Y ZA

Country:
USA.
Writing system:
Latin.

Competition category:
Display, single font.
Manufacturer/distributor:
Joachim Müller-Lancé.

THIS IS THE DREAM
THAT I DREAMED LAST NIGHT·

THE HEAVENS ROARED· AND EARTH RUMBLED BACK AN ANSWER: BETWEEN THEM STOOD I BEFORE AN AWFUL BEING· THE SOMBRE-FACED MAN-BIRD: HE HAD DIRECTED ON ME HIS PURPOSE· HIS WAS A VAMPIRE FACE· HIS FOOT WAS A LION'S FOOT· HIS HAND WAS AN EAGLE'S TALON· HE FELL ON ME AND HIS CLAWS WERE IN MY HAIR· HE HELD ME FAST AND I SMOTHERED: THEN HE TRANSFORMED ME SO THAT MY ARMS BECAME WINGS COVERED WITH FEATHERS· HE TURNED HIS STARE TOWARDS ME· AND HE LED ME AWAY TO THE PLACE OF IRKALLA: THE QUEEN OF DARKNESS· TO THE HOUSE FROM WHICH NONE WHO ENTERS RETURNS· DOWN THE ROAD FROM WHICH THERE IS NO COMING BACK· THERE IS THE HOUSE WHOSE PEOPLE SIT IN DARKNESS: DUST IS THEIR FOOD AND CLAY THEIR MEAT· THEY SEE NO LIGHT· THEY SIT IN DARKNESS· I ENTERED THE HOUSE OF DUST AND I SAW THE KINGS OF THE EARTH· IN THE HOUSE OF DUST WHICH I ENTERED WERE HIGH PRIESTS AND ACOLYTES· PRIESTS OF THE INCANT- ATION AND OF ECSTASY: THERE WERE SERVERS OF THE TEMPLE· AND THERE WAS ERESHKIGAL THE QUEEN OF THE UNDERWORLD: AND BELIT-SHERI SQUATTED IN FRONT OF HER· SHE WHO IS RECORDER OF THE GODS AND KEEPS THE BOOK OF DEATH· SHE HELD A TABLET FROM WHICH SHE READ· SHE RAISED HER HEAD· SHE SAW ME AND SPOKE: 'WHO HAS BROUGHT THIS ONE HERE?' THEN I AWOKE LIKE A MAN DRAINED OF BLOOD WHO WANDERS ALONE IN A WASTE OF RUSHES: LIKE ONE WHOM THE BAILIFF HAS SEIZED AND HIS HEART POUNDS WITH TERROR·

THE DEATH OF ENKIDU· FROM: THE EPIC OF GILGAMESH· MMDCC B·C·
EXCERPTS FROM THE TRANSLATION BY N· K· SANDARS

Pesaro (after a city in Italy) was originally begun over 18 years ago as my first piece in letterform design class, at the Basel School of Design. My ambition as a freshman, of course, was a Roman style 'more Roman than the Romans': finding shapes as ideal and elegant as I could imagine – and I still think the same way, finally digitizing this ancient idea with newer, better skills. The idea of exploring ligatures stems back to letterforms seen carved on medieval sarcophagi at the cathedral of Basel. The choice of ligatures was developed systematically by first sketching all 676 possible combinations.

Typeface name:
Pigiarniq.
Designer:
Wm Ross Mills.

▽ Å △ Ȧ △̇ ▷ Ḃ ◁ ◁̇ ∀ Å̇ ∧ Ȧ̇ > >̇ < <̇
∪ ∪̊ ∩ ∩̇ ⊃ ⊃̇ C Ċ ᑫ ᑭ P Ṗ d ḋ b ḃ ᑐ ᑌ̇
Γ Ṙ J J̇ L L̇ ᑎ Ṙ̊ Γ Ṙ ᓀ ᓘ L L̊ ᓕ σ σ̊ σ̇
ᓄ ᓇ ᓈ ᓂ ᓃ ᓯ C Ċ C ᓴ ᓱ C C ᓕ ᔨ̊ ᔨ ᔩ
ᓕ ᓕ̇ ᓕ̣ ᓕ̇ .ᔨ ᔨ̇ ᔨ̇ ᔨ̇ ᔨ̊ ᑦ ᒐ ᒐ ᒐ̇ ᒐ ᒌ̇ ᒪ̣ ᔪ ᔪ̇ ᔫ ᔭ̣ ᔮ̇
ᔫ̇ ᔪ̣ ᔭ ᔪ ᑐ ᑏ̊ ᑎ ᑏ ᑏ̇ ᑭ ᑮ ᒋ ᒌ ᕙ ᕚ̊ ᒣ ᒤ̇ ᒣ ᕦ
ᕕ ᑉ ᑈ̇ ᒥ ᒦ ᒨ̇ ᒫ ᒫ̇ ᒣ ᒧ ᓚ ᓛ ᕽ ᕽ̇ ᓓ ᓕ ᓕ̇
ᓕ ᕁᕟ ᕁᕟ̇ ᕁᔪ ᕁᔪ̇ < ᑕ ᒥ ᒧ ᑫ ᒣ ᓕ ᕙ ᑦ ᕝ ᓗ

A B C D E F G H I J K L M N O P Q R S T
U V W X Y Z a b c d e f g h i j k l m n o p
q r s t u v w x y z A B C D E F G H I J K L M N
O P Q R S T U V W X Y Z À Á Â Ã Ä Å Æ Ç
Đ È É Ê Ë Ì Í Î Ï ɟ Ł Ñ Ò Ó Ô Õ Ö Ø Œ
Ř Š Ù Ú Û Ü Ÿ Ý Ž Þ à á â ã ä å æ ç ð
è é ê ë ġ ì í î ï ɟ ł ñ ŋ ò ó ô õ ö ø œ κ ř š ù
ú û ü ý ÿ ž µ ı þ ß 0 1 2 3 4 5 6 7 8 9 0 1
2 3 4 5 6 7 8 9 $ € £ ¥ ƒ & @ ¡ ! ¿ ? - -
— / , . : ; + ÷ × + § ¶ † ‡ ‹ › « » " " ™ ©
® ½ ¼ ⅔ ¾ ¹ ² ³ ⁴ ª º | fi ffi ff fl ffl fj

Wm Ross Mills was born in Vancouver and grew up in
rural British Columbia. In 1994 he co-founded Tiro
Typeworks with John Hudson, and has been involved
in the design and production of multilingual typefaces for Microsoft Corp., Linotype Library, and
the government and aboriginal land claims body for
the Canadian territory of Nunavut. He is currently
working on an extension of Pigiarniq, Euphemia,
which will include syllabic characters for non-Inuit
Canadian native languages, and Latin and Cherokee script support for all written North American
aboriginal languages.

304

Country:
Canada.
Writing system:
Canadian Aboriginal Syllabics,
Latin

Competition category:
Text, family.
Manufacturer/distributor:
Tiro Typeworks.

---

piatsiniq   246   pigianngatuq

piatsiniq ᐱᐊᒼᓂᖅ
(*piaksiniq*) Amerindian to-
boggan. *5* 'Wood (?) that one
holds behind one's back while
the others tighten the cord
around a drum.' (?) *6 bl*

piattuq ᐃᐊᑦᑐᖅ
(*piaktuq*) (1) what slides well
(slippery object, not the surface
on which it slides) sled runner (2)
which has a slight salty taste,
(said of water). *5*

piagaarpuq ᐱᐊᖔᖅ
(*piagaaqpuq*) to stay up late,
part of the night (not all night:
see: qautainnasitsijuq). *5*

pigaatni ᐱᖃᑎ
(when relating his experience, he
said) when I was a ... *6p*

pigangnaq ᐱᖕᖕᖅ
off-shore wind (south south-
west) (see: pinangniq &
qavannganiq, *5e*). *6bl* (not *5e*)

pigangniq ᐱᖕᖕᓂᖅ
off-shore wind (south south-
west). *6p*

pigatuaq ᐱᖓᑐᐊᖅ
(& possessive) the only thing
owned by... *5h, i, j*

pigialirqipaa ᐱᕆᐊᓕᖅᑭᕚ
(*pigialiqqipaa*) he begins it over
again (=vi.& -mik, pigialirqipuq). *5*

pigialirqituq ᐱᕆᐊᓕᖅᑐᖅ
(*pigialiqqituq*) begins over again.*5*

pigiallapaa ᐱᕆᐊᓪᓚᐸ
he does it a little more. (=vi. &
-*mik, pigiallanippuq*). *5*

pigiallatuq ᐱᕆᐊᓪᓚᑐᖅ
he progresses a little, increases
a little, does, becomes a little
more. *5*

pigiamaittuq ᐱᕆᐊᒪᐃᑦᑐᖅ
which has not yet begun, what
has not yet been attended. *5*

pigiannganiliurpaa –
ᐱᕆᐊᖖᒐᓂᓕᐅᒪᐅᔾ
(*pigiannganiliuqpaa*) he makes
the start of a spiral row of blocks
(adds it to the snowhouse he
is making) (= vi. & -*mik,
pigiannganiliurivuk*). *5*

pigiannganiq ᐱᕆᐊᖖᒐᓂᖅ
the real start (of s.t.) :
specifically: the start of the
spiral of a snow house on the
ungalik, or even flat circle of
blocks. *5*

pigianngapaa ᐱᕆᐊᖖᒐᕙ
he starts it, does it (in
that circumstance) (=vi. & -*mik,
pigianittuq*). *5*

pigianngatuq ᐱᕆᐊᖖᒐᑐᖅ
he begins, does it for the first
time before several others.

Pigiarniq is a family of multiscript fonts commissioned by the Canadian territorial Government
of Nunavut as part of an initiative to implement
Unicode support for the Inuktitut syllabic writing
system. In addition to Unicode text support, there
was also a need for quality fonts that could be
utilized under a wide range of circumstances, from
web pages to typeset documents. The Government
and its various departments produce documents in
up to four languages, so the design harmoniously
combines the Latin and syllabic scripts without
overemphasizing particular stylistic elements.

ABCDEFGHIJKLMNO
PQRSTUVWXYZabcd
efghijklmnopqrstuv
wxyzÀÁÂÃÄÅÆÇÈÉ
ÊËÌÍÎÏŃÒÓÔÕÖØ
ŒÙÚÛÜŸàáâãäå æ
çèéêëìíîïńòóôõöø
œßùúûüÿ&fiflﬆ,;
:.… -!¡?¿''""‹›«»/|—
••()[]{}*†‡§¶`´ˆˇ˜¨
‾˘˚˝·˛˓ˆ˜„\©®™@€$¢
£ƒ¥ᵃᵒ#1234567890
0/%‰+-÷=≠°'">＜

Andreu Balius (Barcelona, 1962) is a graphic and
type designer, creator of the type project Garcia
fonts & co., and co-founder of the Typerware
studio in Barcelona (Spain). He studied Sociology
and Graphic Design in Barcelona. He divides his
time between studio work and the development
of typographical projects. At present he is also
associated professor at Pompeu Fabra University
in Barcelona. Countering the lack of knowledge
that still exists about the craft of typography and
Graphic Arts in Spain, he has pursued an interest
in 18th-century Spanish typography.

Country:
Spain.
Writing system:
Latin.

Competition category:
Text, family.
Manufacturer/distributor:
Andreu Balius.

PRADELL

Roman, *Italic* & **Bold**
Latin text family inspired from 18th century spanish type specimens
by **Andreu Balius**

Eudald Pradell was born in Ri

Eudald Pradell was born in Ripoll *(Catalunya-Spain)*, *a little village under the Pyrenees*, in 1721. He pertained to a family

Eudald Pradell was born in Ripoll (Catalunya, Spain), a little village under the Pyrenees in 1721. He pertained to a family of *gunsmiths* and learned **the practice of being an armourer** with his father, adquiring the knowledge of *making punches*. **Pradell** established his own works

Eudald Pradell was born in Ripoll (Catalunya, Spain), *a little village under the Pyrenees*, in 1721. He pertained to a family of *gunsmiths* and learned the practice of being an armourer with his father, adquiring the knowledge of making punches. **Pradell** established his own workshop in Barcelona. Despite he was illiterate, he was able to produce one of the most appreciated typefaces ever cut in Spain. His fame as a punchcutter increased and King Carlos III gave him a pension in order to provide new type designs at the *Imprenta Real* in Madrid, where he finally moved and set up his foundry. **Although he is completely unknown nowadays, I consider him one of the greaters** 18th century punchcutters in Europe.

Pradell is the result of two-years of research, and is an homage to the Catalan punchcutter Eudald Pradell (1721–1788). Although Pradell is almost completely unknown today, he was the most important punchcutter at the end of the 18th century in Spain. He was granted the right by King Carlos III to provide new typefaces to the Imprenta Real in Madrid. 'Pradell' is a transitional typeface that gently reveals the evidence of a new modern era in typography. I have kept those details that best exemplify the work of Eudald Pradell, while seeking to make a typeface suitable for modern reading.

Typeface name:
Prensa.
Designer:
Cyrus Highsmith.

ABCDEFGHIJKLM
NOPQRSTUVWXYZ
abcdefghijklm
nopqrstuvwxyz
ÀÁÂÃÄÅÆÇÈÉÊËÌÍÎÏŁÑ
ÒÓÔÖØŒŠÙÚÛÜÝŸŽÐÞ
àáâãäåæçèéêëìíîïłñ
òóôöøœšßùúûüýÿžðþ
&fiflffffffifflfjft,;:....-!¡?¿
''""‹›«»/|¦^\——••
()[]{}*†‡§¶©®@™
€$¢£ƒ¥ªº#1234567890+−×÷=
€$¢£ƒ¥ªº#1234567890+−×÷=

Cyrus Highsmith is a senior designer at Font
Bureau in Boston. He studied briefly at the School
of the Art Institute of Chicago, and longer at the
Rhode Island School of Design, where he received
a BFA. At Font Bureau, he spends his time drawing
typefaces for custom clients and retail publications. In addition, Cyrus teaches at RISD.

Country:
USA.
Writing system:
Latin.

Competition category:
Text, family.
Manufacturer/distributor:
Font Bureau.

FAMILIAR LANDMARK

MEMORIAL ERECTED ON THIS SPOT IN 1926

Permanent

Impossible to relocate; we tried

RESTORATION

STATUE MISSING LOWER TORSO

History Buff

Young expert arrives for consultation

EXPENSES

TOWN OVERCHARGED

Bank Loans

WE REALLY CAN'T AFFORD THIS

Collateral

Prensa (Spanish for 'press') is a new series from Cyrus Highsmith. He describes designing this type as 'wrapping outside curves around the inside, deliberately creating tension between the two,' a technique introduced by W.A. Dwiggins with Electra. Highsmith particularly relies on it for vitality in the italics, stripping down the forms to an effective simplicity through a broad range of weights.

Typeface name:
Quadrat Grotesk.
Designer:
Vladimir Pavlikov.

A B C D E F G H I J K L M
N O P Q R S T U V W X Y
Z A B C D E F G H I J K L M
N O P Q R S T U V W X Y Z
А Б В Г Д Е Ё Ж З И Й К
Л М Н О П Р С Т У Ф Х Ц
Ч Ш Щ Ъ Ы Ь Э Ю Я А Б
В Г Д Е Ё Ж З И Й К Л М Н
О П Р С Т У Ф Х Ц Ч Ш Щ
Ъ Ы Ь Э Ю Я & Fi Fl Œ Œ
Æ Æ , ; : . … - ! ? ' " ' ' " " ‹ ›
« » / | - — • · ( ) [ ] { } * † ‡ § ¶
^ ~ ¦ \ © ® ™ @ € $ ¢ ƒ £ ¥
¤ № # 1 2 3 4 5 6 7 8 9 0
¹ ² ³ ½ ¼ ¾ % ‰ + − ± × ÷
= ≠ ≈ < > ≤ ≥ ¬ µ π ∆ Ω ∏ ∑

Vladimir Pavlikov was born in 1978. In 2000, he graduated from Moscow University of Printing Arts. He is active in type design and graphic design. Awards: The Type Directors Club's type design competition (New York) in 2001, for Zentra; the TypeArt type design competition (Moscow) in 2001, for Smena; the fourth :output student design competition (Frankfurt) in 2001, for the graphic design project 'Calendar'.

Country:
Russia.
Writing system:
Latin, Cyrillic.

Competition category:
Display, family.
Manufacturer/distributor:
ParaType.

THE PUBLISHING DETA
ILS STATE THAT THESE
HAVE BEEN 'REWORKED
IN COLOUR' BY THE DESI

QUICKLY
ROAD
TOY
WINDOW
JUNE
MARGIN

49751

НО ОБЛАСТЬ ПРИМЕНЕ
НИЯ ИНФРАХРОМАТИЧ
ЕСКИХ ФОТОМАТЕРИАЛ
ОВ ОГРАНИЧЕНА РЯДО

ПАЖ
ЗАВТРАК
ВОДА
ЗИМОВЬЕ
ФЛАГ
КРОКУС

HAMBURGE
FONSTIV

ЖАДНЫЙ
BOARD

Quadrat Grotesk is a display typeface whose
design is based on wooden poster types of the first
half of the 20th century. Quadrat Grotesk consists
of three typefaces: Regular, Bold, and Black.

Typeface name:
Raghu.
Designer:
R.K. Joshi.

Independent vowels

अ आ इ ई उ ऊ ए ऐ ओ औ अं अः

Full form consonants

क ख ग घ ङ च छ ज झ ञ
ट ठ ड ढ ण त थ द ध न
प फ ब भ म य र ल व श
ष स ह ळ क्ष ज्ञ

Dependent vowel signs

ा ि ी ु ू ृ े ै ो ौ

Half form consonants

क् ख् ग् घ् ङ् च् छ् ज् झ् ञ्
ट् ठ् ड् ढ् ण् त् थ् द् ध् न्
प् फ् ब् भ् म् य् र् ल् व् श्
ष् स् ह् ळ् क्ष् ज्ञ्

Conjunct ligatures

श्र श्री क्त क्न क्र क्र कृ त्र स्त्र स्त्री
ह्ला ह्न ह्र ह्यौ ह्ला द्र द्धु श्र छं ष्ट्री में

Matras of different widths

ति रि कि टि मि खि

Numerals

१ २ ३ ४ ५ ६ ७ ८ ९ ०

Punctuation marks

. , : ; + - ' ' ( ) ॰ ऽ । ॥

R.K. Joshi is a type designer, calligrapher, typographer, poet, researcher, and design teacher. After a 30-year career in the mass communication industry, Mr. Joshi taught post-graduate design courses for fifteen years at IDC/IIT, Mumbai. At present, he works as visiting design expert at the National Centre for Software Technology (NCST) in the area of language technology. He has collaborated to develop font-design software and Indian-language word-processing packages, and has designed fonts in the context of Indian tradition and advanced digital technologies.

Country:
India.
Writing system:
Devanagari.

Competition category:
Text/display, single font.
Manufacturer/distributor:
NCST Mumbai

ॐ

श्रीमद्भगवद्गीता

प्रथमोऽध्यायः

धृतराष्ट्र उवाच
धर्मक्षेत्रे कुरुक्षेत्रे समवेता युयुत्सवः
मामकाः पाण्डवाश्चैव किमकुर्वत सञ्जय ॥1.1॥

सञ्जय उवाच
दृष्ट्वा तु पाण्डवानीकं व्यूढं दुर्योधनस्तदा
आचार्यमुपसङ्गम्य राजा वचनमब्रवीत् ॥1.2॥

पश्यैतां पाण्डुपुत्राणामाचार्य महतीं चमूम्
व्यूढां द्रुपदपुत्रेण तव शिष्येण धीमता ॥1.3॥

अत्र शूरा महेष्वासा भीमार्जुनसमा युधि
युयुधानो विराटश्च द्रुपदश्च महारथः ॥1.4॥

धृष्टकेतुश्चेकितानः काशिराजश्च वीर्यवान्
पुरुजित्कुन्तिभोजश्च शैब्यश्च नरपुङ्गवः ॥1.5॥

युधामन्युश्च विक्रान्त उत्तमौजाश्च वीर्यवान्
सौभद्रो द्रौपदेयाश्च सर्व एव महारथाः ॥1.6॥

अस्माकं तु विशिष्टाः ये तान्निबोध द्विजोत्तम
नायका मम सैन्यस्य सञ्ज्ञार्थं तान् ब्रवीमि ते ॥1.7॥

भवान्भीष्मश्च कर्णश्च कृपश्च समितिञ्जयः
अश्वत्थामा विकर्णश्च सौमदत्तिस्तथैव च ॥1.8॥

Raghu was the first Devanagari typeface to be designed for the OpenType format. The font contains a wide range of letters (more than 700) and the composition rule tables to facilitate the rendering of complex structures and text composition in Indian languages using Devanagari script. Based on the traditional calligraphic model of the flat-reed pen, this simple style has been designed for continuous text. Raghu is available in the public domain for platforms that use OpenType technology; it can be downloaded from the NCST site: <rohini.ncst.ernet.in/indix//download/font>

Typeface name:
Rayuela.
Designer:
Alejandro Lo Celso.

A B C D E F G H I J K L M
N O P Q R S T U V W X Y Z
a b c d e f g h i j k l m n o p q
r s t u v w x y z À Á Â Ä Ã Å
Æ Ç È É Ê Ë Í Ì Î Ï Ñ Ò Ó Ô
Ö Õ Ø Œ Ù Ú Û Ü á à â ä ã å
æ ç é è ê ë í ì î ï ñ ó ò ô ö õ ø
œ ß ù ú û ü ÿ y g & fi fl ffi ffl
, ; : . ... - ! ¡ ? ¿ ' ' " " , „ ‹ ›
« » / | – — • · ( ) [ ] { } * † ‡
§ ` ´ ^ ˇ ~ ¨ ˉ ˘ ˚ ˝ ¸ ˛ \ © ® ™
@ € $ ¢ £ ƒ ¥ ª º # 1 2 3 4 5
6 7 8 9 0 % ‰ + - ÷ = < > ° "

Alejandro Lo Celso (1970), a graphic and type
designer born in Córdoba, Argentina, has been
art director in publishing media, and has taught
Typography at the University of Buenos Aires. In
2000 he completed his MA in Typeface Design at the
University of Reading (UK). In 2001 he obtained a
post-diploma at the *Atelier National de Recherche
Typographique*, Nancy (France). He has worked as
a freelance designer in London and has written
several articles on typography and graphic design
for *tpG* magazine. He currently lives in Córdoba,
Argentina, where he runs his own digital foundry.

Country:
Argentina.
Writing system:
Latin.

Competition category:
Text/display, system.
Manufacturer/distributor:
PampaType.

En uno de sus libros Morelli habla del napolitano que se pasó años sentado a la puerta de su casa mirando un tornillo en el suelo. Por la noche lo juntaba y lo ponía debajo del colchón. El tornillo fue primero risa, tomada de pelo, irritación comunal, junta de vecinos, signo de violación de los deberes cívicos, finalmente encogimiento de hombros, la paz, el tornillo fue la paz, nadie podía pasar por la calle sin mirar de reojo el

Type can be a hopscotch!

Rayuela™ family is inspired in the ludic atmosphere of literature by Argentinean novelist & poet Julio Cortázar.

The appearance of his novel *Rayuela (Hopscotch)* in 1963 deeply changed the way Latin American literature had been written and read. All chapters in *Rayuela* may be read in a linear order or in another, suggested by the

by hopping from one chapter to the other as you do in the hopscotch. So two novels can be read in one book.

There is a deep playful sense of life in Cortázar's literature, which I tried to convey into this type.

The family consists of three text faces (roman, italic & small caps) within both regular & light colors, plus an extra heavy face, absolutely suitable for

chocolates packaging

& magazines titles of dramatically heavy content

plus a fair tribute to the Roman monumental letterforms, an illuminating

« OPEN FACE »

plus a sort of SCRABBLELIKE? *font which comes whith these nice rosettes!*

tornillo y sentir que era la paz. Uno de ellos lo guarda, quizá lo saca en secreto y lo mira, vuelve a guardarlo y se va a la fábrica sintiendo algo que no comprende, una oscura reprobación. Sólo se calma cuando saca el tornillo y lo mira, se queda mirándolo hasta que oye pasos y tiene que guardarlo presuroso. Solución demasiado fácil. Quizá el error estuviera en aceptar que ese objeto era un tornillo por el hecho de que tenía la forma de un tornillo. Todo es escritura, es decir fábula. (Julio Cortázar, *Rayuela,* 1963)

Rayuela (Spanish for 'Hopscotch') is inspired by the literature of Argentinean writer Julio Cortázar. Though it is suitable for long texts, a certain informality and irreverence can be seen in its half-serif single stroke, which resembles handwriting, and in the deliberate alternation of some characters, which defies current consistency. The family consists of three text faces (roman, italic, and small caps) within both regular and light colors, plus three display fonts.

Typeface name:
Really.
Designer:
Gary Munch.

ABCDEFGHIJKMNOPQRSTUVWXYZabcdefghijklmnopqrstuvwxyz
ÀÁÂÃÄÅÆÇÈÉÊËÌÍÎÏÑÒÓÔÕÖØŒÙÚÛÜŸàáâãäåæçèéêëìíîïñòóôõö
øœßùúûüÿ&fifl,;:.....-!¡?¿'""''‹›«»/|-—–_•·()[]{}*†‡§¶ˇˆ˜¨˙˚˝·¸^~\©®™@
€$¢£ƒ¥ªº#1234567890⁄%‰+±÷=<>≤≥≠≈¬◊∂∆∏∑√∞∫°'″μΩ

ΑΒΓΔΕΖΗΘΙΚΛΜΝΞΟΠΡΣΤΥΦΧΨΩαβγδεζηθικλμνξοπρστυφχψως
ΆΈΉΊΪΌΎŸΏάέήΰϊόύϋώΐΰ,;:.....-!?'""''«»/|-—–_·()[]{}*†ˇ`˙¨§^~¦\©®@
$£¥#1234567890¹²³½%-+±÷=<>≤≥≠≈¬·°'″

АБВГДЕЁЖЗИЙКЛМНОПРСТУФХЦЧШЩЪЫЬЭЮЯабвгдеёжзи
йклмнопрстуфхцчшщъыьэюяѓґђєѕіїјќљњћўџ ЃҐЂЄЅІЇЈЌЉЊЋ
ЎЏ,;:.....-!',‚'„"«»/|-—–•()[]{}*†§¶&`^~\©®™@$£ƒ€№1234567890
+±÷=<>¬≠≤≥≈∞'″μ

ABCDEFGHIJKMNOPQRSTUVWXYZÀÁÂÃÄÅÆÇÈÉÊËÌÍÎÏÑÒÓÔÕÖØŒÙÚ
ÛÜŸabcdefghijklmnopqrstuvwxyzàáâãäåæçèéêëìíîïñòóôõöøœßùúûüÿ&fi
fl,;:.....-!¡?¿'""''‹›«»/|-—–_•·()[]{}†‡§¶ˇˆ˜¨˙˚˝·¸^~\©®™@€$¢£ƒ¥ªº#*
1234567890⁄%‰+±÷=<>≤≥≠≈¬◊∂∆∏∑√∞∫°'″μΩ

ΑΒΓΔΕΖΗΘΙΚΛΜΝΞΟΠΡΣΤΥΦΧΨΩαβγδεζηθικλμνξοπρστυφχψωςΆΈΉΊΪ
ΌΎŸΏάέήΰϊόύϋώΐΰ,;:.....-!?'""''«»/|-—–_·()[]{}†ˇ`˙¨§^~¦\©®@$£¥#*
1234567890¹²³½%-+±÷=<>≤≥≠≈¬·°'″

АБВГДЕЁЖЗИЙКЛМНОПРСТУФХЦЧШЩЪЫЬЭЮЯабвгдеёжзийклмн
опрстуфхцчшщъыьэюяѓґђєѕіїјќљњћўџ ЃҐЂЄЅІЇЈЌЉЊЋЎЏ,;:.....-
!',‚'„"«»/|-—–•()[]{}†§¶&`^~\©™@$£ƒ€№1234567890*
+±÷=<>¬≠≤≥≈∞'″μ

Really*Really***Really***Really*

Linotype Really Latin and Munchfonts Really Cyrillic and Greek · 1999–2001 Gary Munch

Gary Munch. See page 216.

Country:
USA.
Writing system:
Latin, Cyrillic, Greek.

Competition category:
Text, superfamily.
Manufacturer/distributor:
Linotype Library, Munchfonts.

Я думаю, довольно трудно создать новый рисунок шрифта, или, раз уж на то пошло, вообще что-либо новое для повседневного обихода. Разработку нового шрифта можно уподобить сочинению музыкальной пьесы. К примеру, ноты неизменны, как неизменны и буквы. Все дело в том, как они выстроены. Важнее всего, чтобы их новизна по-своему отражала и вписывалась в строй мысли нынешнего поколения графиков-дизайнеров. В новом произведении должно быть нечто, что заставило бы вероятного пользователя встрепенуться, обратить внимание. Эти типографические качества могут создать общественный спрос; однако нужно помнить и о том, что такая популярность преходяща. По-моему, в этом нет ничего плохого. Конечно, все мы думаем, что над нашими шрифтами время не властно; но ведь многие вещи — как музыка — тоже не вечны; это все равно, как „нынче здесь, а поутру забыт". В любом случае, в одном мы с вами можем быть уверены: шрифтов наверняка будет больше.
Эд Бенгет, цитата из «Ю-энд-Эл-Си»

I think it's rather difficult to create a new typeface design, or for that matter, to create a new anything that's in everyday use. A new piece of music would parallel the creation of a new typeface. For example, the notes of music don't change, and the letters of the alphabet don't change, either. It's a matter of how they're put together. The most important feature must be that its newness has a reflection all its own and fits into the pattern of today's generation of graphic designers. The new creation must have something in its character that makes the potential user sit up and take notice. These typographic traits could create a popular demand but we must also consider that this popularity may only be temporary. Personally, I don't think there's anything wrong with that. I know we all feel our designs will last forever, but some things like music don't last either. It's like "here today and forgotten tomorrow." Anyway, you and I can be sure of one thing: the number of typefaces will surely increase.
Ed Benguiat, as quoted in U&lc

Νομίζω ότι είναι ιδιαίτερα δύσκολο να δημιουργηθεί μια καινούργια γραμματοσειρά, όπως είναι δύσκολο να δημιουργηθεί ένα καινούργιο ο,τιδήποτε που χρησιμοποιείται καθημερινά. Η δημιουργία μιας νέας γραμματοσειράς αντιστοιχεί σε ένα καινούργιο κομμάτι μουσικής. Για παράδειγμα, οι νότες της μουσικής δεν αλλάζουν, όπως δεν αλλάζουν και τα γράμματα του αλφάβητου. Το θέμα είναι πώς συντάσσονται. Το πιο σημαντικό χαρακτηριστικό πρέπει να είναι ότι η καινοτομία της είναι αυτόφωτη και ταιριάζει με το ρεύμα της σημερινής γενιάς σχεδιαστών. Η νέα δημιουργία πρέπει να έχει κάτι στο χαρακτήρα της που τραβάει την προσοχή του πιθανού χρήστη. Αυτές οι τυπογραφικές τάσεις θα μπορούσαν να προκαλέσουν τη ζήτηση του κόσμου, πρέπει όμως να σκεφτόμαστε και ότι αυτή η δημοτικότητα μπορεί να είναι μόνο προσωρινή. Προσωπικά, δε νομίζω ότι υπάρχει τίποτα κακό με αυτό. Ξέρω ότι όλοι νιώθουμε ότι οι γραμματοσειρές μας θα ζήσουν αιώνια, αλλά μερικά πράγματα, όπως και η μουσική, δε διαρκούν για πάντα. Σαν να λέμε: «σήμερα είναι κι αύριο δεν είναι». Όπως και νά 'χει, εσείς κι εγώ για ένα πράγμα μπορούμε να είμαστε βέβαιοι: ότι ο αριθμός των γραμματοσειρών σίγουρα θα αυξάνεται.
Εντ Μπενγκουιετ, από το «Γιού-αντ-Ελ-Σι»

Really*Really***Really***Really*

Linotype Really Latin and Munchfonts Really Cyrillic and Greek · 1999–2001 Gary Munch

Really Cyrillic and Greek followed the Latin fonts of Linotype Really. There are so many fascinating details of rhythm and finish that are different among the three scripts, and having followed able commentary from Alexander Tarbeev, Maxim Zhukov, and Gerry Leonidas (not on these, but on other faces), I'm pleased that I got most of the details correct. The different scripts are harmonious in their appearance but not slavishly locked to the Latin base design; each script is allowed its peculiarities of expressions: the Greek looser and gestural, the Cyrillic structured and architectural.

Typeface name:
Relay.
Designer:
Cyrus Highsmith.

ABCDEFGHIJKLM
NOPQRSTUVWXYZ
abcdefghijklm
nopqrstuvwxyz
ÀÁÂÃÄÅÆÇÈÉÊËÌÍÎÏŁÑ
ÒÓÔÖØŒŠÙÚÛÜÝŸŽÐÞ
àáâãäåæçèéêëìíîïłñ
òóôöøœšßùúûüýÿžðþ
&fiflfffffiffflfjfttß,;:...-!¡?¿
'''""‹›«»/|¦^\–—•·
()[]{}*†‡§¶©®@™★
€$¢£ƒ¥ªº#1234567890+−×÷=

Cyrus Highsmith. See page 308.

Country:
USA.
Writing system:
Latin.

Competition category:
Display, family.
Manufacturer/distributor:
Font Bureau.

CRYSTAL GAZING

Live in the future, forget about the past

MYSTERIOUS FORCES

Palm readers

BLACK CATS KEEP CROSSING MY PATH

FUTURE

I am plagued by an ancient curse

WALKING THE EARTH

No place to stop and rest

DOOMED FOR ETERNITY

Old soothsayers warned me to be careful

ominous visions

Relay reaches back to the middle of the last century for inspiration. In England, Edward Johnston and Eric Gill applied humanist proportions and shapes to the geometric sanserif and established a trend within European art deco. In the United States, C.H. Griffith and W.A. Dwiggins at Linotype achieved a similar effect with Metro, influencing American lettering from diner to comic book. Cyrus Highsmith has designed a spirited new series within this American tradition.

Typeface name:
Requiem.
Designer:
Jonathan Hoefler.

ABCDEFGHIJJ
KLMNOPQQR
STUVWXYYZ
abbcddefghhijkkllmn
oppqqrstuvwxyyzzz
1234567890
(¡!&¿?) [ÆæŒæß]
{ÅÇÉÑÒÔÛŸåçéñìoûÿ}
fb ffb ff fh ffh fi ffi fj ffj fk ffk fl
ffl ffffl fr ffr ft ffft fy ffy fta fte fti
ftr fty ch ck ct cta cte ctf ctfi cti
ctr cty sf sfi sfr sfy sh sk sp sp st
sta ste sti stf stfi stfj stfr stfl str
sty ta tta te tte tf ttf tfi tfl tfj tfr
ttfr ti tti tr ttr tt ty tty tz ;Th Th

ABCDEFGHI
JKLMNOPQR
STUVWXYZ
ABCDEFGHIJKK
LMNNOPQQRR
STTUVWXYYZ
abcdefghijklm
nopqrstuvwxyz
1234567890
(¡!¿?&&) {$£¥ƒ€¢}
[◖§†‡*@KNQRTY]
ÆæŒœfiflffffiffl ct st ß
ÅÇÉÑÒÔÛŸåçéñìoûÿ

❧❧❧❧✿❀❁❀✚

ABCDEFGHIJKLMNOPQRSTUVWXYZ

ABCDEFGHIJKLMNOPQRSTUVWXYZ

Jonathan Hoefler. See page 242.

Country:
USA.
Writing system:
Latin.

Competition category:
Text/display, system.
Manufacturer/distributor:
The Hoefler Type Foundry.

Pinturicchio

The Florentine

REQUIEM FINE ITALIC

REQUIEM

Renaissance

REQUIEM FINE ROMAN

Dactylic Hexameter

Calligraphic Development

REQUIEM DISPLAY ITALIC

LACRIMOSA DIES

Humanist Miniscules

REQUIEM DISPLAY ROMAN

Ludovico Vicentino degli Arrighi

La operina di Ludovico Vicentino, da imparare
de scrivere littera cancellarescha con molte altre
nove littere agiunte, et una bellissima ragione di

REQUIEM TEXT ITALIC

Chancery Cursive Lettering

REGOLA DA IMPARARE Scrivere varii
caratteri de littere con li suoi compassi
et misure. Et il Modo de Temperare le

REQUIEM TEXT ROMAN

REQUIEM TEXT ORNAMENTS

Quo usque tandem ab
Catilina, patientia no
Quamdiu etiam furor

REQUIEM ✠ ORNAMENTS

BEAD ENDS   MINARETS

TRUMPETED TERMINALS

Quo usque tande
tere, Catilina, pati
nostra? Quamdiu

Iste tuus nos eludet? Qu
quem ad finem sese effre
iactabit audacia? Nihiln

FLAT ENDS   FLEURONS

ETIAM furor iste tu
nos eludet? Quem a
finem sese effrenata

Nihil urbis vigiliae nihil tim
populi, nihil concursus bono
omnium, nihil hic munitissi
habendi senatus locus, nihiln

ARABESQUE ❋ ENDINGS

TRUMPETED TERMINALS

TE NOCTURUM praes
Palati, nihil urbis vigilia
nihil timor populi, nihi
concursus bonorum on

Horum ora voltusque moverunt,
Patere tua consilia non sentis con
iam horum omnium scientia tene
conjurationem egeris, ubi fueris,

CROWNS   CROWNS

❋ FLEURONS   FLAT ENDS

NIHIL HIC munitissimu
habendi senatus locus, nih
horum ora voltusque mov
Patere tua consilia non se

Quos convocaveris, quid consuli ceper
quem nostrum ignorare arbitraris. O
Tempora, O Mores! Senatus haec int
videt, hic tamen vivit. Vivit! Immo ve
etiam in senatum venit fit publici con

SCROLL   BANNER

ARABESQUE ❋ ENDINGS

SCIENTIA TENERI conjurati
egeris, ubi fueris, quos convoc
quid consuli ceperis, quem nos
ignorare arbitraris. Senatus ha
intellegit, consul videt, hic tam

Requiem is based on a font of engraved capitals
probably cut by Ugo da Carpi, and featured in
Ludovico Vicentino degli Arrighi's *Il Modo de Tem-*
perare le Penne, published in 1523. The lowercase is
new, as Arrighi offered none, although its style is
inspired by the work of Arrighi's contemporaries,
Giovanni Cresci and Giambattista Palatino.

Typeface name:
Retina Agate.
Designer:
Tobias Frere-Jones.

AaBbCcDdEeFfGgHhIiJjKkLlMmNnOoPpQqRrSsTtUuVvWwXxYyZz

¶$§£€¥#ƒ 0123456789%‰©®Ⓟ¢°¿?¡!& (/)[\]{|}†‡* ÂÇÉÎÑØÙŸ

RETINA AGATE ONE

AaBbCcDdEeFfGgHhIiJjKkLlMmNnOoPpQqRrSsTtUuVvWwXxYyZz

¶$§£€¥#ƒ 0123456789%‰©®Ⓟ¢°¿?¡!& (/)[\]{|}†‡* ÂÇÉÎÑØÙŸ

RETINA AGATE TWO

AaBbCcDdEeFfGgHhIiJjKkLlMmNnOoPpQqRrSsTtUuVvWwXxYyZz

¶$§£€¥#ƒ 0123456789%‰©®Ⓟ¢°¿?¡!& (/)[\]{|}†‡* ÂÇÉÎÑØÙŸ

RETINA AGATE THREE

AaBbCcDdEeFfGgHhIiJjKkLlMmNnOoPpQqRrSsTtUuVvWwXxYyZz

¶$§£€¥#ƒ 0123456789%‰©®Ⓟ¢°¿?¡!& (/)[\]{|}†‡* ÂÇÉÎÑØÙŸ

RETINA AGATE FOUR

AaBbCcDdEeFfGgHhIiJjKkLlMmNnOoPpQqRrSsTtUuVvWwXxYyZz

¶$§£€¥#ƒ 0123456789%‰©®Ⓟ¢°¿?¡!& (/)[\]{|}†‡* ÂÇÉÎÑØÙŸ

RETINA AGATE FIVE

Tobias Frere-Jones. See page 238.

Country:
USA.
Writing system:
Latin.

Competition category:
Text, system.
Manufacturer/distributor:
The Hoefler Tyoe Foundry.

SMALL CAP ISSUES

YTD %CHG	52 WEEKS HI	52 WEEKS LO	STOCK (SYM)	DIV	YLD %	PE	VOL 100S	LAST	NET CHG
+19.6	83.4	46	**AKZ** AkzidenzGrot	...		dd	10033	20.8	+0.94
- 5.3	83.8	55.6	**AltG** AltrntGothic	...		dd	10996	74.9	-1.78
-18.5	16.9	5.6	**ANTQ** AntiqOlive	...		dd	9690	42.8	-1.20
+26.4	82.7	25.5	**AvtG** AvantGarde	...		7	6213	78.1	+1.64
+28.5	99	28.8	**BANK** BankGothic	...		dd	8911	28.4	+1.54
+ 5.1	63.2	21.7	**BASE** BaseNine	...		dd	1862	47.5	+0.39
- 3.1	83.6	37.5	**BASK** Baskerville	...		dd	938	14.5	-0.45
-10.1	94.1	54.9	**BDNI** BauerBodoni	...		cc	2206	47.3	-1.46
-13.1	106.3	90.1	**BELL** BellGothic	...		dd	10453	36.6	-0.19
-17.8	65.2	7.4	**BKMN** Bookman	...		...	5626	9.1	-1.05
-12.2	93.4	32.1	**BMBO** Bembo	...		dd	5156	40.9	-1.14
-10.0	31.2	11.7	**BRSH** BrushScript	...		6	9881	62.2	-1.07
-15.1	52.3	6	**CASL** Caslon540	...		dd	9029	64.9	-1.82
-13.2	105.9	14.7	**CNTR** Centaur	...		dd	9587	91.2	-0.41
+26.4	**95.1**	**19.5**	**CHMP** ChmpnGthc	.64	1.8	dd	1509	40.2	**+1.17**
+ 2.5	109.2	5	**CLRN** Clarendon	...		dd	2587	77.1	+1.81
+ 8.3	98.2	26.1	**COOP** CooperBlack	...		dd	5612	54.3	+0.56
+ 8.6	46.6	11.2	**COUR** Courier	...		dd	8931	41.8	+1.20
+ 6.1	**89.4**	**23.3**	**DIDO** DidotHTF	.80	1.6	cc	6467	4.2	**+1.03**
-29.1	89.6	83.7	**DIN** DINGrotesk	...		dd	1558	6.0	-0.48
- 4.0	99.8	32.3	**DOM** DomCasual	...		26	7451	57.0	-1.88
+18.0	73.8	16.1	**EGIZ** Egiziano	...		dd	2789	61.6	+1.53
- 9.7	32.7	18.5	**EURO** Eurostile	...		9	1449	99.5	-1.15
+ 9.4	69.6	59.4	**FKTR** FetteFraktur	...		dd	3944	87.0	+1.01
+ 7.5	66.8	2.8	**FRNK** FrnklinGthc	...		dd	11712	48.8	+0.55
- 4.3	17	7	**FRUT** Frutiger55	...		...	1814	34.5	-1.31
+14.8	35.8	15	**FUTU** FuturaBook	...		18	11325	20.5	+0.42
-19.1	52.3	10.1	**GDY** GoudyOldStyl	...		dd	2685	46.5	-1.77
+ 4.6	95.3	26.8	**GILL** GillSans	...		dd	10748	72.3	+0.39
-18.7	96.2	35.4	**GLRD** Galliard	...		26	1566	1.1	-0.46
-16.4	72.7	9.6	**GMND** Garamond	...		27	2376	62.3	-0.71
-18.3	102.3	20.7	**GROT** Grotesque9	...		47	6147	8.0	-1.66
+ 4.0	87.8	19.1	**HLV** Helvetica	...		dd	3009	63.3	+0.35
+28.0	79.3	35.6	**HOBO** Hobo	...		dd	5981	25.2	+0.79
+19.4	**97.3**	**56.9**	**HTXT** HoeflerText	.5e	1.3	dd	4548	93.7	**+0.99**
+29.3	**85.1**	**11.4**	**INTR** Interstate	.32	2.1	dd	10127	19.3	**+1.86**
+10.2	72.7	59.1	**JNSN** Janson	...		17	8065	63.2	+1.11
- 5.3	84.8	68.7	**KIS** KisJanson	...		dd	4641	80.9	-0.29
+ 8.5	65	7.9	**KSMK** FFKosmik	...		20	510	26.3	+0.92
+22.8	35.9	8.9	**LTHS** LithosBlack	...		dd	1669	39.8	+0.19
+16.5	104.7	1.5	**LtrG** LetterGothic	...		dd	8091	20.6	+0.06
+10.7	96.9	30.8	**MEMP** Memphis	...		...	11742	64.0	+1.16
-21.5	78.4	61.6	**META** FFMeta	...		9	5229	69.6	-0.41
-23.3	54.1	31.1	**MTRO** Metroblack	...		10	4162	97.5	-1.44
+ 3.1	85.9	27.7	**MrsE** MrsEaves	...		dd	8850	21.3	+0.72
-19.7	93.7	71.3	**NEWS** NewsGothc	...		...	6615	72.5	-1.68
+ 8.9	27	1	**OCR** OCR-A	...		dd	10166	93.4	+1.87
-22.7	110	72	**OPTM** Optima	...		dd	4906	63.6	-0.18
+ 8.8	54.1	16.4	**PALA** Palatino	...		34	10695	10.4	+0.93
+29.2	91.2	23.5	**PKAV** ParkAvenue	...		...	4006	95.6	+0.67
+22.7	**62.2**	**48.7**	**REQ** RequiemHTF	.02	.44	dd	3691	74.8	**+0.78**
- 9.2	61.1	37.2	**RTIS** Rotis	...		dd	9562	0.0	-1.33
-21.1	97.7	56	**SCLA** FFScala	...		cc	2176	35.5	-1.23
-26.7	60.6	51.3	**SNEL** SnellRndhnd	...		dd	502	60.1	-1.45
+ 6.1	99.2	1	**THES** FFThesis	...		6	8966	23.9	+1.70
+ 1.5	60.5	43.6	**TMS** TimesRoman	...		dd	9682	1.2	+1.98
- 0.8	107.5	74.2	**TJN** Trajan	...		...	674	6.6	-0.65
- 6.1	70.3	7.1	**TRXE** FFTrixie	...		dd	2343	77.8	-0.96
+ 9.3	93.7	31.5	**UNIV** Univers55	...		10	7603	3.8	+1.29
-17.4	85.3	2.4	**WLBM** Walbaum	...		dd	746	52.4	-1.24
+ 8.6	**45.9**	**45.8**	**WTNY** Whitney	.44	.1	dd	3856	4.3	**+1.10**
-20.0	94.9	45.5	**ZAPF** ZapfChancry	...		...	1757	72.6	-1.32

Retina Agate takes on one of the most hostile typographic environments, stock listings in newspapers. Retina was conceived from the start as an 'agate' face. Notches cut into each intersection and join bear the brunt of ink spread on press, and preserve the clarity of individual shapes. Fine increments of weight allow a newspaper to choose its own particular degree of 'bold' emphasis, as well as anticipating press behavior. All ten weights are drawn to a common set of widths, so the weight of a single word or line can be altered without disrupting the page grid.

Typeface name:
Rouble.
Designer:
Andrey Belonogov.

! @ # $ % & ( ) – +

˝ : . , ; = [ ] / |

1 2 3 4 5 6 7 8 9 0

£ ¥ € — ˷ ? _

A B C D e F G H i j

K L M N O P q R S t

U V W X Y Z

А Б В Г Д е Ё Ж З И

Й К Л М Н О П Р С Т

У Ф Ж Ц Ч Ш Щ Ъ Ы Ь

Э Ю Я

Andrey Belonogov. See page 246.

Country:
Russia.
Writing system:
Latin, Cyrillic.

Competition category:
Display, single font.
Manufacturer/distributor:
Andrey Belonogov.

Rouble was my first experience in type design. Its
Cyrillic part was created in 1999; Latin glyphs were
added in 2001. The name of the typeface reflects
its nature: rublenyi ('chopped') means 'sans-serif'
in Russian type terminology; thus, no relation to
the currency. It is a display design. I think it works
best in larger-size headlines, and also in longer
display texts set with minimal leading.

Typeface name:
Seria & Seria Sans.
Designer:
Martin Majoor.

FF SERIA

ABCDEFGHIJKLM
NOPQRSTUVWXYZ
abcdefghijklm
nopqrstuvwxyz
O I 2 3 4 5 6 7 8 9 ? ! &
ABCDEFGHIJKLM
NOPQRSTUVWXYZ
0 1 2 3 4 5 6 7 8 9 :; § ¶

·,·… ¿¡ - -— _ ' ' " " ,, ‹ › « » (/) [\ ] { | } * † ‡ ° ' "
0123456789 ¹ ² ³ / ¼ ½ ¾ ⅓ ⅔ $ ¢ € ₤ ¥
ƒ % ‰ # @ ® © ℗ ™ Æ Œ Ø Á À Â Ã Å Ç
Ð É È Ê Ë Í Ì Î Ï Ł Ñ Ó Ò Ô Ö Õ Š Þ Ú Ù Û Ü
Ÿ Ý Ž æ œ ø á à â ä ã å ç ð é è ê ë í ì î ï ł ñ ó ò ô
ö õ š þ ú ù û ü ÿ ý ž ª º & ff ffi fi fj fl ffi ffl ſt ß ?
! ¿ ¡ Æ Œ Ø Á À Â Ã Å Ç Ð É È Ê Ë Í Ì Î Ï Ł Ñ Ó Ò
Ô Ö Õ S T Ú Ù Û Ü Ÿ Y z δ √ ∫ ₡ Δ Σ Ω Π π μ
→ ← ↑ ↓ ↗ ↘ ↙ ↖ ★ ☆ ● ○ ■ □ ▶ ▷ ◀ ◁ ⓔ ☏ ✆ ✇

FF SERIA SANS

ABCDEFGHIJKLM
NOPQRSTUVWXYZ
abcdefghijklm
nopqrstuvwxyz
O 1 2 3 4 5 6 7 8 9 ? ! &
ABCDEFGHIJKLM
NOPQRSTUVWXYZ
0 1 2 3 4 5 6 7 8 9 :; § ¶

·,·… ¿¡ - -— _ ' ' " " ,, ‹ › « » (/) [\ ] { | } * † ‡ ° ' "
0123456789 ¹ ² ³ / ¼ ½ ¾ ⅓ ⅔ $ ¢ € ₤ ¥
ƒ % ‰ # @ ® © ℗ ™ Æ Œ Ø Á À Â Ã Å Ç
Ð É È Ê Ë Í Ì Î Ï Ł Ñ Ó Ò Ô Ö Õ Š Þ Ú Ù Û Ü
Ÿ Ý Ž æ œ ø á à â ä ã å ç ð é è ê ë í ì î ï ł ñ ó ò ô
ö õ š þ ú ù û ü ÿ ý ž ª º & ff ffi fi fj fl ffi ffl ſt ß & ?
! ¿ ¡ Æ Œ Ø Á À Â Ã Å Ç Ð É È Ê Ë Í Ì Î Ï Ł Ñ Ó Ò
Ô Ö Õ S T Ú Ù Û Ü Ÿ Y Z + ± − = ≠ ~ ≈ < > ≤ ≥ ∞ ∅
× · · ¤ ◊ ^ ¬ ¦ δ √ ∫ ₡ Δ Σ Ω Π π μ ⓔ ☏ ✆ ✇

FF SERIA ITALIC

ABCDEFGHIJKLMNOPQRST
UVWXYZabcdefghijklmn
opqrstuvwxyz0123456 7
8 9 & A B C D E F G H I J K L M N O P Q
R S T U V W X Y Z 0 1 2 3 4 5 6 7 8 9 :;

FF SERIA SANS ITALIC

ABCDEFGHIJKLMNOPQRST
UVWXYZabcdefghijklmn
opqrstuvwxyz0123456 7
8 9 & A B C D E F G H I J K L M N O P Q
R S T U V W X Y Z 0 1 2 3 4 5 6 7 8 9 :;

FF SERIA BOLD

ABCDEFGHIJKLMNOPQRST
UVWXYZabcdefghijklmn
opqrstuvwxyz0123456 7
8 9 & A B C D E F G H I J K L M N O P Q
R S T U V W X Y Z 0 1 2 3 4 5 6 7 8 9 :;

FF SERIA SANS BOLD

ABCDEFGHIJKLMNOPQRST
UVWXYZabcdefghijklmn
opqrstuvwxyz0123456 7
8 9 & A B C D E F G H I J K L M N O P Q
R S T U V W X Y Z 0 1 2 3 4 5 6 7 8 9 :;

FF SERIA BOLD ITALIC

ABCDEFGHIJKLMNOPQRST
UVWXYZabcdefghijklmn
opqrstuvwxyz0123456 7
8 9 & A B C D E F G H I J K L M N O P Q
R S T U V W X Y Z 0 1 2 3 4 5 6 7 8 9 :;

FF SERIA SANS BOLD ITALIC

ABCDEFGHIJKLMNOPQRST
UVWXYZabcdefghijklmn
opqrstuvwxyz0123456 7
8 9 & A B C D E F G H I J K L M N O P Q
R S T U V W X Y Z 0 1 2 3 4 5 6 7 8 9 :;

Martin Majoor has been a type designer since
the mid-1980s. In 1991, FontShop International
released the award-winning typeface Scala and
Scala Sans. In 1994, Majoor designed the telephone
directory for Dutch PTT. He also designed a complete new typeface for it, Telefont, which is still
in use. Majoor's third serious typeface, Seria and
Seria Sans, was released in 2000. It was awarded a
'Certificate of Excellence' during the International
Typographic Awards 2001 in London. Majoor has
taught typography at several schools of fine art
and lectured at TypeLab/ATypI conferences.

Country:
The Netherlands.
Writing system:
Latin.

Competition category:
Text, family.
Manufacturer/distributor:
FSI FontShop International.

WARSAW AUTUMN 2001
september 21-29

44th International Festival of Contemporary Music

USTVOLSKAYA
Symphonies

THE LAND OF ULRO I
about Swedenborg:
Padding/Haverkamp

YOUNG GENERATION
Komsta, Gryka,
Talma-Sutt, Arnhold,
Głowicka, Krcha, Zubel

BASSO OSTINATO
commissions, premieres

CONTINUA
NIGHT WAVE
DUTCH POLDER
VARIA

WARSAW AUTUMN 2001 2001 JESIEŃ WARSZAWSKA

LEAFLET COVER FOR WARSAW AUTUMN 2001 (REDUCED)

Poul Ruders

was born 1949. He started his musical career as a member of the famous Copenhagen Boys' Choir. He studied at the Odense Academy of Music (piano and organ), then at the Royal Conservatory in Copenhagen. Ib Norholm taught him composition, but the first impulse that awakened his interest in writing music was hearing Threnody by Penderecki when aged 16. After graduation he took up a full-time post as a church organist. He has received commissions from famous European ensembles such as the London Sinfonietta, the Danish Radio Orchestra, the BBC Symphony Orchestra, Capricorn Ensemble and Ensemble InterContemporain; he has also written for Yuri Bashmet and Heinrich Schiff.

Principal works: 3 string quartets (1971, 1979, 1979), Medieval Variations for chamber ensemble (1974), Stabat Mater for tenor, mixed choir, percussion, piano and organ (1974), Pestilence Songs for soprano, guitar and piano (1975), Capriccio Pian e Forte for orchestra (1978), Wind-Drumming for brass quintet and percussion (1979), Violin Concerto No. 1 (1981), 3 motets for mixed choir (1981-88), Manhattan Abstraction, symphonic poem (1982).

176

Aleksandra Gruca is a graduate of the Music Academy in Katowice, where she studied voice with Henryka Januszewska. In 1996 she won Third Prize and a special award for the best interpretation of Polish songs at the Vocal Competition in Duszniki-Zdrój. A year later she won the top accolade at the 7th Ada Sari Vocal Competition in Nowy Sącz and several special awards, including a prize for the interpretation of works by Mozart and Szymanowski and a critics' award.

She was a holder of a grant from the Ministry of Culture and Art (1995-97).

Wanda Wiłkomirska was born on 11 January 1929 in Warsaw. She made her public debut at the age of seven. In 1947 she graduated from the State Higher School of Music

in Łódź where she studied with Irena Dubiska. She later perfected her skills with Ede Zathureczky at the Liszt Academy in Budapest (1949), Eugenia Umińska and Tadeusz Wroński in Warsaw and with Henryk Szeryng in Paris. She is a prizewinner of four international competitions: in Geneva (1946), Budapest (1949), the Bach Competition in Leipzig (1950) and the Wieniawski Competition in Poznań (1952).

She has performed in five continents, giving recitals and appearing with leading orchestras under such renowned conductors as Klemperer, Bernstein, Giulini, Barbirolli, Masur, Sawallisch, and Mehta. She has also developed a fine career in chamber music, performing with her brother and sister in the Wiłkomirski Trio, as well as with Martha Argerich, Daniel

THE LIGATURES OF SERIA

ct ff fi fj fl ffi ffl st

FF Seria + FF Seria Sans
MM
Designed by MM, in the year MM

UPRIGHT ITALIC CAPITALS (MAGENTA) COMPARED TO THE REGULAR CAPITALS (CYAN)

ABGJKNQRTXYZ

FF Seria (designed in the years 1996–2000) is a large family with a serif version and a sans serif version. Much love and attention has gone into the 'special sorts' like small caps, non lining figures, ligatures, and all sorts of extra characters. The combination of a serif and a sans version makes Seria especially suitable for complex pieces of typography such as annual reports. When it is used as a display typeface, however, the much-refined details of the Seria family could give book covers, leaflets, and posters a distinctive appearance.

Typeface name:
Serp'n'Molot.
Designer:
Tagir Safayev.

Tagir Safayev is a Russian type and graphic designer. Safayev is a staff designer at ParaType, and he designed the typefaces PT Freeset (1991–2000), LEF Grotesque (1999), PT Hermes (1995), Bitstream Humanist Cyrillic 521 (1999), ITC Kabel Cyrillic (1993), Meta+ Cyrillic (2000), Mirra (1999), ITC New Baskerville Cyrillic (1993), ITC Officina Sans Cyrillic, ITC Officina Serif Cyrillic (1995), PT Proun (1993), PT Rodchenko (1996), ITC Stenberg (1993), Swift Cyrillic (2002), PT Yanus (1999), and Serp'n'Molot (2001). He received a Certificate of Excellence in Type Design from TDC² for Mirra in 2000.

Country:
Russia.
Writing system:
Cyrillic, Latin.

Competition category:
Display, single font.
Manufacturer/distributor:
ParaType.

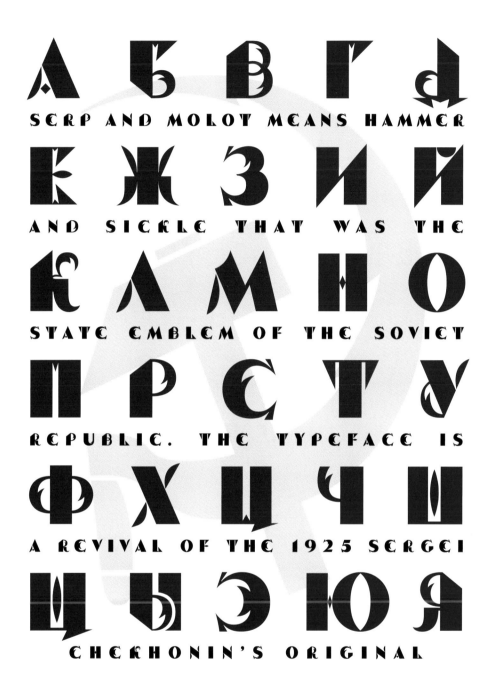

АБВГД
SCRP AND MOLOT MCANS HAMMCR
КЖЗИЙ
AND SICKLE THAT WAS THE
КЛМНО
STATC CMBLCM OF THE SOVICT
ПРСТУ
RCPUBLIC. THC TYPCFACC IS
ФХЦЧШ
A RCVIVAL OF THE 1925 SCRGCI
ЩЬЭЮЯ
CHCKHONIN'S ORIGINAL

Serp'n'Molot means hammer and sickle: the State
Emblem of the Soviet Republics. The typeface was
inspired by some of the Cyrillic letterforms of
Sergey Chekhonin (1878–1936). Chekhonin belonged
to the Mir Iskusstva (World of Art) group, which is
so closely associated with the flowering of Russian
book and theatre design at the beginnig of the
20th century. He was a virtuoso in the drawing of
vignettes, head- and tail-pieces, and illuminated
letters, and the task of designing trademarks for
the first Soviet publishers was therefore one close
to his heart.

A B C D E F G H I J K L M N O P Q
R S T U V W X Y Z a b c d e f g h
i j k l m n o p q r s t u v w x y z &
1 2 3 4 5 6 7 8 9 0 À Á Â Ã Ä Å
Æ Ç È É Ê Ë Ì Í Î Ï Ł Ñ Ò Ó Ô Õ Ö
Ø Œ Š Ù Ú Û Ü Ý Ÿ Ž Ð Þ à á â ã
ä å æ ç è é ê ë ì í î ï ł ñ ò ó ô õ ö
ø œ š ß ù ú û ü ý ÿ ž ð þ fi fl £ €
$ ¢ ƒ ¥ ¤ @ © ® ™ a o † ‡ § ¶ * !
¡ ? ¿ . , ; : … · ' ' " " , „ ‹ › « » ( ) [ ]
{ } | ¦ / \ - - — _ • ` ´ ^ ˇ ~ ¨ ‾ ˘ ° "
˙ ¸ ˛ # / % ‰ ¼ ½ ¾ ¹ ² ³ ' " ° µ +
− × ÷ = < > ≤ ≥ ± ≠ ¬ ^ ~

Jeremy Tankard. See page 214.

Country:
United Kingdom.
Writing system:
Latin.

Competition category:
Text, family.
Manufacturer/distributor:
Jeremy Tankard Typography.

If you have cooked your turkey in the same way year after year, why not change the menu? Give your guests a choice of easy to slice, fresh turkey breast crown or succulent glazed gammon.

simplicity and unity

Cougette Linguine

(serves four)
3 cloves garlic, minced
3 tablespoons extra virgin olive oil
1 onion, diced
2 red bell peppers, diced
2 courgette, cut into ½ inch wheels
2 summer squash, cut similarly
salt and papper
fresh dill, chopped
10 large kalamata olives, sliced (optional)
juice of 1 lemon
450g linguine
4 tbsp sour cream

Lightly brown the garlic in the olive oil in a large skillet, on medium heat. Add the onion and red peppers, and sauté until soft. Add the courgettes and summer squash, and sauté until soft but not wilted. Salt and pepper to taste. Finally, add the dill, lemon juice and olives. Toss together and remove from heat. Toss the mixture with al dente linguine. Garnish with sour cream.

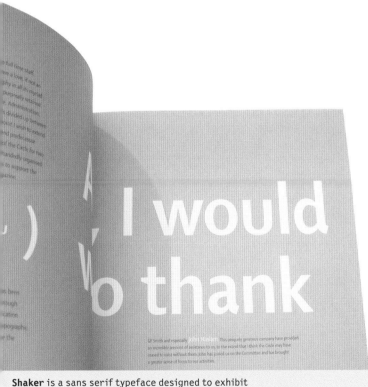

Shaker is a sans serif typeface designed to exhibit the simplicity of style and form that is a hallmark of the original Shaker communities and their famous furniture. This is a 24-font family consisting of condensed, regular, and wide widths, with sets ranging from light to heavy in weight. Shaker was designed from the start to feature uncluttered form, clear headline use, excellent copy setting, and above all to be a versatile digital typeface. The typeface is available in PostScript and TrueType formats for the Mac OS and PC Windows. It has been an immediate success with designers.

Typeface name:
The Shire Types.
Designer:
Jeremy Tankard.

Jeremy Tankard. See page 214.

Country:
United Kingdom.
Writing system:
Latin.

Competition category:
Display, family.
Manufacturer/distributor:
Jeremy Tankard Typography.

THE LETTERFORMS OF THE SHIRES CHANGE STYLE AS YOU MOVE AROUND THEM AND, LIKE PEOPLE, ARE NOT TIED TO ANY ONE PLACE BUT CAN TRAVEL FREELY FROM SHIRE TO SHIRE AND MIX WITH THEIR NEIGHBOURS.

a typeface designed to match a time when england's midland counties were changing. a time when parts of rural england changed the plough for the steam hammer and the shire horse for the steam engine. the resulting shire types bring together the heavy, solid feel of the industrial revolution, whilst creating a set of letters simply designed with clear legibility.

The Shire Types were designed to be used as a tool whereby typographers/designers could create a dense textural mass of lettering. The Shire Types are made up from six typefaces; there are no ascenders or descenders, and accented characters shrink to fit the text height. The capital letters can be mixed with the lowercase ones, as they are all the same height. All six fonts are completely interchangeable with each other. This makes the Shire Types a truly versatile design tool with which endless ideas can be created.

Typeface name:
Shirokuro.
Designer:
Joachim Müller-Lancé.

Joachim Müller-Lancé. See page 290.

Country:
USA.
Writing system:
Japanese, Latin.

Competition category:
Display, family.
Manufacturer/distributor:
Joachim Müller-Lancé.

'Shirokuro' means 'black and white' in Japanese.
The Kanji is named 'Higashi' (East), and the Latin
'Nishi' (West). As positive and negative shapes
interlock, inseparably describing one another,
the interplay of black and white is pushed to the
extreme. My idea dates back ten years, but only
materialized through learning Japanese, where
it offered itself in the composed nature of Kanji
characters. As modern Japanese has a need for
matching Latin styles, 'Nishi' also uses the square
underlying Kanji design.

Typeface name:
Shuriken Boy.
Designer:
Joachim Müller-Lancé.

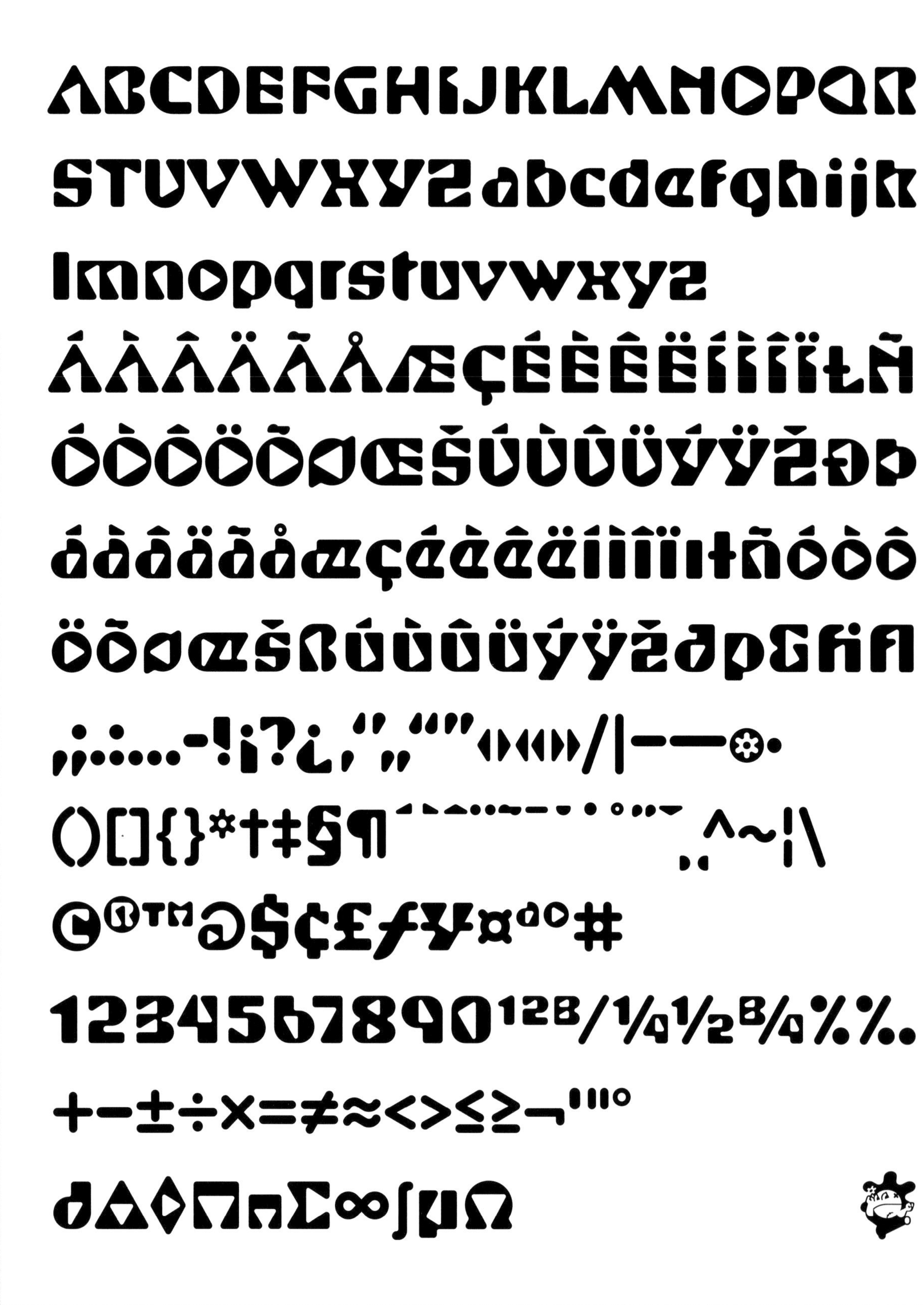

ABCDEFGHIJKLMNOPQR
STUVWXYZabcdefghijk
lmnopqrstuvwxyz
ÁÀÂÄÃÅÆÇÉÈÊËÍÌÎÏŁÑ
ÓÒÔÖÕƏŒŠÚÙÛÜÝŸŽÐÞ
áàâäãåæçéèêëíìîïıłñóòô
öõəœšßúùûüýÿžðþßfifl
,;:.…-!¡?¿‚'",„""‹‹‹›››/|––—❋•
()[]{}*†‡§¶`´ˆˇ˘¯˙¨˚˝˜.¸^~¦\
©®™@$¢£ƒ¥¤º°#
1234567890¹²³/¼½⅛¾%‰.
+−±÷×=≠≈<>≤≥¬'""°
∂∆◊∏∩∑∞∫√Ω

Country:
USA.
Writing system:
Latin.

Competition category:
Display, single font.
Manufacturer/distributor:
Joachim Müller-Lancé.

Shuriken Boy grew out of playing with elementary shapes, and took form over the course of 3 years. First approached as a free play of triangles in dozens of variations, it developed a rigid design system in its final stage. All shapes are drawn on a square grid, with slants at strict angles, and a limited set of curves. As this design is entirely composed of geometric 'patches' punched through each other, it questions the very essence of the usually stroke-based nature of letterforms. The result reminds of letters only vaguely: some shapes only become clear in the context of words.

abcdefghijklmnopqrstuvwxyz

ABCDEFGHIJKLM
NOPQRSTUVWXYZ

1234567890

Å¡Ĉ´Ï"Ó^Ô ÒÂ˜ØŒ‰Í´¨ „¸Á¸
`⁄‹›fifl‡°·‚—±» '"ÆÚ¿˘˝åçd´ƒ©
·˙^°Ñ˜øœ®ß†¨¥`ì™£¢∞§¶·ª°—≠«ˇ"'‹œ…÷≥≤

gjmsty
AFJHIRT

Ronna Penner. 'Having always been an artist, I decided at the age of 33 to learn graphic design. While in college, I discovered an interest in typography: the focus of most everything I did (and do) was on type. For three years, I designed greeting cards for one of the largest companies of its kind in Canada. It was well-suited to me because type is such large part of the design. I've since moved on to a freelance career, and I've expanded my creative focus to encompass the area of web design and multimedia. Of course, typography remains a large part of my design process.'

Country:
Canada.
Writing system:
Latin.

Competition category:
Display, single font.
Manufacturer/distributor:
Bitstream Inc.

Friends~They are kind to each other's hopes,

friendship hopes dreams kindness

hopes dreams kindness friendship

cherish each other's dreams

they cherish each other's dreams.
~Thoreau

Sketchley first came from handwriting I saw and was intrigued by. I am a graphic designer always on the lookout for new and interesting fonts. While working at a greeting card company, I was looking for a particular typeface in the style of Sketchley. I never found one, so, I made it myself. First reactions to the font were, 'It's really weird', or 'Interesting. You made that?' I liked it so much I decided to submit it to Bitstream. Apparently they liked it too. It was released January 2002.

Typeface name:
Sun.
Designer:
Luc(as) de Groot.

Sun designed by Luc[as] de Groot published by LucasFonts.com

CHARACTERSETABCDEFGHIJKLM
NOPQRSTUVWXYZABCDEFGHIJK
LMNOPQRSTUVWXYZabcdeffifflg
hijklmnopqrsßtuvwxyz01234567
890123456789!?¿¡$£¥ƒ€ß¢@&
ÀÁÂÄÃÅÆÇÈÉÊËÌÍÎÏIÑÒÓÔÖÕØŒÙ
ÚÛÜŸÀÁÂÄÃÅÆÇÈÉÊËÌÍÎÏIÑÒÓÔÖ
ÕØŒÙÚÛÜŸàáâäãåæçèéêëìíîïiñò
óôöõøœùúûüÿªºµπ∂∫∏∑√ΩΔ◊#
∞=÷≈+±≤≥¬<>%‰†‡§°·•¶®©™*
®©@™*°!?¿¡$£¥ƒ¢&∂∫∑€≠≤≥†‡§
,…:;({[|]})/0987654321zyxwvut
ßsrqponmlkjihgffifⅼedcbaZYXW
VUTSRQPONMLKJIHGFEDCBA

Luc(as) de Groot. See page 222.

Country:
Germany.
Writing system:
Latin.

Competition category:
Text/display, system.
Manufacturer/distributor:
Lucasfonts.

Sun & Sun Condensed designed by Luc[as] de Groot published by LucasFonts.com

1 Condensed Black 54,5 pt
2 ExtraBold Italic 51,2 pt
3 Bold 47 pt

4 Condensed Bold/Bold Caps 40 pt
5 SemiBold 40 pt
6 Regular Caps 40,7 pt

7 ExtraLight 45,2 pt
8 ExtraLight Caps 30,3 pt
9 Cd ExtraLight italic 30 pt

1 23 Streamline Wizards

2 Grijswaardeanalyse

3 Federal Bureau closed

4 PHARCYDE/2MCS LEFTFIELD

5 Honululu *& the Supersurf*

6 POTSDAMMER WILD SEED

7 Electronic Bodhidharma

8 ARRONDISSEMENT DE NEUCHÂTEL

9 A tener encuenta durante la manipulacion

9/10.8 pt cd extralight unter eine Schütze mit Brot- beziehungsweise Wassersack durchgestschritten eine Saccharose- Pfütze. Zwar waren sie gottlos, aber zäh wie Lackette. Der Schütze sprach: „Wir müssten sie entwässeren. Nur so wird sie zu gutem Scheuersande. Jedoch kann ich sie schwerlich trockenbessern. Mein Sack enthält den falschen Gurgenstand." Der Holzschuhmacher sprach: „Oh, ich vermutete, du willst meinem so sittsam frommen Beutelbrot — auf daß es zuckernd sich zu Tode blute und selbstvergessen stirbtet den Opfertod." „Mein Gott, du laberst wie und ein Schütze mit Brotbeziehungsweis Wassersack durchgeschritten eine Saccharose- Pfütze. Zwar war sie gottlos,

9/10.8pt regular entwässern. Nun soll wird sie zu gutem Scheuersand. Einem schwulenden Pfaffen, dem man seinen Wäschebeutel klauen will. Ist dir denn klar, daß ich es doch niemals schaffe? In deinem Sack ist Brot und in meinem Müll!" „Du bist ein Mösewicht, Sadist und Schlächtere und willst meine Brot als dein süßest Opferlamm. Der ärgste Tempelräuber ist gerecht. Dieses Brote verdammt, ist heiliger. Und Schwarm! So zogen sie den lauthals Schreienden weiter, teils sakrosankt, teils niedersäbelnd schroff. Noch heute singen siebe dem Anstaltsleiter das Lied vom Pfüter

9/10.8 pt bold/italic im unter Schütze mit Brot- beziehungsweisend Wassersack durchschrittend eine Saccharose-Pfütze. Zwar war sie gottlos, aber zäh wie Lack. Deim Schützen sprach: „Wir müssen sie entwässern. Nur so wurde sie zum guten Scheuersanden. Jedoch kann ich sie schwerlich trockennsern. Mein Sack enthält einen falschen Gegenstand." Holzschuhmacher sprach: „Oh, ich vermute, du willst mein sittsam frohmmes Beutelbrot — *auf daß es zuckernd sich zum Tode bluten und selbstvergessen stirbt den Opfertod."* „Mein Gott, du laberst wie ein Schal"

Sun was developed in consultation with Sun Microsystems Art Director Chris Haaga. Sun wanted a display face that was typical of a headline style in a US newspaper, that is, rather condensed and heavy. I did not work with a translational contrast principal this time, so I had nothing but trial and error to get the subtle weight differences in character strokes to harmonize with each other. They also put me under real pressure, asking for normal and italic versions two weeks before the deadline. After the exclusivity period expired, I expanded the Sun family for use by the newspaper *Jungle World*.

Linotype Syntax

ABCDEFGHIJKLMNOPQRSTUVWXYZabcde
fghijklmnopqrstuvwxyzÀÁÂÃÄÅÆÇÈÉÊËÌÍ
ÎÏŁÑÒÓÔÕÖØŠÙÚÛÜÝŸÐÞáâãäåæçèéêëìí
îïłñòóôõöøœšßùúûüýÿžðþ&fifl,;:....-!¡?¿''""
‹›«»/–—•·()[]{}*†‡§¶`´^~¨¯˘°"„.,.^~¦\©®™@
€$¢£ƒ¥¤ªº#1234567890¹²³/¼½¾%‰+−±

Linotype Syntax Serif

ABCDEFGHIJKLMNOPQRSTUVWXYZabcde
fghijklmnopqrstuvwxyzÀÁÂÃÄÅÆÇÈÉÊËÌÍ
ÎÏŁÑÒÓÔÕÖØŠÙÚÛÜÝŸÐÞáâãäåæçèéêëìí
îïłñòóôõöøœšßùúûüýÿžðþ&fifl,;:....-!¡?¿''""
‹›«»/–—•·()[]{}*†‡§¢`´^~¨¯˘°"„.,.^~¦\©®™@
€$¢£ƒ¥¤ªº#1234567890¹²³/¼½¾%‰+−±

Linotype Syntax Letter

ABCDEFGHIJKLMNOPQRSTUVWXYZabcde
fghijklmnopqrstuvwxyzÀÁÂÃÄÅÆÇÈÉÊËÌÍ
ÎÏŁÑÒÓÔÕÖØŠÙÚÛÜÝŸÐÞáâãäåæçèéêëìí
îïłñòóôõöøœšßùúûüýÿžðþ&fifl,;:....-!¡?¿''""
‹›«»/–—•·()[]{}*†‡§¶`´^~¨¯˘°"„.,.^~¦\©®™@
€$¢£ƒ¥¤ªº#1234567890¹²³/¼½¾%‰+−±

Hans Eduard Meier (1922, Horgen, Switzerland)
trained as a typesetter from 1939 to 1943, and as a
graphic artist at the Kunstgewerbeschule in Zurich,
1943–1948. He attended the Académie Grande Chau-
mière and the École Estienne in Paris in 1948, and
freelanced for various publishers and agencies in
Paris. Since 1952 he has been a freelance designer
in Zurich, where he teaches design and drawing.
He is best known for Syntax, but his other type
designs include the notable Barbedor and Syndor.
In addition to the new Syntax Serif & Letter, he has
recently designed a display face, Syntax Lapidar.

Country:
Switzerland.
Writing system:
Latin.

Competition category:
Text, superfamily.
Manufacturer/distributor:
Linotype Library GmbH.

Robert,
Here's an alternate page layout, using
Hans Eduard Meier's new Syntax faces.
The text face harmonises very well with ~~l superellipse,~~
the sans serif. Yr thoughts?

~~swelled rules~~
~~...al fonts~~ and have frequently
~~been~~ added, by mistake or by design, to alphabets with which
they don't belong — historical revivals of the printing types of
Garamond and Baskerville for example.

Analphabetic
Symbols

If you are forced to work with a font whose parentheses fall
below standard, borrow a better pair from elsewhere. And whatever parentheses you use, check that they are not too tightly fit-
ted (as in recent fonts they very often are).

5.3.2   *Use upright (i.e., 'roman') rather than sloped parentheses,*
square brackets and braces, even if the context is italic.

Parentheses and brackets are not letters, and it makes little sense
to speak of them as roman or italic. There are vertical parentheses and sloped ones, and the parentheses on italic fonts are
almost always sloped, but vertical parentheses are generally to be
preferred. That means they must come from the roman font, and
may need extra spacing when used with italic letterforms.

This rule has been
broken more often
than followed since
the end of the 16th
century. It was fol-
lowed more often
than broken by the
best of the early
typographers who
set books in italic:
Aldus Manutius,
Gershom Soncino,
Johann Froben,
Simon de Colines,
Robert Estienne,
Ludovico degli
Arrighi and Henri
Estienne II.

$$(efg)\ (efg)$$

The sloped square brackets usually found on italic fonts are,
if anything, even less useful than sloped parentheses. If, perish
the thought, there were a book or film entitled *The View from My*
[sic] Bed, sloped brackets might be useful as a way of indicating
that the brackets and their contents are actually part of the title.
Otherwise, vertical brackets should be used, no matter whether
the text is roman or italic: 'The View from My [sic] Bed' and '*the*
view from my [sic] bed.'

85

Linotype Syntax is a reworking and extension
of the original Syntax, developed by Hans Eduard
Meier in 1968 and presented by the font foundry
D. Stempel AG. The original Syntax is widely regarded as the model 'humanist' sans serif. The inclina-
tion to the right lends the font a dynamic feel. Its
figures are based on oldstyle characters but have
a distinctive, modern design. Now the much-loved
Syntax shows off its new clothes: two new weights
for the sans, and new serif and informal letter
designs, all available in six weights.

Typeface name:
Tanya.
Designer:
Olga Overchuk.

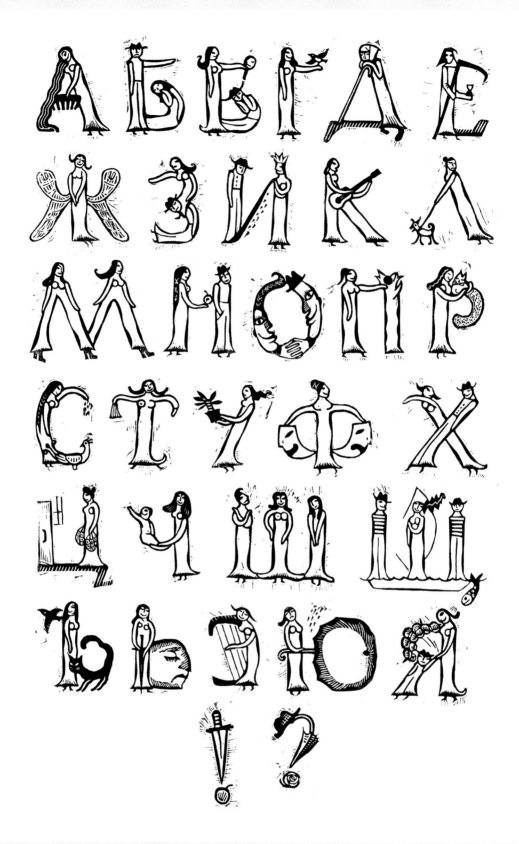

Olga Overchuk was born in 1970 in Donezk, Ukraine. She graduated from Donezk Art College in 1990 and Kharkiv Academy of Arts and Design in 1998. She was a participant in the 'Miniprint' exhibition (Barcelona, Spain) in 1999. At present she works as a graphic designer.

Country:
Ukraine.
Writing system:
Cyrillic.

Competition category:
Display, single font.
Manufacturer/distributor:
Olga Overchun.

ЯКИМИ ОЧИМА МИ ДИВИМОСЬ НА СВІТ

Борис Ступка

влення про біологічну роль вітаміну D3 в організмі за останні десятиріччя значно поповнилися новими відомостями. Отримані докази, які дозволяють розглядати D3 як вітамін, необхідний для регуляції в організмі не тільки мінерального обміну, але й багатьох інших життєво важливих процесів, що значно розширює можливості його використання в медицині. Ми займаємося вивченням впливу вітаміну D на обмінні процеси, розповіла одна з відомих українських біохіміків фахівців з вітаміну D, завідувач лабораторії медичної біохімії Інституту біохімії НАН України Лариса

Апуховська, з'ясовуємо його фізіологічну функцію в організмі. Ось зараз ми досліджуємо дуже важливе питання про правильне призначення вітаміну D в період вагітності, позаяк з'явилося чимало публікацій про те, що саме цей вітамін є відповідальним за формування плоду. Тому дуже важливо добирати дози застосування рецарату. Ми займаємося також питанням зв'язку вітаміну D та цукрового діабету. Розробляємо готові форми препарату вітаміну D останньої генерації комплекси, які взаємн о

підсилювали 6 фізіологічний ефект.Крім того, паралельно не тільки розв'язуємо медичні завдання, але і йдемо у сільському господарстві таким самим шляхом, оскільки необхідність у таких препаратах для тваринництва в Україні стоїть дуже гостро. Ми тісно співробітничаємо з Київським вітамінним заводом. Мета отримати вітамінні препарати, які відповідали 6 усім міжнародним вимогам.Для того, щоб правильно застосовувати вітамін D3, треба розв'язати два завдання: перше мати добрий препарат вітаміну D3, друге мати сучасні методичні рекомендації щодо його застосування.

Сюди ж варто додати й побажання здійснювати популяризаторську роботу, яка в Україні практично відсутня. Достатньо сказати, що останні рекомендації стосовно застосування вітаміну D у колишньому Радянському Союзі були видані 1990 року в їх складанні брали участь відомі вітамінологи та педіатри. Проте, на жаль, найважливіші методичні рекомендації не дійшли до України.У результаті в Україні лікарі їх не мають, а користуються медичними рекомендація м и двадцятирічно ї давнини. При бурхливому розвитку подій у

вивченні ролі вітаміну D3 це неприпустимо. У старих рекомендаціях хибно поставлені два найважливіших питання: там написано, що застосовуються препарати вітаміну D2... А зараз у цілому світі вітамін D2 вже не застосовують, позаяк установлена його низька біологічна активність. Він узагалі є

чужорідною речовиною для організму. Його застосування або дає дуже малий ефект, або зовсім не дає результату. Але натомість він має достатньо великі побічні дії окислюється, утворюються перекисні сполуки і все це негативно впливає на організм.Друге дози, які призначалися, були завеликими. Тепер показано, що лікувальна доза не повинна перевищувати 5000 МО. Великі дози є неприпустимими, оскільки вітамін D діє на біологіч н і процеси дозозале ж н о. Тобто при малих

дозах він діє позитивно, а при великих утворюється багато гормонально активних форм і дія є протилежною.У зв'язку з усім цим лікарі насторожено ставляться й до вітаміну D3. Ця насторожениість викликана здебільшого відсутністю

сучасних знань про те, що сьогодні досягнуто і як з усім цим можна працювати.Третя причина це те, що в Україні лікарі вважають, що потреба у вітаміні D може бути задоволена за допомоги їжі та сонячних променів. Це зовсім не так!Міфи навколо вітаміну D3Давно встановлено численними дослідами, що у шкірі під впливом сонячного світла синтезується вітамін D3.I все ж широко

розповсюджена думка, що для задоволення потреби організму у вітаміні D3 достатньо короткочасного ультрафіолетового опромінення рук та обличчя, є глибоко помилковою. Новими дослідженнями встановлено, що тільки якщо все тіло дорослої людини зазнає природної інсоляції впродовж двох годин, в її організмі відзначається певне підвищення рівня вітаміну D3. Проте через 24 години все повертається до вихідного рівня. Тому і в літній період забезпеченість вітаміном D3 лише дещо вища, ніж узимку, але недостатня для повного задоволення організму.Небезпечною помилкою є думка про те, що брак вітаміну D3 в організмі

56

Light	SemiLight	Regular	SemiBold	Bold	ExtraBold	Black
ABCDE fghijkl 123456	ABCDE fghijkl 123456	ABCDE fghijkl 123456	ABCDE fghijkl 123456	ABCDE fghijkl 123456	ABCDE fghijkl 123456	ABCDE fghijk 123456

Italic	Italic	Italic	Italic	Italic	Italic	Italic
ABCDE fghijk 123456	ABCDE fghijk 123456	ABCDE fghijk 123456	ABCDE fghijk 123456	ABCDE fghijk 123456	ABCDE fghijk 123456	ABCDE fghijk 123456

Caps	Caps	Caps	Caps	Caps	Caps	Caps
ABCDE FGHIJK 123456	ABCDE FGHIJK 123456	ABCDE FGHIJK 123456	ABCDE FGHIJK 123456	ABCDE FGHIJK 123456	ABCDE FGHIJK 123456	ABCDE FGHIJK 123456

ABCDEFGHIJKLMNOPQRSTUVWXYZ
abcdeffiflfffifflfbfhfjfkghijklmnopqr
sßtuvwxyzÆÀÁÂÄÃÅÇÈÉÊËÌÍÎÏÑÒÓ
ÔÖÕØŒÙÚÛÜŸàáâäãåæçèéêëìíîïñò
óôöõøœùúûüÿABCDEFGHIJKLMNOP
QRSTUVWXYZÀÁÂÄÃÅÆÇÈÉÊËÌÍÎÏÑ
ÒÓÔÖÕØŒÙÚÛÜŸ012345678901234
56789!?!?¿¡¿¡$£¥ªºƒ€¢¢@&&µπð∫∏
∑√ΩΔ◊#∞=÷≈+±≤≥¬‹›%‰†‡§°·•¶
®©™*.,…:;({[|]})//„""«»‚''‹›"‴´˘˙˚¯¯˜¯¯
•º˝˝ˇˆ
˛ˌ

designed by Luc[as] de Groot at FontFabrik.com 1998-1999 published by LucasFonts.com

Country:
Germany.
Writing system:
Latin.

Competition category:
Text/display, family.
Manufacturer/distributor:
Lucasfonts.

NOVA COMPVTOGRAPHICA

twenty one typefaces

Luc(as) de Groot's TheAntiquaB

ABCD

EXTRABOLD 10 PT OUR WORDS ARE LETTING US DOWN.
They still serve for parochial gossip; but they have become so specialized

BOLD 8 PT WHEN THAT HAPPENS, THERE ARE STILL TWO WAYS OF PUTTING THE NEWS OR MESSAGE
across any chasm of misunderstanding in our so-called English Language. One is the slow way: stop and define
every sense-shattered word until it does mean the same thing at both ends of the plank. The other is the quick
way of metaphor. One *"pictures"* something by a figure of speech; and the picture makes sense to people
who are no longer *"talking the same language"*.

LIGHT 6 PT WHEN ENOUGH PEOPLE HAVE DESPERATELY
resorted to any particular metaphor, it loses its vivacity as an
allegory and becomes just a way-of-saying-things.
But the "picture" is still there, for those who care to look.
Historians have reason to do so. Why don't a new generation, or a
new century, abandon certain inherited figures-of-speech by
common consent, and substitute different ones?

REGULAR CAPS 7 PT WHEREAS THE TYPOGRAPHER IS TRYING TO
MAKE PEOPLE READ, AND THEREFORE FINDING OUT ALL HE CAN
ABOUT LEGIBILITY, HIS OPPOSITE-NUMBER IN SCIENCE IS TRYING TO
FIND OUT ABOUT LEGIBILITY; AND TO THAT END IS IN FACT MAKING
PEOPLE READ - UNDER CONTROLLED CONDITIONS, IN ORDER THAT
HE MAY OBSERVE HOW THEY PERFORM...

REGULAR 9,7 PT em popu non novit auindi, Hoc legat et lecto carmine doctus amet. Arte citae
veloque rates remoque moventur, Arte leves era currus: arte regendus amor. Cureautomedon
lentesque erat arptus habenis, Tiphys in Haemonia puppe maglister erat: Me Venus artificem
tenero praefecit Amori; Tiphys et Automedon dicar Amoris ego. Ie quid quidem ferus est qui
mihi saepe repuignet: Sed puer est, aetas mollis et apta regi. Phillyrides puerum cith perfecit
Achillem, Atqu animos placida contuduit arte feros. Qui totiens socios, totiens exterruhostes
Creditur annosum pertimuisse senem. Quas Hector sensur erat poscete magistro erberitubus
iussas praebuit ille manus. Aeacidae Chiron, ego sum praeceptorat Amoris: Sae uterque puer,
natus uterque dea. Sed tamen et tauri cervix oneratur axterruratro, Fagnani dentele teruntur

designed by Luc[as] de Groot at FontFabrik.com 1998-1999 published by LucasFonts.com

TheAntiquaB is the big family that emerged, after
years of development, from TheSerif (part of the
extended Thesis family). It is a modern text face
with an extensive range of weights to handle complicated typography. The AntiquaB was a winner in
the 1999 Type Directors Club competition.

Typeface name:
Tourist.
Designer:
Julian Bittiner.

ABCDEFGHIJKLMNOPQRSTU
VWXYZabcdefghijklmnopq
rstuvwxyz0123456789¢$£¥
€&¤%‰ÀÁÂÄÃÅÇÈÉÊËÌÍÏÎ
ÑÒÓÔÖØÙÚÛÜŸàáâäãåçèé
êëıìíîïñòóôöõøùúûüÿ¶§†‡
ƒÆŒœæfiflß@®©™ª°ˆ#*,.…:
;¿?¡!_'"""''„,/|\–—·«»~{([])
}<>+÷=≈Δ±≤≥◊°•∞µΣΠπ∫Ω¬√

Tourist

Julian Bittiner is a global citizen with roots in
Switzerland, Italy, and now San Francisco, working in both print and new media at MetaDesign. He
also co-operates Office, a studio geared towards
less tangible endeavors. Prior to working in San
Francisco, Julian earned two degrees in fine art
and graphic design from the Art Center College of
Design. Being vain, he also aspires to acting.

Country:
USA.
Writing system:
Latin.

Competition category:
Text, single font.
Manufacturer/distributor:
Julian Bittiner.

CONVALIDA

CONVALIDA

LIRE

6000

€ 3,10

Actv Venezia
Società per Azioni

Biglietto di bordo Ord.

GEN	FEB	MAR	APR	MAG	GIU
LUG	AGO	ET	OTT	NOV	DIC

GIORNO						ORE				MIN
1	7	13	19	25	31	1	7	13	19	00
	8	14	20	26		2	8	14	20	15
3	9	15	21	27		3	9		21	
4	10	16	22	28		4	10	16	22	30
5	11	17	23	29		5	11	17	23	
6	12	18	24	30		6	12	18	24	4

I biglietti, salv... ...izati entro due

• rispettare le ... ...rso di dubbio,
rivolgetevi ... ...l'eventuale

Il biglietto convalidato non è cedibile, va conservato
fino al termine del viaggio e presentato ad ogni
richiesta del personale di controllo.
p. Iva 00762090272

CS10

V2 № 92988

Tourist is a hybrid letter form, sitting somewhere
between European Modern and American Postmodern typographic ideologies. The typeface also
reflects its dual purpose, namely, to be both contemporary and unique in form while still remaining
highly legible. The slab-serif genre seemed to offer
the possibility of combining these often opposing
qualities. Tourist thus combines geometric and
humanist forms, as well as elements of sans-serif
and serif typefaces.

Typeface name:
DTL Unico.
Designer:
Michael Harvey.

ABCDEFGHIJKLMNOPQRSTU
VWXYZ &ŒÆÇØ
abcdefghijklmnopqrstuvwxyz
œæfiflßçøáàâäãåéèêëñóòôöúùûü
([{1234567890/1234567890}])
!?:;€$£¥¢§¶†®%@™
ABCDEFGHIJKLMNOPQRSTUVWXYZ
&ŒÆÇØ 1234567890

ABCDEFGHIJKLMNOPQRSTU
VWXYZ &ŒÆÇØ
([{1234567890/1234567890}])
abcdefghijklmnopqrstuvwxyz
œæfiflßçøáàâäãåéèêëñóòôöúùûüÿ
!?:;€$£¥¢§¶†®%@™
ABCDEFGHIJKLMNOPQRSTUVWXYZ
&ŒÆÇØ 1234567890

Michael Harvey (London, 1931) worked as an engineering draughtsman until Eric Gill's *Autobiography* inspired him to become a lettercutter. From 1955 until 1961, he assisted Reynolds Stone, carving inscriptions in slate, stone, and wood. He has since carved many inscriptions. Michael Harvey began to design lettered bookjackets in 1957, and since then has produced at least fifteen hundred for leading publishers. He has designed typefaces for the Ludlow company, the Monotype company, Adobe Systems, and the Dutch Type Library. He is the author of a number of books on lettering and calligraphy.

Country:
United Kingdom.
Writing system:
Latin.

Competition category:
Text, family.
Manufacturer/distributor:
Dutch Type Library.

THE INVENTION OF PRINTING FROM MOVABLE TYPES WAS ONE OF THE CHIEF EVENTS AF-fecting the history of European civilization. The task of duplicating texts without variance was impossible before Gutenberg equiped the scholar with the accuracy of type. Prejudiced connoisseurs in the *FIFTEENTH CENTURY DEPLORED THE NEW MASS-PRODUCTION OF BOOKS, BUT MEN OF letters eagerly hailed the printing press as a method of disseminating knowledge in permanent form; and the earliest printed books soon rivalled in beauty, as they superseded in econ-*

THE INVENTION OF PRINTING FROM MOVABLE TYPES WAS ONE OF THE chief events affecting the history of European civilization. The task of duplicating texts without variance was impossible before Gutenberg *EQUIPED THE SCHOLAR WITH THE ACCURACY OF TYPE. PREJUDICED CON-noisseurs in the fifteenth century deplo-red the new mass-production of books, but men of letters eagerly hailed the*

THE INVENTION OF PRINTING FROM MOVABLE TYPES WAS ONE OF THE CHIEF events affecting the history of European civilization. The task of duplicating texts without variance was impossible before Gutenberg equiped the scholar with the accu-*RACY OF TYPE. PREJUDICED CONNOIS-SEURS IN THE FIFTEENTH CENTURY DE-plored the new mass-production of books, but men of letters eagerly hailed the printing press as a method of disse-minating knowledge in permanent form; and the earliest printed books soon rival-*

THE INVENTION OF PRINTING FROM MOVABLE TYPES WAS ONE OF the chief events affecting the his-tory of European civilization. The task of duplicating texts without variance was impossible before Gutenberg equiped the *SCHOLAR WITH THE ACCURACY OF TYPE. PREJUDICED CONNOISSEURS in the fifteenth century deplored the new mass-production of books, but men of letters eagerly hailed the printing press as a method of dis-*

THE INVENTION OF PRINTING FROM MOVABLE TYPES WAS one of the chief events af-fecting the history of Euro-pean civilization. The task of duplicating texts without variance was impossible be-fore Gutenberg equiped the scholar with the accuracy of type. Prejudiced con-

THE INVENTION OF PRINTING FROM MOV-able types was one of the chief events affecting the histo-ry of European civi-lization. The task of duplicating texts

DTL Unico is an 'all purpose' typeface, very useful in both book production and office work. The design was made with a wink at the eighteenth century, and owes its name to that: DTL Unico is named after the Dutch composer Graaf ('Count') Unico Wilhelm van Wassenaer (1692–1766). This composer was re-discovered in the 1980s, when some famous compositions, whose origin had been uncertain, were ascribed to him. The name Unico also refers to current developments in font technology, namely Unicode. DTL Unico will be a very extensive type-face family, supporting many codepages.

ABCDEFGHIJ

ABCDEFGHIJKLMNOPQRSTUVWXYZabcdefghijklmnopqrstuvwxyz1234567890 *ABCDEFGHIJKLMNOPQRSTUVWXYZabcdefghijklmnopqrstuvwxyz1234567890*

Vesta light

KLMNOPQRS

ABCDEFGHIJKLMNOPQRSTUVWXYZabcdefghijklmnopqrstuvwxyz1234567890 *ABCDEFGHIJKLMNOPQRSTUVWXYZabcdefghijklmnopqrstuvwxyz1234567890*

Vesta regular

TUVWXYZ&

ABCDEFGHIJKLMNOPQRSTUVWXYZabcdefghijklmnopqrstuvwxyz1234567890 *ABCDEFGHIJKLMNOPQRSTUVWXYZabcdefghijklmnopqrstuvwxyz1234567890*

Vesta medium

abcdefghijkl

ABCDEFGHIJKLMNOPQRSTUVWXYZabcdefghijklmnopqrstuvwxyz1234567890 *ABCDEFGHIJKLMNOPQRSTUVWXYZabcdefghijklmnopqrstuvwxyz1234567890*

Vesta semi bold

mnopqrstuv

ABCDEFGHIJKLMNOPQRSTUVWXYZabcdefghijklmnopqrstuvwxyz1234567890 *ABCDEFGHIJKLMNOPQRSTUVWXYZabcdefghijklmnopqrstuvwxyz1234567890*

Vesta bold

wxyzæœß/@

ABCDEFGHIJKLMNOPQRSTUVWXYZabcdefghijklmnopqrstuvwxyz1234567890 *ABCDEFGHIJKLMNOPQRSTUVWXYZabcdefghijklmnopqrstuvwxyz1234567890*

Vesta extra bold

Ø(–).,:;!?€¥§

ABCDEFGHIJKLMNOPQRSTUVWXYZabcdefghijklmnopqrstuvwxyz1234567890 *ABCDEFGHIJKLMNOPQRSTUVWXYZabcdefghijklmnopqrstuvwxyz1234567890*

Vesta black

1234567890

Gerard Unger. See page 289.

352

Country:
The Netherlands.
Writing system:
Latin.

Competition category:
Text/display, family.
Manufacturer/distributor:
Gerard Unger.

'We take a little of this

[...]'the chef might be French, Spanish, Choctaw,

'What it's

and a little of that,

Cuban, Yoruban, Brazilian, Sicilian, Haitian or

trying to do

mix it all up,

Dr. John, introduction to 'Creole moon', 2001

West African, and that's like our music, that's

is make you

and what you get

like our global culture, that's like our city,'[...]

timeless.'

is musical gumbo.'

Vesta was an early proposal for the Rome-project: to design a typeface for the Jubilee in the year 2000, a design that projects the 2000-year-old tradition of public writing in Rome into the new century. In the end, my serif design Capitolium was chosen, but at an earlier stage I researched whether a sans serif design could be connected to the Roman tradition, based upon samples of republican lettering, as on the temple of Vesta at Tivoli. As sans serif is internationally established as the style for signs, the possibility of a sans for Rome should be seriously looked into.

Typeface name:
Waters Titling Pro.
Designer:
Julian Waters.

A B C D E F G H I J K L M N O P Q R S
T U V W X Y Z & Þ

TALL CAPITALS

A Æ B C D E F G H I J K L M N O Œ
Ø P Q R S T U V W X Y Z

ALTERNATES & LIGATURES

Æ ÆA ÆS CA CÆ CC CE CO CŒ CT DC
DG DO DŒ E E EA EÆ EE EO ES EY J K
K KS LA LÆ NN Œ ŒA ŒS OC OG OO
Q R R RS ST T T TH TT TY Þ V W Y Y
ZA ZÆ & *an and at for from in of the to*

ACCENTED GLYPHS

Á Â Ä À Å Ã Ç Ð É Ê Ë È Í Î Ï Ì İ Ł Ñ Ø
Ó Ô Ö Ò Õ Š Ú Û Ü Ù Ý Ÿ Ž Ă Ā Ą Ć Č
Ď Đ Ě Ė Ē Ę Ğ Ģ Ī Į Ķ Ĺ Ľ Ļ Ń Ň Ņ Ő Ō
Ŕ Ř Ŗ Ś Ş Ş Ť Ţ Ű Ū Ų Ů Ź Ż

MISCELLANEOUS GLYPHS

0 1 2 3 4 5 6 7 8 9 $ ¢ £ ¥ *f* ¤ € # ¼ ½ ¾ ^
~ · + ± < = > | ¦ × ÷ − ∂ μ π Δ Π Σ Ω √ ∞ ∫ ≈
≠ ≤ ≥ ◊ ¬ ℓ ° ª º ( ) [ ] { } / \ * ·
§ † ‡ ¶ © ® ™ @

Julian Waters has been a professional lettering artist for more than 20 years. He was a typographic consultant to Maya Lin during the construction of the Vietnam Memorial, and his clients have included the National Geographic Society and the U.S. Postal Service. A member of the faculty of most of the annual international calligraphy conferences since 1982, Waters has taught and lectured all over North America and Europe, including substituting for Hermann Zapf in his two-week calligraphy master class at the Rochester Institute of Technology.

Country:
USA.
Writing system:
Latin.

Competition category:
Display, family.
Manufacturer/distributor:
Adobe Systems.

WATERS TITLING PRO

30-POINT LIGHT AND SEMIBOLD WITH TALL CAPITALS, ALTERNATES, AND LOWERCASE WORD LIGATURES

THE HOUND *of the* BASKERVILLES

THE ORIGIN *of* SPECIES

THE MYSTERY OF EDWIN DROOD

A PASSAGE TO INDIA

THE HOUSE OF MIRTH

JOURNEY *to the* CENTER *of the* EARTH

THE COUNT *of* MONTE CRISTO

ALICE *in* WONDERLAND

DEATH *in the* AFTERNOON

THE FOOD *of the* GODS

THE BROTHERS KARAMAZOV

LIGHT	**SEMIBOLD**
LIGHT CONDENSED	**SEMIBOLD CONDENSED**
LIGHT SEMICONDENSED	**SEMIBOLD SEMICONDENSED**
REGULAR	**BOLD**
CONDENSED	**BOLD CONDENSED**
SEMICONDENSED	**BOLD SEMICONDENSED**

Waters Titling Pro (1997). This broad-edged pen design is related to other historically-based titling alphabets but offers a wider range of weights and widths, making it extremely versatile for movie titles, book jackets, posters, banners, calendars etc. Waters Titling is rooted in the timeless Roman monumental inscription forms of almost 2000 years ago, but it is infused with contemporary vigor and flair. The design exhibits a strong calligraphic thick-thin stroke weight contrast and flowing, subtly-bracketed serifs.

**ABCDEFGHIJKLMNO
PQRSTUVWXYZabcd
efghijklmnopqrstuv
wxyzÀÁÂÃÄÅÆÇÈÉÊ
ËÌÍÎÏŁÑÒÓÔÕÖØŒÙ
ÚÛÜÐàáâãäåæçðèé
êëìíîïłñòóôõöøœßùú
ûü&fifl,;:....-!¡?¿''""
,„‹›«»/|–—•·()[]*
†§¶`´^˜¨°¸\©®™
@€$£€#1234567890
¹²³/¼½¾%‰+=°'"**

ABCDEFGHIJKLMNO
PQRSTUVWXYZabcd
efghijklmnopqrstuv
wxyzÀÁÂÃÄÅÆÇÈÉÊ
ËÌÍÎÏŁÑÒÓÔÕÖØŒÙ
ÚÛÜÐàáâãäåæçðèé
êëìíîïłñòóôõöøœßùú
ûü&fifl,;:....-!¡?¿''""
,„‹›«»/|–—•·()[]*
†§¶`´^˜¨°¸\©®™
@€$£€#1234567890
¹²³/¼½¾%‰+=°'"

Yellow Bold

Yellow Regular

Country:
Germany.
Writing system:
Latin.

Competition category:
Text, family.
Manufacturer/distributor:
Jürgen Weltin.

.... **Borough Green** **882396**
.... **Sevenoaks** **454377**
.... **Ticehurst** **201229**
s-On-Sea....... **Hastings** **442838**
.... **Hastings** **444758**
St........ **Hastings** **437880**
rds-On-Sea.... **Hastings** **422514**
.... **Hastings** **424500**
.... **Hastings** **432267**
.... **Uckfield** **760999**
Uckfield **761001**
.... **Peasmarsh** **230281**
ough......... **Hildenboro** **833232**
.... **Knockholt** **533171**
.... **Ide Hl** **750310**
s-On-Sea...... **Hastings** **439117**
.... **Sevenoaks** **454434**
.... **Crowboro** **654796**
.... **Hastings** **446037**
.... **Heathfield** **862053**
.... **Tun Wells** **536761**
.... **Crowboro** **603461**
.... **Crowboro** **654009**
.... **Biggin Hill** **572920**
.... **Newick** **723293**
.... **Hastings** **428308**
.... **Heathfield** **867491**
e........ **Langton** **864742**
.... **Rye** **223372**
rough.......... **Tun Wells** **523111**
Tun Wells **524993**
.... **Cranbrook** **712089**
.... **Otford** **522847**
.... **Otford** **522903**
.... **Sevenoaks** **761023**
.... **Tenterden** **762227**
.... **Northiam** **253224**
.... **Tun Wells** **548412**
.... **Hurst Green** **861394**
.... **Hastings** **423449**
ham.......... **Chiddingly** **872406**
.... **Cooden** **843817**
.... **Bexhill on Sea** **219413**
.... **Sevenoaks** **453393**
Green... **Paddock Wood** **835966**
.... **01892** **686148**
.... **Hastings** **434055**
.... **Hastings** **421686**
.... **Cranbrook** **713634**
.... **Hastings** **431996**
.... **Cranbrook** **713460**
Sea........ **Hastings** **436241**
een.......... **Sevenoaks** **456123**
.... **Tenterden** **762788**
.... **Hawkhurst** **753233**
.... **Lamberhurst** **890279**
.... **Sevenoaks** **457831**
.... **Paddock Wood** **832079**
.... **Hastings** **851066**
.... **Bexhill on Sea** **224275**
.... **Hastings** **442406**
.... **Tenterden** **766033**
.... **Hadlow** **850267**
.... **Buxted** **732191**
.... **Hadlow Down** **830485**
.... **Sevenoaks** **761503**
.... **Hildenboro** **833975**
.... **Tun Wells** **514517**
.... **Tun Wells** **528662**
.... **Paddock Wood** **836064**
.... **Tun Wells** **522864**
athly.............. **Halland** **840208**
.... **Nutley** **712808**
Rd............ **Tonbridge** **360129**
.... **Hastings** **444158**
s-On-Sea....... **Hastings** **424095**
n Hill........ **Biggin Hill** **572448**
.... **Ide Hl** **750328**
Shoreham........ **Otford** **525428**
n-Sea........... **Hastings** **461800**
.... **Hastings** **421195**
and.............. **Rye** **227080**
.... **Westerham** **563245**

Golding Hop The,Sheet Hill,Plaxtol........ **Borough Green** **882150**
Granville Tavern The,2 St. Georges Rd........ **Hastings** **429044**
Green Man Inn The,
The Green,Horsted Keynes,Haywards Heath........ **Danehill** **790656**
Greyhound Hotel The,St. James Square........ **Wadhurst** **783224**
Greyhound The,Charcott,Chiddingstone Causeway.. **Penshurst** **870275**
Greyhound The,123 Shipbourne Rd........ **Tonbridge** **354473**
Greyhound The,Upper Grosvenor Rd........ **Tun Wells** **524713**
Grove Tavern,19 Berkeley Rd........ **Tun Wells** **526549**
Guinea Butt The,Calverley Rd........ **Tun Wells** **546877**
Gun Inn,Gun Hill,Horam........ **Chiddingly** **872361**
Half Moon,144 Tonbridge Rd........ **Hildenboro** **832153**
Half Moon The,Friars Gate........ **Crowboro** **661270**
Halfway House The,Rose Hill........ **Isfield** **750382**
Halfway House The,London Rd........ **Sevenoaks** **457108**
Hare & Hounds,391 Old London Rd........ **Hastings** **422349**
Hare & Hounds The,The Street........ **Framfield** **890327**
Hare & Hounds The,Main Rd,Rye Foreign........ **Peasmarsh** **230483**
Hare & Hounds The,
95 Bidborough Ridge, Bidborough........ **Tun Wells** **529870**
Hare The,Langton Rd,Langton Green........ **Langton** **862419**
Harrier The,Link Hill,Rye Rd........ **Sandhurst** **850323**
Harrow Inn The,Maidstone Rd........ **Hadlow** **850386**
Harrow Inn The,Harrow Rd........ **Knockholt** **532168**
Hastings Arms The,2 George St........ **Hastings** **722208**
Havelock The,27 Havelock Rd........ **Hastings** **425742**
Heale R C,The Greyhound Hotel,High St........ **Wadhurst** **784090**
Henry Simmons The,4 Wrotham Rd........ **Borough Green** **882016**
High Brooms Tavern,102 High Brooms Rd........ **Tun Wells** **528543**
Highway Man The,
The Heath Maidstone Rd,Horsmonden........ **Brenchley** **722215**
Hogshead & Compasses,45 Little Mount Sion........ **Tun Wells** **530744**
Hogshead On The Walf,Lyons Crescent........ **Tonbridge** **357506**
Hollington Oak,
Wishing Tree Rd, St. Leonards-On-Sea........ **Hastings** **854104**
Hooden off the Stage,66 St. Johns Rd........ **Tun Wells** **619376**
Hop House (Tom Cobleigh),
Knights Park,Knights Way........ **Tun Wells** **617443**
Hop Pocket The,Maidstone Rd........ **Paddock Wood** **832857**
Hopbine Inn,Petteridge Lane,Matfield........ **Brenchley** **722561**
Horns The,66 High St........ **Otford** **522604**
Horse & Cart Inn,School Lane........ **Peasmarsh** **230220**
Horse & Groom,........ **Rushlake Green** **830320**
Horse & Groom The,
4 Mercatoria,St. Leonards-On-Sea........ **Hastings** **420612**
Humphrey Bean The,94 High St........ **Tonbridge** **773850**
Hungry Horse,Rose & Crown,Turkey Rd........ **Bexhill on Sea** **214625**
Huntsman The,Eridge Rd,Eridge Green........ **Langton** **864258**
Imperial The,119 Queens Rd........ **Hastings** **435465**
Imperial The,29 London Rd,Southborough........ **Tun Wells** **528757**
Inkerman Arms The,Rye Harbour Rd........ **Rye** **222464**
Ivy House The,199 High St........ **Tonbridge** **352382**
Jack Cade The,Cade St........ **Heathfield** **862209**
Jacobs Well,Golden Cross,Hailsham........ **Chiddingly** **873173**
Johns Cross Inn,Battle Rd........ **Robertsbdge** **882154**
Junction Inn The,Station Rd,Groombridge........ **Langton** **864275**
Kelsey Arms,105 St. Johns Road........ **Tun Wells** **518721**
Kent Cricketers,Moor Hill........ **Hawkhurst** **752306**
Kent Hounds The,Well Hill,Chelsfield........ **Knockholt** **534288**
Kentish Rifleman The,
Silver Hill,Dunks Green,Shipbourne........ **Plaxtol** **810727**
Kentish Yeoman,10-12 High St,Seal........ **Sevenoaks** **761041**
Kicking Donkey Inn The,Witherenden Hill........ **Burwash** **883379**
King William IV,87 Hastings Rd........ **Pembury** **823108**
Kings Arms,Church St,Shoreham........ **Otford** **523100**
Kings Arms The,Leaves Green Rd,Keston........ **Biggin Hill** **572514**
Kings Arms The,High St........ **Rotherfield** **853441**
Kings Arms The,High St,Brasted........ **Westerham** **562975**
Kings Head,25 Courthouse St, Old Town........ **Hastings** **439292**
Kings Head Inn,East Grinsted Rd,North Chailey........ **Newick** **722870**
Newick **724370**
Kings Head The,Udimore........ **Brede** **882349**
Kings Head The,1 High St,East Hoathly........ **Halland** **840238**
Kings Head The,61 Rye Rd........ **Hastings** **423767**
Kings Head The,Badsell Rd,Five Oak Green..... **Paddock Wood** **832070**
Lamb Inn The,Hooe........ **Cooden** **847891**
Langham The,Elphinstone Rd........ **Hastings** **420858**
Laughing Fish The,........ **Isfield** **750349**
Little Brown Jug The,Chiddingstone Causeway........ **Penshurst** **870318**
London Trader,4-7 East Beach St........ **Hastings** **429684**
Lord Nelson,East Bourne St........ **Hastings** **423280**
Lord Warden The,73 Manor Rd........ **Hastings** **420055**
Malvern Pub The,Malvern Way........ **Hastings** **440330**
Man of Kent The,1 Sandy Lane........ **Sevenoaks** **452977**
Man of Kent The,14 East St........ **Tonbridge** **371921**
Manor The,114 Manor Rd........ **Hastings** **422697**
May Garland Inn,Horam Rd........ **Horam** **812249**
Maypole Inn,Hurstwood Rd,High Hurstwood........ **Buxted** **732257**
Middle House Hotel The,High St........ **Mayfield** **872146**
Millers Arms The,38 Winchelsea Rd........ **Hastings** **439075**

North Star The,Clarence Rd,St. Leonards-On-Sea...... **Hastings** **436576**
Oak & Ivy The,Rye Rd........ **Hawkhurst** **753293**
Oak Tap The,Upper High St........ **Sevenoaks** **458783**
Oak The,33 High St,Rusthall........ **Tun Wells** **536952**
Oldfellows Arms The,397 Old London Rd........ **Hastings** **423242**
Old Bell Inn The,33 High St........ **Rye** **223323**
Old England,45 London Rd,St. Leonards-On-Sea...... **Hastings** **722154**
Old Golden Cross The,56 Havelock Rd........ **Hastings** **424716**
Old House The,Redwell Lane,Ightham........ **Borough Green** **882383**
Old Jail The,Jail Lane........ **Biggin Hill** **572979**
Old King John,39-41 Middle Rd,Ore........ **Hastings** **443310**
Old Ship The,Westmore Green,Tatsfield........ **Biggin Hill** **577315**
Opera House The,88 Mount Pleasant Rd........ **Tun Wells** **511770**
Orson Welles,Grove Hill Rd........ **Tun Wells** **530723**
Padwell Arms The,Stone St,Seal........ **Sevenoaks** **761532**
Papa Jo's,Carlisle Parade........ **Hastings** **432646**
Papermakers Arms,The Street........ **Plaxtol** **810407**
Peace & Plenty Inn,Peasmarsh Rd,Playden,Rye........ **Iden** **280342**
Peacock Inn The,
Goudhurst Rd,Iden Green,Goudhurst........ **Goudhurst** **211233**
Peacock Inn The,Shortbridge,Piltdown........ **Uckfield** **762463**
Pig In Paradise The,White Rock........ **Hastings** **439444**
Piltdown Man The,Piltdown........ **Newick** **723563**
Pipemakers Arms The,2 Wish Ward........ **Rye** **223064**
Plough & Horses The,Walshes Rd........ **Crowboro** **652614**
Plough Inn The,Hastings Rd........ **Crowhurst** **830310**
Plough Inn The,49 Priory Rd........ **Hastings** **717832**
Plough Inn The,The Moor,Westfield........ **Hastings** **751066**
Plough Inn The,Leigh Rd,Hildenborough........ **Hildenboro** **832149**
Plough The,Plough Hill,Basted........ **Borough Green** **885689**
Poacher The,Hartlake Rd,Tudeley........ **Tonbridge** **358434**
Tonbridge **358934**
Polhill Arms The,Polhill,Halstead........ **Knockholt** **534232**
Primrose The,112 Pembury Rd........ **Tonbridge** **358699**
Prince Albert,28 Cornwallis St........ **Hastings** **425481**
Prince of Wales,High St........ **Hadlow** **850224**
Prince of Wales,9 Camden Rd........ **Tun Wells** **527433**
Prince of Wales The,High St........ **Cranbrook** **713058**
Prince of Wales The,Hailsham Rd........ **Heathfield** **862919**
Pub 31,Pett Level Rd,Winchelsea Beach........ **Rye** **225965**
Punch & Judy The,11 St, Stephens St........ **Tonbridge** **352368**
Queen Adelaide The,20 West St........ **Hastings** **430862**
Queens Head Inn,Parsonage Lane,Icklesham........ **Hastings** **814552**
Queens Head The,
Five Oak Green Rd,Five Oak Green........ **Paddock Wood** **832073**
Queens Head The,The Green,Seddlescombe...... **Sedlescombe** **870228**
Railway Bell,25 Priory Rd........ **Tonbridge** **362979**
Railway & Bicycle The,Tubs Hill........ **Sevenoaks** **452477**
Railway The,1 Kings Rd,St. Leonards-On-Sea........ **Hastings** **461083**
Rainbow Trout The,Broad Oak........ **Brede** **882436**
Red House,The Red House Higham Lane........ **Tonbridge** **358527**
Red Lion,45 Sevenoaks Rd........ **Borough Green** **882410**
Red Lion,Hooe,Battle........ **Ninfield** **892371**
Red Lion,Sparrows Green........ **Wadhurst** **782628**
Red Lion The,14 High St........ **Biddenden** **291347**
Red Lion The,82 Lower Green Rd,Tunbridge Wells... **Tun Wells** **520086**
Rifleman The,30 Camden Rd,St. Johns........ **Sevenoaks** **460723**
Ringles Cross,Ringles Cross........ **Uckfield** **762510**
Rising Sun The,173 Battle Rd,Hollington........ **Hastings** **427030**
Rising Sun The,Twitton Lane........ **Otford** **525489**
Robert De Mortain,373 The Ridge........ **Hastings** **751061**
Robin Hood Inn,Main Rd,Icklesham........ **Hastings** **814277**
Robin Hood The,Sandhurst Rd........ **Tun Wells** **521383**
Rock & Fountain,Rock Hill,Chelsfield........ **Knockholt** **534335**
Rock Inn The,Chiddingstone Hoath,Edenbridge........ **Penshurst** **870296**
Rock Robin The,Station Hill........ **Wadhurst** **783776**
Rose & Crown,Otford Lane,Halstead........ **Knockholt** **533120**
Rose & Crown,High St,Fletching,Uckfield........ **Newick** **722039**
Rose & Crown,Northiam Rd,Beckley........ **Northiam** **252161**
Rose & Crown,47 Grosvenor Rd........ **Tun Wells** **522427**
Rose & Crown Inn,Fletching St........ **Mayfield** **872200**
Rose & Crown The,High St,Wrotham........ **Borough Green** **882409**
Rose & Crown The,Ham Lane........ **Burwash** **882600**
Rose & Crown The,87 Carpenters Lane........ **Hadlow** **850242**
Rose Revived The,Ashes Lane........ **Hadlow** **850382**
Royal Albion,Marine Parade........ **Hastings** **432658**
Royal George The,London Rd........ **Hurst Green** **860200**
Royal Oak,Highgate Rye Rd........ **Hawkhurst** **752184**
Royal Oak,Whatlington........ **Sedlescombe** **870492**
Royal Oak Inn,Main St,Rye........ **Beckley** **260312**
Royal Oak The,Pett Rd,Pett........ **Hastings** **812515**
Royal Oak The,1 Church Rd........ **Newick** **722506**
Royal Oak The,216 Henwood Green Rd........ **Pembury** **822958**
Royal Oak The,Lower Hayesden Lane........ **Tonbridge** **350208**
Royal Oak The,82 Shipbourne Rd........ **Tonbridge** **359357**
Royal Oak The,92 Prospect Rd........ **Tun Wells** **542546**
Royal Oak The,80 Speldhurst Rd,Southborough...... **Tun Wells** **520444**
Royal Sovereign The,15 Sea Rd........ **Bexhill on Sea** **213427**
Royal Standard The,East St........ **Hastings** **420163**
Royal Standard The,14 High St........ **Westerham** **562925**

Yellow needed to be extremely economical with space, to be clear and highly readable at very small sizes, and to be used with negative leading. The outcome was a sans serif distinguished by simplicity of design and condensed letterforms with a very large x-height. To avoid drawing deep cut-ins where vertical and horizontal strokes join, I designed sharp horizontals to gain more white space around the joining strokes. This treatment is essential to the design and its functionality, and it allowed me to keep the symbols very open.

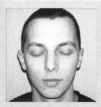

Olivier Umecker is a graphic designer who divides his time between Strasbourg and Lyon (France), and works for public institutions and historical exhibitions. He studied graphical industries and communication in Strasbourg. During this period he researched the history of typography in France and Germany during the Second World War. He is keen on primitive signs, invented languages (Klingon, Tengwar), and gardening. His creations in the typographical field are essentially symbols, such as Modulo, published by Linotype Library, and Insects, which won an award in the 1998 *U&lc* competition.

Country:
France.
Writing system:
N/A

Competition category:
Pi, family.
Manufacturer/distributor:
Olivier Umecker.

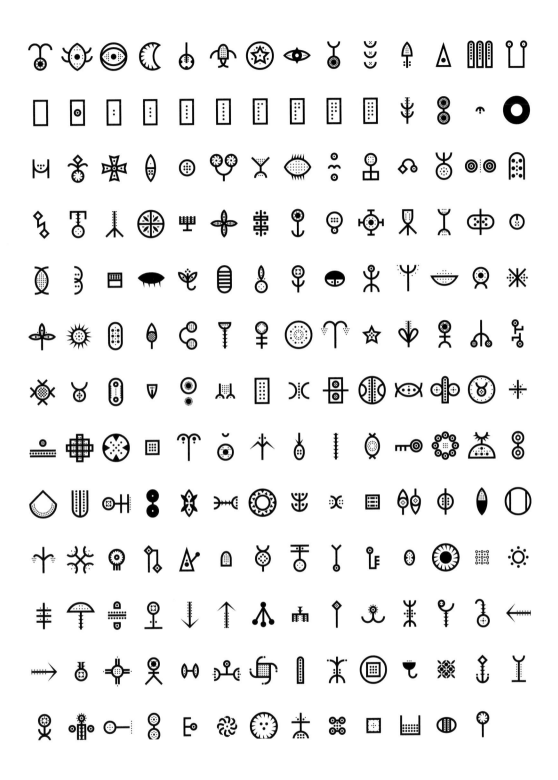

Yisana is a free and contemporary interpretation
of diverse symbols from African sources. Each symbol is available in two forms: plain and elaborated.

Typeface name:
Zentra.
Designer:
Vladimir Pavlikov.

Vladimir Pavlikov. See page 310.

Country:
Russia.
Writing system:
N/A

Competition category:
Pi, single font.
Manufacturer/distributor:
Vladimir Pavlikov.

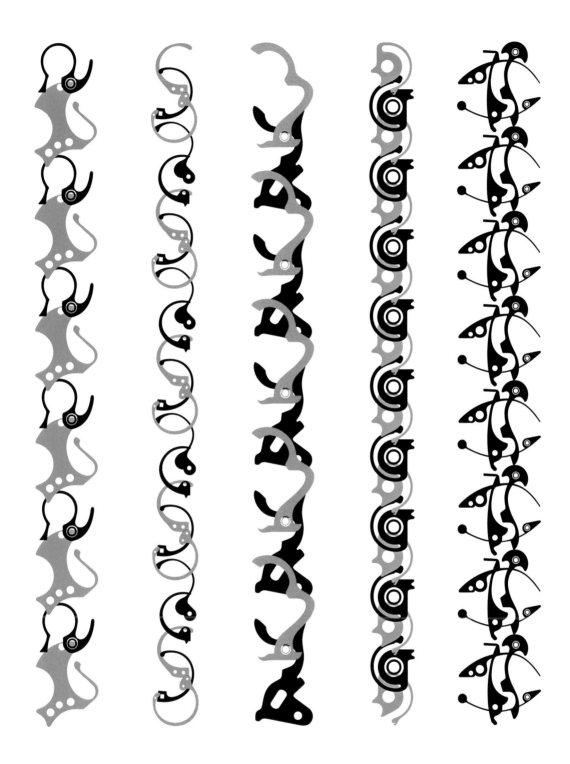

Zentra is an abstract view of mechanical forms, an
exploration of my interest in abstract shapes and
machine details. It discovers new plastic purport
in the objects around us. It opens up forms with
new characters and associations. Zentra designs
may be used in combinations – for example, in ornaments it make a contrast of fantastic forms and
strong rhythm – or as isolated signs.

Typeface name:
Zigzag.
Designer:
Yurij Lila.

Yurij Lila was born in 1973 in Komsomolsky, Kharkiv Region, Ukraine. He graduated from the Kharkiv Academy of Arts and Design in 2000. He has participated in exhibitions under the auspices of the Academy.

Country:
Ukraine.
Writing system:
Cyrillic, Latin.

Competition category:
Display, single font.
Manufacturer/distributor:
Yurij Lila.

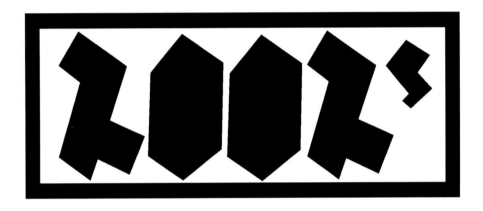

Zigzag was a course project under the supervision
of Professor Vladimir Lesnyak at Kharkiv Academy
of Arts and Design. The design combines elements
of early Soviet Constructivism with a postmodern
image, creating original and laconic typeforms.

Typeface name:
Zubizarreta.
Designer:
Joan Barjau.

zubizarreta tosca

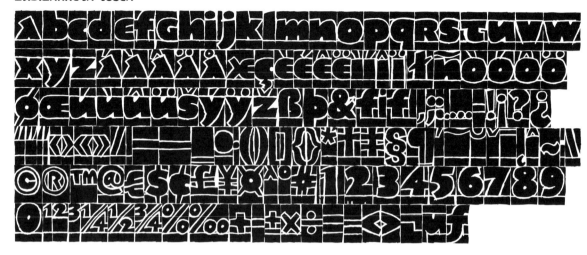

zubizarreta regia

abcdefghijklmnopqrstuv
wxyzÁÀÂÄÅÆÇÈÉÊËÌÍÎÏłÑÒÓ
ÔÖØŠÚÙÛÜÝŸŽßÞ&fifl,;:....-!¡
?¿""''‹›«»/|——_•·()[]{}*†‡§¶˜˘
¯ˆ~,'\©®™@€$¢£¥¤°^#12345
67890¹²³¼½¾%‰+-±×÷=<>¬µf

zubizarreta sobria

abcdefghijklmnopqrstuvwx
yzÁÀÂÄÅÆÇÈÉÊËÌÍÎÏłÑÒÓÔÖØŒŠ
úùûüýÿžß&fifl,;:....-!¡?¿""''‹›«»
/|——_•·()[]{}*†‡§¶˜˘¯ˆ~,'\©®™@
€$¢£¥¤°^#1234567890¹²³¼½¾
%‰+-±×÷=<>¬µf

Joan Barjau (Barcelona, 1950) practises graphic
design in its widest sense: sketch, humour, illustration, painting, animation. Presently he works in his
own studio, as both graphic and type designer. He's
the designer or co-designer of the typefaces Ivà,
Jeune Adrian, Memima, Sniff, Talqual, Tschicholina,
Xiquets Primis, and Zubizarreta.

Country:
Spain.
Writing system:
Latin.

Competition category:
Display, family.
Manufacturer/distributor:
Type-O-Tones, FSI.

Zubizarreta was 'sculpted' out of an initially black background, as in the traditional engraving technique used for the fabrication of lead types. Zubizarreta Tosca (rough) was born by emptying maps of pixels by hand, in order to achieve a rough drawing profile. I continued carving until Zubizarreta Regia (regal) and Zubizarreta Sobria (sober) were formed. This font is also characterized by the structure of its characters, which do not differentiate between upper and lower case. It is inspired by early 'unicase' experiments of Jan Tschichold and Adrian Frutiger.

Contributors

MISHA BELETSKY first fell in love with design attending night classes at Moscow Printing Institute in Russia. At the age of seventeen he moved to the United States with his family. While studying illustration at Rhode Island School of Design, he apprenticed with David R. Godine, Publisher, and there became infatuated with a well-made book and its typography. Upon graduating, he joined the design department of Alfred A. Knopf, Publisher. He recently returned to New York from a sabbatical he took to study the Talmud in Jerusalem, and presently designs books for Abbeville Press Publishers.

ROBERT BRINGHURST is a poet & typographic historian living in Vancouver. His book *The Elements of Typographic Style* (2nd ed., 1996) is widely used as a textbook and serves as a standard reference in the field. He is also the author, with Warren Chappell, of the revised and updated *Short History of the Printed Word*.

JOHN HUDSON designs type and is co-founder, with Wm Ross Mills, of Tiro Typeworks, an independent digital font company specialising in text faces for multilingual and scholarly typography. Tiro's clients include Microsoft, Linotype Library, and Apple Computers. He has received awards in Cyrillic type design, and for his 'outstanding contribution to the development of Cyrillic typography and international typo-graphic communication'. He writes and lectures on type technology and font software, and as co-chair of the ATypI Technology Committee he organises the annual ATypI Font Technology Forum. Most recently, he has designed new Cyrillic, Greek and Hebrew types, and helped revise an Arabic newspaper face.

AKIRA KOBAYASHI (*see* p. 165).

GERRY LEONIDAS (*see* p. 165).

SAKI MAFUNDIKWA is the founder and director of the Zimbabwe Institute of Vigital Arts (ZIVA) in Harare. He holds a degree in telecommunications and fine arts from Indiana University and an MFA from Yale, and served as an adjunct professor at the Cooper Union School of Art in New York. He worked for several years at Random House in New York as a designer of books, Web sites, and multimedia. In 1997, after twenty years in the United States, he returned to his homeland with a focused vision of the contribution that he could make to the future of Zimbabwe. He has lectured and taught in several countries, and he is currently finishing a book on *Afrikan Alphabets: the story of writing in Afrika*.

THOMAS MILO incorporated DecoType in 1985 with two partners. Tom has studied Old Church Slavonic, Russian, Bulgarian, and Macedonian; Ottoman Turkish, Modern Turkish, Azeri, and Yakut Tur-kic; and Modern Standard Arabic as well as Egyptian, Lebanese, and Moroccan Arabic. He worked in Saudi Arabia for a Dutch trucking company (1976–77), and did two tours of duty as an Arabic-speaking officer in the United Nations Interim Force in Lebanon. DecoType contributes fonts and Arabic Calligraphy applications to Microsoft Office Arabic Edition; for Adobe PageMaker Middle East, DT provides a special interface for Calligraphic typesetting; to the Mac OS 9, it contributes Arabic fonts. Together with Barco Graphics, DecoType is working on a complete implementation of its design strategy for authentic Arabic.

FIONA ROSS (*see* p. 165).

ADAM TWARDOCH has been engaged since 1990 in multilingual typography, type design, web design, and software development. He has created Central European versions and custom extensions for over fifty fonts, as well as several of his own typefaces. In 1999 he joined ffo agentur GmbH in Frankfurt (Oder), where he is currently responsible for typography and new media. Since mid-2000, he has been typographical consultant to MyFonts.com. He is the Polish country delegate to ATypI, and is a member of ATypI board.

VLADIMIR YEFIMOV (*see* p. 165).

MAXIM ZHUKOV (*see* p. 165).

Index to essays

The text of the essays has been set in 11-point Fenway, a typeface designed by Matthew Carter in 1998 for *Sports Illustrated* magazine. The design of Fenway was inspired by the types of two illustrious punchcutters who worked for the Enschedé Type Foundry at Haarlem in The Netherlands: Johann Michael Fleischmann (1701–1768) and Jean-François Rosart (1714–1774).

ABCDEFGHIJKLM*NOPQRSTUVWXYZ*
abcdefghijKLMNOPQ*rstuvwxyz*

The custom version of Fenway used in this book was developed, in OpenType format, by John Hudson of Tiro Typeworks, Vancouver, BC. Fenway's character set was significantly expanded to accommodate the numerous special sorts necessary for the typesetting of this book; many of these additions to the original font complement were created by the originator of Fenway, Matthew Carter, at the request of the book production team.

ABCDEFGHIJKLM*NOPQRSTUVWXYZ*
abcdefghijklm*nopqrstuvwxyz*

Fonts belonging to the Vincent family – Vincent Medium (above), Vincent Display, and Vincent Banner Drop – have been used for all display elements in this book's essay section, its front and back matter (for larger-size headings, titles, initial capitals), and also its cover. Vincent, designed by Matthew Carter in 1996, was first used in *Newsweek* magazine in 1999. Vincent's design is based on an early type of Vincent Figgins (1776–1844), an English punchcutter whose foundry remained in operation until 1908.

ABCDEFGHIJKLM*NOPQRSTUVWXYZ*
abcdefghijklm*nopqrstuvwxyz*

PT New Letter Gothic has been used for the typesetting of the text and headings in the bukva:raz! section of this book. PT New Letter Gothic was designed by Gayaneh Bagdasaryan for ParaType, Moscow, in 1999. Its design is based on Letter Gothic, a typeface originally developed by Roger Robertson in 1956–1962 as a single-weight, monospaced font for IBM electric typewriters. PT New Letter Gothic comes in two versions: Latin and Cyrillic.